THE BLACK HEART BOOK II   Released November, 2008

After a visit to Pine Mountain, Kentucky and the Big Laurel Cemetery where her great grandfather, Alex Turner, and her grandmother, Judy Turner-Smith, are buried, the author felt led to write *The Black Heart Book*. *The Black Heart Book II* is a sequel and covers the time period between 1921 and 1930. This true story is about sin and redemption, and it chronicles events that affected the Turner family and their lives in the Kentucky Highlands.

THE BLACK HEART BOOK I   Released November, 2004

There were no secrets among the folk who lived in the Pine Mountain Region of Kentucky. Everyone knew that Alex Turner was an old man with strange powers. They also knew that his daughter Judy could shoot like a man and had the same powers. **But no one knew about The Black Heart Book!** Between courtroom cases, turkey shoots, the attacks of moonshiners and rabid dogs, the author reveals with stunning insight the struggles of her great grandfather and of her grandmother, a fiercely independent woman, who overcame the adversities of abandonment and divorce to carve a path to success for herself and her two young daughters.

WALKING FREE: THE LIFE OF NELLIE ZIMMERMAN   October, 2008

Together with legally blind Reverend Doctor Daryl C. Greene, Richmond, Indiana, Rosezelle Boggs-Qualls wrote a landmark book about a totally deaf and totally blind lady from Massillon, Ohio entitled, *Walking Free: The Life of Nellie Zimmerman.*

Nellie was locked away in a mental hospital for nineteen years against her will only because no one knew how to communicate with her. Nellie was the disabilities pioneer that prompted the passage of the Federal Olmstead Act that now makes what happened to her illegal.

Nellie had a deep abiding faith in God. Mentally, her IQ was in the genius range. After her release from the mental hospital in her 70's, she went to college, lectured all over northeast Ohio, and became an award winning life skills teacher of deaf/blind teenage boys.

OUR CAT FAMILY   Released July, 2008

This true story is about eight rescued cats and how their individual stories intermingle with the events that impacted the lives of their human family. You will learn how different circumstances resulted in rescues of the cats and how each of them joined the ranks of the author's cat family.

SIXTY FIVE ROSES: THE RICHARD GANNON STORY   Released March 2008

This true story, documented by his family, chronicles the life of Akron, Ohio native Richard C. Gannon. Born in 1952 with Cystic Fibrosis, and a life expectancy of age 11, as an adult he becomes financially independent, operates his own business, and is an award winning boatman, hunter and fisherman.

Sixty Five Roses: The Richard Gannon Story pays tribute to the medical skill of his doctors, and tells how a man's courage, faith in God, the awesome power of prayer, and his family's love and support enable him to overcome incredible life threatening challenges. In January, 2007, Richard is the oldest known living person who was diagnosed with Cystic Fibrosis as an infant.

To the best of the author's knowledge, this is a true story. It is based on family lore as related by Judy Turner-Smith, 1884-1976. The events described herein have been confirmed by other members of the immediate Turner family and in recorded history of Perry and Harlan County, Kentucky. Some names have been changed for confidentiality purposes.

Published by
Ascended Ideas
www.ascendedideas.com

ISBN 978-0-692-00063-2

The Black Heart Book II
Copyright 2008
By Rosezelle Boggs-Qualls

Manufactured in the United States of America on acid-free paper.

To
Ernestine Brown

THE

BLACK HEART BOOK

II

God bless you,

Rosezelle Boggs-Qualls

By

ROSEZELLE BOGGS-QUALLS

Edited by Karen Wilson-Zenner
Akron, Ohio
For their encouragement, inspiration,
and kind assistance, I extend my deep
appreciation to the following relatives
and friends:

Esther Berlyoung, Navarre, Ohio
Chuck Bianchi, Baxter, Kentucky
Reverend Titus Boggs, Laurel Mission, Big Laurel, Kentucky
Bela Bognar, PhD, Wright State University, Dayton, Ohio
Carl Brun, PhD, Chair, Social Work Department
        Wright State University, Dayton, Ohio
Barbara Brunk, Cuyahoga Falls, Ohio
Timothy Campbell, Cawood, Kentucky
Terri Campbell, Cawood, Kentucky
Judie Golden, Stow, Ohio
Anne Rose Greene, Richmond, Indiana
Curtis and Nancy Greene, Columbus, Ohio
Reverend Doctor Daryl C. Greene, Richmond, Indiana
Emmanuel Greene, Indianapolis, Indiana
Emily Street Hensel, Navarre, Ohio
Judith Victoria Hensley, Loyall, Kentucky
Ineda Lewis-Howard, Putney, Kentucky
Mildred K. Howard, Loyall, Kentucky
Donna Jones, Miamisburg, Ohio
Bobbie Maggard, Cumberland, Kentucky
Gayle and Lee Miller, Navarre, Ohio
Jim and Norma Partin, Tipp City, Ohio
Howard A. and Mary Francis Young-Qualls, Cawood, Kentucky
Thomas S. Qualls, North Canton, Ohio
Vickie Qualls, Mary Alice, Kentucky
William A. (Buck) Qualls, Cawood, Kentucky
Leroy and Kathy Schindler, New Lebanon, Ohio
Sharon E. Stanford, Union, Ohio
Shirley Tropea, Massillon, Ohio
Karen Wilson-Zenner, Akron, Ohio

ABOUT THE AUTHOR

From the rugged mountains of Southeastern Kentucky comes one of the twenty-first century's most powerful writers. Her written word will both educate and entertain you.

Rosezelle Boggs-Qualls grew up in Sunshine, a small coal mining village just south of Harlan, Kentucky. A born tomboy, she spent her days exploring the trails, streams, caves and abandoned mines of the Cumberland, Big Black and the Pine Mountains. For High School, Rosezelle attended the Pine Mountain Settlement School, Pine Mountain, Kentucky. In spite of a serious hearing impairment, she graduated from high school at age 16. In 1946, she met and married William A. (Buck) Qualls. Her husband is totally deaf.

When they were first married they lived in Cawood, Kentucky. However, in 1947, Harlan was a depressed area and in order to find employment they were forced to leave the mountains they loved and move to Dayton, Ohio.

Rosezelle earned a Bachelor of Science Degree in Social Work at Wright State University, Dayton, Ohio. Her graduate work in Applied Behavioral Science was also at Wright State. For more than 35 years she was employed in the Child Welfare Field in both the Dayton and Akron, Ohio areas. After her retirement in 2004, she and Buck came back home to relocate in Harlan and now live in Cawood, Kentucky. They have one son, Tom, and three grandchildren.

In 2003 Rosezelle was given the prestigious Wright State University *Social Worker of the Year Award,* and the Wright State University College of Liberal Arts *Outstanding Alumna Award.*

Also, Rosezelle served a six-year appointment by Bob Taft to the Ohio Governor's Council on People with Disabilities 1998-2004. She is serving her second appointed term by Steven L. Beshear to the Kentucky Governor's Council on Independent Living for People with Disabilities. She is also serving her second term as Board Chair for the Southeastern Kentucky Regional Agency of Pathfinders for Independent Living whose offices are in Harlan.

In 2007 she organized and is now serving her third term as President of the Harlan Writers' Guild.

TABLE OF CONTENTS

CHAPTER	TITLE	PAGE

PROLOGUE

I CHANT THE KENTUCKY MOUNTAINS SUBLIME

I chant the Cumberland Mountains, the Pine Mountains,
Big Black Mountain and the myriad of
Other mountains of the Appalachian region.
I chant the geography of the Cumberland River, formed by
The junction of Martin's Fork, Clover Fork, and Poor Fork,
At the town of Harlan. And the innumerable spring fed creeks,
Branches and rivulets that flow into them.

I chant the peaks, the gorges, caves, rugged cliffs, and the rocky walls
Beneath whose frowning faces many acres of rocks are piled high.
I chant the cool shady ravines and the springs flowing from the earth
Where the hunter slakes his thirst and the traveler rests in the shade.

I chant the trembling ferns in the coves, the flowers in the glens, the
Dogwood in bloom. The tall trees, the big trees, the cool shade
Beneath them, the hollows filled with honeysuckle vines, wild
Mountain Laurel and sheltered vales of ivy and moss covered logs.
I chant the haunts of the turkey, the hawk, the trilling songbirds, the quail,
The squirrel, raccoon, opossum, fox, deer, and panther, black and brown bear,
Wildcat and the little animals that burrow in the ground.

I chant the winding trails over the mountains, the lonesome trails,
Traveled by men and women, the trails made by the patient steps of
Mountain people and their horses, cattle, goats, and sheep.
I chant the dangers posed in deadly poisonous serpents that are
Abundant in the forests, in the clearings and in the flowing waters.
I speak of the copperhead, the rattlesnake, and the water moccasin.

I chant the Indians of these mountains, the red men and women who
Lived here for eons of time, and were here when the white men came.
Left behind were tomahawks, stone axes, arrowheads, beads, pottery,
Encampments, walking trails, and burial grounds.
I chant their honesty and honor, their reverence for nature, their
Friendship for white men, and their reluctance to give up their land.

I chant the white men for moving west and occupying Indian land,

Clearing forests, and erecting a new civilization upon the old.
I chant the wise men and women of these mountains, the strong
Robust people, who with not much more than their bare
Hands, wrestle a living from an unforgiving land.
I chant the silent people of these mountains, who ride along the silent
Trails, over the tall mountains, the hills, through gaps and valleys.

I chant the boisterous people of these mountains,
Who write funny rhymes about their neighbors and tell funny jokes.
And can still laugh long and loud at themselves.
I chant the pious men and women of these mountains, who read their
Bible, love God, listens to the preacher on Sunday, and let their souls
Sway to the emotion of the sermon and to the songs of faith.

I chant the heroic fighting men and women of these mountains,
Who stand strong on their honor and their proud history of facing
The enemy and never turning their backs on their foe.
I chant the farmer of these mountains, who clears and fences
New ground, plants crops and orchards, and builds his flocks and herds.
I speak of the stalwart people who fell the virgin forests, build their
Homes and barns, and usher in a new era of quiet farm life.

I chant the spice wood tea, the boneset tea, the sassafras tea, and all
The drinks made from the herbs and shrubbery of these mountains.
I chant the clouds, the sky, the sun that shines, the rains, the moon in
Dreamy mood and all the elements of nature that bless this land.
I chant the men, women, and children of these mountains, the Black, the
White, the Red, and all who live in harmony with nature. I speak of the high,
The low, the good, the bad, the reverent, and the sad.

I chant the dreams of stalwart mountain men, pure mountain womanhood,
And the life-long love they share with each other.
I chant this world, my world,
The mountains of southeastern Kentucky.

By
Henry Harvey Fuson, 1933

Edited, with permission, by
Rosezelle Boggs-Qualls, 2008

FORWARD
(The story thus far from "The Black Heart Book I")

The setting for this true story is in Harlan County near the Leslie County Line in the Southeastern Kentucky Mountains near Big Black Mountain, the tallest peak in the Kentucky highlands. This story is about the author's great grandfather, David Alex Turner (1822-1929), as related by her grandmother, Judy Turner-Smith (1884-1976). Alex owned a huge homestead that spanned large acreages on both sides of the Little Greasy Creek near Big Laurel. The Little Greasy Creek Trail wound along through Big Laurel and Little Laurel. It was about four miles further south that you turned left onto the Laden Trail to go up and over tall Pine Mountain to come down into the small logging town of Putney. The only way to travel on the narrow trails was by horseback, and the only way to transport anything was with a long narrow runner sled pulled by a mule.

In June 1898, Alex, with his oldest son, Rob, defended himself against a frivolous law suit brought by a cousin that involved property lines. Alex won that case and still managed to be friends with his cousin. However, he was bitterly disappointed in the man and decided he would do whatever it might take to guard against those who wanted to do hurt to him or to his family.

Alex answered an ad in a Pittsburgh, Pennsylvania newspaper that promised a two-dollar book would reveal the secrets of life. He sent the requested two dollars in postage stamps, and waited. Three weeks later, he took his young daughter, Judy, with him on the Laden Trail up and over tall Pine Mountain to Putney. The book arrived at the Putney Post Office wrapped in coarse, brown paper. It was addressed to Alex Turner, but with no return address.

Alex tore open the package and held the book in his hands. The title was in red calligraphy, *Black Heart – The Secret of Life.* It was a long ride over the mountain and down the Little Greasy Creek Trail to Big Laurel. He had to cross the Leslie County Line and follow a creek-bed trail up to the head of Alex's Branch (named for him) to reach his cabin. He could hardly contain his impatience to begin reading his new book.

The "Black Heart" book gave him instructions that enabled him to possess certain powers. It assured him that with these powers he would be able to "take charge of his life." However, the book instructed him to commit a terrible sin against God. Alex had a strong faith in God. He loved Jesus and had lived his life as a devout Christian. But, the temptation outlined in the *Black Heart* book was overpowering.

Alex gave in to the temptation. He climbed to the top of Big Black Mountain and at midnight on October 30, 1898, he committed the terrible sin. He was immediately repentant and did not carry out any further instructions. In fear and sorrow, he rushed down the mountain toward his home. It was a bright moonlit night. He was wearing a hard hat with his carbide light hooked to it so he could see the trail. About half way down the mountain side he came to a stretch of cliffs and a very narrow section of the trail. There was only room for one person and a misstep would send one over into a thousand foot drop off.

He turned the sharp corner of the first switch back in the trail and found his path blocked by a horrifying large, black dog. Already crazed with fear and sorrow, Alex heard the horrid dog speak, with a rumbling deep in its throat. It distinctly said, "Alex, go back. There is more. You must go back. I order you to go back!"

"No!" Alex screamed and backed up far enough past the sharp turn in the cliff path so that he couldn't see the black dog anymore.

Alex waited a long time. It seemed like an hour. When he again went around the sharp turn to continue on down the mountain, the black dog was gone. When he arrived home he burned the *Black Heart* book. He fasted and prayed for three days and nights. He felt that God forgave him and he received redemption for his sin. He was at peace within his soul.

It wasn't long afterwards that Alex discovered he did have some of the powers described in the *Black Heart* book. He vowed to use them only for good and never in the heat of anger.

Alex's youngest daughter was Jona or Jonie. Next to Jonie in age was Judy. Alex doted on Judy. His three older daughters were Rana or Rainie, who married Israel Miniard; Sarah or Sadie, who married Bishop (Bish) Boggs; and Emily, who married Robert Lewis. Robert is the brother of Enoch, who courted and married young Jonie. All four of his sons-in-law had land of his own. Alex had five sons, Rob, the oldest, then Dave, Alex, Liege, and the youngest one, Preston.

The youngest daughter, Jonie, married Enoch Lewis at age fourteen. She was married long before Judy. Stacy Elizabeth, Alex's wife, was very worried about Judy. She was convinced that Alex had ruined Judy because he allowed her to compete with men at turkey shoots all over the area. Judy could ride and shoot like a man, and better than most men. Her mother believed Judy would never find a man she would respect enough to be a good, obedient wife.

In danger of being called an "old maid," Judy finally did fall in love and marry. Her husband's name was Robert Smith, a man who had only worked at a day job and had no real interest in applying himself to a dawn-to-dusk running of a successful hard-working farm. Alex gave Robert and Judy the land they needed to make a good living. Under the Commonwealth of Kentucky law of property, he had to make out the deed giving Robert full ownership of the land. However, Robert let Judy do all the work while he did little or nothing. He didn't like guns. He wouldn't hunt, trap, or fish, but he was a constant complainer about the work.

When Judy was pregnant with her first child, Alex placed a "spell" on Robert that changed him. Suddenly, to Judy's amazement, Robert loved their land and became a kind and hard-working husband. This change in him lasted about five years.

Judy and Robert had three daughters, Mary, the oldest, then Stella, and the youngest, Della. Little Stella died before she was two years old. Soon after the birth of Della, Robert was struck by lightening and realized the calluses on his hands were from doing work he hated. Robert was filled with rage. He deserted his family and moved to Clay County.

The farm was in Robert's name. His hate for his wife and father-in-law caused him to advertise and sell not only the farm, but all of the tools and equipment, live stock, and the two years' supply of preserved food that represented months of hard work. His intention was to sell everything, leaving Judy with nothing for herself and their children.

At this time, in 1915, Pine Mountain Settlement School was being built south of Big Laurel and about a mile from the Laden Trail. The builders were two missionary women, Ethel Delong and Katherine Pettit. Miss Delong was Presbyterian and Miss Pettit was Catholic. William Creech and his wife, Sally Dixon-Creech, donated more than seven hundred acres of mountain land to them for the building of the school. The couple was known as Uncle William and Aunt Sal Creech. Alex went with Judy to see them about the possibility of her getting day work at the new school.

Judy had barely a second-grade education, but she was hired and began working in the kitchen in Laurel House at the school. Her job was to teach children cooking, food preservation, and to help prepare three meals a day for about one hundred people. Miss Delong very kindly taught Judy to read well enough to follow the recipes and measurements needed to cook for that many people. Judy learned even more by reading her Bible and asking Miss Delong questions about words and concepts that she didn't understand.

Judy had her own sleeping quarters in Laurel House, the largest building at the school that housed the kitchen and dining room. Mary and Della were allowed to attend the school and live at Big Log, the dormitory for younger girls. Mary was nine and Della was six, but because neither of them had ever been to school, they both began in the Primer. Within a few weeks, Mary and Della were promoted to the first grade. By Christmas, Mary was in the third grade and planning to be moved from Big Log to live with the older girls.

Mary was twelve on November 26, 1919. When she graduated from the sixth grade the following May, she was placed in the town of Hazard with a minister's family to help care for their four children. She was treated like one of the family and allowed to continue her education. Della was ten on April 30, 1920 and would be in the fourth grade in the fall. She stayed at Pine Mountain School with her mother.

In 1921 as Alex grew older, he taught Judy some of the special powers that he only used for good. Judy promised him she would continue to do the same. Alex was now more than one hundred years old and living with his youngest daughter, Jonie Lewis, and her family on their farm near the mouth of Alex's Branch and located near the Leslie County line.

While on a trip to Harlan with the missionaries to buy supplies for the school, Judy was taunted by an evil man about being a grass widow because her husband deserted her and later had divorced her. For the first time, she realized she had the undeserved reputation through vicious local gossips of being a woman with loose morals who couldn't hold her man.

In the summer of 1921, while on a trip with Miss Pettit to Hazard to visit Mary and her foster family, Judy went out alone and walked around downtown. She went into several restaurants to learn how they prepared their different meals. One particular place that fascinated her was the Hazard Hotel and Restaurant, owned by Bill Jenkins. She introduced herself as Mrs. Judy Smith and asked if she could see his kitchen. He asked, "Why do you want to see where we do the cooking?"

She explained, "I work at the Pine Mountain Settlement School near Big Laurel in Harlan County, and I prepare three meals a day for more than a hundred people. I wanted to see if I could learn something new to use on my job!"

He laughed, and said, "Ma'am, I'm happy to show you our kitchen, and you're just who I've been looking for. If you ever want to leave that school for another cooking job, come and see me."

Shortly after Judy's trip to Hazard, a group of church people arrived from the East Coast for a visit at Pine Mountain School. They were an important financial sponsor of the school. The vicious gossips made it their business to inform them of the grass widow working with the children in the school kitchen.

Although the leader of the church people was sympathetic with Judy's situation, he told the missionaries he had no choice. "A divorced woman should not be around very young children because it gave the young girls a bad example of womanhood. You have to let Mrs. Smith go or our group will withdraw as financial sponsors of the school."

When Judy was informed by Miss Pettit that she had to leave the school, she was sure that God had led her to visit Mr. Jenkins' Hotel and Restaurant. It was a two-day trip by horseback from the school to Hazard. Judy left right away. She saw Mr. Jenkins and was immediately hired as the restaurant manager.

She was allowed to leave Della at the school until her graduation from the sixth grade. Della was in tears as she watched her mother leave the school. She stood and watched until Judy was out of sight.

The story continues in The Black Heart Book II.........

Chapter One
COURAGE, FAITH, AND HOPE

Judy was unaware that her younger daughter, Della, hadn't moved from the spot where they said goodbye. With eyes swimming in tears, Della watched her mother pass through the entrance gate, leaving her behind at the Pine Mountain Settlement School. Judy was riding her beloved horse, Curly, and leading a pack mule that was carrying her personal belongings. Della expected her to turn and wave before she rode out of sight, but Judy didn't look back.

Della's older sister, Mary, left Pine Mountain School when she graduated from the sixth grade. Miss Pettit, one of the missionaries in charge of building the school, arranged for Mary to live with the Reverend Ethan Brownlett and his family in Hazard. Mary was very happy in her placement with the minister. She was treated as one of the family and enjoyed going to the local school and helping to take care of the family's four children.

Because vicious gossips had informed school sponsors and financial benefactors that Judy was divorced (through no fault of her own) and unfit to be around young girls, she had been asked by Miss Pettit to leave her job as the school cook. So, now she was leaving Pine Mountain School to begin a new job as manager and chief cook for Jenkins' Restaurant in Hazard. Della knew that her mother would be living near Mary. She couldn't help the gulping sob that escaped from her throat at the thought that she was now alone.

However, Della only stood there for a few more moments feeling abandoned. Then she squared her shoulders and, with thoughts coming fast and running together, she said, "Oh, well, I'm 'mong friends here with my teachers and the students. Ma 'spects me to make the best of it, and I will! Aunt Jonie and Grandpa Alex are always willin' to visit me, and every once in awhile I see Aunt Becky and my other cousins. So, I'm not really alone! I've got two more years 'til I graduate and then I'll go live with Ma and Mary in Hazard."

With these thoughts to reassure her, Della walked rapidly toward Laurel House. Her assigned job for nine weeks was to clean the hardwood floors in the dining room using dust down (oiled sawdust). She needed to hurry if she was going to get it done before they set the tables for the noon meal.

As Della resolutely walked toward Laurel House, Judy continued on down the Little Greasy Creek Trail. Her youngest sister, Jonie, and her husband owned a large homestead in Leslie County, just over the Harlan County line. It wasn't on her way to Hazard, but she needed to go there to add more of her personal belongings to the already heavily burdened mule.

Judy dearly loved Jonie. She was closer to her than to any other of her four sisters. Her father, Alex, made his home with Jonie. Judy wouldn't have time to see and say goodbye to her sister-in-law and dearest friend, Becky, who was married to her brother, Rob.

Judy didn't tarry long. When the mule was packed and its burden secured, she turned toward Jonie and Alex with brimming eyes, "You both know that I hate to leave you. Leavin' little Della was one of the hardest things I've ever done. I'll try to visit at Christmas. Pray for me that I'll be able to do this new job. I love you so very much, but now I must go."

Jonie was crying as she handed a burlap bag up to Judy. "I made you 'nuff food to last you through the morrow."

Alex, too, had brimming eyes as he said, "You'll be in my thoughts and prayers continually 'til we see each other again. I'll look forward to Christmas. Try to bring Mary with you. I really love and miss the child. We promise we'll visit Della at the school. Now go on with you or you'll never get there!"

Again, Judy left without looking back. She felt terribly mixed emotions as she rode along. She felt sadness because of the necessary separation from her young daughter at Pine Mountain School and from her own beloved family. Yet uncontrolled elation bubbled up at the thought that she had a good job waiting for her. She was determined to do her very best. She had built a good nest egg with the money she received when the farm was sold and from her wages at the school. As soon as Della graduated she planned, with God's help, to make a home for herself and her two daughters.

It was pushing it to make the trip by horseback over the mountains to Hazard in two days. The first day passed without incident. She was more than half way to Hazard when she stopped at dusk and made camp. With her evening prayers still on her lips, she went to sleep and slept soundly through the night.

The next morning, she was up before daybreak, ate breakfast, and packed up to leave. With her new-day prayers finished, she said aloud, "And, God bless Jonie for the fine food bag she gave me. It really saved me a lot of time."

She had to grin a little sheepishly after she said that, because she was sure God didn't have time to worry about her saving time. Then she said, "I'm sorry, Lord, that was sure nervy of me!"

Judy was anxious to be on her way. With the campfire well drowned, she mounted Curly and reached for the mule's lead rope. If all went well she would be in Hazard by nightfall. Her plan was to go directly to Reverend Brownlett's home and spend the night with his family and Mary. She could check in with Mr. Jenkins at the Hazard Hotel tomorrow morning.

She passed through Hyden and turned northeast into a little traveled trail that would take her directly to Hazard. After riding about a mile, she overtook two shifty-eyed, heavily-bearded men who were going the same way. Ordinarily, she welcomed company, but she instinctively distrusted these two men.

They greeted her warmly, saying they were two brothers from over Hazard way and their names were Josh and Gabe Blevins. "Our Maw and Paw have a home-place on the east side of town, near the Kentucky River."

She responded, "Well, fellers, it's good to meet you. I'm from near the Harlan County Line, near Big Laurel. My name's Judy Turner-Smith. I'd welcome your company, but I'm in a hurry to reach Hazard afore dark. Please move over so I can pass. "

"What'd you say, Gabe, shall we let her pass?"

"No, Josh, she's got more than jus' supplies on that mule. She should pay us if she wants to pass. I know she's got cash money hid somewhere."

Without hesitating, Judy reached over Curly's side, pulled her rifle free and aimed it at the brother, Josh. "You two boys are makin' a big mistake if you think you can hold me up and make me pay you for nothin'. My name's Judy Turner-Smith from Big Laurel. I think you've heard of me from the turkey shoots in Leslie and Harlan County. You don't want to mess with me! If you want to keep your ears, fingers, and toes, don't do somethin' you'll regret!"

"Gabe, back off, I've heard of Judy Turner afore she added Smith to her name. She hits dead center anything she aims at. Let her pass. Don't do nothin'!"

The two brothers pulled over into the underbrush of the trail and allowed Judy and her mule plenty of room to pass between them. They were muttering obscenities under their breath. She did a half turn in the saddle so she could keep an eye on both of them until she passed around a bend in the trail. Then she kept a steady trot going for the next mile or so. When Judy figured she was far enough ahead of them to be safe, she slowed down to her normal pace.

She said aloud, "Thank you, God, for keeping me safe. If I'd shot 'em, it would've been self-defense. I'm sure glad I'll be at Reverend Brownlett's home soon. I wouldn't want to camp out tonight with those two on the prowl. If I see 'em again, I hope they'll be in front of me where I can watch 'em. I sure wouldn't want to have to worry about 'em bein' behind my back!"

During the rest of the trip that day, Judy didn't meet anyone else on the narrow trail. When she arrived in Hazard, she went immediately to Reverend Brownlett's home and received a warm welcome from his family and Mary.

She spent that first night with the Brownlett's and ended the long day with prayer before going to sleep. "Thank you, Lord Jesus for keeping me safe from the Blevins boys today. If that was their real name! Please bless Reverend Brownlett and his family. Bless my little Mary and keep her safe. Be with my little Della so far away at school. Help her to not be too lonely or sad. Be with my Pa, Jonie, and her family, and dear Becky and her family. Bless them for all their help and love. Be with me tomorrow as I begin my new job. Help me to always do my best and to keep a prayer in my heart as I learn new things. I'll give you all the praise. Dear Jesus, I love you! Amen."

Early the next morning Judy rode Curly and led the pack mule into town. She tied them to the hitching rail by the long front porch and climbed the eight steps leading to the front entrance. She didn't have to look for Mr. Jenkins. He met Judy as she came through the ornate, double doors of the Hazard Hotel.

Mr. Jenkins was an aging, stocky, broad-shouldered, bushy-haired man. Today he was all smiles as he welcomed Judy. "Lordy, Mrs. Smith, I'm so glad to see you're finally here!"

Judy was embarrassed by his enthusiasm and worried that she was late in reporting to him for the new job. "It's not been a week since we agreed that I would work for you. Am I really that late?"

"Oh, no, Mrs. Smith, you're not late at all. It's just that I'm that anxious to have someone reliable take over running the restaurant for me. If you'd got here two days ago, it wouldn't have been too soon!"

He continued on in a raspy, breathless voice, "Let's get you settled in. I remember that I told you your room would be a corner one where you could easily see both ways when looking down on Main Street."

Mr. Jenkins banged on a shiny metal bell that was on the front desk of the hotel and suddenly an older man shuffled up to them. He muttered, "Yes sir, Mr. Jenkins. Do you want somethin'?"

The hotel owner reddened in sudden anger, but controlled his voice perfectly as he smiled through clenched teeth and his jaw muscles worked, "Yes, Lance, this is Mrs. Judy Smith. She's the new Restaurant Manager. That's her pack mule tied outside at the rail. I want you to move her things into the corner room on the second floor overlooking Main Street. She'll show you where she wants to put everything."

Then he turned to Judy and said, "After you've settled in, come and see me. We'll talk about our plans for you to begin work tomorrow."

The older man slowly moved along with Judy out to the patiently waiting mule and helped her to unload her possessions and put them on the front porch, ready to take upstairs to her room.

"Lance, I need a good livery stable. I'll return my mule to the livery behind the hotel. That's who I rented him from. I need my horse put up, but I want him well fed and kept clean. I would 'preciate you telling me the best place in town where I can board him."

"Miss Judy, the best place in town is where you rented your mule. It's the next block over, behind the hotel. It's the Hazard Feed and Livery, and run by Raff Pennington and his sons. Tell 'em Lance sent you. They'll take good of your horse. I've been looking at him and he's mighty fine. I can tell you take good care of him. What's his name?"

"His name's Curly and he's real special to me. I've had him since he was a colt and he's 'bout twenty years old now. If you'll take my bundles up to my room,

I'll go ahead and take him and the mule to the Livery. You've been mighty nice and, Lance, I do want to thank you!"

"You's more than welcome, Miss Judy."

As Judy rode Curly and led the mule around to the back of the Hazard Hotel, she was smiling. Thanks to Lance, a big worry about what to do with Curly while she was busy in town was solved. She liked the kindly older man.

Judy grinned happily, "I think I've made a good friend."

She rode Curly through the wide, double doors of the livery and dismounted. She was met by an aging, portly, pleasant looking fellow with a handsome mustache, "Well, good mornin' Ma'am. What can I do for you?"

"Are you Mr. Raff Pennington?"

"Yes, Ma'am, I shore am! And, who might you be?"

"My name's Judy Turner-Smith, I'm the new cook at the restaurant in the Hazard Hotel. A nice man named Lance told me to tell you he sent me. I'm returning your mule, but I need to board my horse, Curly, by the month. I want to be sure he's well cared for. Do you have room for him and how much do you charge for his board?"

"Well, Miss Judy, it's a pleasure to meet you. Board for your horse will be $2.00 a month. We'll feed and treat him good. He'll have his own clean stall. When weather permits, we turn our boardin' animals loose in the corral out back. To keep him healthy, you'll need to exercise him daily. If we do it for you, it's a dollar extra a month."

"I'm goin' to pay you a month in advance for Curly's board and exercisin'. Since I'm startin' a new job, I don't know how much extra time I'll have each day. After a month, I may exercise him myself. I'll come over every day, though, to talk to Curly. He and I have a understandin' 'bout that."

Judy gave Mr. Pennington $3.00 for a month's board and special care. He thanked her, and said, "You're welcome to come and talk to your horse any time you want. Now, you say you're Jenkins' new cook? Me and my boys eat there 'most every day. I'm sure lookin' forward to some real good cookin'!"

"That's fine, Mr. Pennington, and I look forward to seeing you there!"

Judy gave Curly a loving goodbye pat and hurried back to the hotel.

She was pleased that her possessions were safely deposited on the floor or on the bed in her room. The corner location gave her a good view of the street and made her feel proud of her new position as restaurant manager. When she compared her new, spacious living quarters to the small underground room she lived in for so long at the school, this room was luxurious!

She hurriedly unpacked her bundles, carefully hanging her few dresses and aprons in the closet. She folded her other clothes away in the chest and dresser drawers. There were only a few toilet items to worry about. She placed her hand mirror, comb, and brush on top of the dresser. On one of the shopping trips to

Harlan with Miss Pettit, she had splurged and bought two different scents of toilet water. She chose the light scent of lilac to wear today. The heavy scent of honeysuckle she would save for nights.

There was a large mirror attached to the dresser and her reflection made her smile in approval. Her long curly black hair was pinned neatly around her oval shaped face and her blue-green eyes were sparkling with excitement. Her complexion was a flawless pearly white, and the work outfit she had changed into was neat and flattering to her slender figure.

Mr. Jenkins was waiting for her when she appeared in the lobby. He was more excited than she was! He jumped up and asked, "Is your room all right? Are you satisfied with everything? Is there anything else that you need or want?"

"Yes, Mr. Jenkins, the room's fine. If I need anything else, I'll tell you. But, I'm anxious to see the kitchen and to know just what you expect from me."

"Now, Judy, I think I told you that we serve three meals a day. Breakfast is our busiest time. The noon dinner is second. Supper draws the lightest crowd.

Say, Raff Pennington has already come by to let me know he thinks you're going to do just fine. You made quite an impression on him because of how much you care for your horse.

Now, as I told you before. You'll work six days and have Sundays off. I'll take care of the restaurant when you're off. I know you have a daughter here in Hazard who's placed with Reverend Brownlett. He's a mighty fine man who's well-liked by everyone. If you ever need to take time off because of your child, just tell me. I can always fill in for you."

"Mr. Jenkins, I want you to know that I do 'preciate what you've done for me. My livin' quarters are very nice. I promise that you'll get full measure from me in my work. I want you to always tell me if I'm doing anything wrong. I'll do my best to make it right."

"Judy, I'm so glad you're here! I think you and I are going to get along just fine. We'll make a good team in running the hotel and the restaurant. Now, let's go see where you'll be working and I'll show you where everything is. You are in charge of ordering supplies and need to make sure we receive only quality meats and fresh fruit and vegetables. It's important that we don't run out of anything we need to prepare our daily menu."

For the first time, Judy felt some uncertainty about what was expected of her. At the school, she wasn't the only one responsible for ordering and maintaining supplies. Mrs. Zande was the overseer and was back-up to Judy's decisions. Now, she alone would be responsible.

She squared her shoulders and said, "I'll learn real fast. Mr. Jenkins, you won't have to worry. When I order supplies and they give me the bills, or invoices, do I just give them to you to take care of?"

"Yes, don't worry about people wanting money. I'll take care of paying everybody. You'll have enough to do. There's an assistant cook, a salad and dessert person, and someone to bus tables and wash dishes. After the first week, if the people working here don't suit you, we'll get rid of 'em. I'll let you make the decisions about who you want to work for us."

The rest of the day was spent in learning where everything was, including the pots, pans, and all the kitchen tools necessary for preparing food. She found the designated storage places on pantry and cabinet shelves for table linens, candleholders, candles, sugar bowls, salt and pepper shakers, glassware, china and silverware. There were special table centerpieces and other decorations stored away that were used for different holidays. There was also a special storeroom for cleaning supplies and equipment. Judy was impressed because she was used to the same kind of efficiency at the school.

When it was time for the noon meal, Mr. Jenkins invited Judy to eat with him. She looked at the menu, but offered as the day's special was an open-faced beef sandwich with mashed potatoes and gravy. Both she and Mr. Jenkins ordered the special, with coffee. When it was served by the young waitress, they both were pleased with the way she presented the food. She smiled, and told Judy her name. Then she asked to be told if they needed anything else.

The only thing that marred the meal and made Judy uncomfortable was when they both heard the cook scolding the young waitress for something he thought she did wrong. Judy frowned and shook her head in disapproval.

"Mr. Jenkins, the people eatin' here should never be able to hear anything unpleasant that's happenin' in the kitchen. If they want a peaceful meal, that alone would spoil it for them. And it looks bad for the restaurant. Besides, I don't believe the waitress did anything that warrants him scoldin' her in public."

"Judy, this is exactly what I want you to do. Remember you're the new manager, not me. What you don't approve of, you fix it to suit yourself. I'll back you all the way. I want our hotel and restaurant to be rated A-1 all the time!"

Judy was in awe of Mr. Jenkins and had to ask, "Why are you dependin' on me like this? I've only talked to you two times. You don't really know me!"

"I talked with Reverend Brownlett, who is a good friend with Miss Pettit at Pine Mountain School. Both of them gave you a glowing recommendation and assured me I couldn't hire a finer person or harder worker. Their word is plenty good enough for me!"

Judy reddened in embarrassment from the high praise. "I thank you with all my heart, Mr. Jenkins. Bless Miss Pettit and Reverend Brownlett, too!"

Mr. Jenkins said, "The afternoon is yours to do as you please. I know you haven't spent much time with your daughter since you arrived here last night. So, why don't you go stay with her awhile and come back in time to order from the supper menu. Then you'll know how we handle the evening meal."

Judy thanked him again and went to the livery stable to saddle Curly. She planned to be at Reverend Brownlett's at about the same time that Mary got home from school. She was elated with the happy prospects of her new job.

Reverend Brownlett's wife, Anne, answered the door when Judy knocked and welcomed her into the parlor.

"Ethan isn't here right now. He has a parishioner that is seriously ill and went to visit with the man's family. He'll return shortly. I've made a fresh pot of tea and baked some fruity teacakes. Let's have our tea and cakes in the kitchen. We can visit until the children get home from school."

Judy smiled and accepted the kind invitation. "Mrs. Brownlett, this is the first time I've heard Reverend Brownlett's first name. Ethan suits him perfectly."

"Tell me about the new job. Do you feel you'll be happy working there?"

"Oh, my, yes! It's a dream come true! I'll be doing what I love to do which is cook, and I have my own room as part of my salary. I'll have Sundays off so I can go to church with Mary. Mr. Jenkins seems to be the loveliest sort of man. That is if a man can be called lovely?"

They both laughed heartily at the thought. Then Anne said, "We are laughing now, but I certainly agree that men who are honest, thoughtful, pleasant, and treat women with respect can be called lovely men!"

Judy responded in a much more somber mood, "The problem is that we have too few men who fit that description. My father does, but I have met way too many who are definitely not lovely men.

That reminds me, Mrs. Brownlett, do you know anything about two brothers named Josh and Gabe Blevins? They said their folks had a farm east of Hazard and near the Kentucky River."

"Well, I have heard some ugly stories about them. Why do you ask?"

"I met 'em on the Hazard Trail this side of Hyden. I had to threaten 'em with my gun afore they'd let me pass on the trail. They were going to rob me."

"What a frightening thing to happen to you! You should tell Ethan when he comes home. Maybe he'll want you to report it to the sheriff's office."

"I'll tell Reverend Brownlett about it, but I don't think it's wise to make worse enemies of these men by bringing in the sheriff. After I made 'em let me pass, nothing else happened. I'll wait. Maybe I'll never see 'em again."

The two women had finished their tea and sweet cakes when Mary and the four Brownlett children came noisily into the house. Mary saw Curly tied up outside and was delighted to find her mother there. However, she excused herself to go upstairs with the children to see that they changed out of their school clothes into play outfits.

Anne smiled and said, "You can see why we love your daughter. She never has to be reminded to do anything. She knows what needs to be done and does it, and always cheerfully. She is so good with our children!"

It wasn't long after the children came home that Reverend Brownlett arrived, too. Judy excused herself and went outside to sit in the porch swing with Mary. She told Mary everything about her first day at the Hazard Hotel.

"Ma, will you really be able to go to church with me on Sunday? We can eat Sunday dinner together. Then, we can have the afternoon to ourselves, or join Reverend Brownlett and his family in some of the special Sunday church doings. Anyway, I'm so happy that we're together again. I miss being with Della. She writes to me every once in a while. I always write her right back using the $2.00 she gave me for stamps."

After checking the time, Judy decided she should head back to the hotel to have supper with Mr. Jenkins. She had much to do to get ready for her first full day of work tomorrow. She hugged her daughter and said goodbye, with a promise to see her on Sunday. "Hey, that's just a few days from now and we'll have the whole day together!"

She rode Curly into the livery stable. She was met by a much younger man this time. He introduced himself, "I'm Tom Pennington. I'm the oldest of the "Sons" part of the business. I'll gladly take care of him for you."

"I'm much obliged. Thank you."

Judy said good night to Curly with a loving pat on his sleek neck.

Mr. Jenkins was sitting in a large rocking chair waiting for her when she climbed the steps to the porch of the hotel. He smiled and asked, "Are you hungry? Let's go have supper and plan your day for tomorrow."

Judy said, "Yes, I am hungry. Thank you for waitin' for me."

She noticed that the long porch was a partial wrap-around that spanned the entrances to the hotel and to the restaurant. There were twin sets of steps from the street to the porch in front of both businesses. But you didn't have to climb them twice if you were staying in the hotel.

"Well, that's sure convenient, Mr. Jenkins, the way you designed the entrances to the hotel and the restaurant. It saves a lot of steps by having them connected this way."

"Judy, you sure do notice things that most folks don't give a second thought about. I like that. I want you to look at the breakfast menu while we have supper. You need to plan to serve people by six tomorrow morning."

They went inside and sat down at a medium-sized round table that was set up for four people. The chairs were cane-bottomed and very comfortable. On each table there were bright red and white checkered cloths and complimenting red and white cloth dinner napkins.

The same young waitress that served them lunch appeared with the dinner menu. Again, she smiled and said, "My name is Sylvia. Do you need a minute to look at the menu?"

Mr. Jenkins didn't look up or respond, so Judy said, "Yes, please. And would you also bring me the regular breakfast menu, and if you have a listing of the breakfast specials, I would like to see that, too?"

Sylvia's eyes grew huge. She extended her hand and said, "You must be Mrs. Smith, our new manager that I've been hearin' 'bout! It's a pleasure to meet you, ma'am. I'll bring you the breakfast menu and our specials right away."

The waitress went behind a long diner-type bar that spanned almost the width of the dining room and retrieved a breakfast menu and the listing of daily specials. She was on her way back to their table, when the cook yelled for her.

"Sylvia, what's takin' you so long? I'm waitin' for their orders! If you don't stop all the chit chat with the customers, you're gonna get yourself fired!"

Embarrassed, the young waitress stopped in her tracks and was red from her collar to her eyebrows. However, she continued to their table and gave the extra menus to Judy. She apologized, "I'm sorry that the cook got mad at me. He didn't know it was you, Mr. Jenkins, or you, Ma'am. Please forgive me."

With that said, she managed a trembling little smile, and asked, "Are you ready to order?"

They made their choices, but both expressed displeasure with the cook's behavior and said almost in unison, "Well, that outburst from the kitchen certainly spoiled my dinner!"

Judy asked, "Mr. Jenkins, when will I officially be in charge here?"

"You were officially the new manager when you arrived this morning!"

"Will you excuse me while I go to the kitchen? I won't be long."

Mr. Jenkins grinned, "Why certainly, Judy. Take all the time you need."

She scraped her chair back, got up and walked resolutely across the dining room and through the swinging half-doors into the large kitchen.

Isaac, the cook was tall, dark-haired, red-faced, and heavy-set; He was a frowning ogre of a man. Judy took into account that he was big man and most certainly a bully because of how he treated the nice young waitress. She smiled at him and offered her hand. Flustered, he did take her right hand. She closed her left hand over his and her lips moved silently.

Then very quietly, but distinctly, she said, "I'm Judy Turner-Smith, your new boss. Your voice carries into the dining room when you're angry and scolding our help. It ruins the appetite of the customers. No matter how good a cook you are, if you're disagreeable and scolding, it ruins the entire meal. Do you agree with what I'm saying? If you don't, come tomorrow, you'll be the one fired, not Sylvia who was just doing her job, and very well, I'm pleased to add."

The cook stammered in surprise, "Why, why, yes, Miss Smith, whatever you say. I'm a good cook. I won't be loud again! I've got a problem with that, but I'll change. I need this job. I'm really pleased to meet you, Ma'am."

Still speaking softly, Judy asked, "What's your name?"

"Oh, my name is Isaac, Isaac Blevins, Ma'am."

"Well, Isaac Blevins, it's a pleasure meetin' you. When the last customer is served, you may leave for tonight. I'll see you tomorrow mornin'."

Isaac smiled pleasantly, showing some relief in his voice as he said, "Thank you, Miss Smith. Yes, Ma'am, I'll see you at 4:00 in the mornin'."

"No, Isaac, I'm changing your hours startin' tomorrow. Report to work at 5:00 and we'll see how things go through the day, then we'll talk some more."

Judy went back through the swinging doors and seated herself again with Mr. Jenkins. "What happened? I kept waiting for a loud explosion from Isaac. I didn't hear a peep."

"No, and I dare say you won't ever again. I explained to him how loud, angry voices upset customers. And, when customers are upset it spoils the taste of his good food. He agreed with me and said it wouldn't happen again. Oh, I see our food's here. Isaac will be leavin' for the day soon and then I can see more of the kitchen and get ready for tomorrow.

At the school, I prepared for the next days breakfast the night before. I plan to do the same here. But now, I have to look at the menu and the daily specials so I can plan what needs to be done."

"Judy lets enjoy our steaks. I don't want to talk any more business tonight. As soon as we finish supper, you're on your own. Come and see me if you need anything!"

The steaks were excellent. Isaac provided a large baked potato, with fresh churned butter and cool sour cream. There wasn't any side salad available tonight. The large round yeasty rolls had already been rolled in butter and were greasy feeling, but went well with the rest of the meal.

Before they finished eating, Judy saw Isaac leaving by the side door. Sylvia came and replenished their coffee and asked about dessert. Both of them declined. Judy asked Sylvia if the dishwasher was still there. She looked quickly at Mr. Jenkins, "I'll see if I can find him. He has to clear the tables, too."

Judy asked, "Sylvia, will you stay over for a few minutes tonight?"

"Yes, Ma'am, I'll be glad to."

Sylvia gathered up a number of dirty dishes and carried them to the kitchen. Judy heard them being scraped and then dropped a few at a time into the hand operated dish-washer. She knew that the dishwasher was long gone and Sylvia was covering for him.

Then she turned to Mr. Jenkins, "The cook said his last name was Blevins. Does he have two brothers named Josh and Gabe?"

"Yes, he does, but don't hold that against him. I've heard a lot of ugly stories about 'em holding up people, and I know you can't trust 'em. Isaac is the only one of the boys that's willing to work. He's a good cook, just needs to learn how to deal with people. It's too bad about his brothers; the old folks are good Christian people. How do you happen to know of 'em?"

"I met up with 'em on the Hazard Trail yesterday. They tried to rob me. I had to threaten 'em with my gun afore they let me pass. I thought 'bout goin' to the sheriff, but nothing else happened. I decided to leave well 'nough alone. I think they're cowards, but dangerous! Do they ever come in here to eat?"

"Yes, they do, but only because their brother's the cook. We've never had any trouble out of 'em, but watch yourself. If they do cause you any more trouble, I'll talk to the sheriff about it myself.

Now, I'm goin' to leave you alone to get ready for tomorrow. Remember, if you need anything, let me know. I'll be at the front desk 'til well after midnight. The hotel and restaurant are pretty safe, because after I go to bed, the sheriff has a deputy who checks on both places off and on all through the night. I'm usually up around three in the morning, but now that you're here, I'll be able to get a decent night's sleep, for a change!"

Judy stayed behind, sitting at the table studying the breakfast menu and the short list of regular morning specials. They looked fairly simple. What was new to her was the large variety. At Pine Mountain School, everyone ate the same thing; they just had to make enough to feed a hundred people.

She soon knew pretty much what she had to do. She went into the kitchen to talk with Sylvia. She was just finishing up the evening dishes.

Judy asked, "Sylvia, who is the dishwasher and where is he?"

"Miss Judy, when I don't do 'em myself, its Mr. Lance who's s'posed to do 'em. He's a sweet older man and I don't want to get him in any trouble!"

Sylvia was almost in tears. "Please don't fire him. He needs a job to live!

I gave him his supper afore you and Mr. Jenkins came in. Lance's old and can't stay awake from six in the mornin' 'til this late at night. He's lying down in the shed where he sleeps. I've been watchin' out for him now for 'most a year."

Judy put her arm around Sylvia, and said. "Now don't you get upset. Lance was very kind to me this mornin'. I know he's aging, but we can change his hours and duties to make it possible for him to make a livin' and not have to worry 'bout gettin' too tired. Where's the shed that he's livin' in? Doesn't he have any family?"

"The shed's where we used to do the hotel and restaurant laundry, but we send it out to the Hazard Laundry now. Lance has used it to sleep at night and to store his few belongin's. He takes all his meals free in the restaurant. I don't know of any family of his. Since I've been watchin' out for him, I feel like I'm his family. Lance reminds me of my Grandpa Johnson. My folks died when I was small and he raised me. I lost him, too, when he was 91. He died over a year ago and now I have no family left."

"Well, don't worry 'bout it anymore. Tomorrow, I'll need you to help me learn where everything is and to line out what has to be done for lunch and dinner. Will you mind doing that for me?"

"No, Ma'am, I'll be pleased to help you in anyway I can, but what 'bout Isaac, the cook. He'll yell at me. He yells at Lance, too. He threatens to fire me all the time."

"Don't you worry about Isaac. I think you'll be pleased at the change in him. We had a talk tonight afore he left and came to an understandin' about how we need to treat other people. What time do you come to work in the morning?"

"I'll be here at five thirty to help get ready to start servin' at six. The restaurant is open to the public from six in the mornin' until eight at night. I live close by and sometimes I go home on slow days to do my washin', ironin', and cleanin'. But, 'til you can do without me, I won't take any time off. I'll wait 'til you tell me when I can leave."

"Let's not worry about that right now. Tell me, are all of the meats kept in the big walk-in cooler or is there a smoke house somewhere nearby for the hams and bacon?"

"As far as I know, all of the meats are kept in the big cooler."

"I'm going inside the cooler to see what all we have on hand. We'll need bacon, sausage, pork chops, ham, and steak to prepare for folks as they order from the menu and the breakfast specials."

Judy went inside the cooler while Sylvia waited outside with the door standing open. There was a good supply of all the breakfast meats, a large standing rib beef roast, pork chops, pork roasts for barbeque, and some of the best cuts of beef. Judy's eyes widened as she spotted a whole side of beef hanging all the way in the back of the large cooler.

"Sylvia, do you know who does the butchering? There's a whole side of beef in here!"

"No, Ma'am, I didn't know when we ever ordered beef by the side. I've never seen any butcherin'. You'll have to ask Mr. Jenkins 'bout that."

"Sylvia, you said your Grandpa's name was Johnson. Was he your father's pa? Is that your name, too?"

"Yes, my whole name is Sylvia Rae Johnson, spelled R-a-e. But, nobody ever calls me that."

"Why don't you take off for the day? I'm goin' to stay here a while and plan the cookin' and servin' of the mornin' meal. I really 'preciate all your help and I'll see you at five thirty in the mornin'."

When Judy was alone in the large kitchen, she began to put together the dry ingredients she needed for biscuits, pancakes, oatmeal, hominy grits, and a simple coffee cake. She filled a basket with potatoes ready to be peeled for home-fries to go with the egg plates. She went back inside the big cooler to locate fresh butter, lard, eggs, buttermilk and sweet milk.

Then she gathered together all the pots, pans, large spoons, egg turners, meat turning forks, and mixing bowls that she and Isaac would need to prepare the food.

The only ingredients that she wanted to use and couldn't find were fresh fruits and tomatoes. She liked to use them as a garnish with fried or scrambled eggs. There were lots of quart and half-gallon jars of tomatoes, peaches and apples, but that wouldn't do for her purposes.

Sylvia would be there early enough to prepare the tables. But, from now on they would get the tables ready the night before. Judy had to smile as she remembered her mother, Stacey Elizabeth, reminding her that, "Good wives spend time at night helpin' out the morrow!"

Then she turned her attention to the beautiful black cast iron cook stove. It was huge and had an electric warming closet all the way across the top of it. She checked it out and found that it was very clean. At the end of the stove on the right side was a holding tank or reservoir full of warm water. In the process of cooking and baking that water would be very hot and just right for doing dishes.

It was one of the first all electric stoves that were made for commercial use. The one in the kitchen at Pine Mountain only had six burners. This monster had eight. There was a large removable grill pan that covered two of the burners. Mr. Jenkins had designed and built a venting system that included an inverted blower in the ceiling. The system carried steam and smoke upward through round insulated tin stove pipes that went all the way up and vented above the roof.

There wasn't anything to do to the stove to prepare for tomorrow so Judy closed up and went to the hotel lobby to say good night to Mr. Jenkins. She found him dozing, almost ready to fall off the chair behind the front desk.

"Mr. Jenkins," she said loudly enough to wake him.

"Oh, Judy, I must have dozed off, but I'm awake now. How'd it go?"

"Everything went very well. I'm ready for the breakfast crowd, but I have a question. When you order a whole side of beef, who butchers it for you?"

"I don't understand. I don't ever order a whole side of beef. I'd be afraid it would spoil before we could use it all. Why do you ask?"

"There's a whole side of beef hangin' all the way in the back of the large cooler. You must have paid for it along with the other bills. We probably need to ask Isaac about it tomorrow. Anyway, I'll see you in the mornin'. Good night!"

Judy made her way up the stairs to her room. Although she was tired from the long, exciting day, after she said her prayers and went to bed, she was wide awake. It was after midnight when she heard a wagon go by the front of the building, turn and go around to the side. Then she didn't hear it anymore and knew it had stopped not far from Main Street.

Worrying that someone might try to break into the side door of the restaurant, she pulled on a housecoat, went out into the hall and down the stairs. Mr. Jenkins was not there. She went outside and walked softly across the front porch and looked around the corner.

The wagon was still there. She heard men's gruff voices. There was almost no light on the street. She could tell that the side door was open. A lit lantern hung from the side of the wagon and in the dim light she saw three men coming out the door carrying what had to be the side of beef.

To her dismay, she heard Gabe Blevins saying, "Isaac, Gol dang it! Your new boss started today and you say her name is Judy Turner-Smith? We met her yest'day on the Hazard Trail. You take it easy with her. Why, I heard she even shot and wounded one of her own kin."

She heard Isaac's panic stricken voice, "We can't do this again! I need my job. I don't care if you are my brothers. You two are evil to force me to do this! Don't you ever ask me to help you steal anything again! Mr. Jenkins has been good to me. I liked Mrs. Smith. Don't you go botherin' her! Let's load this beef and get out of here afore that deputy comes snoopin' 'round. I'll lock the door and meet you 'round in back."

Gabe demanded, "What's the matter with you? This has never bothered you afore. What do you care about old man Jenkins? We'll talk 'bout this later!"

Judy shrank back against the wall. She was completely in the shadows. She prayed, "Dear Lord, please don't let 'em see me!"

Two of the men climbed in the wagon and drove it around the back of the building, out of her sight. She watched as Isaac looked both ways, locked the door and sprinted to the corner to meet up with his brothers.

They made good their get-away. Only she had seen them. Mr. Jenkins had to be told in the morning. When he checked his invoices he would find that he'd been tricked into paying for a side of beef that now had been stolen by a trusted employee and his dishonest brothers. It would be up to Mr. Jenkins to decide what he wanted to do about it.

From what she overheard, Isaac wasn't a willing participant in the scheme. Somehow his brothers had forced him to go along with them. He also had some loyalty to Mr. Jenkins. She said to herself, "When I shook his hand and invoked the powers to mellow him in how he treated others, that didn't include making a dishonest person, honest. I'll have to think 'bout this!"

Again, Judy climbed into bed. She would get about three hours sleep because she'd set the Big Ben alarm clock for 4:30. Sleep came almost as soon as her head hit the pillow.

As soon as the clock sounded its alarm, Judy's feet hit the floor. Her excitement in facing this first day on the job overcame any sleepiness. She dressed quickly, with a prayer on her lips. She asked God to be with her through the day, and to help her to be worthy of the trust Mr. Jenkins had placed in her.

Judy had to make a decision about her witnessing the theft of the side of beef, and she mulled over in her mind the fact that Isaac was guilty of the crime of pilfering by helping his two brothers to steal from Mr. Jenkins. But, there was also the fact that she overheard him saying he was forced to help them and that he wasn't going to do it again. God would lead her to whatever decision she made and what she would say to Mr. Jenkins.

For this first day on the job, she wore a flattering navy blue ankle-length gathered skirt and a white middy blouse. Then she put on an attractive blue and white checked apron that covered the front of her clothes and most of her back. Light brown stockings and sturdy, medium-heel, high-laced black shoes completed her work outfit.

Judy never felt she needed to wear much cosmetic make up. Her flawless complexion looked like fine white porcelain china. Today, she patted just a sprinkle of Pond's loose powder on her face to take away the shine on her nose. The light scent of the lilac toilet water was her choice for this morning.

At 5:00 a.m. she was in the restaurant ready to begin her first breakfast experience in Hazard.

Alec and Stacy Turner (Great-great Grandpa and Granny)

Chapter Two
TRIALS AND TRIUMPHS

While Judy was getting settled into her new position as manager of the
Hazard Restaurant, Della was struggling with her feelings of abandonment. She
knew her leaving wasn't due to any fault of her mother's. In her young heart she
felt a raging anger against the Helton family that lived near Big Laurel on a farm
that was in a hollow near the Little Greasy Creek Trail.

Al Helton was the name of the man who dug the big hole for their
swimming pool. He was so mean he was forced to leave the school grounds. Dora
Mae Helton was the name of the mean-talking girl who hurt her feelings so badly
when she lived in Big Log. Only the quick action on the part of Mrs. Zande saved
her from being further embarrassed had the girl been given a chance to spread her
nasty insinuations about Judy to the other students and teachers.

Della's many questions seemed to have no answers. She remembered what
her mother told her when Dora Mae's accusations stung her heart and she asked,
"Why are people like the Heltons 'lowed to get by with hurtin' others?"

Judy told her, "Honey, there's always goin' to be people like them in your
life. That's how the world is and in order to fight them we must not stoop down
to their level. We're hard-workin' God-fearin' people. That's our defense! Good
Christian people who know us will never believe the lies they tell."

This was the first night that Della was alone at Pine Mountain School. She
lay wide awake in her bed with her pillow wet with tears. She resolved that no one
would know how terrible she felt. She was alone, but she knew she was strong
enough to withstand her feelings of despair. In the darkness of her dormitory
room, as she listened to the slow, steady breathing of the other three sleeping girls,
she remembered the advice her mother gave her. Remembering her mother's calm
and soothing voice helped her cope with her awful loneliness. She began to talk to
herself and it helped! "Ma told me when I needed help and someone to talk to, I
could talk to God. He'll always be there and talkin' to Him will help me make
right decisions about everything."

Taking heed of her mother's advice, Della spoke softly to God in prayer,
"Dear God, it wasn't Ma's fault that my Pa was mean and sold our home. It was
his fault that we had no place to go but here at Pine Mountain School. Ma told us
that losin' our home place was Your will. She said we should be grateful. You have
a plan for each of us that 'cludes me and Mary gettin' a good education and able to
earn our way in life. I know Ma's right. I miss her awful, and Mary, too. Please
take care of them. Help me to do my best. In Jesus' name I pray. Amen."

It was such a welcome relief finally to calm her fears and feelings of
loneliness. Talking to God and coming to grips with the reality that He was
guiding her life gave her such comfort that she was able flip her pillow so that it

was dry to her cheek. Then, she turned over on her right side, facing the window, and was soon sound asleep.

Six o'clock came too soon. All four girls bounded up, ready for the day! Before they could leave the dormitory, their beds had to be made, their room neat and free of any clutter. Then they had to get dressed for work and school. Laurel House was a quarter of a mile away and breakfast was ready to be served at 6:30.

Each student was assigned a specific duty to be completed in two hours on each school day. On Saturdays they worked five and a half hours, and on Sundays, one and a half hours. Each assigned job was for a period of nine weeks and then a different job was scheduled. For this particular nine weeks, Della's assigned job was cleaning the large dining room floor each day after breakfast. To do this she tipped up the loose tops of the round dining room tables and pushed them and one hundred and forty chairs against the walls. Beginning at the south end of the large room, she scattered the oily dust down over the floor and swept it over the hardwood floor with a wide, long handled push broom.

Each morning, to make the job less boring, Della pretended she was making a seven-layer applesauce stack cake. As she cleaned the floor and replaced the first row of tables and chairs, she had a big smile on her face because that represented one layer on her imaginary cake that was now done!

She completed each layer of the 'cake' until she had all of the tables and chairs back in place and a gleaming hardwood floor.

On Saturdays when she had five and a half hours for work, Della also cleaned the spacious social room that was connected to the large dining room. She shoved all the sofas, occasional chairs, and end tables against one wall and again used the oily dust down to clean that hardwood floor. When she was finished, she replaced all the furniture exactly as it had been before.

Each school day, after her work assignment was completed, she walked back to her dormitory to wash up. There was only half an hour before the bell would ring for them to report to their first class in the large white school house. It was even farther away from her dormitory than Laurel House. The days were so crowded with work and classes that Della didn't have time to feel her loneliness until she was in bed and "lights out" was called for the night.

Each night when she said her prayers, she talked to God, telling him of her feelings and any problems that were bothering her. She asked God to watch over her mother and Mary, and to keep them safe.

Judy had only been gone a week when Della received a letter from Mary. She told her about their mother's job and how happy she was to be working there. Mary always gave a glowing report on how well she was treated by Reverend Brownlett and his family. She was happy to be going to school in Hazard and would be graduating from Junior High School next May and going into the ninth grade in September.

On Sunday afternoon, Della sat down and answered Mary's letter. She asked her to remind her mother to write to her, too. Although she understood her mother had little free time, and she knew her mother loved her very much, she still wanted and needed to get a letter from her.

It was another long week before she got the letter she craved. Judy echoed what Mary had said. "Honey, my job is a dream come true. I thank God every day for leading me here. Yes, I was right. I don't have to wash pots and pans. Hooray!

I love you so very much. You do your best in your work and in your classes. We'll be together at your Aunt Jonie's and with your Grandpa Alex this Christmas. I'll get a whole week's vacation so I can stay until New Year's Day. We'll have a great good time!"

Della was thrilled to get her mother's letter. She was pleased when she heard from Mary, but this was the very first letter she had ever gotten from Judy. She read it over and over until she had every word memorized and then she put it in her Bible to keep it safe.

Judy and Isaac were finished filling the orders for her first day's lunch crowd. It was 2:00 in the afternoon. All the tables had been cleared of the noon meal. Sylvia put out the red and white checked tablecloths in preparation for the supper crowd. Isaac was still there. Early that morning Mr. Jenkins listened carefully to all that Judy reported to him about the theft of the side of beef. He went through his meat invoices and found he had been tricked into unknowingly paying for the side of beef just three days before Judy came to work there.

Then he walked over to the sheriff's office.

Walt Middleton sat in a squeaky armchair behind an old beat-up walnut desk. Tim Jones, his deputy, was busy putting coal into a pot-bellied stove. He had a big granite coffee pot ready to put on top of the stove for perking the strong coffee they both drank all day long.

On the wall behind the sheriff were the dozen or so wanted posters he had punched through and hung on three nails. The sheriff designated the first nail as holding wanted men he labeled "Dangerous." The next nail was designated, "Maybe Dangerous." The third nail wasn't labeled at all, but it only held a couple of wanted posters. Evidently there wasn't a serious crime involved with them because the sheriff considered these two men not worth his bother.

When Mr. Jenkins arrived he walked in without knocking. "Howdy Walt, could I see you for a minute, alone?"

"Good morning to you, Bill. Sure thing. Tim, before it gets too late in the day, go on over to the restaurant and get us both a breakfast special plate. We're hankering to try out your new manager's cooking!"

"Walt, I think you'll like her cooking fine."

Mr. Jenkins waited until Tim had closed the door behind him and he and the sheriff were alone. Then he said, "Walt, I've got a real problem with one of my employees. I've trusted him so much that he has keys to all the doors in the hotel and restaurant. Last night after we closed the restaurant for the day, Judy, Mrs. Smith, questioned me about a full half side of beef she found hanging in the cooler. Now you know that I'd never order that much beef at one time. After midnight last night she heard a wagon being driven around to the side of the restaurant. When she heard it stop not far from Main Street, she came down to the front porch. Without being seen by them, she watched as Isaac and his two brothers carried the side of beef outside and put it in the wagon. His two brothers drove the wagon around back of the building while Isaac locked the side door and then ran to meet up with them. An hour ago I went through last week's meat invoices and found that I was tricked into paying for that side of beef."

"Bill, what's the problem? Judge J.T. Farmer will sign a warrant. Just tell me you're bringing charges of theft by deception, or pilfering, against all three brothers and I'll take the warrant for their arrest to the Judge to sign. Then, I'll go and arrest all three of 'em!'

"Walt, it's not that simple, Dad Gum it! Judy overheard Isaac telling his brothers that he wouldn't let them force him to do this again. That he needed his job and that I'd been good to him. I don't know what they did that forced him to betray my trust. I like Isaac. He's a good cook! Judy wants me to consider giving him another chance. Do you have any ideas about how I can bring charges against just his two brothers and not include him in the arrest warrants?"

"Bill, I can arrest all three of 'em, but I'll separate Isaac from the other two. I'll give him a chance to confess and implicate his two brothers. In exchange for his testimony, charges against him can be dropped. We can work this out with the prosecutor and Judge J.T. But, are you sure this is what you want to do?"

"I trust Judy's instincts about Isaac because I feel the same way. We may never know how he was forced to go along with the theft, but Judy and I think he's worth saving this time."

"Okay, you sign these papers and I'll go get the warrants from the Judge. I'll pick up Isaac first, but I'll do it so no one will know he's being arrested. After I talk with him, I'll go find his brothers."

Mr. Jenkins finished signing three forms authorizing charges to be brought against all three men when Tim came through the door bringing their breakfasts. Mr. Jenkins left them to enjoy their food. He was leaving it up to the sheriff and hoped Isaac would cooperate so he could save his job.

It was about 2:30 that afternoon when Judy looked up as a man with a sheriff's badge came through the door. She felt a pang in her heart because she guessed he was there to arrest Isaac. She walked toward him and instantly liked what she saw. He was a handsome man, tall, slim, with dark hair and eyes. He had a smile on his face as he held out his hand to her in greeting, "I'm Sheriff Walt Middleton. You must be Judy Smith, Jenkins' new manager. I sure did enjoy your breakfast special plate. My deputy will bring your dishes back later today. Right now I need to have a talk with Isaac Blevins. Will you tell him to come out here to see me?"

"Yes sir, I will, but please listen to what he has to say before you judge him. I think he's basically a good man."

Judy went into the kitchen to talk to Isaac. He was cleaning all evidence of the lunch cooking off the large grill in preparation for the supper crowd.

She approached him and said, "Isaac, the sheriff, Walt Middleton, asked for you to come out to the dining room to see him. He wants to talk to you."

Isaac visibly paled, but clinched his teeth in a forced smile. He searched Judy's face for some clue that would tell him if she or the sheriff knew about what happened last night. However, Judy's face was relaxed. She smiled at him and then he relaxed, too. She led the way into the now deserted dining room. Sheriff Middleton motioned for Isaac to join him at a table against the far wall.

They sat and talked for quite a while. Then the sheriff left and Isaac came back to the kitchen.

She sighed in relief. Judy knew that she might have had to handle the supper crowd alone today. It had all depended on what the sheriff did with Isaac.

She asked, "Is everything all right, Isaac? I was afraid something had happened to your folks."

"No, Ma'am, everything's all right. The sheriff just needed to ask me something about my brothers."

A few minutes later, Mr. Jenkins came to talk with Isaac. After a fifteen minute conversation at the same table where he had sat with the sheriff, Isaac came back into the kitchen. Without a word to anyone, Mr. Jenkins went back to the front desk in the hotel.

It was about 4:00 o'clock that afternoon when Sheriff Middleton and his deputy, with Josh and Gabe Blevins, rode up to the jail. Both brothers were in irons. The sheriff followed a hunch that the two brothers would be at their folks' place butchering the side of beef. He did find them there and they were caught red handed! They had told their folks they worked for a farmer over in Hyden and he paid them with the slaughtered beef.

The way the sheriff was able to handle the case meant that Judy's name was kept out of it. What the public knew about Isaac's role in the theft was also kept to a bare minimum. Josh and Gabe never knew it was Judy that had turned them in. They admitted their guilt and avoided a jury trial. Judge Farmer sentenced both of them to three years in prison.

Mr. Jenkins learned a valuable lesson. He carefully read the invoices he received for goods, supplies, and services for his business before he paid them.

Sylvia proved to be invaluable to Judy by informing her about important customers, needed supplies and services for the dining room, and any impending problems that she knew about. Judy used her as an assistant and influenced Mr. Jenkins to increase her salary from three dollars a week to five dollars. Isaac's salary was increased from seven dollars a week to ten. Lance's pay was almost doubled. This enabled him to rent a small sleeping room close to the hotel.

Judy told Mr. Jenkins, "I want to thank you for trustin' me enough to follow my advice and raise these people's pay. They're the key to the successful operation of the hotel and the restaurant. I promise you we'll see a profit that'll more than triple the amount their raises are costin' you."

Within a month, the profit that was shown in the restaurant was enough that Mr. Jenkins took Judy aside and said, "For the first time since I've been in business, I'm going to give each employee a Christmas bonus. Your ideas have paid off handsomely. Even Isaac goes around smiling and being nice to everyone. For Christmas, we'll have a party and invite all the help and their families to celebrate with us. At the party, I'll give out the money for the bonuses.

Go to the ten-cent store and buy what you need to make the restaurant look nice. Pick out some decorations for the hotel lobby, too. We'll put them up the weekend after Thanksgiving! Maybe we should get a tree for the lobby, too. Who do you want to help you with the decorations?"

"I think Sylvia will be great at picking out the decorations, and I'll ask both Isaac and Sylvia to help me put them up. Saturdays are usually slow after the lunch crowd, so we'll begin then and my Mary can help finish up on Sunday after church. You know, Mr. Jenkins, this'll make us feel more like a family!"

With her room included as part of her pay and being able to have all of her meals in the restaurant, Judy was able to save almost all of her salary. Out of the $48.00 a month she earned, she managed to save about $40.00. She didn't trust banks. Her money was kept hidden away in a dainty, beribboned lady's money-sack that she had tied around her waist under her clothes.

She still had almost all of the money she received from Mr. Philpot for the stock, equipment, and preserved food supplies when he bought her farm. Also, she had saved most of her salary from Pine Mountain School. Each time she managed to save another hundred and twenty dollars, she went to the bank and had the smaller bills changed into fifties or a hundred. It was just a week before Christmas that she finally reached a savings goal of one thousand dollars.

Next week she and Mary would go to Harlan County to spend Christmas with her father, her sister Joni's family, and little Della. She didn't want to travel with that much money so she decided to trust her precious savings to a bank and opened an account at the Hazard Savings and Loan.

When she deposited five hundred dollars into her new account, she received a tiny little yellow book with her name on the front of it. There was a number written in ink, too. The bank teller said it was her account number. Inside the little book were the date, the amount of her deposit, and the same amount over in the last column that showed her balance.

The man behind the teller's bars explained that each time she made a deposit she needed to bring the little book so they could record the amount and her new balance. "If you withdraw, or take money out of your account, that will be recorded, too. The withdrawal is subtracted from your balance."

Judy frowned, and exclaimed, "Oh, I won't be taking any out!"

Mr. Jenkins' holiday party was held on the eighteenth, the last Sunday before Christmas. The restaurant and hotel lobby were beautifully decorated. Sylvia and Isaac took a real delight in doing almost everything themselves. Lance shuffled in and out, watching their progress, and nodding his approval.

The daily repeat customers had been so pleasantly surprised that they brought their families and friends in to eat and see the decorations. Mr. Jenkins laughingly teased Judy that she knew that would happen, "You planned it this way so the extra profit we make will pay for the decorations!"

He literally whooped with glee, "We've started a tradition at the Jenkins' Hotel and Restaurant. The amazing thing is that all of our decorations are paid for and everything but the live trees can be stored and re-used every year!"

He bought Lance a Santa Claus costume and told him, "I'll tell you when it's time for you to go change and come back as Santa!"

The restaurant salad person, vegetable preparer, and overall cook's helper brought their families. Sylvia and Isaac didn't bring any family. Judy brought Mary. Mr. Jenkins had no family living in Hazard. He did invite the sheriff and his deputy to stop by for refreshments. It did Judy's heart good when Sheriff Middleton, without any hesitation and a big grin on his face, walked up to Isaac and vigorously shook his hand. All together there were about twenty people who partook of refreshments, sang carols, told Christmas stories, and generally enjoyed socializing with each other.

It was almost dark when Lance in his Santa suit came walking through the door with a big sack on his back. He had toys and candy for the dozen or more children. Judy watched in amazement as he got right into the role of Santa. He was in his element. Every child there wanted to sit on his lap and plant a kiss on his cheek until he was in danger of losing his white bushy glued-on beard!

Each employee received a long white envelope with their name written on it. When they opened their envelopes, each was in total shock. Everyone received a single bill that represented close to a month's pay. Judy, Isaac, and Sylvia each received a fifty-dollar bill. The rest of the employees received twenty-dollar bills. Their gratitude made Mr. Jenkins all misty-eyed. Every adult in the room turned to gaze at him.

He had a wide grin on his face as he rose to his feet to make a speech. "I want to tell you all how pleased I am that you've honored me with your presence here at our first Annual Jenkins Hotel and Restaurant Employee Christmas Party. I believe every child here received a toy and enough candy to spoil several dinners. The envelopes that the hotel and restaurant employees received represent my gratitude to them for work well done. The money inside is their Christmas bonus. I know you're all anxious to get home before it gets too late, so I'll shut up. I've said enough! Merry Christmas to each of you!"

Chapter Three
A FAMILY CHRISTMAS IN THE PINE MOUNTAINS

Judy noticed that Isaac and Sylva paired off at the party and spent the entire time in each other's company. Isaac had changed. He was clean-shaven each morning when he came to work. His new hair style was shorter so the hair was out of his eyes and trimmed to just below his ears. He had the barber taper his hair in the back so it hung neatly just below his collar.

He used to wear the same apron until it was ready to stand up by itself, but now he changed to a clean one every morning. His manners toward Sylvia were of respect and consideration. He smiled at the customers and went out of his way to make the plates of food look more attractive.

If Judy requested anything specifically from Isaac, he did his best to do it the way she wanted. The three of them became a hard-working team. Each day they served more than a hundred separate meals and they made the work seem easy. Mr. Jenkins couldn't have been more pleased.

Nothing was ever said about the theft of the side of beef. Josh and Gabe Blevins were in prison. A younger unmarried sister was living at the old home place and caring for Isaac's aged parents.

Judy knew Isaac was free for the first time in his life. She hoped something good would come of the budding romance between Sylvia and him.

The morning after the First Annual Jenkins Employee Christmas Party, Mr. Jenkins asked Judy, "Is Mary out of school now for the holiday break?"

"No, since Christmas comes on Tuesday next week, her last day is Wednesday, the nineteenth. Then, she doesn't go back to school 'til January second. We need to leave Hazard early Friday morning since we plan to spend my week off with Della and my father. He's a hundred and one and lives with my youngest sister, Jonie Lewis and her family. They live in Leslie County, almost on the Harlan County line, near Big Laurel. He's in fairly good health. We're lookin' forward to seeing all of them!"

"Judy, what's your father's name?"

"Alex Turner. He owned a big homestead at the head of Alex's Branch, which was named for him. Alex's Branch is fed by mountain springs and is part of the headwaters of Little Greasy Creek. There's some of the best huntin' and fishin' in the world there."

He was being kind and truly interested in Judy's background, He smiled and said, "You're known hereabouts as Judy Turner-Smith. You're working and raising your two daughters alone. What happened to your husband?"

"My father gave Robert Smith, my ex-husband, and me enough land to make a good living workin' it. Robert refused to work it with me. He refused to hunt, trap, or fish. He refused to do anything that would help support our family. He

31

deserted us soon after little Della was born, and after about a year and a half of not knowing where he was, I was served with divorce papers by mail. Then he sold the land that my father gave us right out from under me. He sold my home and his children's home, lock, stock, and barrel, leaving us homeless.

That's how I happened to be working as the kitchen instructor at Pine Mountain Settlement School. My distant cousins, Uncle William and Aunt Sally Dixon-Creech convinced Miss Pettit to hire me and provide schoolin' for my little girls. After working there over four years, some mean-talking gossipin' people named Helton that live in Big Laurel cost me my job at the school, but it didn't cost me the trust and friendship of Miss Pettit and Mrs. Zande. They knew me and that I do have high morals and a love of God within me. They didn't believe the vicious gossip that was spread by the Heltons.

The missionaries had no choice but to ask me to resign when the gossips spread their lies to members of a Mission Board that financially supported the school and questioned the wisdom of having a divorced woman working around the young mountain girls. But, the good Lord had a plan for me. He led me to you last June and I'm grateful to you for hirin' me. You never need to worry 'bout trustin' me because you have my undying gratitude!"

"Judy, you don't have to worry about my trusting you. You've become the daughter I never had. My wife, bless her soul, and I never had any children. She passed on more than ten years ago. I have a married brother who has a passel of children and lives in Florida, about half way down near a town called Orlando. Early next spring, I want to take two weeks off to visit him and see if I like where he lives enough to move down there some day. Before I leave on my visit, though, I'll train you to take care of the hotel while I'm gone. There's not that much to it, but there are some hostelry laws that have to be abided by.

Now, that's enough of this business talk! You get ready to go visit your father and the rest of your family. Let Mary know you'll be leaving the first thing Friday morning. Let Raff Pennington know you'll need Curly saddled and ready to go. Plus you'll need the pack mule you're used to. I think his name's Ned. Am I right? I have presents for your two girls, but save them for Christmas morning. Take some time off this afternoon or tomorrow if you want to go shopping for presents for your father and the rest of your family."

Judy couldn't stop the tears that sprang into her eyes. She wasn't used to anyone being so kind to her and it really touched her heart. Standing on her tiptoes, she hugged his neck and kissed his cheek. She exclaimed, "You're really too good to me, Mr. Jenkins!"

"Here now! Don't you go and get all soft on me. We're just talking business here. And, by the way, from now on call me Bill, the same as I call you by your first name."

Judy had to gulp to swallow the lump in her throat and dry up her tears. She smiled up at him and said, "I'll call you Bill, but not in front of the customers in the restaurant. I don't feel like that's respectful enough. Yes, I'd like to do some shopping afore I leave on Friday. I'll get to my sister's Saturday night, God willin'. I'll spend a whole day with them before Christmas Eve."

"I think you should take an extra traveling day coming back. You can be back to work on Saturday. Just tell Isaac and Sylvia to watch things while you're gone. You should give them part of the day off tomorrow so they can go shopping. We can watch the restaurant while they're gone. Now, you stop worrying about things! Just you be extra careful traveling on the mountain trails."

Judy went to the Brownlett home to tell Mary they were leaving Friday morning. She found them very excited about a "love offering" of money and goods for Pine Mountain School. The Reverend smiled and asked, "Are you going to rent a pack mule from the Hazard Livery Stable for your trip home?"

Judy said, "Yes, I think I'll rent Ned again. He and I get along fine."

"Will you mind taking along with you the goods that were donated by members of my congregation for the missionaries at the school? I'll pack them on your mule when you're ready to leave."

"No, I don't mind at all. I'll be by early to pick up Mary. I appreciate your offer to help me pack the donated goods on Ned. I'll have some things already packed, but I'm sure he'll be able to manage a lot more."

"That's wonderful, Judy, you're a Godsend to us! We'll be ready and looking for you. Mary's excited about this trip. I doubt she'll get much sleep between now and Friday!"

Mary came bounding down the stairs to greet her mother. Judy hugged her close, "Honey, you need to be ready to leave afore daylight Friday morning. I'll come even earlier so Reverend Brownlett can pack some things on Ned to take to Pine Mountain School. We'll deliver them when we go to pick up Della. You get a good rest afore our trip. I'll see you first thing on Friday morning!"

Judy's alarm clock sounded its shrill call at 5:00 a.m. on Friday. It was still pitch-black outside. She got dressed and walked over to the livery to get Curly and Ned. A very sleepy Tom Pennington greeted her as he led Curly out of his stall. He was saddled and there was a lead halter on Ned. Tom asked, "Mrs. Smith, where on God's good earth are you goin' so early in the mornin'?"

Judy grinned broadly and said, "Good morning, Tom. Mr. Jenkins has given me a week's vacation. My daughter, Mary, and I will spend Christmas with my younger daughter, my hundred and one year old father, and my sister's family. They live near the Harlan County line. I'll return Ned when I get back."

Tom smiled, tipped his hat to her, and said, "Have a safe trip, Ma'am, and Merry Christmas!"

Judy rode Curly and led the mule around to the front of the hotel. Her packed travel-sacks of clothes and presents for the family were already waiting on the front porch. Ned was packed in a matter of minutes and she headed out to The Brownlett's to pick up Mary.

When she arrived, Mary was standing on the porch with her small bundle. Ethan had saddled a small roan mare for Mary. Her bedroll containing a thin pillow and blankets was already secured behind the saddle. Judy tied Mary's bundle to another one about the same size and slung them over the little horse's back. She secured them with a rope that was knotted underneath the mare's belly.

Reverend Brownlett showed Judy the donated goods he needed to pack on Ned. Most of it consisted of patchwork quilts and wool blankets. There were a few knitted and crocheted mittens, scarves, and toboggans for small children. Although the packing consisted mostly of lightweight stuff, it was bulky. To make more room for the church's donations, Judy took some of her sacks off Ned and fitted them securely on Curly's back.

When Ned was packed, Ethan gave Judy a fat, sealed brown envelope and told her it was the monetary donation from the church for the school. Judy put the envelope in her saddlebag, "I'll give all of this to the school when I pick up Della. I'll ask Miss Pettit to count the money, and give me a receipt showing the total. You'll have something to show your church members. I'm sure they'll also get a proper thank you letter from the school. God bless you, Reverend!"

Ethan took Judy aside and handed her another small cloth sack. "This is something from me and my family for you, Mary, and your daughter, Della. Wait until Christmas morning to open them. Have a safe journey. You'll be in our thoughts and prayers."

Judy and Mary were both dressed in layers of clothing for warmth. As they left Hazard, it began to spit tiny snowflakes. The ground was too warm for the snow to stick, but Judy knew a wet trail through the mountains meant a slow trail. She urged Mary to keep up and put Curly to a slow trot, while leading a heavily-packed and reluctant Ned.

It was about noon when they stopped, dismounted, and tied the animals to low hanging branches. They ate, and drank from their canteens. This took about a half an hour and they were on their way again. Judy had in mind a certain spot that was the half way mark. Here she planned to make camp. There was a large overhanging rock close to the trail. She figured they could build a warm fire and camp under it for shelter in case it rained or snowed again in the night.

Their luck held. They reached the half way camping place well before dark. She found plenty of dry wood and had a roaring fire going in no time. The overhanging rock made a perfect shelter. The large rock formation located at their back, reflected the heat from the fire and added to their comfort.

They each had a bowl of warmed beef stew that Judy packed from the restaurant along with buttered yeasty rolls. Mary said, "Ma, this is a feast. We need to say thank you to God before we eat."

Judy smiled and said, "Honey, you go ahead and say your prayer out loud and it'll be for both of us."

Mary's childlike prayer was beautiful in its simplicity, "Dear Lord we thank you for this good food. Keep us safe as we make this journey. We'll give you all the praise. In Jesus' name, Amen."

Judy echoed with a heart felt, "Amen."

They quickly ate their supper. After feeding and watering the animals, Judy made sure that Curly and the other two were securely tied and hobbled. She knew they would sound an alarm if any intruder, four-legged or two, came near while they slept. Judy asked Mary to clean up the campsite while she gathered plenty of firewood to last through the night. Judy pulled her rifle from the side of her saddle and put it by her side under her covers. Then they rolled their tired bodies in their blankets and sank into a deep sleep.

It was about six the next morning when Judy threw back her covers expecting to see snow. "Thank you, Lord," she prayed. "Our luck is still holdin'. The ground is dry. Dear God, please be with us today. Keep safe. I love you, Lord Jesus. Amen."

They didn't take time to cook anything for breakfast. The buttered yeasty rolls from last night were still good. They ate them as they broke camp, drowned the campfire and packed everything back on the mule. It was just breaking daylight when they struck out on the last half of the Harlan Trail.

Judy knew where the half way mark was for the second day's march. They stopped there, built a fire to warm their bodies, and heated up the last of the beef stew. It did them good to have warm food to eat. After cleaning up and re-packing everything on Ned, they continued their journey. Judy said, "Honey, if everything goes well, we'll be at your Aunt Jonie's well before dark."

All went well; they were riding into Jonie's yard an hour before nightfall. Judy estimated it was about five o'clock. Jonie saw them coming through her farm gate. Shouting a gleeful welcome, she ran to meet them. Alex struggled to get to his feet from his "low-to-the-floor" cane-bottomed porch chair. He wanted to be standing so he could properly greet his daughter and little Mary.

Jonie called her older boys to come and greet their Aunt Judy and Cousin Mary. She used a stern voice to give them orders, "Otis, come here and take care of their horses. Gib, come and help your Aunt Judy unpack this mule!

Honey, what in the world do you have loaded on this poor mule?"

Judy laughed out loud, "Jonie, honey, that stuff's not as heavy as it looks. It's a love offering from Reverend Brownlett's church for Pine Mountain School. I'm takin' it to them when I pick up Della. If it wasn't so late, I'd go get her now, but I think it'll be better if I wait and get her the first thing in the mornin'. Mary, honey, you want to go with me, don't you? You and your sister can ride double on the trip back."

"Yes, Ma, I want to go with you so I can tell Reverend Brownlett that I saw Miss Pettit. And I'll be able to thank her properly for helping me to be placed with him and his family. They've been real good to me. And, Aunt Jonie, I'm treated like one of their own children!"

Judy was so anxious to see Della she found it hard to get to sleep. She prayed that Della was all right. Always in the back of her mind was the worry that the Heltons would cause them more problems. Whenever she was troubled, she remembered Alex's advice. "Tell it to the Lord. He will worry for you. If you give it to Him, then you have to trust Him and leave it there! "

Judy closed her eyes to talk silently to God, "Dear Lord, You know what's in my heart and what's troublin' my mind afore I tell You. You know that my Della is here alone. Please protect her from the mean-talkin' gossips that did all of us harm. Bless Miss Pettit and Mrs. Zande for agreein' to watch over Della for me. She has just one more year after this one at Pine Mountain School and then she'll be livin' with me in Hazard.

And, thank you, Lord, for being with me today. I'm close to my old home right now and the years I spent workin' that farm were the happiest days of my life. You cured my grief. I know you have a plan for me. I'm living that plan. You helped me to put aside my deep feeling of grief over being asked to leave Pine Mountain School. I now know that was part of your plan for me, too. The Hazard Hotel and Restaurant are now the focus of my work and my life. My work in the restaurant and the wellbeing of my daughters are the most important things to me. Thank you for watching over me, Della and Mary. Thank you for your blessin's, dear Jesus, I love you. Amen."

She felt a sense of relief and that a burden had been lifted. "I'll do what Pa says now and let God take care of my worries for me."

Within three minutes Judy's eyes closed and she was sound asleep.

The next morning they ate a good old-fashioned farm breakfast. Jonie prepared cured ham, fried eggs, red-eye gravy, fried potatoes, and buttermilk biscuits. Judy pushed herself away from the table. "Jonie, honey, Curly won't be able to pack me if I gain a hundred pounds eatin' like this!"

Jonie grinned delightedly. "It does my heart good to see you and Mary eatin' your fill of good home cookin'. Do you think you'll be back in time for dinner? We eat about 12:30, but we'll wait 'til you get here."

"I think we'll be back by then, but don't hold up dinner waitin' for us. We can always eat when we get here. All I'm goin' to do is give the church donations to Miss Pettit and get a receipt; pick up Della and head back here."

Judy went to the barn to saddle Curly and the little mare. She re-packed Ned and looked to make sure she had the sealed envelope. Then they mounted their horses and, leading Ned, began the trip to Pine Mountain School.

Judy didn't know what kind of welcome she would receive from Miss Petit and Mrs. Zande. She was determined not to tarry long. After she delivered the donations and got her receipt, she meant to find Della and leave the school as soon as she could. Her memories of the school were now bittersweet. She would never forget the years of love and joy she felt working there and she could never forget being asked to leave without saying goodbye to anyone.

Leading Ned, she and Mary rode through the school's entrance gate. As they neared Old Log, they saw Mrs. Zande come out the door and start walking toward the school's office building. Mary called, "Mrs. Zande, wait!"

Mrs. Zande stopped dead in her tracks and turned toward them. "Oh, Mary, child, I'm delighted to see you and here is our Judy. You both get down this instant and let me hug you! My dear blessed Lord, what all do you have packed on this poor mule?"

Judy laughed and said, "What I have is a love offering from Reverend Brownlett's church in Hazard. Ned has packed them a long way to get here. Really, there isn't anything very heavy on him, just very bulky. But, he'll be happy when you unpack all of the gifts and free him from his burden. I came to bring the donations and to get Della. How is she? Tomorrow's Christmas Eve. Is she free to leave? Her Grandfather Alex is most anxious to see her! "

"Della's just fine. She works hard and is an excellent student. And, yes she's free to leave anytime for the holidays. I have a feeling she's been packed and waiting for days! I think Kathryn is in the school office. We'll stop there and I'll get one of the older boys to unpack poor Ned."

Judy and Mary remounted their horses and, leading Ned, accompanied Mrs. Zande on around the slight curve in the road to the little one-story building that was the school office. On the right side of the road was the small branch of water that fed the swimming pool. Judy had to smile as she remembered all the mush and grits the children ate to pay for that pool. The path up to the front door of the office building was very steep. Rustic steps had been cut in the ground and lined with deep set "stepping" stones. The stones were taken from the tall mountain behind the building and curved up from the road on two sides. They were designed and built in that fashion to save steps no matter from which direction you approached the office building.

Miss Pettit looked out the window and saw them coming. Before they dismounted again she flung open the office door and called to them. "Welcome to you both, my dear Mary and our Judy! Do come in and let me look at you! It's delightful to see you. What a wonderful Christmas surprise. But, tell me Judy, what on earth do you have packed on that poor mule?"

"Miss Pettit, Ned is getting so much undeserved pity that he's goin' to be ruined. He's packin' donations to the school. They're light-weight, but they're bulky. Reverend Brownlett's church sent the school a love offering. I need someone to unpack him, though, and carry the donations up to the office. Also, I have an envelope with money donations from the church. I'll need you to count it and give me a receipt to return to the Reverend."

"I'll be more than happy to do that. My dear Ethel, please go in the office and get Jimmy to come and unpack the mule. Judy, you may get the envelope of money for me now, and I'll count it. Have you come to pick up Della? Mary, why don't you go to Laurel House to find your sister? Go with her to her dormitory and stay there while she gets ready and we'll meet you both at Laurel House as soon as we finish here."

Mary dutifully answered, "Yes, Ma'am, Miss Pettit!"

A tall, slender, neatly dressed young boy came out from one of the back rooms of the office building. He smiled shyly, and waited to be told what Miss Pettit wanted him to do. Without hesitation, he walked down the little hill to Ned and began loosening the packing ropes. He loaded his arms full of gifts and brought the first of them in and put them on the end of Miss Pettit's big desk.

"My dear Ethel, lets open the gifts and see what all we have here."

Together, as gleeful as two of their students, they tore through some wrapping paper and cut binding string with scissors to open the many boxes. There were three colorful hand-sewn and quilted bed covers. Then they found the two large woolen blankets. A large bundle of laundered and carefully ironed brightly-colored flour sacks brought squeals of delight.

Miss Pettit exclaimed, "We've got enough flour sacks for every girl in the Home Economics class to have her own sewing project!"

Then they found the smaller travel sacks. One held the hand-made mittens, scarves, and toboggans that were sized for the younger children. Another sack had three sets of hand-made embroidered pillowcases and dresser scarves. There was a sack that held several women's hand made neck scarves and bandannas. Last of all, there was a sack that held about a dozen men's work neckerchiefs in red and blue polka dots.

Judy retrieved the envelope from her saddlebag. She had to laugh as Ned, now shed of his over-sized burden, snorted and did a little two-step dance sideways. He turned his head and nuzzled her neck as a thank you! "Okay, I love you, too! It'll be a much easier trip for you goin' back home."

She took the envelope up to Miss Pettit and waited while she counted the money. There was almost a hundred dollars in bills stacked on her desk. Then she dumped out a small pile of silver coins and counted them. Judy carefully placed the receipt she received from Miss Pettit in her saddlebags.

The two missionaries thanked her for bringing the donations and invited them to stay for dinner in Laurel House. Judy was grateful for the invitation, but said, "I'm sorry we really can't this time. I promised my family we'd have dinner with them. I'd like to get Mary and Della now and we'll be on our way."

Mrs. Zande said, "I have to go up to Laurel House to check on the cooking. I want to talk with Mary. So, Judy, dear, I'll see you up there."

In a warning tone, Miss Petit reminded Judy, "Della has to be back the day after New Year's and maybe the three of you can take a meal with us then."

"Miss Pettit, I may have to bring her back even sooner, unless my sister can bring her on that Wednesday. Mary and I must be back in Hazard on Friday next week. Will that be all right?"

"Judy, my dear, you do whatever's most convenient for you. If you can, next week, while you're here, maybe you can come during one of the days and we can eat together and chat. I want to hear about your job and how you're doing, and all about Mary. In another year, we'll be planning what Della will do after her graduation."

"I'll see how it goes. I wanted to make a trip to Harlan this week."

"I'll be going to Harlan, myself, on Wednesday after Christmas. Why don't you plan to be here by 9:00 and you can go with me? Mr. Wilder will be with us and that'll give us plenty of time to visit."

"I'll plan on doin' that. I thank you for invitin' me. I'll be here around 9 o'clock on Wednesday morning."

"Good! Now go get little Della. I wish you all a very Merry Christmas!"

Judy fumed that she had taken a lot more time talking to Miss Pettit than she intended to. She tied Ned to the hitching post by the road and put Curly to a brisk trot to go up to Laurel House to meet Mary and Della.

She didn't see them at the front of the large, lovely building, so she rode on around to the back. Della, Mary, and Mrs. Zande were standing on the narrow ramp-like back entrance next to the kitchen. Della had a small sack of clothes with her. She squealed in delight, "Ma, oh Ma, I'm so glad to see you. I'm all ready to go. Mrs. Zande said I could stay with you and Aunt Jonie until way next Wednesday, the day after New Year's! You and Mary comin' to get me is the best Christmas gift I could hope for."

Judy dismounted quickly and caught Della up in her arms for a huge bear hug. "And, bein' with you, honey, is the best Christmas present ever for me! Bein' with you and Mary both at the same time is extra special. Your Grandpa Alex is waiting to see you. They're holdin' dinner for us. Goodbye, Mrs. Zande! I'll see you on Wednesday."

Mrs. Zande hugged and kissed both girls, and said, "I wish you all a truly Merry Christmas!"

Della climbed up behind Mary on the little mare and locked her arms around her sister's waist. Judy mounted Curly and they trotted over to the office building to the hitching post to get Ned. It was seven miles to Jonie's, but Judy figured they would be there in plenty of time for dinner.

Mary and Della kept up a steady chatter about school, teachers, and Christmas. Listening to their lively conversation made the miles melt under Curly's feet. It was noon when they rode into the barn at Jonie's. Gib met them and offered to put up their horses, including Ned. He would feed, water, and rub them down. Judy thanked him. Then she asked, "Have you had dinner?"

"Yes, Aunt Judy. Mam had me eat early so I could meet you when you came. She's got dinner ready for you. Cousin Della, I'm sure glad to see you! After you eat, I'll meet you and Mary down in the orchard. If there are any apples that didn't freeze last night, we'll gather 'em up and put 'em in the barn."

After they ate a big meal of Jonie's good cooking, the children all went down in the orchard to play and gather any late fruit that was still good to eat. Judy, Jonie and Alex were left alone to catch up on each other's news. Judy gave a glowing account of her job as restaurant manager and of her employer, Mr. Jenkins. "I'm learnin' more all the time. After the holidays, he's goin' to teach me how to run the hotel so I can take it over when he goes out of town."

Alex listened thoughtfully to all that Judy said. Then he reminded her of the vision he had about a year ago. "The Lord has been good to you, little Mary, and my precious Della. I've only got to see Della twice, but Jonie has seen her at the school once a month. She hasn't complained. Della's a brave little girl!"

Jonie and Enoch had been quiet while Judy told them about her life in Hazard. She assured them the placement Miss Pettit secured for Mary couldn't have been better. Mary would be ready for high school next fall, and could stay with the Brownlett's as long as she wanted. Also, Della would be graduating from Pine Mountain School at the end of next year.

Judy continued, "I don't know yet what Della wants to do when she comes to Hazard to live with me. The Good Lord will lead us. Because Mary's placement worked out so well, Della may want to work for a family if they allow her to continue her education. Miss Pettit said we need to discuss Della's future for when she graduates. I think that means she already has a family in mind."

Jonie asked, "Judy, honey, do you think you can be that lucky twice? Mary has a wonderful placement with the Brownlett's, but little Della might get into a bad situation that she won't be able to get out of. But, like you said, we will have another full year yet afore you have to decide.

Let's enjoy the time we have and get ready for Christmas. Did you bring any gifts to put under our tree? The young'ins worked hard cuttin' out paper bells and angels. They cut out and colored a long zig-zaggy chain to wrap around the tree. I strung a long rope of popcorn last night so they'll have that to put on the tree, too. We have a few toys for Clara, Mellie, Dolly, and baby Delphia. Enoch bought some farm tools for Otis and Gib. They all have some new clothes. I went to Harlan and bought oranges to go with our apples and nuts for their stockin's. And, I'm making black walnut fudge so all of 'em can ruin their supper."

Judy said, "You asked me if I brought gifts for Mary and Della. Yes, I did. I got them a few things afore I left Hazard. Then Mr. Jenkins and Reverend Brownlett's family gave me some gifts to put under the tree for them. I'm goin' to Harlan with Miss Pettit the day after Christmas. There'll be sales on dresses, skirts, blouses, and shoes. I want to get Della two complete outfits that she can switch around and make four sets of school clothes." Next week I'll get Mary her new clothes at the after Christmas sales in Hazard. They know that the new clothes are part of their Christmas week celebration!"

Jonie said, "I'm glad you're gettin' Della some new clothes. She's grown like a bad weed these last six months. Mary now looks like she's the younger and Della's the older! But, I know Mary's over three years older than Della. Now, let's talk about Christmas day!"

"Jonie, what're we havin' for Christmas Dinner?"

"I thought I'd do most of the cookin' and let you enjoy your vacation from preparin' food. But, knowin' you, honey, you won't be able to keep your hands off the fixin's.

We're havin' chicken and dumplin's, a baked cured ham, and a pork loin roast, stuffed with cornbread dressin'. That's the meat. Then, I'm fixin' creamy mashed Irish taters, candied sweet taters, canned green beans and shucky beans, both seasoned with my own salt bacon, cornbread and biscuits. And, we're havin' sweetened canned t'maters, turnip greens cooked with cured bacon fat, and buttered sweet spring peas. I'm makin' an applesauce stack cake that'll have six layers. I think we'll have 'nough to feed everybody!"

"My dear sweet Jesus, Jonie, you'll have enough to feed a good sized army. But, I can hardly wait!"

The next day passed quickly. When it was gone and night was falling, Alex said, "Judy, honey, I'm glad you came a day early. I know tomorrow you and Jonie will be so busy cookin' we won't be able to visit much. But, I'll probably sleep most of the day anyway."

Jonie and Judy spent a lot of time in the kitchen on Christmas Eve doing everything they could in advance so they were, as their mother, Stacey Elizabeth, used to say, "helping out the morrow."

Jonie's oldest daughter, Alta, helped them get everything ready and then she joined the younger children who were so full of excitement that they could barely contain themselves. Jonie draped a bleached cotton cloth around the bottom of the decorated long-needled, white-pine Christmas tree.

At about 9 o'clock, she shooed all the children to bed saying, "Now, you know Santy can't come if you're awake. He'll know if you ain't asleep. Mellie, let Della and Mary sleep with you and your sisters. There's plenty of room in your big bed. I don't want to hear any yammering or giggling out of you girls after I blow out your lamp."

Then she looked at Otis and Gilbert. "Boys, you'd better go to bed. I'll need your help on the morrow to keep my cook stove blazin' hot to make all this good food. We want to have Christmas dinner by 2:00 o'clock. Everyone will be starvin' just from the smells comin' from the kitchen!"

The two brothers grinned and Gib said, "Mam, we hear you. When I get up in the morning I'll split some more wood and bring it in for the wood box, and I'll get you two more buckets of coal. I sure don't want that stove to get cold! Goodnight, Mam, Grandpa, Pa and Aunt Judy!"

Jonie laughed, "Go on with you. Goodnight boys!"

Alex said, "I'm goin' to turn in early. I'm gettin' too old for all this 'citement. Good night to all!"

Enoch, Jonie, and Judy sat awhile, sipping on some sweetened hot sassafras tea. Later, when they checked and found all the children sound asleep, they began to set out the Christmas gifts they had accumulated.

Jonie had two hand-sewn, "low waistline" dresses each for Alta, Clara, and Mellie. She had sewn three long-legged "romper" outfits for Dolly and Delphia. There were four sets of girls' handmade scarves and mittens. There was a warm, crocheted cap for the baby. On each trip to Harlan, Jonie had added more items to her little hoard of Christmas gifts. She had a soft, rubber doll for the baby. Then there were four identical, except for their hair, store-bought huggable rag dolls. In order for the girls to tell them apart, each doll's hair was a different color of yarn thread. Jonie had chosen blonde, light brown, dark brown, and the fourth one was a red head.

From Newberry's Ten Cent Store she had bought one pretty miniature tin tea-set for all the girls to play with. Judy added the two dolls and clothing items she had bought just two days ago in Hazard for Mary and Della. Also, she put the wrapped gifts under the tree for them that were from Mr. Jenkins and the Brownlett's. She forgot they had given her gifts, too.

Then it was time to put the two boys' gifts under the tree. Judy laughed out loud and said, "My goodness, Enoch, you and Jonie are sure giving Otis and Gib a lot of work. There's a hoe, shovel, pick, mattock, and a garden rake. Hey, each tool has both of their names on them."

Enoch laughed, too, "Well you know, Judy, Mam is just bein' practical! The boys always want to use the same tool at the same time. Now we have two of everything. That's not all we got 'em! Don't you agree that sometimes practical makes good sense?"

"I have a gift for each of them, too. And, I got you and Jonie somethin' to put under the tree. It's gettin' late and we have to get up early to start the cookin' if we want to eat dinner at 2 o'clock. By our soakin' the shucky beans all night, they should cook done in time for dinner. Let's get the young'ins up at daylight. That way we'll have fun watchin' them find their gifts. Good night!"

Jonie sang out in her sweet voice, "Good night to you, too, honey."

Christmas always filled Judy with a feeling of peace and joy. As she lay in the back bedroom, near Jonie's full-to-overflowing pantry room, her thoughts drifted back to the Christmas celebrations she had taken part in at Pine Mountain School. Before she lived at the school, she didn't have time to learn much about Christ's birth. She learned to read after she began to work at the school. She mulled over in her mind the meaning of this time of the year.

She prayed softly, "Dear God, this holy night and day is the celebration of the birth of the sweet Lord Jesus. Even though He was born almost two-thousand years ago, His birth is just as real today as it was then. His mother, Mary, and Joseph took shelter in a stable, where He was born.

The exchanging of gifts is in memory of the gifts brought in homage to the baby by the three wise men. The three kings from the East found Him by following a star that You set in the heavens to show them the way to His bed. His bed was in a manger in a stable in Bethlehem and it was surrounded by shepherds from the fields and the angels who summoned them.

Also, there were several four-legged creatures gathered there in the humble stable. You gave man dominion over all the creatures of the earth, but that don't mean man can be cruel to 'em. That means we're s'posed to respect and take good care of all of God's creatures.

Dear Lord, I have just sort of rambled on tonight. Thank you for watchin' over me, my little Mary and Della. I'll give you all my praise, In Jesus' name, Amen."

Judy sighed as she thought of her dogs, Trixie, Bootsy, and Sam, that her brother Rob took to keep when she left the farm. She still loved them and always missed them, especially when she went hunting in the mountains around Hazard. They were part of God's great and small earthly creatures. She would like to see them and Becky, and their young'ins. Jonie and Enoch, nor Alex, had mentioned Rob at all. Her last thoughts before sleep was, "I want to see Becky and Rob while I'm here and I'll ask about them in the mornin'."

Christmas morning was cold, with a brisk wind blowing. Judy rose early and went outside to look at the sky. It was cloudless with the moon just disappearing over the mountain. When she came back in the house, Jonie was at the stove laying the fire on top of the thin layer of ashes that were still warm from last night. She sang out, "Merry Christmas, Judy, honey. You beat me in gettin' up. I'm puttin' on the coffee and a kettle of oatmeal. I thought we could eat a bowl of oats, and have coffee with some of my sweet cakes. That'll be quick and, then I'll get the ham and pork roast in the oven. Is that all right?"

"Jonie, that's just fine. We can make the cake early and have that job out of the way. The smell of the cake baking will wake the young'ins and they'll come running to see what they have under the tree!"

"I'm goin' to let Enoch and Pa sleep 'til they wake up on their own. But, you're right; the young'ins will wake 'em by all the noise they'll make."

Jonie only had three cake pans, so she made three layers at a time. When the first three pans were filled and put in the hot oven, it wasn't but a few minutes until the delicious smell went all through the house.

Judy heard the girls' feet hit the floor and they appeared as if by magic in the kitchen. Jonie looked at their bare feet and said, "No body goes near the tree 'til all of you are dressed and have your shoes on!"

All six girls did an about face and raced back to the bedroom to see who could get dressed first.

With all the commotion the girls made, Enoch, Gilbert, and Otis became wide awake and got dressed, even to their work shoes, before Mellie made an appearance in the kitchen. She was the first of the girls to get dressed. Jonie quickly took the first three cake layer pans out of the oven and sat them on the windowsill to cool. "Judy, honey, I hear the baby, but let's let Pa sleep."

"Now," she said, "Lets all go see what Santy brought us!"

Jonie carried baby Delphia while Alta, Clara, Mellie, Dolly, Della, and Mary, all came trooping out of the bedroom and raced into the front room to gather around the Christmas tree. Enoch did the honors of passing out presents. Each of the girls squealed in delight over their dolls. Then, Clara, Dolly, Nellie, and Mellie sat down on the hardwood floor to examine the tea set.

Gib and Otis hung back waiting to be given a present. Their eyes grew huge when their father handed them the garden tools. "Pa, you're joshing, right?"

"No, Boys, now you each have your own set of tools. You can decide who gets to use the old ones and who gets to use the new ones, or you can just trade back and forth."

Gib looked forlorn as he asked, "Mam, is this all we got for Christmas?"

Jonie winked at Judy, "Well boys, I think there are two boxes hangin' on the back of the tree under that paper chain that has your names on 'em."

The brothers almost knocked the tree over in their haste to find the hidden presents. Gib tore the paper off the small box and was the first to open his gift. His jaw dropped. He held up a handsome pocket watch with a dark, brown cowhide watch-fob attached to it. Otis found an identical watch in his gift box. His watch-fob was made of medium brown cowhide.

Both boys hugged and kissed their mother's cheek. They were too old to kiss their father, but they heartily shook his hand. Both were exclaiming, "Oh thank you Mam and Pa!"

All the clothing and outerwear gifts were opened and examined. The fruit, nuts and candy were a big hit. Jonie had made knitted, wool-lined mittens, a scarf and a wool toboggan for Enoch. She had also hand-sewn a Sunday best shirt for him in a sky-blue cotton broadcloth. From Judy and Jonie, Alex received hand-sewn and store-bought gifts, including two flannel nightshirts, a warm, pointed night cap, and two pair of heavy, wool socks to wear in bed.

Enoch gave Jonie two packages with each holding enough material for new dresses. One of them was a brilliant red. Her eyes grew huge as she gazed at the gaudy material. Enoch said, "Now, Mam, don't you give me no sass 'bout that dress material. With your dark hair, dark eyes, and complexion, red should be your favorite color!"

"Pa, I do thank you."

That's all that Jonie said at the time. Judy grinned and thought, "Wait 'til she gets him alone!"

Judy's present from the Brownlett's was a lovely handmade shawl. The gifts the grown-ups gave each other were all hand-sewn or embroidered linens for the bedrooms. They were either pretty pillowcases or dresser scarves.

While the children were busy with their treasures, Jonie and Judy began preparing the Christmas feast. At 2:00 on Christmas day the table was loaded with lovingly prepared food when they called the family in to eat.

Enoch feasted his eyes on the beautiful food. He exclaimed, "Judy, Mam, if this table could talk, all it would do is groan!"

A half an hour later, everyone complained they had eaten so much they didn't have room for the applesauce stack cake. Jonie said, "Don't nobody worry about that. Afore dark, we'll have the cake with coffee for us, and with sweet milk for the young'ins."

Judy felt a pang of sadness as darkness fell on Christmas day. It had come and gone all too soon. She was looking forward to her trip to Harlan tomorrow with Miss Pettit and Mr. Wilder. Della had grown more than an inch and she could tell that her shoes were too small and pinched her feet. Mary didn't seem to grow much at all. Della was almost a head taller than her older sister.

On Monday morning Judy was up early, had a warm breakfast with Jonie, and was on her way to Pine Mountain School by seven. The days were so short now, that daylight was almost an hour away.

To be sure she was warm enough, Judy had layered her clothing. Over her regular outfit, she wore a warm buttoned up sweater. There was a thick woolen scarf around her neck. Over her other clothing she wore a heavy long woolen split tail riding coat. On her head was another scarf that covered her ears, and over that was a becoming lady's riding hat. She would be warm now and when she returned in the dark later tonight. She never went anywhere in the mountains without her rifle. It was securely attached to her saddle. Curly was in good spirits and covered the distance between Jonie's and the school with time to spare. Miss Petit was mounted and waiting for Mr. Wilder. Judy was glad she was waiting for him and not her!

Mr. Wilder led two pack mules to carry the school's supplies they would buy on this trip. Judy only intended to buy school clothes and a pair of shoes for Della. Her purchases would easily fit on Curly's back. All was ready and the three riders stepped out at exactly 9:00 o'clock.

They followed Little Greasy Creek toward the Divide where they turned left onto the Laden Trail to go over tall Pine Mountain. On the crest of the mountain they passed by the busy logging camp. Judy marveled that the logging company was able to lay a railroad track in the mountain terrain to transport the cut timber. They planned to extend the track all the way to Big Laurel!

About half way down the mountain on the other side, they passed by the mammoth sized Rebel Rock. They reached the large lumber company and sawmill of Putney in record time. Miss Pettit said, "We're here and it's not yet eleven. Let's stop at the boardinghouse for a quick dinner and if we don't dally, I think we'll be in Harlan by around two."

Judy agreed, "I think that's a good plan. While you do your shopping in Harlan, I'll do mine. I'm just going to the ten cent stores for Della's school clothes, but I'll go to Powers and Horton to buy her shoes. I'll meet you at the A&P Store. That way, we should be on our way back to the school afore three."

Mr. Wilder warned, "The days are so short now. It'll be dark when we get to the school. Judy, will you be all right goin' on to your sister's that late?"

"Yes, I have my rifle with me. My Curly can outrun any horse. The moon should be almost full tonight and the sky's clear. I'll be able to see well enough to be all right. I know it's goin' to be cold, though."

They rode into Harlan well before two. Miss Pettit left Judy at Newberry's Store and rode to the A&P where they all agreed to meet in an hour.

Newberry's had a whole section of girl's dresses, skirts, and blouses. Judy found two complete outfits of pretty, matching gathered skirts and middy blouses. In addition to them, she bought Della one nice Sunday dress. At Scotts' she found step-ins (bloomers), petticoats, and stockings. She was pleased with her purchases, but to find Della's shoes, she walked to Powers and Horton.

Almost none of the streets in Harlan were completely level, and she walked slightly uphill until she reached the top and then crossed the street to go to Powers and Horton. They had the best quality of children's shoes in Harlan. They were also expensive!

Mary had very small feet, but Della needed a larger size than most girls her age wore. She knew the size she wanted, but was debating about getting two pair. Della needed a pair of high-top, buttoned shoes for every day, and a pair of low-cut laced-up oxfords for Sunday best.

When Judy opened the heavy door, she accidentally bumped into a woman who was coming out. The woman saw Judy coming in, but didn't wait for her to clear the door before attempting to leave the store. Judy exclaimed, "Oh, pardon me, please!"

"You better watch where you're goin'!"

"I'm sorry that I bumped you. I didn't see you comin' out of the store."

"Say, you're that Judy Smith woman that used to work at Pine Mountain School, ain't you? I thought you'd left these parts!"

"I'm sorry, again, that I bumped into you." Judy extended her hand, "Yes, I'm Judy Turner-Smith."

The woman ignored her offered hand and drew back and away from her. Judy ignored the insulting body language. She reached out and gently took hold of the woman's left arm. Judy's lips moved silently and then she released the arm and stepped back.

Then she asked, "Have we met afore? I don't think I know you. What did you say your name was?"

"I didn't say! I want nothin' to do with the likes of you! My name is Loretta Helton; I'm Dora Mae's mother. Yes, Dora Mae, she's my daughter that you and your good-for-nothin' girl kept from gettin' in Pine Mountain School. But we got her in a good school anyways. She's goin' to Red Bird School!"

Judy's eyes grew huge and then narrowed. Judy's mind was racing, but her thoughts were calm, "Here in my face is the woman whose mean-talking gossip cost me my job and forced me to live so far away from my family."

Judy smiled sweetly and said, "I hope she does right well at Red Bird. Now, excuse me, I have more shoppin' to do. I wish you a Merry Christmas!"

Loretta Helton lifted her nose high in the air and snorted, "Humpf!"

Judy pushed through the heavy door of Powers and Horton and went directly to the Children's Shoe Department. She found exactly what she was looking for and promptly bought Della two good-looking pairs of shoes.

Loaded down with her packages, Judy went looking for Miss Pettit. She saw her standing on the sidewalk outside of the A&P Store. Judy stopped in her tracks and pretended to be looking in a furniture store's front window. Miss Pettit was talking with the rude Loretta Helton.

Judy didn't want another confrontation with the woman, especially not in front of Miss Pettit! She kept looking in the store window until she saw the Helton woman walk away. Then she walked on up the street to the corner and joined Miss Pettit. Mr. Wilder hurried toward them as he came around the back of the large store building leading the heavily loaded mules.

Judy's thoughts were busy trying to justify what she did when she touched Loretta Helton's arm and invoked the powers in the way her father taught her. It wasn't revenge she wanted, but some small measure of justice.

For the next week, Loretta was going to have nothing in her daily life go just right. There wasn't anything going to happen that could physically harm her or hurt anyone else, but the woman would be deeply frustrated when everything she did at home, especially in her kitchen, turned out badly.

Mr. Wilder led the mules and was well ahead of them on the Putney Trail. Making sure he was out of ear shot, Miss Pettit asked, "Judy, did you see me talking to Mrs. Helton?

"Yes, I did. What did she want?"

"She wanted to warn me to have nothing to do with you or she would write to the Mission Board back East and cause the school trouble!"

"Miss Pettit, this is the first time I've ever seen the woman to know who she is. Why does she hate me so much?"

Miss Pettit had nothing but compassion in her voice, "Judy, there's no way to understand the spiteful meanness in some people. God never promised us a perfect world. Although it can hurt us to the depths of our soul, we must try to forgive them and turn what is hurtful into a positive situation. All this trouble the Heltons caused you started with vicious gossip. They saw that you were almost defenseless and vulnerable. In their meanness, they took advantage of that to hurt someone who couldn't fight back."

"I'm not sure I know what the word vulner'ble means. I think you mean that I was someone they knew they could hurt, and yet they went ahead and did their mean-talkin' gossip, anyway."

"Yes, Judy, that's right. And now they know that the school is vulnerable because we depend on the Mission Board's financial support to exist."

"Miss Pettit, what you're sayin' is that it's better for me and the school if we don't give 'em any ammunition to use 'gainst us. Then, don't you think that it'll be best if I don't visit the school until Della's finished with the sixth grade? I can have my sister, Jonie Lewis, continue to visit her in my place. I want you to write to me like you've been doin', to tell me how her school work is progressin' and if she needs anything special."

"Yes, I think you know I'll do that anyway. When Della's ready to graduate, I think you should come for her graduation, regardless of the Heltons.

Judy, I'll be in touch with Reverend Brownlett about a possible work/study placement for her in Hazard. I think we can find a good Christian family who'll pay her to work for them, provide room and board, and allow her to continue her education. Della's a bright child and it would be a shame if she couldn't go on to high school like Mary. I'll put my thoughts on this subject in my 'Progress Report' letters that you receive at the end of each semester."

Judy said, "The Brownlett's have been wonderful to Mary. I worry that we can't find a good placement for Della. But, if we can't, she can stay with me in the Hazard Hotel and go to school. You know that I won't stand for her to be mistreated by anyone.

Miss Pettit, I know that she and Mary are very different. Della is so independent that she fights her own battles most of the time. Mary will tell on somebody in a heartbeat if they get out of line with her. But, my little Della keeps things locked in her heart and soul, and doesn't tell anyone when she's hurt."

"I promise you that Ethel and I will keep a close eye on her for you. We'll protect her from the Helton clan. When I write to you, please write back. We need to keep in touch both ways!"

"Miss Pettit, I'll do that. I do thank you and Mrs. Zande for all you've done for me and for my girls. When we reach the turn off to the school, I'll keep on going so I can be at my sister's as soon as I can. It'll be dark and it's turning much colder. I'll need to hurry."

Judy left Mr. Wilder and Miss Pettit as planned and reached Jonie's well after dark. Her hands and feet were numb from the cold. She was starved, too, and even though it was mostly leftovers from yesterday's feast, she relished the delicious supper that Jonie had saved for her.

"Jonie, honey, I left my packages in the travelin' sacks in the barn with Curly. I'll have Della try on everything in the mornin'. I hope that nothin' has to be returned to the stores in Harlan, but if there is, could you do that for me the next time you go to town? I'll need you and Enoch to take her back to the school on Wednesday. Mary and I need to leave early Friday morning. We need to be in Hazard Saturday night."

"Yes, I'll be glad to do whatever's needed."

"Where is Pa? Has he gone to bed already?"

"Yes, he gets real tired early in the afternoon. He does whatever he wants. By usin' his walkin' stick, he can go out and wander 'round in the orchard, and in and 'round back of the barn. He likes to stop on his wanderin's to pet and have long talks with the animals. He eats good. Pa's happy here with us. And, he feels safe."

"Judy picked up on her last remark, "Why wouldn't Pa feel safe just 'bout anywhere?"

"Well, you know that he and Rob have been on the outs ever since he sold his farm and came to live with me. Brother Rob did something real bad. Something I wouldn't have thought possible. We never told you, but after Pa and Mam moved in with me, Rob got roaring drunk and came here screamin' for Pa to come out and face him like a man."

Judy was aghast, absolutely dumb-founded, "What did Pa do?"

"He went out on my front porch and faced him. Rob screamed at Pa, accusin' him of robbing his first born of his birthright. He wasn't making much sense. Pa didn't answer him a'tall. That seemed to make him madder! Without any warnin', Rob shot twice over Pa's head. Pa ducked low and came back into the house. Then Rob yelled for me to come out, but Enoch went instead and told Rob to go on away from here or he'd sue him for trespassin' and damagin' private property. Even drunk, Rob knew what bein' sued would mean. He left. He hasn't come to see me or his pa since."

"Have you seen him or Becky? Is she all right? I meant to ask you 'bout them when Mary and I first got here and kept forgettin' to."

"I've seen Becky just twice since Rob did that. She was in Harlan. She doesn't go very often. She said that Rob's moods are worse since he's older. He won't do any work. He plans to sell his place as soon as the last of their young'ins are grown and have left home. Becky's not well. You and I both know she's worked herself to death, raisin' her husband and them eleven young'ins."

"If you see her again, give her my love. I do love Becky with all my heart. If you can slip it to her, give her my address at the hotel. Maybe she could write me and have one of the older boys mail the letter for her."

"I'll do that. Pa didn't do anything to Rob. He said 'My first born is now dead to me!' He's not spoken Rob's name aloud to any of us since then. It makes me sad. There was a final sound in Pa's voice. He meant every word he said."

Judy told Jonie and Enoch of her run-in with the Helton woman in Harlan. She warned them about the evil that was in that entire family. "When Della visits you, make sure she goes nowhere near any of them! I really believe they'll not hesitate to do any of us harm."

The next morning, Della squealed in delight when she tried on each of her new school outfits. The dress for Sunday church looked darling on her. The shoes fit perfectly, with room for her feet to grow. She beamed with pleasure when she saw her new underwear and stockings. Jonie laughed, "I won't have to return a thing. It all fits perfect and looks very nice on Della."

Mary's face was etched with jealousy as she watched her sister trying on school clothes. Her sour mood didn't escape Judy's eagle eye. She hugged her and said, "Don't you worry. When we get to Hazard, we'll buy your new school clothes. We both agreed to give poor Ned a rest on the trip back, didn't we?" Well, that's what we're doing. There'll be sales going on in Hazard all next week. You'll have the same number of new outfits as Della."

Mary was placated. Her Aunt Jonie's questioning and unbelieving look because of her rude behavior made Mary uncomfortable. She eased her feelings by apologizing to her mother. "Ma, I'm sorry if you thought I was jealous of Della. I know we didn't want to have Ned carry a lot of unnecessary bundles back with us. We'll be all right and I'll love goin' shopping with you next week!"

Judy had to smile at the skillful, back-handed apology that came from Mary. But, she let it slide this time. The day passed quickly, but she was able to relax and get some real rest for the first time since she left Hazard.

Late Thursday afternoon, Mary helped carry their Christmas presents out to the barn. All of the travel-sacks were tied securely with rope and ready to load on Ned early the next morning.

On Friday morning they rose early so they could leave before daylight. Jonie packed them a special bag filled with enough food to last two full days. Then she added more to the bag, saying, "You don't know what the weather will be like on Saturday. If you have to stay another night on the trail, you'll have plenty to eat. I'm askin' the good Lord to watch over you on your journey!"

"Jonie, honey, thank you for all you and Enoch have done for us. We've had a wonderful Christmas! I don't know when we'll get to see you again, but you'll be in our hearts, in our thoughts, and in our prayers! All of the young'ins are asleep. We told Della and Pa goodbye last night. I don't want to wake 'em. Goodbye, now. We love you all so very much!"

Then, Curly, the little mare, and Ned stepped out on the first leg of their long journey back to Hazard. Judy didn't look back. Her eyes were filled with tears and she didn't want to see Jonie crying, too. She prayed silently that she and Mary would have a safe journey and that the weather would hold. It was very cold, but the trail was still dry.

Chapter Four
DELLA'S DILEMMA

When Della woke up that morning, Judy and Mary had been gone for about two hours. She couldn't help feeling abandoned. To feel better, she made a solemn vow. "I'll do my best to make Ma proud of me. In a year and a half, I'll be living with her and Mary in Hazard. Until then, I'll have a goal for each day. It'll be like using my imaginary cake to get through a boring job at school. This time, the days will be different. They'll turn into weeks, months and years. I won't think beyond graduation. That's my goal and when I'm finished, my life will change. After that, I'll know what God has planned for me."

Alex awoke feeling a new keening in his heart. It was a lonely, lost feeling because both Mary and Judy were gone. He felt in his bones and deep in his soul, their sweet hugs and warm kisses on his cheek. On Wednesday, little Della would be leaving with Jonie to go back to school. It was hard not to feel alone and depressed, but he made himself feel better by thinking of all that was good in his life. He prayed silently, "Thank you God for Jonie and her family. If it wasn't for them, I'd have no way of knowin' what your plan is for me. Be with Judy and Mary on their journey to Hazard. Please keep my family safe. In Jesus' name I pray. Amen."

Judy promised Alex she would write to him. He needed to hear from her. All of his children were busy with their families. He missed them. In particular, he missed his daughter, Rana, (Rainie), who married Israel Miniard and died in childbirth when Israel, Jr. was born. Her widowed husband, and her son, Israel, Jr. (called Id) his wife, Rhoda (Rhodie), with their children lived farther down on Little Greasy Creek, deeper into Leslie County. They stopped to see him and Jonie each time they went to Putney or to Harlan.

The rest of his family, including Dave, Liege, Sadie (Bish) Boggs, and Emily (Robert) Lewis, lived in different directions away from him and had to make a special trip if they came to visit. There was Rob and Becky, but he never saw them any more. He knew it would probably be next Christmas before he saw Judy, Mary, and Della again. Alex smiled as he thought of Emily and Jonie. The two sisters had married the Lewis brothers, Enoch and Robert. All of their children were double first cousins!

His smile turned into a frown as he remembered that Judy talked with the Helton woman in Harlan and worried that the Heltons might try to harm Della.

Alex's worries were not lost on Jonie. She responded to his furrowed brow, "Pa, are you worried about Della being alone at school and what the Heltons might try to do? Now, don't you fret about Della. She's stronger'n any of my girls and can hold her own. Anyways, every time I go to Putney or Harlan, I'll stop to see her and take her some good eats to keep in her room."

Wednesday morning dawned bright, but cold. Jonie bundled Della into layers of warm clothing for the ride to Pine Mountain School. She climbed into the saddle of her tall black horse, "Night," and reached down to swing Della up to sit in front of her. Della's new clothes and Christmas presents were tied in bundles and swung over Night's broad back. Jonie packed another sack with fruity cakes and cookies for Della to snack on and share with her roommates.

They made good time and arrived at the school well before dinnertime. As they rode up to the older girls' dormitory, Della grinned, "Aunt Jonie, you couldn't have planned this better. After dinner the rest of the day is free until the supper bell rings. Do you have to go or can you come in with me?"

Jonie hugged her tight and said, "Honey, I'd better head back home. Alta is watching her sisters and the baby, and she's fixin' them dinner. Remember, I love you and I'll be back to visit real soon. You work hard and be a good girl. Your Mam loves you and we love you. I have to say goodbye!"

Della stood on the front steps of her dormitory and watched her beloved Aunt Jonie until she was out of sight. For the first time since her mother moved to Hazard, she didn't feel lost and alone. She turned and quickly climbed the stairs leading to her room. The many bundles that held her new clothes, the pretty doll, Aunt Jonie's cakes and cookies, and the other Christmas gifts were clutched tightly in both hands. In about thirty minutes she had to go to Laurel House for dinner, but she took time to put everything away.

It was with a completely new and positive attitude that Della faced the prospect of being without her mother. She had a plan for getting through the long months over the next year and a half. As she worked at her scheduled job assignments her goal was to memorize every Old English ballad that they sang in Assembly, at special events, and to celebrate holidays. She would surprise Aunt Jonie and Grandpa Alex by singing their favorites for them all the way through. She reassured herself, "I'll memorize one song a week as long as I stay here! I'll follow our "Ballad Song Book" and memorize them in the same order as they're printed in the book. I'll do the same with my favorite church hymns."

Della began immediately to carry out her plan to memorize all of the Old English folk songs they sang at school. She took a special secret delight in knowing she didn't have to look at the printed page of her ballad book when they sang the songs she knew. Only Mrs. Zande seemed to notice that Della held her head high and didn't even glance down at the songbook when she sang. Della's voice was loud, sweet, and clear. It seemed to come natural for her to use a unique mountain twang to emphasize the intense feelings of some of the lyrics. Her singing stood out over the voices of her classmates.

It was an early April morning after a regular school assembly that Mrs. Zande approached her, "Della, I've noticed that your singing has greatly improved. Have you been practicing?"

Della didn't want to reveal that she was memorizing all of the songs that they sang, so she said, "Yes ma'am, Mrs. Zande! I've been memorizing the ballad songs and some of the church hymns that are my favorites."

"Are you staying at the school during Easter week?"

"Yes ma'am, I'm stayin' and workin' that week so I can pay more on my tuition. I've already told my Aunt Jonie, but she said they would come to church here in the Chapel on Easter Sunday."

"That's really nice. Have them plan to stay with you for Sunday dinner. I would like it very much if you would practice a special song with me that we'll sing during the Easter Services. Will you do that for me?"

Della's eyes grew huge, "You want me to sing with you, alone, in the Chapel? What would we sing?"

I've been practicing "I Love to Tell the Story" on my dulcimer. Let's you and I meet this Sunday afternoon about two o'clock in the social room and see how it goes. Is that all right?"

"Yes ma'am. Do I need to dress up?"

"No, honey, just be comfortable."

Della was almost giddy with excitement. She enjoyed taking speaking parts in the skits they performed that told the stories of some of the more popular ballads, but she never sang in front of an audience before. As the day wore on, she began to have self-doubts about her voice. "Was she good enough; could she sing loud enough? What would her classmates think, or say to her?"

That night she remembered what her mother and grandpa Alex told her about talking things over with God, that He would always lead her to make right decisions. Her bedtime prayer was almost the same each night. She knelt by her bed and prayed, "Dear Lord, I thank You for this day. I thank You for watchin' over me and takin' care of me. Bless Ma, Mary, and Grandpa Alex. Keep them safe. Bless Aunt Jonie, Uncle Enoch and all my cousins. Bless Aunt Becky. Keep her safe. I love You, Lord Jesus. Amen."

With her prayer finished, she arose and got under the bed covers. She lay very still. Her bed was next to a window and she could see a half moon slowly moving across the night sky. She began to have a very important conversation with God. "You know I've never done anything like this before. You know that I'm scared that my voice ain't good enough. I'm scared I'll make a bad mistake and people will laugh at me. Mrs. Zande thinks I'm good enough to do this or she wouldn't have asked me to practice that song with her. "I Love to Tell the Story" is one of my favorites. I know it by heart and I love to sing it when I'm workin' and alone. Dear Lord, if Mrs. Zande thinks I can do this, then I have to believe that I can do it, too. I'm goin' to trust You in that I'm makin' the right decision. Thank You, dear Lord, for leading me through this hard thinkin'."

With that settled, Della sighed, turned toward the rising moon, closed her eyes and was soon sound asleep.

Sunday afternoon finally came and she walked from her dormitory to Laurel House to meet with Mrs. Zande in the social room. Della was dismayed to find that Miss Pettit was there busying herself by looking through the small library of books on the shelves lining the north side of the large room.

Della lifted her head high and mumbled, "I don't care if Miss Pettit is here. I'll just do my best to please Mrs. Zande. Miss Pettit can think whatever she wants. As long as Mrs. Zande likes my singin', that's all that matters!"

The practice went better than Mrs. Zande had expected. There were just two short verses and a chorus to the song and Della's sweet clear voice beautifully emphasized the lyrics' key words in the expressive mountain twang. Miss Pettit's jaw dropped the first time she heard Della sing. There was no doubt. Della's strong voice would carry to the far corners of the Chapel.

Easter week came. Only a few students stayed to work during their spring break. Della received her work schedule from Miss Pettit. She saw that for the first four days she worked eight hours a day. On Good Friday, she only worked three and a half hours. Saturday was visitor's day and a free-day.

For her first assignment, Della was given the job of "spring cleaning" the older boys' dormitory. Twenty boys lived there. On the morning of the first day, she swept and wet mopped the entire building, stripped twenty beds, gathered fresh bedding to remake them, and hung twenty pillows on the clotheslines to air.

A thorough cleaning meant breaking down each boy's bed, and dragging the mattresses and bedsprings outside to be cleaned and aired. Two older boys came early and moved the beds, mattresses, and bedsprings outside and leaned them against the building. She beat the mattresses on one side and then turned them over to be beaten on the other. She was told that each individual coil of the bedsprings had to be cleaned with a long, pointed hard-bristle brush. Della counted the number of coils in each row and multiplied them by eleven rows. She exclaimed, "Wow, that's seventy-seven coils to each bed and then multiply that by twenty!

Della was tall for her age, but was just ten years old. She would be eleven on April thirtieth. The work she was doing on that one day alone would have exhausted an adult woman. After working just two hours, she couldn't help grumbling, "This is way too much to do in the six hours I have left to work today. I'll try to get as much done as I can before the dinner bell rings and then finish up before five tonight."

She fluffed the pillows before hanging them on the line to air. The mattresses were clean on both sides. She looked at the long line of twenty bed springs and breathed a deep sigh. With a determined look on her face, she picked up the stiffly-bristled, sharply-pointed brush, and began running it all the way through the deep coils. Each set of springs became an imaginary eleven-layer cake. She stopped when the dinner bell rang to walk to Laurel House for the noonday meal. She came back to her job at one o'clock and had finished cleaning ten of the bed springs when Miss Pettit came by to check on her work.

"My dear Della, what a wonderful job you're doing! At three-thirty this afternoon I'll send one of the older boys over to take the springs and mattresses back in and put them on the bed frames for you. Then, you can make up all the beds using the fresh clean linens. I'm looking at the springs you've done already. I think it'll be best if you go over all of them again. I believe you'll have time to do that before three-thirty. Don't you think so, dear?"

Although seething inside, Della answered, "Yes ma'am, Miss Pettit!"

"Thank you, Della. I'll see you at supper tonight!"

Without a backward glance, Miss Pettit marched down the road past the Chapel and on toward Laurel House. Della looked closely at the ten bed springs she had already cleaned. She ran her hand over several of the coils. There wasn't any kind of soil on them. In fact they looked brand new!

Della fumed, "I agreed to do them twice, but I think its unnecessary work. On top of what I've done today, it ain't fair! It's after two now. I'd have to really rush to finish the next ten and then do all twenty of them over again."

She picked up the hard-bristle brush and slowly cleaned each coil. By pacing herself, she finished the last ten bed springs at exactly three-thirty. The older boy appeared and struggled mightily to get the springs and mattresses inside and up the stairs to the bedrooms. Della took down all the pillows and carried them upstairs, four at a time. She had finished making up all the beds when Miss Pettit suddenly appeared. With a look of pleasure on her face, she surveyed the freshly made up beds. "Della, my dear, you have worked splendidly today! Don't you feel much better about your work since you cleaned the bed springs twice?"

Della didn't feel even one twinge of guilt as she dutifully responded, "Yes ma'am, Miss Pettit!"

Saturday was a free day! Also, it was Visitor's Day for the students that worked through Easter Week. There were people from the surrounding community visiting on the school grounds. It had been more than two years since Della had seen Dora Mae Helton, but the second she laid eyes on her she knew who she was. She was near the back door by the kitchen at Laurel House when Della spotted her. Immediately, Della turned her back to Dora Mae and the woman she was with. Della decided that the woman was the girl's mother. She wanted nothing to do with either of them.

Because she spotted Dora Mae before the girl saw her, she managed to avoid her all day. At the end of visitor's day, Della went back to her dormitory until time for supper. Afterwards, she was meeting Mrs. Zande again at Laurel House for one more practice before her solo in church tomorrow.

That evening, both Della and Mrs. Zande were satisfied that they would be 'good' together during the Easter service. One of the men schoolteachers, a retired missionary named Reverend Henri Lattimore, would lead the service and deliver the sermon. There was a mixed choir of both boys and girls who would take part in the program. After the choir sang the first song, then Della was to sing the second hymn with Mrs. Zande accompanying her on the dulcimer.

Easter Sunday dawned with a brilliant sunrise. Della put on her Sunday dress and the black patent leather shoes. She had a pretty green checked ribbon for her curly black hair. The ribbon deepened the color of her blue/green eyes. Della walked to the Chapel with Mr. and Mrs. Zande. She was to sit with them until time for her solo.

After the choir finished the first song, she and Mrs. Zande walked to the front of the Chapel and faced the audience. Way in the back of the church, Della spotted Dora Mae and her mother. Across the aisle, on the other side of the church were her Aunt Jonie and Uncle Enoch. Della kept her eyes glued to Jonie's sweet face. She silently said a prayer, "Thank you Lord for Aunt Jonie. Help me get through this. Please don't let the Heltons know who I am. Amen."

Then Mrs. Zande began to play sweet, mellow tones on the Dulcimer and, right on cue, Della began to sing. Her voice was strong, loud, clear, and sweet as she sang the beloved old hymn "I Love To Tell The Story."

Della's use of her natural mountain twang served to emphasize the intense feelings that were prominent throughout each verse and in the short chorus. She noticed several heads bobbing in time with the music. The lovely old hymn was obviously a favorite of many members of the audience as Della sang:

"I love to tell the story of unseen things above,
Of Jesus and his glory, of Jesus and his love,
I love to tell the story because I know it's true,
It satisfies my longings as nothing else would do.
    Chorus
I love to tell the story; Twill be my theme in glory,
To tell the old, old story of Jesus and his love.

I love to tell the story for those who know it best,
Seem hungering and thirsting to hear it like the rest.
And when, in scenes of glory, I sing the new, new song,
Twill be the same old story that I have loved so long.
    Chorus
I love to tell the story; Twill be my theme in glory,
To tell the old, old story of Jesus and his love.

Della watched Jonie's face and was pleased to see her mouthing the words to the old hymn. She knew the words by heart and while smiling and nodding encouragement to Della, silently sang it with her all the way through.

They finished their special music and started to return to their seats. Della walked down the church aisle with Mrs. Zande, but left her side and joined Jonie and Enoch to sit with them. She forced herself to look straight ahead and didn't even glance in the direction of the Heltons.

After church Jonie, Enoch, and Della walked together to Laurel House for the Easter Sunday dinner. Della looked at the tables and her mouth watered. Each table was set for nine people and loaded down with a large, pre-sliced ham on a platter, along with a brimming-full gravy boat. In the middle of the table were several large serving bowls filled with mashed potatoes, green beans, turnip greens, candied sweet potatoes, and canned sliced peaches. Also, there was a plate with nine individual pieces of chocolate-iced yellow cake.

Mrs. Zande invited Della and her family to sit at her table and was lavish with her praise of Della's solo. Jonie nodded, "We're all proud of our Della. She's good at everything she does, but we didn't know she could sing like that!"

Enoch asked, "Della, honey, have you been practicin' singin' and not tellin' anybody?"

Della turned a becoming shade of pink, "Uncle Enoch, you're embarrassing me. Did you and Aunt Jonie really think I did good? I've never sung in front of people before."

Mrs. Zande laughed, "Well, Della, my dear, I've a feeling that you'll be taking music this next term and will soon be singing in front of a lot of people."

Della beamed with pleasure. It wasn't often that she was singled out for high praise. She would write her mother after Aunt Jonie and Uncle Enoch left and tell her all about church today.

As soon as the meal was over Jonie said, "Della, honey, we'll have to be headin' home. We left Alta in charge agin. I had everything ready to put on the table, but she and the boys had to manage the Sunday dinner all by themselves. I'm so glad we came, I wouldn't have missed hearin' you sing for anything."

"Aunt Jonie, and you, Uncle Enoch, I love you both so much. Give Alta and all the girls a hug for me. Tell the boys I love 'em, too. I'll look forward to seein' you again, soon!"

Della stood in front of Laurel House and watched Jonie and Enoch until they rode out of sight. Then she turned around to go back to her dormitory. About half way up the fairly steep roadway she stopped and turned aside to take a little used shortcut path that ran between several trees and small boulders. The reason Della decided to use the path now was because she saw the Heltons standing near the back door by the kitchen talking to Miss Pettit. From their body language, Della could tell they were badgering Miss Pettit about something.

She was well hidden among the trees and rocks on the small path and sat down on a stone step to watch. For the first time she had a chance to get a good look at Dora Mae and her mother. They had identical scowls on their faces as they rudely talked over Miss Pettit's calm attempt to placate them. Miss Pettit finally raised one hand as a signal to them to be quiet. Della couldn't see her face, but she was sure that Miss Pettit had heard enough from the Heltons.

Miss Pettit suddenly raised her voice in exasperation, "No. Della Smith is a student here. She's one of our best students and a hard worker. I will not tolerate your insinuating otherwise. The Mission Board has approved Della's living and attending school here until she graduates. Now, this subject is closed. You're welcome to stay as long as you like, but please excuse me!"

Miss Pettit turned abruptly and quickly walked away from the Heltons. They stared after her in disbelief. Then the woman slowly turned away and with her daughter in tow, they walked to their horses. Both of them mounted and prepared to leave. Della stayed in her hiding place and watched until they rode out of sight. They would be just a few minutes behind Jonie and Enoch on the Little Greasy Creek Trail.

That night in her dormitory, Della wrote a long letter to Judy. She gave Mrs. Zande most of the credit for the success of their joint musical presentation. Because she didn't want to worry her mother, she made no mention of the Heltons and their confrontation with Miss Pettit. She would wait until they were together again to tell Judy about them. She closed her letter by asking her mother to tell Mary she loved her and to remind her sister that she owed her a letter.

No one knew that Della overheard part of the Heltons' conversation with Miss Pettit. Della could only imagine what dreadful thing they were demanding the school to do to her.

Before she went to sleep that night, she talked over her troubles with God. "Dear Lord, I'm so grateful to Miss Pettit for standing up to them and for standing up for me. From now on I'll be on guard against them 'cause mean-talkin' people are dangerous. Ma always told me to take my troubles to You and leave them there. That's what I'm doin' now, but I'll still be watchful. Thank you for today. The dear Lord Jesus' Easter service was beautiful. You answered my prayers that nothing would go wrong with my singin' and Mrs. Zande's music. Bless Ma, Mary, Aunt Jonie, Uncle Enoch, my cousins, and Aunt Becky. Amen"

Chapter Five
TRUSTING AND BELIEVING

When Judy left her sister's home and her beloved father to return to Hazard with Mary, she had a deep sadness in her heart, but a pleasant thrill in her soul. The feeling was bittersweet. Her father's birthday was in June and he would be a hundred and two years old. Because she now lived a long way from home, Each time she was with him, she worried that it would be the last. Only God knew how much time Alex had left. She murmured, "I pray that God lets Pa live to see his vision for me come true."

The two-day trip to Hazard was without incident. The weather cooperated and they had a dry trail all the way. Fourteen-year-old Mary chattered all the way about the fashionable school clothes, hat, and shoes that she wanted to buy in Hazard. "Ma, I'm older now and I want to look like the other girls in my class. I know you pick out all of Della's clothes for her, but will you let me pick my own school outfits and Sunday dress? I need some Ponds loose face powder and a small bottle of toilet water. I like lilac and lavender scents."

Judy turned her head away from her daughter so she wouldn't see the delighted grin that lit up her face. Yes, her older daughter grew up while she wasn't looking. She heard everything Mary said. Judy wanted her to be happy in her situation and she would try to provide whatever Mary needed to blend in with the other schoolgirls.

Judy erased the wide grin and turned a serious face toward Mary. She said, "Honey, it depends on how much things cost. Be mindful that I work hard for my money. Try to choose nice things that are on sale. Yes, besides your school clothes, I want you to buy a pair of high top shoes for school, and a pair of low patent leather ones for church. And, yes, you do need a new Sunday hat.

We'll go shopping late Tuesday afternoon. The stores are closed Monday for New Year's. You'll need to make the 'rangements with Reverend Brownlett for Tuesday, and I'll ask Sylvia and Isaac to watch the restaurant for me."

Mary was so delighted that she hugged herself in her excitement. "Ma, I can hardly wait. We'll have fun, too. Maybe we can stop at the pharmacy on Main Street and have an ice cream soda. Reverend Brownlett takes us there some times and the sodas are so good! Have you ever had an ice cream soda?"

"Yes, Mary, I had a vanilla soda once when Miss Pettit treated me. Yes, let's plan on that as soon as we finish our shoppin'!"

When Judy dropped Mary off at the Brownlett's, she helped put her bundles on the porch. "I'll have to leave you now and go on to the hotel. Take care of your horse before you do anything else. Make sure you feed her, give her fresh water, and rub her down. I'll see you on Tuesday."

Judy rode to the livery stable to return Ned and to have them put Curly up for the night. All of a sudden she was tired. She was glad she didn't have to be on the job until tomorrow. It had been a wonderful week for her because she was with her daughters, her father, and her sister Jonie's family. Also, Miss Pettit and Mrs. Zande made her feel so special. She would treasure the memories of this one week in her heart forever!

She walked around to the front of the hotel and climbed the steps to the front entrance. When she walked through the double doors into the lobby Mr. Jenkins jumped to his feet and came toward her with open arms. Astonished, Judy stopped in her tracks. "Judy, honey, I'm so glad to see you! Come and tell me about your visit home. I missed you something awful. Now maybe I can get a good night's sleep again!"

Judy couldn't resist the temptation to tease him, "Mr. Jenkins, did you really miss me, or your sleep?"

He came right back with a retort, "Both, dad gum it! I missed both!"

"Did everything go all right in the restaurant? I wanted you to rely on Isaac and Sylvia more so it would be easier on you. I told them to help you in any way they could. Did they?"

"Yes. They're both Godsends. They told me you've been teaching them a lot about how to please the diners. Some customers are now three-times-a-day repeaters. If we keep growing like this, I'll have to give them another raise."

Judy beamed her pleasure. With a wide grin she said, "No. We won't give any new raises just yet. It's too soon. About the first of July would be a good date to give each of them a raise. We'll see how business is by then and decide how much when the time comes."

"That sounds like a plan. You have travel sacks to unpack. Go on and get settled in. When you're ready, come and have supper with me. I still want to hear about your father and your other daughter, Della. We had good weather here, so I wasn't too worried about your traveling on the mountain trails."

"Mr. Jenkins-Bill-I'd like that. I'll be ready for supper in 'bout an hour. I want to freshen up and change clothes."

When she went into the restaurant for supper, Sylvia and Isaac gave Judy a warm welcome back, saying they had missed her. Judy felt like she had come home. All the people she worked with were like family. In a way they were her new family, and she cherished them as such.

After they ordered supper, Bill smiled and said, "Now, I want us to plan for my trip to see my brother in Florida. I've checked the schedules and find that I can go all the way by train, but there isn't any express train. All that's available are what I call whistle-stops. It'll take the better part of three days, one way! Even so, that's the fastest way to travel when going that far. I got a letter last week. He said the best time to come was late February or early March before the stormy season.

The summers there are brutal hot, but he said he manages to stay cool. He didn't tell me how he does that, though.

I told you I'd train you to handle the hotel while I'm gone. I'll pay you extra for that. I'd like to begin your training early next week. We'll play that by ear. I'm planning to leave about the twenty-fifth of February and return on the fifteenth of March. That's eighteen days altogether, but six of them will be spent in travel. That means I'll have twelve days with my brother and his family."

He paused in his long explanation to grin and say. "Oh, well, twelve days is long enough to wear out my welcome!"

Judy listened carefully to Bill. Then she protested, "Mr. Jenkins-Bill-you don't need to pay me any extra for doing this for you. I'm glad to do it. How about if I come over to the hotel during the slow-time in the mid-afternoons? That way we could use an hour a day for you to teach me."

"Judy, that's a real good idea. But you're going to get paid extra during the time I'm away. That's only fair."

Sylvia brought their orders. They stopped talking to enjoy the food. Isaac had outdone himself. Not only was the food delicious, but it was dressed up with a winter-greens garnish and a wedge of fresh tomato to make the plate attractive. The small loaf of hot bread was no longer slathered with grease, but was crusty, very tasty, and easy to spread with butter. Bill's grin was his stamp of approval.

After they ate he excused himself to get back to the hotel. As he left the room, he turned and said, "Judy, I'm so happy you had a good trip, but I'm happier that you're back safe. We'll talk some more later. Don't stay up too long. You get some rest. I'll see you in the morning."

After briefly talking with Isaac and Sylvia, she told them to call it a day and go home. She and Mr. Jenkins had been the last ones there for dinner and now the dining room was empty. It didn't take long for her to make the preparations for tomorrow. She locked up exactly at nine o'clock.

Mr. Jenkins was seated behind the front desk and she waved at him as she began to climb the stairs to her room. Her Big Ben alarm clock was set for four a.m. After her bedtime prayers, she climbed in between the cool, clean sheets and was asleep as soon as her head hit the pillow.

Bill Jenkins was delighted with Judy's ability to learn and do everything she set her mind to. The laws governing the hostelry business were not as clearly written as one might expect. He explained how he personally interpreted them, and admitted that he had called Frankfort a few times himself for clarification of the flowery language used by the Legislature in writing Kentucky law.

The most important rule was that everyone who stayed in the hotel, one or more nights, had to register in the big book kept at the front desk. There were no exceptions. No one received a room key until they signed the book.

Then he explained the duties of the cleaning crew and the maintenance man. Their duties overlapped between the hotel and the restaurant. Thelma Brackett was the lead housekeeping person. She was overseer for two other housecleaning ladies and kept them on a tight schedule. The previously occupied rooms were made up as soon as the people checked out. They were ready for new customers by one o'clock each day. Also, people staying more than one night, on request, would have their room refreshed with clean linens each day before two o'clock. Thelma was also responsible for seeing that the restaurant was thoroughly cleaned every night. So far Judy had no reason to complain.

Anything in the hotel that needed repairing or refurbishing was the responsibility of a "jack of all trades" man named Roy Jackson. He was a tall, burly, full-bearded, jolly fellow. Each time Judy saw him, he was dressed in a red and white or blue and white checkered shirt and carpenter's bib overalls. The many specially designed pockets of the overalls held the tools of the maintenance trade. He had marking pencils, a note pad, chalk, and a plumb line in the bib of his overalls. From specially sewn cloth loops at and below his waist hung a medium sized square, wooden collapsible measuring tool that could be opened up to measure anything up to ten feet long, and a claw hammer.

His toolbox had two long open compartments. A heavy rope was attached in such a way that Roy could put the rope over his shoulder and carry the box up a ladder. The two compartments separated the myriad of tools that he stored neatly in their nesting places. Besides his large collection of nails, screws, nuts, and bolts, it was filled with several different sized pipe wrenches, a medium sized hand turning auger and a good collection of auger bits, screw drivers, nail sets, a "soft headed" mallet, and hammers of various sizes.

Judy guessed that Roy's toolbox must have weighed well over fifty pounds. To carry that up and down a ladder and from one repair job to another all day took a lot of strength. She was happy he was her friend.

Over the next three weeks, Judy spent at least an hour a day going over her new duties while Mr. Jenkins was on vacation. He made sure Judy knew every facet of the hotel business. She was to involve the sheriff or his deputy if she had trouble with a guest. "Don't feel bad if you have to call them. I've had to several times when a troublesome customer disturbed others or refused to pay for a room. Call the sheriff, too, if some one gives you their name and you find out later that they're called by another name. They may be 'wanted' and the sheriff needs to check them out."

He showed Judy where he kept a shotgun hidden inside the front desk. There was a secret compartment with a false front that made it look like a long drawer. The false front was anchored in place by a piano hinge that was as wide as the gun's nesting place. The "drawer" knob turned just slightly to allow the false front to swing down, exposing the gun and the twelve gauge shotgun shells.

He explained, "Roy built that into the front desk for me about five years ago. Only he and I know about it. Now you do. You handle yourself real well around guns so I'm not worried about that. I've learned to anticipate trouble and when I see it coming, I get the gun out ahead of time and load it so I'm ready for anything. If you wait until the trouble is on top of you, there won't be time to get to the gun and load it. You can get killed by being too slow to act."

"Bill, I know exactly what you mean. Don't you worry about me. I'll be fine. I've always been pretty good at headin' off trouble."

"Judy, honey, I think you're as ready as you can be to take over for me. I'll be leaving early on the morning of the twenty-fifth. I'll want you to begin to run the hotel on the twenty-third so I'm free to prepare for the trip. Also, be prepared to still run the hotel for another two days after I get back."

"Bill, you know I'm going to miss you while you're gone. I want you to enjoy this time with your brother's family, but please do be careful. Even if you're on a train, you'll need to be watchful of other people who may be just plain evil and can hurt you."

"I've been in the hotel business long enough to spot evil in people pretty good. I'm always careful. I'm sure I'll be all right. I'm beginning to get excited about this trip. When I get back I'll tell you all about Florida!"

While Judy was being trained to run the hotel for Mr. Jenkins, she and Mary spent every Sunday together. Sometimes just the two of them would go riding after church and dinner with the Brownlett's. Other times they joined the minister's family on their outings. They both wrote regularly to Della.

It was in late February that Della wrote, "I'm going to stay here at the school over Easter Week to work toward my tuition. I remember that Mary had a lot of money left over because she worked through vacations and the summers. I want to do the same thing. Aunt Jonie knows I'm doing this. She and Uncle Enoch are coming here to spend Easter morning and go to church in the Chapel."

Early on February twenty-fifth Judy went with Mr. Jenkins to the train station to see him off. She had spent two days at the front desk of the hotel. Judy was excited about her new responsibilities and grateful to Bill for trusting her. She didn't expect any trouble from the overnight guests, but was grateful for the watchful eye of Sheriff Middleton and his deputy, Tim Jones. Also, she could depend on Roy Jackson and even Raff Pennington, if she needed them.

She talked with Sylvia, Isaac, and Lance and asked for their help, "I'll need you to be responsible for makin' sure everything's all right in the restaurant while Mr. Jenkins' gone. He's asked me to run the hotel in addition to managin' the restaurant. Sylvia, it'll be helpful if you and Isaac meet with me in the hotel lobby for an hour every afternoon at 2:00. Lance, I'm asking you to watch the restaurant each day while we meet. Is that all right with you?"

Lance spoke first, "Miss Judy, 'course I'll do anything you ask me to do. If you need me for anything a'tall, just let me know."

Isaac said, "I think you know you can depend on me. Anything you need, all you have to do is ask."

Sylvia was nodding her head to everything that was said. Then she said. "I'll help you any time, and in any way I can. Just tell me what you want me to do. I think I can speak for all of us when I say we owe you more than we'll ever be able to repay you. We feel like we're family and you're the head of the family. You're not old enough to be called Ma, but you just wait!"

Judy was delighted. She laughed along with the rest of them. "Yes, indeed, I do feel like we're all one family. I'm so grateful to all of you. We have a lot of work to do over the next few weeks, and I have a lot to learn. Sylvia, each day for our afternoon meetings, you and Isaac need to write out a list of things to talk about. I'll make a list, too. Our first meeting will be tomorrow afternoon."

Judy sat behind the hotel's large front desk until it was time for dinner. There had only been two guests all morning. Both men were drummers who booked two nights each and paid in advance. She made sure both men registered by signing their names, home addresses, and their business name in the large book. She didn't know the men. After she gave each of them the key to their assigned rooms, she invited them to eat at the hotel's restaurant. They thanked her and later she noted that each of them had taken her up on her invitation.

She placed a "Gone to Lunch" sign by the guest registration book on the front desk and went to the restaurant. The dining room was almost full and everything was running smoothly. She ordered the day's special. It was the open-faced roast beef sandwich with mashed potatoes.

Sheriff Walt came through the front door and stopped at her table. She invited him to join her. He smiled and sat down. "Well," he asked, "How's your first day going as hotel manager with Bill actually gone?"

"Really, Sheriff, it's going just fine. I've only had two registered guests so far this mornin'. I'm sittin' against the wall so I can watch the street. I'll see anybody that comes into the hotel and anybody that leaves."

Sylvia appeared and Walt asked, "Judy, what did you order?"

"The open-faced beef sandwich special, apple pie, and coffee."

"That sounds good, Sylvia, bring me the same."

Walt turned to Judy. "Who were the two people that registered?"

"They were drummers. One was sellin' farm equipment, and the other was sellin' barrels of whiskey. They both paid in advance for two nights."

"After we eat dinner, I'll come over and look at their names and see where they're from. Then I'll check out who they've called on so far today to get orders for what they're selling."

"They looked like ordinary drummers to me. I didn't see any guns. Both were polite. Although they didn't come in together, they know each other 'cause the second one asked for an adjoinin' room to the first guest. It has a connectin' door. We've only got one set of rooms like that in the hotel."

"They're probably just who and what they say they are. But it never hurts to be careful with strangers in town."

The sheriff and Judy finished their pie and coffee at the same time and both scraped their chairs back and went over to the hotel. No one had come in over the dinner hour. Sheriff Middleton turned the book around and looked at the last two names and where they were from.

"You're right, they're strangers. I don't recognize their names. When they come back to the hotel, send Lance to get me. I want to see them for myself. If I've got a wanted poster on them, I'll know it."

Judy felt she had to be concerned for the comfort of the hotel's guests. She readily agreed to send Lance to get him when the two men came back. Then she asked, "Walt, when you come to take a look at 'em, why don't you do that while they're seated in the restaurant eatin' supper? That way, if they're who they say they are, you won't have to approach 'em at all. I want 'em to come back and stay at the hotel again if they're honest men."

The sheriff laughed, "Judy, don't worry your head. I'll be as nice as I can be. I'll even shake their hands and welcome 'em to Hazard. How'll that be?"

"I knew I wouldn't have to worry about you. When they come back I'll find out if they plan to go to supper at the restaurant. If they do, I'll put that in a note to you and have Lance take it to your office. In the meantime, if you find out anything bad about 'em, come and let me know."

"I'll do that."

The sheriff left Judy pondering the situation. Within a few minutes after Walt was gone, an older couple with a teenaged granddaughter came in. They registered to stay three nights. The lady was very talkative, "We're here to visit my mother. Ma is ninety-two years old and lives alone on the edge of town. Her house is real close to the river. Her birthday is in July, but we won't be able to come then. I haven't seen her for three years. Ma always insists on cookin' 'nough to feed a small army and she's not able to do that any more. We thought we'd bring her to this restaurant to eat with us at least twice. Then she'll know we're gettin' fed."

Judy laughed, "I know what you mean. My Pa's almost a hundred and two years old, but he still insists on doing whatever he takes a mind to. When you come to eat, let me meet your Ma. I'll consider it an honor!"

The couple had been gone to their room for just a few minutes when the sheriff came hurriedly through the double doors. Judy was intent on studying the registration book, and looked up in alarm. Instinctively, she turned the knob on the secret compartment and exposed the shotgun and shells.

"Judy, I got a good look at them. They're on wanted posters for armed robbery. If they come back, try to keep them here. I'll look around town to see if I can spot them. We'll try to arrest 'em away from the hotel and without any gunplay. If you can help it, stay out of it completely, but be on guard!"

The first place that Walt checked on was the Hazard Bank. The banker said he hadn't seen anyone suspicious, but he would be alert. The next place he checked was the Hazard Freight Weigh Station and Telegraph Office. There was nothing there to be concerned about.

However, with his next stop he found what he believed was the reason the two men were in Hazard. Both the Blue Diamond Coal Company and the U.S. Steel Corporation Coal Company had large mining operations in the mountains that surrounded Hazard, Hyden, and Harlan. He checked and found they both had large payrolls scheduled to come to their Hazard offices by a special armed courier service the next day.

The payroll shipment didn't consist of just cash money, but also of banded stacks of specially printed paper script with values from a penny to two dollars and rolls of script that were company manufactured light-weight tin alloy coins representing dollars, half dollars, quarters, dimes, nickels, and pennies. Script was the money medium that miners could use to trade for goods and services in the mining camps. Most of the miners were paid in cash, but when they borrowed by getting advances on their pay, or ran up debt in the company store, they were paid in the company script that was accepted as a money exchange, but always with an extra charge that benefited the company.

Each large mine operation was a small town within itself. The mining company owned the camp houses that they rented to their employees. Often there were a hundred or more of the clapboard houses. Besides the tipple and several small out-buildings that were necessary to the operation of the mine, there were other buildings that included a bathhouse, boardinghouse, doctor's house and office, barber shop, and a large company-owned general store.

If the outlaws' plan worked, they not only would be gaining the cash money that was included in the shipment, but they would profit by selling the company script to miners for a lesser value on the dollar.

Walt quietly approached each of the two coal mine operators and explained his suspicions. They agreed with him that he was very probably right. If he was right it meant someone with knowledge of the courier service's schedule had tipped off the two wanted outlaws. They needed to find out the identities of the dishonest men, and whether they worked for the two mining companies or if it was just one person who worked for the courier company.

While the sheriff was meeting with the two mine operators, Judy was waiting to see if the two men came back to the hotel separately or together. She wasn't at all surprised when she looked up and watched them come through the double doors together. She smiled sweetly at them and said, "You both look as if you had a good day. Are you going to have supper in the restaurant tonight? The steaks are good and the prime rib's even better."

Both men hesitated only a moment, then the younger one said, "Well, why not. Bob, what are you hungry for? I think I'll have a steak."

Bob replied, "Let's eat now. I'm already hungry and this way we'll be done eatin' afore the place gets crowded."

They didn't take time to go upstairs to their rooms. Instead, they went into the restaurant and sat down at a far table that allowed Bob to have his back to the wall. As far as Judy could tell they were not armed.

She said under her breath, "I'm thinkin' they've left their guns in their rooms. If that's so, it'll be easier to take them. I've got the shotgun loaded and ready in case I need it to help the sheriff to arrest them. Now if he'll just come afore they finish eatin'!"

Judy rang the bell on the desk to summon Lance. When he came, she gave him a note to take to the sheriff or to give to Tim, the deputy. She said, "Lance, make sure they read it. It's important that they get the note right away. Don't stop to talk to anyone. Come straight to see me when you come back."

"Yes ma'am, Miss Judy, I'll do just as you say!"

She kept an anxious eye on the restaurant door and prayed that the two outlaws would take their time over supper. After about a half an hour, she walked across the porch and looked in the restaurant window. She saw that the men had ordered dessert and Sylvia was refilling their coffee cups.

She turned to go into the hotel when she saw Lance coming down Main Street and about thirty yards behind him was Walt and Tim. Judy stood still until Lance was safely inside the hotel lobby. Then she went behind the desk and retrieved the shotgun. Lance's eyes grew huge as he stared at the big gun. She motioned to him to sit in one of the overstuffed chairs and told him to stay there. With the shotgun in her hands, she walked through the double doors to the porch. She positioned herself just out of sight of anyone inside the restaurant, but close to the front door. She waited to see what Walt and his deputy would do.

Sheriff Middleton and Deputy Tim went into the restaurant one at a time. The sheriff seated himself at the table closest to the two men on the side nearest the front door. Tim came in and seated himself on the other side of the men, but at the next closest table. They had the two men situated between them just the way Walt wanted. Neither of the men seemed to notice that anything out of the ordinary was happening.

Sylvia began to approach Walt and Tim to take their orders, but stopped to clear off a table when the sheriff showed her his gun drawn and hidden under the table. She looked at Tim and saw that his gun was also drawn. She hurriedly stacked the dirty dishes and went into the kitchen. She whispered to Isaac,

"There's something wrong out front. Sheriff Middleton and Tim are about to arrest those two drummers that were in here this mornin'."

Isaac said, "We'll stay here in the kitchen 'til it's over. If we do anything else, it might get somebody hurt."

Both of them stayed out of sight. They resisted the urge to look out at dining room using the "pass through" opening.

The man called Bob finally became aware of Walt sitting next to them. First, he saw the sheriff's badge and then he looked directly into Walt's unblinking stare. As the outlaw's right hand darted inside his coat, Walt brought his gun up above the table and it was leveled at the man's chest. The other man came alive to what was happening and he pulled a gun from somewhere beneath the table. Tim yelled, "Hold it! Now, drop it! You, Bob. That's your name, ain't it? Bring your gun out, slowly. Put it on the table with your buddy's gun."

Both of the outlaws were red from their collars to their eyebrows. They looked from Walt to Tim and eyed the two guns pointed at them.

Then Judy moved closer to the doorway so they could see the barrel of the shotgun. They saw the gun but they couldn't see who was holding it. They raised their hands above their heads, stood up and began to walk toward the door with Walt and Tim behind them. Walt shouted, "Hold it right there!" Tim you keep them covered while I secure their hands. We don't want any accidents between here and the jail."

Judy slowly withdrew, backing out of sight. When Walt came into view, she was busy behind the front desk in the lobby, acting oblivious to the whole thing. The two outlaws didn't have a clue about the role that Judy had played in their capture and the ruining of their plans to rob the mining payrolls.

With the two outlaws safely locked up in his jail, Walt came back to the hotel to go through their belongings to see if he could find a clue as to who had tipped them off to the payroll delivery schedule.

He did find a map with a route marked on it. At a remote crossroad there was an "X" marked in the middle of it. In the margin was a date, time of day, and a short note saying that the time given was when they should be at that crossroad. The note said that they should meet him at five o'clock outside of town on the river road, by the bridge. The note wasn't signed, but there was the initial "JB."

Walt went back to the restaurant for supper, leaving Tim with the prisoners. He promised to bring supper back to him. He told Tim, "We'll take turns standing watch through the night. Then, we'll go together tomorrow to keep the date with the third man, this J.B. We'll arrest him, too! Tim, I want you to know that you did real good today!"

"Walt, tell me, who was holding that shotgun outside the door? It was seeing that shotgun barrel pointed at 'em that made 'em give up so easy!"

"It was Judy holding the shotgun. She's an expert with guns and she was a real help today."

Tim's jaw dropped. "I can't believe that was our Miss Judy, no way!"

"Yes, her full name is Judy Turner Smith. She can shoot better than most men and used to win every turkey shoot in three counties."

Late the next day, Judy saw Sheriff Middleton and Tim ride by with another man in irons. They had captured the third man who was involved in the plan to rob the miners' payroll shipment.

Wanted posters were usually issued by the Kentucky Attorney General's office in Frankfort. Sheriff Middleton informed them with a telegram that he had captured the two outlaws that had wanted posters on them.

It was eight days later that he came to see Judy and handed a long white envelope to her. She looked at the return address and said, "What's this for? It's from Frankfort."

"Open it. It's for you because of your help in capturing the two outlaws last week. It's a reward that was listed on the wanted posters to be given to anyone helping in their capture."

Judy's eyes grew huge as she pulled the one-thousand dollar bank draft out of the envelope. "Why are they giving me this? I didn't do anything to deserve this much money."

"Judy, you told me that the two men knew each other because the second one asked for an adjoining room to the first man. If you hadn't noticed that, found it unusual, and told me, I probably wouldn't have acted fast enough to catch them. So, yes, you do deserve the five-hundred dollar reward that was offered for each of them. There may be an additional amount come from the courier company. If they do send some reward money, you'll get that, too."

"Sheriff Middleton, do we have to let other people know I got this money? I didn't want anyone to know that I had anything to do with capturing those two hotel guests. It's not good for Mr. Jenkins' business."

"The only other one that knows about it is Tim. I've told him to not say anything, and he won't. He sure does admire you, though!"

"How do I handle this bank draft? If I take it to the bank, they'll know where I got it."

"There's no name on it. I'll put my name on it, and get cash for it. Then I'll bring the money to you. That way no one will know it's for you. I'll explain to the folks in Frankfort that the recipient wants to be anonymous. If there's a reward from the courier company, I'll do the same thing. Is that all right?"

"What does anonymous mean?"

"It means you want to remain an unknown person."

"That'll be perfect. Walt, I'll be forever grateful! I don't want to ever do anything to hurt Mr. Jenkins or his business."

Later that same day, Walt came to the hotel and brought Judy a bank envelope with ten one-hundred dollar bills in it. She remained calm on the outside, but inside she was ecstatic. The sheriff asked her if she was free to have an early supper with him and she said, "Yes."

It was a week later that Walt came by the hotel to give Judy another bank envelope that contained five one-hundred dollar bills.

She had seen him coming through the double doors with a big grin on his face and knew that something good was happening.

Her eyes grew huge when he handed her the envelope. "Walt, do they know who I am?"

"No. I handled it the same way I did the other. Only Tim knows of your involvement. He won't tell anyone."

This time, Judy couldn't hide her delight. She exclaimed, "Oh, my dear Lord! I can't believe this is happenin' to me. Walt, you are one of God's angels! I am forever in your debt!"

"No. Judy, I'm in your debt. So, since I'm hungry again, how about an early dinner with me?"

Judy and Walt were now best friends. He had the utmost respect for her. In turn, she had the utmost respect for him. Walt had proven that he was an honest man. He respected women. He was mannerly and considerate of others. He had the courage it took to perform his duty as sheriff. He was exactly all that she and Anne Brownlett would call a "lovely" man.

Chapter Six
MYRT

Judy kept her new riches under her clothes in her fashionable lady's money-sack. However, she didn't want to keep that much money on her person for long. She planned to continue going to the bank once a month to make a good-sized deposit into her account. Her savings were easy to keep track of because each deposit was entered in her little yellow bankbook. She figured that by depositing just so much each month it would take about a year to transfer the reward money into her account. She hoped no one would ask about all that cash.

The three weeks Mr. Jenkins spent in Florida passed by quickly. There was one other memorable thing that happened while he was gone. The couple and their granddaughter that came to visit the ninety-two year old lady did bring her to the restaurant to dine with them. They introduced her as Myrtle Baker. She and Judy hit it off immediately. She said, "I want to call you Judy and I want you to call me Myrt! I never dreamed that restaurant cookin' was this good! I could be happy eatin' here three times a day!"

Myrt had an infectious grin. Unlike a lot of mountain women, she had all of her teeth and wasn't afraid to show them in a smile. Her good-natured banter with her daughter's family rubbed off on the other diners. After her first meal at the restaurant, Judy invited her to sit in the hotel lobby to wait until her family was ready to take her home. In talking with her, Judy discovered she had kin that lived near Big Laurel in Harlan County. The Bakers that she knew from there were good Christian folks. She told Myrt, "My brother Dave Turner married the daughter of the Bakers that live near the Leslie and Harlan County Line. That makes you and me related by marriage."

Myrt said, "I'm the last of my generation. My brothers and sisters have passed on. I ain't able to travel to visit nieces and nephews. It's been a long time since I've seen anyone but my daughter and her family."

Judy knew that she had found another good friend in Myrt. When the couple and their granddaughter checked out, Judy promised the woman that she would look in on her mother about once a week or whenever she rode out along the river while exercising Curly.

Bill Jenkins couldn't have been more pleased with the report he got from Judy about her operation of the hotel and restaurant in his absence. He also got a glowing report from Sheriff Middleton and Deputy Tim Jones. Walt was true to his promise and told no one, not even Bill, about Judy's role in the capture of the outlaws. However, he did say, "Bill, Judy was real serious when she asked me not to arrest two men in the hotel because she was afraid it would hurt your business. She said she would never knowingly do anything to hurt you, the hotel, or your business. I believe you made a real wise choice when you hired Judy as the restaurant manager. I hope you know that?"

"You bet I know that, Walt. She's been a Godsend to me. I think of her now as the daughter I never had."

Mr. Jenkins didn't say anything to Judy about his conversation with the sheriff. He had heard from Raff and his sons at the Livery Stable, too. It seemed all who knew and had dealings with Judy went out of their way to be sure that he knew she did a fine job for him while he was gone.

It took two whole days for him to rest up from his long train ride from Florida. On his third day back, Bill resumed responsibility for the operation of the Hazard Hotel. At about 4:00 in the afternoon, he went over to the restaurant and invited Judy to have an early supper with him.

After they ordered, he said, "I want to tell you about Florida. I sure don't want to go by train again because after you get out of the mountains, it's boring. But, I don't know any other way to get there right now. I don't think I wore my welcome out 'cause they invited me back and asked that I stay a month or two the next time. What do you think about that?"

"Bill, even though you're still tired from the long train ride, I think it did you a world of good to spend some time with your family. I truly believe that a person's family is the most important thing in our life. I know I miss my little Della terribly and thank God every day that my Mary is here in Hazard with me.

While you were gone I met an older woman named Myrt Baker. She lives on the edge of town, out by the river. Some of her family stayed two nights at the hotel. My brother, Dave Turner, married a lady named Baker whose family lived in Big Laurel. So, now I have another one of my kin livin' here. She's ninety-two years old and has no family here. I promised her daughter that I would check on her when I exercise Curly and ride out that way."

"I don't think I know her. Why don't you rent a buggy from Raff on Sunday, take Mary with you, and go get her. We'll all eat in the restaurant, my treat. That way I'll get to meet her."

"That's a good idea! I should've thought of doin' that myself. When I see her, I'll make the 'rangements. Mary will enjoy an outin' like that, too."

The following Sunday, Judy stopped to see Myrt and found that the lonely older woman had a full Sunday dinner ready and waiting. As Judy tied Curly to the hitching post in the front yard, Myrt came out on the porch. She was beaming her welcome, "Judy, I'm so glad to see you. Come in, Come in!

I've got dinner ready for us. I was in hopes that you'd come today. I've got something I want to talk over with you."

Judy was surprised that Myrt had prepared a full meal for just the two of them. "How did you know I'd be hungry? I am, you know. And everything looks and smells delicious!"

They sat down at the groaning table and enjoyed a pleasant hour together. Judy said, "Now, you let me do the dishes real quick and then we can talk. You sit here at the table and tell me where everything goes."

It didn't take Judy more than fifteen minutes to make quick work of the dish washing chore. She sat down at the kitchen table and faced Myrt with a questioning look on her face. Myrt laughed and said, "Judy, my dear, don't look so serious. All I want is your opinion about what I should do with the rest of my life. I'll be ninety-three years old in July. I don't think it's safe for me to live alone anymore. Sometimes I don't see anybody for days."

Judy interrupted her, "Don't you have a friend that could live with you? Do you know someone that would be willing to help you with the farm and do other work just for their room and board?"

"No, I don't. That's my problem. I have to be able to trust someone to be good to me-to take care of me if I get sick. I know of no one that I can really trust. I wrote to my family that lives in Big Laurel, but none of them can just pack-up and move to Hazard."

Judy was quiet for a few moments, and then asked, "Myrt, you seemed to have already made a plan when I butted in and stopped you from tellin' me what you want to do. What do you want to do?"

"I've got seventy five acres, more or less, of mostly good bottom land here. This old house is still solid. There's a good orchard. There's a sound barn. I don't have any stock because I sold off all of 'em."

"Are you tryin' to tell me you want to sell your farm?"

"Yes, I wrote my daughter last week, but I've not mailed the letter yet. I wanted to talk to you first. I told her I wanted to sell the farm and use what money I get to live in your hotel and eat in your restaurant for the rest of my life. But, I need to ask you to be there to take care of me in my last days. Would you be willin' to do that for me?"

Judy's face was a puzzle. Her jaw dropped. She was stammering, "Why ...Myrt, honey, are you sure? It would be a priv'ledge to have you live near me, and of course I'll help you in any way I can. You're a dear person. It's like I said afore, 'cause of my brother, Dave, we are kin to each other, even if it's just by marriage. But, even if that wasn't true, I'd feel the same way about you."

"Judy, I want you to mail my letter for me. Then, I want you to talk with the hotel man to find out what he would charge me by the month to live there. Then, would you give me a special low rate if I take all my meals in the restaurant? Once I know how much all that will cost, I can decide what price I'll need to put on my farm so I can live in the hotel."

"Myrt, I'll mail your letter tomorrow mornin'. Let's wait 'til you hear from your daughter afore we make permanent plans. You're right, though; you need to know what livin' in the hotel will cost. I'll talk to Mr. Jenkins tomorrow and let you know what he says. Oh, I almost forgot. He asked me to invite you to eat supper with us at the restaurant next Sunday. I'm renting a buggy. I'll bring my little Mary with me when I pick you up. We'll both bring you home."

Myrt's eyes grew huge as she raised her eyebrows, "Oh, you see, my dear, I feel so sure that what we just talked 'bout is God's plan for me now. I feel so much more at peace 'bout leavin' my farm. Tell Mr. Jenkins I'm much 'bliged to him and look forward more than ever to next Sunday!"

The next morning, after the breakfast rush was over, Judy mailed Myrt's letter to her daughter. When she returned she went next door to talk with Mr. Jenkins. He was seated behind the front desk and smiled as she came through the double doors. She said, "I invited my new friend Myrt Baker to have supper with us next Sunday like you wanted. She was delighted and is lookin' forward to meetin' you. She wants me to talk to you 'bout what it would cost for her to live in the hotel permanent. How much would it cost by the month? What would it cost for her to take all of her meals in the restaurant? Could she get a special rate? You're not sayin' anything. Do we ever have anyone live here permanent?"

"It's been 'bout two years since we had an older gentleman live here with an arrangement like that. When he got sick, I took care of him until he passed away. Yes, we can work out a special monthly rate for room and board. Where's she going to get that kind of money, though? We'd need a guarantee that she can afford to live at the hotel."

"If we can work out an arrang'ment that she feels she can afford, she'll pay for her room and board by sellin' her seventy-five acre farm. It's a good farm, so I don't think she'll have any trouble sellin' it. She's written to the daughter that stayed here in February. She wants to wait 'til she hears back from her 'afore she goes ahead with anything."

"I'll tell you what, let's have supper together tonight. You work on what you think she should pay for both room and board. I'll work up some figures, too. Together, we'll decide what's fair. How old did you say she was?"

"She'll be ninety-three in July. Thanks, Bill. I'll see you at supper."

Judy spent part of the afternoon, using both her head to do the figuring and her heart for compassion, to arrive at a proposal for Myrt. She reminded herself they were running a business and needed to make a profit. It was 1923. Hazard prices were somewhat higher than the prices she remembered in Harlan. Drummers paid up to seventy-five cents a night. Men could get a bath, shave, and a haircut at the City Barber Shop, but there wasn't any place for ladies to get a bath outside of the hotel. The same arrangements as applied to her would have to be made for Myrt, including carrying the warm bath water up to the second floor.

Judy was talking to herself, "I wonder what it would cost to make a new room on the first floor? We could make a hallway to run off of the lobby. Then we could either enclose a space, or open up a wall and build a room toward the back of the hotel. It wouldn't be too hard to put in a water closet by linin' it up with the one on the second floor. I'll talk to Mr. Jenkins about that."

Judy put some figures down on paper. For a room on a monthly basis, she put down thirty cents a night which came to about nine dollars a month. Breakfast cost twenty-five cents for the special. So she put down fifteen cents. Dinner specials were thirty-five cents. So she put down twenty cents. Supper specials were forty-five cents. So she put down thirty cents. That made board sixty-five cents a day or about twenty a month. From her figures, for about thirty dollars a month Myrt could live there with no other expenses for housing and food. This would add up to about three-hundred and sixty dollars a year. If Myrt lived in the hotel for five years, it would cost her about eighteen hundred dollars.

Judy was anxious to see the figures Mr. Jenkins came up with. Also, she was putting together in her head an argument for the sleeping room and water closet that she thought would be useful to have on the first floor.

After they were seated and had ordered, she was pleasantly surprised when Mr. Jenkins showed her his figures. He agreed with her figures for room and board. Then he said, "Since Miss Myrt is going to be a permanent guest for the rest of her life, we'll trim the three-hundred sixty dollars down to a flat three-hundred dollars a year."

Then Judy asked, "Bill, what would you think about us buildin' a room and water closet on the first floor to be used by older guests who can't easily climb steps? We've got some store rooms that we don't use that much. I think it would be easy and not too costly for us to use the space to fix up a sleepin' room arrangement. If we line up the water pipes with the water closet we have upstairs, it wouldn't cost much. As Myrt gets older, a room on the first floor might be a real convenience for all of us. And later on, when we need it for someone else, we'll be glad we have it,"

Mr. Jenkins's face was a study as he took time to consider Judy's proposal. Judy knew she had her answer by the broad grin that spread across his face. "Dad gum it, Judy, I say let's do that. I don't know why I never thought of it myself. Over the years I've had to help a lot of older folks climb up and come down from the upstairs rooms. I'll talk with Roy Jackson about it right away. We'll put him in charge of getting it done."

"Bill, I'd like to have a hand in how it's done. Is that all right with you?"

"Yes, I want you to. It's your idea, so you fix up our first floor sleeping room how you see fit."

"We don't know how long Myrt will live here, but I want her to be as comfortable as we can make it for her."

"Judy, honey, I hope Miss Myrt lives to be a hundred. We don't know how much she'll get for her farm. But whatever it is, she'll be taken care of right here by both of us. That's a promise. After I meet her on Sunday, I'd like to ride along when you take her home and look at the farm buildings and the land. We don't have to say anything yet, but if she does decide to sell, I'll talk to the bank and some people I know who might be interested in it as an investment."

After church and Sunday dinner with the Brownlett's, Judy and Mary drove the rented buggy out to Myrt's farm to pick her up. She was ready and waiting on her front porch. She was dressed in a soft-blue and white checked gingham dress, trimmed in lovely handmade crocheted lace. Judy complimented her on her dress. "It's very becomin' to you with your pretty snow white hair. You should wear a lot of blue. Did you make the lace, too?"

"Yes, I did, I like to crochet, tat, and embroider pretty things. Now that I can't do any heavy work, I have lots of time to do other things that I love. Mary, honey, do you like handwork?

Mary blushed because she wasn't expecting to be included in grown-up talk. She managed to respond, "Yes ma'am, I learned how to do all those things at Pine Mountain School. But, since I'm livin' here, goin' to school, and workin' for Reverend Brownlett's family, I haven't been doing any handwork."

Judy, Mary, Myrt, and Mr. Jenkins had a very pleasant time together. After supper they used the buggy to take Myrt back to her farm. Mary was happy to be included. This was the most time she had spent in a single day with her mother in a long time. Mr. Jenkins was riding along with them to look at the farm. Myrt was just happy to have the company.

Judy promised Myrt she would be back to see her by the middle of the week to go over some of the plans they had talked about.

After they dropped Mary off at the Brownlett's, Bill said, "I really liked everything that I saw at the farm. It's been a hard working farm for a lot of years. By Miss Myrt's not being able to plant anything, it's lain fallow and become enriched again. That's good black dirt. Great for growing almost anything! As soon as she gives us the go-ahead, I'll talk to the bank about appraising the property, and to a couple of friends of mine about buying it for an investment."

It was the following Wednesday before Judy could get away to exercise Curly. She rode out toward the river road and went to see Myrt. She took along some figures to show her and a written note from Mr. Jenkins that offered her room and board for $300.00 a year.

Myrt's face was a study. "That's a mighty low amount. In my room at the hotel, wouldn't everything be furnished? I wouldn't have to worry about heat in the winter. And I would eat in the restaurant for every meal. Will I be 'lowed to order what I want, within reason?"

Judy laughed, "Yes, you can order the daily specials, or anything else that you want. You don't have to worry about goin' hungry. You met Sylvia on Sunday. You'll grow to love her. She'll take good care of you, I promise!"

Myrt's face became serious, "Will you check at the Post Office in town for mail that comes for me? I should be gettin' an answer from my daughter any day. We can't really plan anything 'til we hear from her. If she fights me on this, I don't know what I'll do. I have to leave the future in God's hands. I know He has a plan for me for my last days."

It was another full week before a letter came for Myrt. The next afternoon, Judy mounted Curly and rode out to deliver the letter. They sat in the kitchen sipping coffee with the unopened letter in the middle of the table. Judy smiled as her friend sipped coffee while getting her courage up to read the letter. Finally, Myrt said, "I am so scared of what she's said. Judy, honey, will you open it and read it out loud to me?"

Judy carefully opened the flap of the small envelope. There were two handwritten pages. The penmanship was beautiful and easy to read.

Dear Ma, I was so surprised and happy to hear from you. We all so enjoyed our visit at the old home. Even my grand-daughter didn't get bored on this trip. I thank God that you are well. We are all fine.

Roger and I have been talking and praying about what we could do to take care of you. Then your letter came and God has answered our prayers. We didn't think that you would ever want to leave the farm.

What you propose to do in order to have the money to live where you will be well cared for is a dream come true. Roger is seventy-five and I'm seventy. Neither of us is well enough to take care of you should you get sick. You would probably end up having to take care of us.

By all means, sell the old farm. Just let us know when you sell it, and when you move to the hotel. We liked the lady who was running the hotel and the people in the restaurant, too. They were very kind to us. I think you will be happy there. We hope and pray that you can sell the farm for enough money to be comfortable. We will come to see you when we can.

Love you, Ma.

Gertrude and Roger

Judy finished reading the letter and looked up at Myrt. Tears were streaming down her cheeks, but she was smiling. She exclaimed, "Thank God, Gertrude understood that I couldn't live with them! They ain't objectin' to my sellin'. I was so 'fraid they'd want the money that I'll get for it, but they don't! Now, I'm free to sell. Judy, honey, you'll need to help me find a buyer."

"Myrt, now that you're free to go ahead with your plans, Mr. Jenkins is willin' to help find a buyer for the farm. Why don't we let him handle it? Neither he nor I will do anything without you approvin' what we do."

Once Myrt's plan was set in motion, it was just a few weeks later that she was deciding what personal items she wanted to take with her to the hotel.

Roy Jackson, the maintenance man, was creating a very nice sleeping room and water closet. The storage room they decided to use wouldn't be missed. There was still plenty of storage space left over.

The farm was to be sold on an "as is" basis, and included the house, all outbuildings, barn, and seventy-five acres, more or less. It was appraised for three-thousand two-hundred dollars. Bill, working with the Hazard Savings and Loan, located an investor who made an offer of three-thousand dollars.

Myrt accepted the offer. With a broad grin on her face and a merry twinkle in her big brown eyes, she said, "I doubt that I'll live to be a hundred and three years old, so at three-hundred dollars a year, three-thousand dollars should take care of me and get me "put away nice" when my time comes."

Judy helped Myrt move to the hotel and get settled in. Either Judy or Bill helped her to come down the stairs and climb back up three times a day. Myrt ate breakfast and dinner alone because that was Judy's busiest time of the day. But she and Judy had supper together almost every night. The older lady was a joy to be around. She always had a smile for everyone, fully appreciated everything that was done for her, and never complained. When the first-floor sleeping room was finished, Myrt was expecting to move into it. She was serious, but smiled as she said, "Judy, honey, once I'm on the first floor, I'll be able to do everything on my own. I won't have to worry 'bout botherin' you and Mr. Jenkins all the time."

"You know it's no bother. But, we'll get you settled in your new room as soon as it's finished and properly furnished."

Judy received a letter from Miss Pettit. Included in the envelope was the usual glowing quarterly report about Della's progress. There were no report cards at Pine Mountain like the regular public schools prepared on each student. Instead, Della had to write a letter telling her mother how she thought she had progressed over the last semester. Judy always smiled when she read Della's opinion of the quality of her work and classes. Della always finished each of her reports with, "I promise I'll do better next semester!"

In Miss Pettit's personal note, Judy learned of Loretta Helton's attempt to have Della expelled from Pine Mountain School. Miss Pettit assured her that she had backed them down. "My dear Judy," Miss Pettit wrote, "I don't want you to worry about this. I informed Mrs. Helton and her daughter, Dora Mae, that we have special permission from the Mission Board for Della to stay at Pine Mountain until she graduates."

Judy was appalled and enraged that a grown woman would attack a child in such an evil way. She wrote to Alex and Jonie, to let them know. She warned them again to be careful of the Heltons and what they might do because they lived just a quarter mile away, on Little Greasy Creek near Big Laurel.

This time, Jonie paid more attention to Judy's worries about the Heltons than she had in the past. The next time she saw Israel and Id Miniard, she invited them to stop in for a minute. Over some fruity cakes and steaming cups of coffee, she told them about all the trouble the Helton family had made for Judy and now was doing spiteful things to hurt eleven-year old Della at School.

Israel's wife had been Rana (Rainie), Jonie's older sister. Rainie had died in childbirth. Israel hadn't remarried. Israel, Jr. was known as Id and was married to Rhoda. Id was the leader of the gang of young toughs who shot up her Brother Rob's house with little Mary and Baby Della inside along with Rob's wife and all of their children. After they finished shooting at Rob's house and were riding away, Judy shot her nephew in his earlobe, mangling his ear.

Surprisingly, there were no real hard feelings between Israel, Id, and Judy. Both father and son said he had it coming. They both felt that because it was Judy who shot him, he was lucky to be alive.

Jonie was not surprised at their reaction of anger and disbelief that anyone could be so evil when they heard about what the Heltons were doing.

Id said, "Aunt Judy was never one to be mean-talkin' about anybody. They've got no call to do what they're doin'. We know their neighbors, the Couch's. They're real fine Christian people. We'll let them know what the Heltons are doin'. Maybe their knowin' will help put a stop to it. Do you all go to see Della? With Aunt Judy so far away, she must be lonely for her Ma."

"We see her at least once a month. She's a good worker, good in school, and you should hear her sing! We're all proud of her."

Israel said, "We'll stop and see her the next time we go to Harlan. She needs to know she has family besides you and Enoch who cares about her."

Jonie was pleased and surprised that Israel and Id showed that much concern about Della. "Israel, I think Della would be happy to see you both. She's not seen you in a long time, so you'll have to make yourself known to the school and to her when you visit."

Id said, "Aunt Jonie, we'll do that. You and Enoch come to see us. Let us know the next time Aunt Judy and little Mary come to visit from Hazard. I know it's hard for Grandpa Alex to travel anywhere, but if you all can't come to our house and can put up with a passel of kids, maybe we can come to yours!"

True to their word, about a week later, Israel and Id stopped at the Pine Mountain School office and asked to see Della Smith. Mrs. Zande very sharply questioned their relationship to Della. "How do you know her? Are you her kin?"

Israel didn't take offense with her tone of voice. He grinned, and said, "I'm her Uncle Israel Miniard. I married her mother's sister, Rainie Turner. This is my son, Della's first cousin, Id. We've not seen her for a long time. We just wanted to let her know that we'll stop to visit whenever we go past here on our way to Putney or Harlan."

Mrs. Zande replied, "Visiting in the middle of a school day is inconvenient for our students. Our regular times for visits are on Saturday or Sunday afternoons. If those times are not possible, we'll make exceptions, but not more than once a month."

Israel said, "That's a fair request."

Then Israel asked, "Is it possible for us to see her now? Then, after today, we'll visit her after church on Sunday, but just once a month."

Mrs. Zande sent an older boy to the large white schoolhouse to ask Della to come to the school office, and to tell her that she had visitors.

When she climbed the stone steps up to the school office, Della was shocked to find her Uncle Israel and Cousin Id there. Her first response was a question, "Uncle Israel, is Aunt Jonie and Uncle Enoch all right?"

He replied, "Della, honey, your Aunt Jonie's fine. We stopped to talk with her last week. We know your Ma's a long way off from here and thought you might like to have more of your family visit with you from time to time."

"Oh, I'd like that very much. But, it can't be on a weekday 'less it's a 'mergency. Or, unless Mrs. Zande says it's all right."

"We're plannin' to see you on Sunday afternoon, once a month. Is that all right with you?"

"I'll look forward to seein' both of you. Say hello to Aunt Jonie. But, I do have to get back to class, now. Thank you for comin' to visit me."

As they rode away, Israel and Id expressed their surprise at how mannerly and grown up Della was. Id asked, "What is she, now? I think she must be about 11 years old? If I didn't know better, I'd say she was about 14. It must be the teachin' and trainin' they get there at the School. I've not seen little Cousin Mary for about three years. I think she's 14, maybe 15 now."

Israel said, "Id, we really needed to stay in closer touch with Judy. I feel bad that it's just been Becky, Jonie, and Enoch that helped her and her girls after Bob Smith pulled that dirty trick on her. Startin' now, we'll make up for it!"

Della was puzzled by the surprise visit from Israel and Id. Since their farm was sold and they moved to Pine Mountain School, only Aunt Becky, Aunt Jonie, and their families had helped and stayed close to them. She murmured, "I guess they were just bein' nice. I shouldn't feel like I can't trust people who haven't been nice, and then all of a sudden show up and say they want to visit!"

She hurried back to class. The subject was one of her favorites and she didn't like having to miss any of it. The retired lady missionary who taught "Reading Bible History" used such a dramatic way of telling the Old Testament stories that it was easy to remember the Bible characters, and what they and God did. The stories were amazing and she made a "hundred" on every test.

The next Sunday, Jonie and Enoch came to visit. They told Della they had heard from her Ma and that the school had let her know about the mean thing the Heltons had tried to do to her. Della was dismayed that her mother found out about it before she had a chance to tell her face-to-face.

"Aunt Jonie, I wanted to tell Ma myself when I see her 'gain."

"Della, honey, you may not see your Ma again 'til next Christmas. Those people are dangerous liars and mean-talkers. If they bother you again, you be sure you tell me, Uncle Enoch, or Uncle Israel."

"Oh, you knew about Uncle Israel and Cousin Id comin' to visit me? They were very nice. But, I hadn't seen them in about three years, maybe longer. At first I didn't know who they were."

"Yes, I told them about the Heltons. They both said they knew the Helton's neighbors, name of Couch. The Couch's are good Christians. Israel thought that the Heltons can be 'shut up' if the neighbors talk to them."

"I wish they wouldn't say anything to them. Miss Petit really stood up to them. She took up for me! I don't think they'll give me any more trouble."

Jonie was very concerned, "Della, honey, you didn't tell me 'bout what happened here, and I didn't know what Miss Pettit did about it. What do you want me to do? Is there anything I can do?"

"I want Uncle Israel to come and visit, but can you stop him from talkin' to the neighbors 'bout me? I don't want them talkin' 'bout me. It'll just stir up more trouble. The Heltons cost Ma her job here. They're liars and mean-talking people. I'm 'fraid they'll just get meaner if someone talks to them 'bout me!"

"All right, honey, when we get home today, we'll go on down Greasy Creek to see them. I don't want you worryin'. But, you've got to promise me you'll tell me when something happens to you. Don't keep stuff to yourself. Remember you've got a family who loves and cares 'bout you!"

Della promised she would do as Jonie asked. But, she still believed the more people she involved in her troubles, the more troubles it caused.

After Jonie and Enoch left, Della was still fuming and mumbling to herself, "I don't want people talkin' 'bout me! Christians talkin' to the Heltons ain't gonna change 'em. They'll just get meaner! The Heltons will do something real bad to me if anyone talks to them. I just know it!"

Della had two hours of free time before supper and Vespers. She used the time to write a long letter to her mother. She explained why she hadn't told her about the Heltons. *I love you Ma. I know you worry about me, but I felt sure Miss Pettit took care of them and protected me. From now on, I'll tell you if anything bad like that happens again. I'm working at the school this summer and that means I may not get to see you. Aunt Jonie said I may not get to see you until Christmas. Take care of yourself and Mary. Tell her she owes me a letter.*

Della felt better after she sealed her letter, and put a stamp on the envelope. It would go out in tomorrow's mail. The Heltons were forgotten. She felt carefree as she hurried to Laurel House for Sunday supper.

83

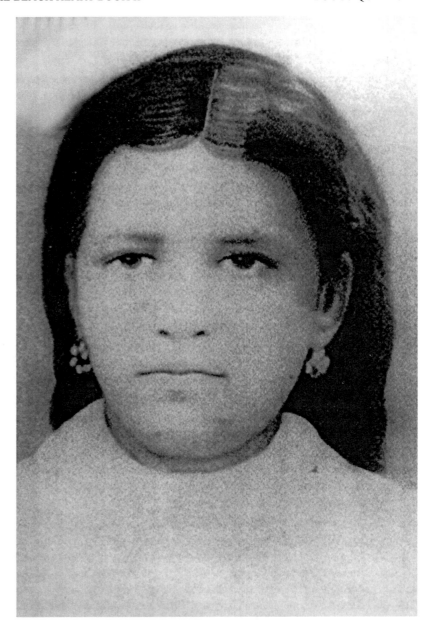

Raina (Rainie) Turner Miniard

Chapter Seven
VISIONS AND DREAMS

The summer was almost over. Della was eleven in April and had worked through the summer to pay her tuition expenses. Every six months, Miss Pettit provided a statement of her account with the school. She figured that after summer was over, she would have almost fifteen dollars to the good.

True to their word, her Uncle Israel Miniard and his son, Id, with his wife Rhoda, had come to visit with her once a month on a Sunday afternoon. Sometimes they came at the same time as her Aunt Jonie and Uncle Enoch. When that happened, using the snack food that Jonie prepared they had a small picnic under the trees in front of Laurel House. Della accepted Israel, Id, and Rhoda Miniard as family and began looking forward to their visits.

As far as she knew, there had been no additional contact with the school by the Heltons. She talked to God about her problem with the liars and mean-talking people, and just as her Ma told her to do, she left her problem with God.

Judy was busy with the restaurant. She was ever mindful of her father's vision of God's future plan for her. In her prayers, she thanked God every morning and every night for leading her to find work in Hazard. Mary was still doing well in her work-study placement with Reverend Brownlett's family. Judy's distant kin and friend, Myrt, was now occupying the newly-created sleeping room (complete with water closet) on the first floor of the hotel.

Judy made a large deposit once a month into her account at the Hazard Savings and Loan. All together, counting her savings and the reward money, she had close to three-thousand dollars. The monthly interest she accrued at the bank didn't amount to a whole lot, but it added to her growing hoard of cash money.

In the middle of October, Miss Pettit wrote Judy a letter, letting her know that she planned to spend Thanksgiving with the Brownlett family. She would stay two days and Della was coming, too. Judy was ecstatic! She would have both of her daughters with her. Miss Pettit wanted Judy and Della to meet Harvey and Sarah Cantrell. They were highly recommended by Reverend Brownlett to be a possible work-study placement for Della after she graduated next May.

Miss Pettit explained in her letter, "The Cantrells are Christian people. They have a large, hard-working farm northeast of Hazard. They have agreed that, if her work is satisfactory, they will pay Della a small amount each month, provide room and board, and allow her to continue her education in Hazard."

The following Sunday, when Judy joined Mary and the Brownlett's for church and dinner, she expressed her concerns about Della's possible work-study placement with the Cantrell family. "How well do you know these people? Do they attend your church? Do they attend church regularly?"

"Judy, that's three questions in one. Yes, I know them well. Yes, they attend my church. Yes, they come to church fairly regular. If they aren't here for Sunday service I believe it means they had a farm related emergency that prevented them from coming. Occasionally, when they've missed three Sundays in a row, I ride out to check on them. I understand that when you're working a farm you can't always get away even to honor the Sabbath."

"Well, you've eased my mind a little. Whether or not Della wants to take this job will be entirely up to her. I'll see her again at my sister's when we spend Christmas with them. We'll decide then what her plans will be. This'll give Della five months to get ready to leave Pine Mountain. Do you want me to plan on taking another Church love offering to give to the school this year?"

"Yes, the members of our Women's Organization have already designated a money amount they wish to donate. And, they've started collecting household and clothing items for the school."

Judy laughed out loud, "Well, I'd better reserve poor old Ned again from the Livery Stable. Last year everyone was sorry for him because they thought he was too heavily burdened with a lot of lightweight, bulky stuff. Ned loved the sympathy he got from everyone we met."

Mary was excited by the prospect of seeing Della at Thanksgiving, and looked forward to taking the long trip with her mother. She asked, "Ma, if you go to Harlan again to trade for Della's school clothes, can I go with you this time? It's been almost three years since I've been to Harlan."

"If I go, and the weather isn't too bad, you and Della can go, too. We may go with Miss Pettit and Mr. Wilder again. Last year I thought the time in Harlan was too rushed by us trying to go and come back in just one day. How would you like to stay a night in Harlan, and come back to Jonie's the next day? This would give us plenty of time to shop in the stores."

"Ma, I would love to do that. My birthday's almost on Thanksgiving this year. I'll be fifteen, and next year I'll be a freshman in Hazard High School. I'll use some of my own money if I want to buy stuff, and I'll be able to say I shopped for my clothes in both Harlan and Hazard!"

"I know you're grown compared to when I was your age, but don't you dare say you want a beau and to get married. You're goin' to be the first girl in our family to graduate from High School, and Della will be right behind you!"

A serious look passed over Mary's face. "Ma, if Della gets to stay two days when she comes with Miss Pettit, couldn't we do some early shopping and trading here in Hazard? There'll be an after Thanksgiving sale because there's one every year. If we do go to the sales, Della can say the same thing: that she got to trade for her school clothes in both Hazard and Harlan!"

Judy looked puzzled, "Mary, honey, why's it so important to you about where we trade that you want to tell anyone about it?"

"Ma, I know you don't care about making good impressions, but it's important to me to make a good impression on the rich girls I go to school with. Some of them know that I work and go to school. Some are scornful and say hateful things. If I can say I'm able to do something that none of them can do, it makes them show me some respect. Am I wrong for wanting to do that?"

"No, honey, I don't think it's wrong, but I do think it's a shame that they make you feel bad about yourself. I think I've told you afore that you're goin' to find a lot of mean-talking people in your life. You'll find that most of the time we can't do a thing about them. The one thing we can do is to not sink down to their level. We're good-Christian people. We work hard and do our best whether it's school or a job. We don't have to drop our head to anyone. Just remember that and hold your head high cause you've earned the right to be proud of what you've done, and what you've yet to do!"

Mary squealed her pleasure and hugged her mother, "Oh, Ma, you always make me feel so special! We're going to have a lovely time when Della's here with us on Thanksgiving. And, it'll be less than a month later when we'll see her again at Aunt Jonie's."

It was almost dark on the day before Thanksgiving when Miss Pettit and Della arrived at the Brownlett's. Judy was already there. She arranged for Isaac and Sylvia to take over for her so she could meet Della and Miss Pettit. She saw them coming almost a block away. Della was riding a small black horse. When they came closer, Judy was grinning delightedly. Della spotted her mother and jumped off her horse, literally dragging the startled animal to the porch hitching rail. Then she ran up the front steps, grabbed her mother in a big hug, and planted a wet, sloppy kiss on her cheek.

When Judy returned the hug and kiss, she was surprised to find Della's cheek wet with tears. But Della was smiling happily. She was so glad to see her mother; she was in 'happy' tears.

Miss Pettit continued to ride her tall horse all the way to the hitching rail. Reverend Brownlett quickly left the porch and assisted her in dismounting. She slowly bent her body forward, and in straightening up, slowly stretched her arms above her head to relieve her tired body from the long day in the saddle.

After cheerfully greeting her host and hostess, Miss Pettit turned her attention to Judy and Mary. "I'm so glad you're here, Judy. And, Mary, you're looking well. Why don't you and your sister go inside and make your plans for tomorrow and Friday while I talk with your mother?"

The two sisters chorused, "Yes ma'am, Miss Pettit!"

Anne Brownlett shepherded her children inside, too. Only Judy, Reverend Brownlett, and Miss Pettit were left outside on the front porch. Miss Pettit said, "Judy, I've corresponded with the Cantrells. They want to meet Della early Friday morning. Ethan, I thought we might use your carriage to ride out to their farm. I want to see where it is and what it's like. Could you go with us?"

He said, "Yes, I'll be happy to take all of you. I've seen their farm. They live in a lovely valley. There are views of tall mountains in all directions. It's mostly a stock farm with lots of cows, pigs, sheep, and horses. They have a lot of good bottomland that they plant in field corn, hay, oats, and other kinds of winter feed. Then I've noticed they have a large home-garden full of vegetables."

Judy asked, "How many extra farm hands do they have workin' there?"

He replied, "There's no one that I've ever seen. I know that they have two older boys, almost men. There're two girls that I believe are a little older than Della. I seldom see any of their children in church. When I inquire about them, they tell me that all the children have chores that have to be done, Sabbath or no. I did inform them that the expectation was that Della would be allowed to accompany them to church."

"Miss Pettit, I'll wait 'til after we meet the Cantrells and see their place afore I make up my mind about placin' Della with 'em. I know you and Reverend Brownlett have said they're good Christian people. I just want to be sure they'll be fair and kind to my daughter."

Reverend Brownlett answered for Miss Pettit, "Judy, I give you my word; I'll keep a watchful eye on Della. If she's mistreated by anyone in their family, she'll need to tell me and I'll deal with it immediately."

Judy said, "That's the problem, Della keeps her troubles locked inside herself. She tries to deal with 'em alone, on an adult level. But, she's just a child! You'll have to visit with her and see for yourself. She's norm'ly a happy, sweet little girl. If she acts hurt and sad, you'll know something's not right."

Miss Pettit echoed what Judy was saying. "Ethan, Judy's right. At school, when anything is amiss with Della, she usually will tell Ethel Zande. But, if Ethel's not available, she won't tell anyone else. She'll try to deal with her own problems. You say you know these people and they'll be kind. However, if we place her there, we'll feel better if you keep a close eye on them."

"Kathryn, let's wait 'til Friday morning. If we decide it's a good placement for Della, we'll go ahead with our plan for her to go there next May. I promise I'll supervise her placement. So, please, stop worrying!"

Ethan changed the subject, "Now, what are our plans for tomorrow? Judy, you and Della are welcome to have Thanksgiving dinner with us."

"I thank you for invitin' us, but that's too much work for Anne. My girls and I will have dinner at the restaurant. We'll have roast turkey, a hickory- smoked ham, baked with raisin sauce, and all the trimmin's."

Ethan laughed, "Let's tell Anne we've changed our plans and we're all going to eat with you at the restaurant!"

Judy grinned, "If you do, you'd better duck real quick. After all the work she's done to prepare for Thanksgiving she's liable to hit you with something!"

When they arrived at the hotel, Judy told the girls to sign the large book on the front desk. "Now, you're registered guests and your room's next to mine!"

She wisely arranged for them to have a separate room. This greatly impressed Mary, but Della would have much rather stayed with her mother. Judy figured that the two sisters would stay awake half the night talking and giggling. She had to be at work by four in the morning and by giving them their own room, she would be able to get the sleep she needed.

Before they did anything else, the girls went to inspect their room. Della said she needed to freshen up and change her clothes. When they came down to the lobby, Mr. Jenkins introduced himself to Della, and then told the girls that their mother was waiting in the restaurant.

Seated at a round table for four were Judy and Myrt. Mary greeted the older woman warmly, giving her a kiss on the cheek. Della hung back, waiting to be introduced. Myrt didn't wait on formalities, but spread her arms in a welcome gesture, saying, "My name is Myrtle Baker, but folks call me Myrt. You've got to be my new best-buddy, Dellie. Your Ma's my very best friend. Come here, child, I need a hug from you."

Della couldn't keep from grinning at the presumptuous older woman. She walked over to her chair and gave her a hug, saying, "Who could resist a greeting like that? I'm so pleased to meet you."

Della was impressed with the importance of the place where her mother worked. She was equally pleased when Judy told her she could order whatever she wanted from the menu. She asked, "Ma, I can really order anything?"

"Yes, honey. What would you like?"

Della looked around the room and her eyes grew huge as she gazed at an open-faced roast beef sandwich with mashed potatoes and brown gravy. "Ma, I want what that man's eatin' over there by the window."

Sylvia came to take their orders. Judy told Della to go ahead and order her food and drink. With pleasure washing across her face, Della lifted her head high and said, "I want the special number three and a glass of milk."

Sylvia repeated, "You must be Della, I'm so happy to meet you at last. Now, you want the special number three, that's the open-faced roast beef sandwich with mashed potatoes and brown gravy. Is that right?"

Della grinned, "Yes ma'am, and I thank you."

Mary was very much the sophisticated young lady when she ordered fried ham, eggs-over-easy, with home fries, cornbread, and a glass of milk.

Judy's face was a picture of happiness and pride in her two daughters. She was thinking, "A little over five years ago we lost our farm and neither of my girls had any schoolin'. Who would believe that in such a short time, Mary and Della would be able to sit proudly in a restaurant, read and order from a menu! This is part of Pa's vision of what God has planned for me and my girls. I Thank God for watchin' over us, and bless Pa for believin' and for his vision."

Judy noticed that while Della was mostly interested in the restaurant's kitchen and how the prepared food was served, Mary chattered away about her school, her school friends, the shopping they were going to do in Hazard on Friday, and how much of her savings she wanted to spend. Della remained quiet, letting her sister do most of the talking. It was plain to see that Della wasn't as enthused as her sister about shopping in Hazard and spending money.

Myrt and Della were really taken with each other. They engaged in their own conversation while Judy, Mary, and Sylvia were discussing the dessert menu. Myrt was answering Della's questions about how she came to live as a permanent resident in the Hazard Hotel. "Miss Myrt, I didn't know anyone could do that. I know Ma lives here, but she works here. Where's your family?"

Myrt chuckled and said, "May the Lord bless you, child, but I'm so old all my close kin are gone 'cept a daughter. I didn't want to be a burden to anyone, so I came here to live. I take all of my meals here in the restaurant. I think your Ma has 'dopted me as her Ma. She looks after me all the time and makes sure I behave myself!"

Della was beaming at the older woman. "I know you behave yourself. You're just joshing me, right?"

Judy interrupted Della and Myrt, "Come on now, what do you two want to order for dessert?"

Myrt winked at Della, turned toward the young waitress, and said, "Sylvia, honey, do you have any of that walnut, spice-cake that I had last night? Della, you should try this cake."

Sylvia beamed at both of them. "Yes, Miss Myrt, we sure do. Della would you like a piece and another glass of milk?"

Della nodded her head, "Yes ma'am, I'll have the same thing that Miss Myrt's havin'!"

The next morning when Judy's Big Ben alarm clock sounded off at three o'clock she quickly got out of bed and, on her knees, said her morning prayers. "Thank you, dear Lord that both of my girls are here with me for this Thanksgivin' Day. Help me to do my best in my work. Keep my family safe. Bless Miss Pettit for carin' 'nough to help us find a good placement for Della. I pray the Cantrells are the right kind of people. Be with us tomorrow when we meet 'em. Lead me to make the right choices. In Jesus' name I pray, Amen."

She planned to let the girls sleep until they woke up on their own. If they weren't down to eat breakfast by nine o'clock, she would wake them. Myrt would be in her usual place at their regular corner table long before eight o'clock.

Judy put a large sign in the restaurant window and another on the dining room wall near the Daily Specials Menu. The signs read: 'Join us for Thanksgiving Dinner at one p.m.'

In smaller print at the bottom of the sign it read: "Roast Turkey, Baked Ham, Mashed Potatoes, Candied Sweet Potatoes, Sage and Cornbread Dressing, Green Beans, Turnip Greens, Yeasty Rolls or Cornbread."

At about twelve-thirty o'clock, Judy noticed that a neatly-dressed man was standing outside the window reading the sign. She noticed him because he was using his finger to underline what he was reading. She watched as his finger moved from one side of the sign to the other. "It's sure takin' him a long time to read what we're servin'! I wonder if he's comin' in to have dinner with us."

The man turned, walked to the door, and pushed it open to come inside. Judy walked toward him, making a mental note that he was around forty years old, had coal-black, wavy hair, and his dark-brown eyes were almost black. He wasn't much taller than she was, and when he smiled, he had white, even teeth.

She greeted him warmly and led him to a table for two near the front window. She noticed he was clean-shaven and that his complexion was a dark, smooth, olive color. She knew of a man in Harlan named Charlie Cabanetis who had a complexion like that. He owned a restaurant. When she asked Miss Pettit about him she told her that Charlie was a foreigner from a country called Syria.

Judy was surprised at herself for letting her mind wander like that. She smiled at the man and handed him a regular menu. She said, "Our Thanksgiving special is the same as you were readin' on the sign outside. There's another sign on the wall, too. The special is only seventy cents and it's all you can eat. So, feel free to order seconds. We have our own pumpkin and mincemeat pie, too. Dessert and your drink are both included in the Thanksgiving special."

The man's smile turned into a broad grin. Speaking with a charming accent, he exclaimed, "Well, I don't think I can go wrong orderin' your special!"

Judy smiled sweetly at him as she beckoned to Sylvia to come and take his order. Then she retreated into the kitchen to see if Isaac needed her help. Isaac and his salad and vegetable staff were in good spirits, laughing and talking as they worked. Judy used the pass-through opening to get another look at the man she had found attractive.

She turned to Isaac and asked him if he knew who the man was that was seated near the front window. He looked and said, "No, I don't know his name, but I saw him real early yesterday mornin' over at the Livery Stable. He was talkin' with Raff. Why, is something wrong?"

"No, there's nothin' wrong. I know that Sheriff Middleton and Tim are comin' here to eat Thanksgivin' Dinner, and they always want to know about any stranger that comes into the hotel or the restaurant."

Isaac asked, "By the way, where are Miss Myrt and your girls?"

"They ate breakfast real late. But, they'll be hungry soon. If they don't come to eat by two o'clock, I'll go hurry them along."

The stranger was having a piece of mince-meat pie and a second cup of coffee when Walt and Tim came in and sat down. At the same time, Myrt, Mary and Della came and sat at the table next to them. Judy walked over to their tables and introduced them to each other, "Della, this is Sheriff Walt Middleton and his Deputy, Tim Jones. Sheriff and Tim, this is my younger daughter, Della."

Della's eyes grew huge. "Mr. Walt, are you really the sheriff? I've never met or seen a sheriff before!"

Walt laughed, "Yes, Della, I'm the sheriff and I've heard a lot about you. It's a pleasure to meet you."

Walt leaned forward to shake her hand. Then Tim did the same. Judy chuckled, but she was so proud that Della didn't hesitate at all but extended her hand as though it was the most natural thing in the world to shake hands with two grown men. Mary was a little put-out because she remembered that her mother hadn't introduced her to the sheriff like she just did for Della.

Judy sat down with the sheriff and his deputy to ask if they knew the man sitting by the front window. They glanced over and Walt nodded his head. "Yes, I know him. He's been here a couple of days. His name's Jim Collins. He told the owner of the boardinghouse where he's staying that he's looking for work. From the looks of him, I'd say he's changed his name. He wants to be seen as an American instead of a foreigner. I think he's Syrian. I'll talk to him and see if I can help him to find a job. First, I have to find out what he can do and what kind of work he's looking for."

Walt looked at Judy in surprise, "Why did you want to know who he is? Has he done something wrong?"

"Oh, no, it's nothin' like that. It's just that I noticed that he's neatly-dressed and mannerly. He must not have any family here in Hazard or he wouldn't be eating Thanksgivin' dinner with us. Maybe they don't they have a Thanksgivin' dinner at the boardin' house?"

Walt said, "I never thought about it before. I guess they don't. Probably the reason they don't is because the men who stay there during the work-week have gone home to spend the holiday with their families."

"Walt, you and Tim enjoy your dinner. When I think we've served our last customer, I'll fill a plate and come and join Myrt and my girls."

By the time Judy came back to the table the man she had found attractive had left. She hoped he would come back again.

The day ended pleasantly for everyone. They gathered in the restaurant for a late supper, but they only had room for dessert and something to drink. After they ate, Mary said she was ready to go to their room. Judy hadn't had a chance to talk with Della about their plans for the next day. She said, "Mary, I need to spend some time alone with your sister to talk about our meetin' with the Cantrells tomorrow. You go on upstairs. She'll be up in a few minutes."

They left the restaurant as the sun was going down. Judy said, "Let's sit in the lobby. There's no one there but Mr. Jenkins."

Judy couldn't stop the worry lines from creasing her forehead. She sat next to her younger daughter so she could put one arm around her, and asked, "Della, honey, what has Miss Pettit told you about workin' for this family?"

"Ma, she told me that they needed someone like me to help out with the farm work. She said I'm younger than their four children. That means I won't have to care for them like Mary does. I'll help milk the cows, feed the stock, cook, wash, iron, or anything else they ask me to do. She said that in exchange for my work, I would be paid some money every month and be allowed to live there with free room-and-board."

"What did she say about goin' to school every day and to church on Sunday? Will you have any days off to spend with me and Mary?"

"Miss Pettit didn't talk to me about that. I think we have to ask Reverend Brownlett what he told them about me stayin' in school. I do want to go to school like Mary does." Then Della grinned, and said, "Ma, I hope I'm never as silly as Mary is 'bout tryin' to impress people who ain't worth impressin'."

Judy hugged Della close, "Honey, we'll have a lot to clear up tomorrow when we meet with the Cantrells. I want to know where you'll sleep. With those older boys still at home, you should have your own room like Mary does. I want to know what they plan to do about you having time off on Sunday to spend with me and your sister.

Now, this is important! I want you to know that you don't have to take this job unless you want to. If you do take this job and it don't work out, or if they're mean to you, you can live here at the hotel with me and go to school. Then, if you want to, I can find work for you to do here in the kitchen."

"Ma, I don't want anyone sayin' that Mary can do something that I can't. I don't care if she's older. I'm bigger than she is. I do want to please Miss Pettit and be a success! I promise that if the job isn't like Miss Pettit says, I'll tell you."

"Della, honey, you know that if I can help it, I'll never allow you to be hurt. But you have to tell me about it. You're too young to handle bad troubles all by yourself. That's why you have me!"

"Oh, Ma, I already said I promise to tell you every time something is not right with me. Now, you've got to believe me. You do believe me, don't you?"

"Yes, honey, now I do. You go on up to bed; we have to get up early in the mornin'. I'll wake you at five o'clock."

Judy watched her younger daughter climb the stairs to go to her room. Della was a head taller than Mary. Almost everyone called her older sister "Little Mary."

Mary was more than three years older than Della. Because she was tall for her age, people thought Della was the older.

Again Judy made arrangements for Isaac and Sylvia to be in charge so she could go with Miss Pettit, Reverend Brownlett, Della, and Mary. Miss Pettit was sitting in the carriage when Judy and her girls arrived. Ethan was smiling when he winked at them, putting them at ease by saying, "Don't you fret; we just got here ourselves. Tie your horses to the rail. Anne will take care of them for you. Now, let me help you get aboard and we'll be off. I feel that this will be a memorable day and it makes me think of one of my favorite Bible verses: 'This is the day that the Lord has made, we will rejoice and be glad in it!' The Lord is good, let's all be thankful for this day."

Judy remembered she had been told that the Cantrell farm was on the east side of Hazard. They traveled through town and about another mile past the city limits. It was pretty country. Ethan turned into a long lane leading to a large farm home. A huge barn and silo dwarfed the other buildings. Judy noted that there were three good-sized corncribs filled with winter feed for stock. She knew a good, working-farm when she saw one and this one was outstanding.

They pulled up in front of a long hitching rail that was near the barn. Harvey and Sarah Cantrell came out of the back door of the house to meet them. Two young men came from the direction of the corncribs. They scattered a large bunch of chickens as they walked right through the middle of them. Their father showed his displeasure by frowning at his sons and the squawking hens. Two young girls came out of the front door of the house. Reverend Brownlett waited until all of the Cantrells had gathered before he helped Miss Pettit and Judy to the ground. Mary and Della hopped down on their own.

Ethan introduced Miss Pettit as the one who corresponded with them. Then he introduced Judy as the mother of Mary and Della. Harvey Cantrell asked, "Which one of these girls is Della?"

Della stepped forward and held out her hand to Mr. Cantrell, "I'm Della, and I'm pleased to meet you."

He pointedly ignored her hand, saying, "I thought you told me Della's the younger one. The other one looks younger to me. Now, Miss Pettit, you did say that Della will be twelve in April. She looks strong enough to me to be a good worker. My girls will be fourteen and fifteen their next birthdays."

Judy asked, "What are your girls' names?"

"The younger one is Lacey and the other one is Winnie."

"What about your sons; what are their names?"

"The older one is 19; he's Harvey, Jr. and Jimmy is 17."

Miss Pettit interrupted to ask, very pointedly directing her questions to the wife. "Mrs. Cantrell, what are you expecting Della to do for you? Will it be both farm chores and housework? Della's a good worker and I'm sure she'll do a good job for you, but we did talk about her being able to continue her school work. She'll also need to have free time to do her school homework, and to spend some time away from the farm to be with her mother and sister."

Sarah Cantrell was red from her collar to her eyebrows. She looked at her husband and then back to Miss Pettit. It was Mr. Cantrell who responded to the question and comments. "We'll see how Della works out. School is more than a mile away. To get there, my girls have to walk, unless I'm goin' into town anyway. She'll have to figure it out herself about any homework. The farm chores will come first. My wife will tell her what has to be done in the house. Has Della ever worked around farm animals?"

Miss Pettit answered, "No, not during the last few years. She knows how to take care of a home, cook, clean, wash and iron. She's a fast learner. I'm sure you'll be pleased with her work. Now, if we're all agreed, I'll bring Della back to Hazard next May after she graduates from Pine Mountain School. Her mother will see about getting her enrolled in the seventh grade here in Hazard. That means that from the end of May until the first of September, she'll be free of school and can work full-time for you. Mrs. Cantrell, what are you prepared to pay her for working for you?"

Again, the woman turned beet red and looked toward her husband. Harvey Cantrell, with his patience sorely tried, carefully explained, "We're providin' her with a good home, room and board. She'll be treated the same as my girls for as long as she stays with us. What she's paid will depend on how much she can do. We'll wait and see. I don't want to commit to any set amount until she's been with us at least a month."

Miss Pettit nodded, "That seems fair. I'm sure you'll be fair."

Ethan asked, "What about church? We talked some time ago about her being allowed to attend church on Sunday and spend time with her family."

"We'll have to wait and see about that, too. Work comes first. Animals have to be taken care of. When me and my wife come to church, we'll bring her with us if we can. Then later that day, her Ma can bring her back to the farm."

Miss Pettit turned to Della, "Do you have any questions?"

"Yes ma'am, Miss Pettit. If I may, I want to ask Mr. Cantrell to tell me where I'll sleep and keep my things? Will I have my own room, or will I have to share a part of a room? If I have to share a room will I have a place just for me where I can keep my belongin's?"

Harvey Cantrell frowned in displeasure, "We'll work all that out when you come to us in May."

Then he turned his attention away from Della, "I believe this 'rangement we've made with Miss Pettit will work out well for us and we look forward to havin' Della become part of our family. Now if you all will excuse us, we have a lot of work that's waitin' to be done."

With that, the whole family began to move away in different directions, leaving Miss Pettit, Judy, Mary, Della, and Reverend Brownlett standing there, feeling awkward. "Well," Ethan exclaimed, "I do believe that we've been unceremoniously dismissed! I can't remember this ever happening to me before!"

Judy was feeling more than a little outraged by the Cantrell's manners. She said, "I had a big hard-working farm that I worked single-handedly with two small children. I was always mannerly to everyone and never rude to anyone."

Ethan helped the two women climb into the carriage. Mary and Della hopped in with ease. After Ethan took his place, he backed-up the team so they could turn around. Still worried, Judy asked, "Miss Pettit, do you still think this can be a good placement for Della?"

"Yes, I do, Judy. You have to remember that not all people are alike. It's apparent that Mr. Cantrell doesn't give his wife a voice in any decisions that affect the farm or his family. He's seeing himself as employer and Della as his employee. To say she'll become a member of his family is a big concession on his part. I think we should give the placement a try. Ethan has promised to keep a sharp eye on them and Della. We'll know right away if she's being mistreated or not being fairly dealt with."

Reverend Brownlett didn't say anything, but there was a deep, furrowed frown on his forehead. Judy looked straight ahead and said nothing until they returned to Ethan's house and were ready to climb down out of the carriage.

Then she asked, "Miss Pettit, what time do you want to leave in the morning? What time do you want me to have Della here?"

"We want to leave before daylight. So I think about six will be fine. She'll be packed and ready to go. Her horse will be saddled and ready for her."

"Ethan, I'll bring Mary back in the morning. The girls are going shopping. There's an 'After Thanksgivin' Sale' at almost every store in Hazard!"

Judy, Della, and Mary rode back to the hotel. Judy said, "We'll take the horses over to the Livery Stable and walk to the stores in town. It's still early and I think we can do all we want in time to get back to the hotel by noon. We'll have dinner with Myrt and you girls can do whatever you like until suppertime. I need to help Isaac and Sylvia. They may want to go shopping, too."

They left the Livery Stable and Judy asked, "Mary, you've not said a word since we met the Cantrells. What are you thinkin' about?"

"Ma, I didn't like any of them. If those boys and girls do go to school in Hazard I've never seen them that I know of. Those rude boys are older than me, but the girls are 'bout my age. I've never seen them at my school. I'm afraid that none of that family will be good to Della. With them livin' way out there, only Reverend Brownlett will be checkin' on her."

Judy interrupted Mary, "Honey, when the time comes, if Della still wants to work for these people, I'll exercise Curly by riding out to see her once a week. If anything's wrong, I'll know it, and I'll deal with it in my own way."

Della laughed, "See, Mary, both Ma and Reverend Brownlett will be looking out for me. Those people will know they'd better be good to me or they'll be in trouble with Ma and the Reverend!"

The two sisters finished their shopping and returned to the restaurant for dinner at about noon. Myrt was seated at the round table set for four. "Come on, my new-buddy, Dellie, and little Mary. Judy, I'm hungry 'nough to eat a horse."

Sylvia came to take their orders, saying, "Today's specials are mostly yesterday's leftovers, but they're delicious!"

Judy said, "Bring me some of the baked ham in raisin sauce, mashed potatoes, dressing, and green beans. Oh, and cornbread, too. I'll need some coffee to stay awake if I eat all that."

Myrt grinned, devilishly. "That sounds so yummy! Bring me the same."

Mary ordered ham and eggs, home fries, cornbread, and milk.

Della said, "Sylvia, if it's all right, I want to be a little different. Instead of ham bring me turkey dark meat, dressing, candied sweet potatoes, greens, and cornbread. Oh, and I want a glass of milk!"

Sylvia laughed out loud, "Della, sweetheart, that is certainly all right!"

The day went so fast Judy hardly had time to turn around before she was saying good night to the girls. She returned to the kitchen to get ready for the morrow. With that done she climbed the stairs to her room. She said her nightly prayers and set the alarm for four in the morning, but when she climbed in between the clean cool sheets, she was wide awake.

It was hard to get to sleep. She felt Della's being placed with the Cantrells was the wrong thing to do. Della wanted to accept the challenge of making the placement work for her in order to be able to say she 'kept up with Mary.' However, the Cantrells were not anything like the Brownlett's. Even when her troubled sleep finally came, there were nightmares.

Judy, Mary, and Della were at the Brownlett's home well before six O'clock. Miss Pettit's horse was saddled and waiting. The pack mule was loaded with their trail gear and ready to go. Mary said a tearful goodbye to her sister and went inside the house. Judy stayed on the front porch with the Brownlett's and watched Miss Pettit and Della until they rode out of sight.

Judy smiled through her tears and prepared to say goodbye to Anne and Ethan. Anne said, "Judy, honey, Ethan told me how the Cantrells talked yesterday. He had trouble sleeping last night. They always put on a different face at church. Whatever Della decides, we'll watch out for her. We have until next May. Anyway, Christmas is coming! You and Mary have to prepare for your trip to Big Laurel to spend the holiday with your family."

Judy had thoroughly enjoyed having Della visit. After she left with Miss Petit on Saturday morning to go back to Pine Mountain School, Judy couldn't help feeling emptiness in her heart. Miss Pettit was self-sufficient enough to have a safe trip through the mountains to the school. Even though she spent most of Sunday with Mary, it wasn't the same without Della. Not having both of her daughters with her was just part of it. It was the lonely life she was living that caused her to feel this way. Her thoughts turned to the interesting man she met at the restaurant. Walt said his name was Jim Collins. She would ask him tomorrow if the man found work, and if he planned to stay in Hazard.

As much as she missed Mary and Della, it was too soon to make long-range plans. Mary had two and a half more years to work for the Brownlett's and finish high school. Della had until May this year at Pine Mountain. After that Della wanted to work for the Cantrells and finish school. What Judy really wanted was for her girls to live with her in the hotel, but that wasn't possible just yet. Even though Mr. Jenkins was good to her, it was too soon to ask him to allow Mary and Della to live there, too. It would be an imposition. She murmured to herself, "I'll just have to wait and see what God's plan will be for us."

Chapter Eight
ALEX'S VISION UNFOLDS

It was Monday morning. Thanksgiving Day passed too quickly and the weekend had been way too slow. Judy was waiting impatiently for Walt to come for his noon meal. She knew he would be late because it was almost ten o'clock that morning when Deputy Tim came for their breakfast carry-outs. Finally, at almost two-thirty the sheriff walked through the front door and seated himself at his usual table in the corner. With his back against the wall he had a clear view of the dining room and the street. This late in the day the dining room was empty.

Sylvia greeted him warmly and took his order. Judy poured herself a cup of coffee and walked over to join Walt. As she started to sit down, she noticed a look of concern wash over his face. Walt's forehead was usually smooth and laugh-lines creased his eyes as he smiled a greeting. Now there was a frown and the pleasant laugh-lines around his eyes were non-existent.

Judy turned immediately and went into the kitchen. She quickly loaded the shotgun she kept under the counter. With the gun aligned with the side hem of her apron it wasn't visible to anyone outside the front door.

Walt looked surprised to see Judy come back with her gun. She laid it across her lap under the table and picked up her coffee cup with her left hand, keeping her right hand on the gun.

Judy asked, "What's wrong? Are you goin' to tell me what's goin' on outside? I see two men out there, but they're just talkin' to each other."

"There's been some bad blood between the two Owens brothers and the man that's walking fast coming down the side street. He told me yesterday that the two brothers cheated him on a horse deal. He made a complaint, but didn't want to wait for Judge Farmer to come here next week. Do you see him?"

"Yes, I see him. Walt, he's carrying a gun. The Owens men see him and one of them's drawn a gun. Now, I see the other brother's got a gun, too! There's goin' to be a shootin'! Sylvia, get in the kitchen and stay there!"

The sheriff left the table, drew his gun and walked through the front door to approach the two Owens brothers. Judy stood just inside the open door with her gun concealed by her apron. From her vantage point she could see quite a way down Main Street. She saw the deputy coming on the run. The two brothers saw Walt and started toward him as he called to them, "There's going to be trouble! Come inside the restaurant, now!"

The man on the side street quickly walked forward a few steps, kicking up yellow dust from the dirt street, and yelled, "All of you stay where you are! Sheriff, you stay out of this. I told you that I wanted my money back from these two thieves. The lame horse they sold me is over at the Livery waitin' for 'em. Now, do I get my money?"

One of the brothers shouted, "No! If the horse's lame now, it's 'cause you did something to him. He was fine when we sold him to you."

The lone man facing them started to bring his rifle up to point it at the two brothers. The older brother shouted, "I'm warnin' you! Don't raise that gun!"

At that moment Bill Jenkins and Lance came through the hotel doors. Both were unaware of the trouble on Main Street. Bill saw all three men with their guns raised, held at arms length, and aimed at each other. He knew the two brothers, but didn't know the third man standing in the middle of the side street.

He turned and saw that Walt was pointing his gun at the two brothers. Lance was slow in understanding what was happening and kept walking toward the edge of the porch. Bill grabbed him by his arm and jerked him backwards. They both ducked inside the hotel and turned around to watch out the window.

The unexpected movement behind him by Bill and Lance distracted Walt for a split second. Two guns fired at almost the same instant. The man standing in the side street slowly fell to the ground. Walt was spun around by a bullet in his left shoulder. When the first man was shot by one of the two brothers, his gun fired wild. It was his bullet that hit the sheriff.

Deputy Tim came running up to the two brothers with his gun drawn. "You're both under arrest until we can sort this out. Sheriff, are you all right?"

The older Owens man barked, "It was self defense! You're not goin' to 'rest us! I won't let you 'rest us!"

Both brothers still had their guns drawn and they each took a menacing step toward Tim. Walt was now sitting up, leaning against the building. His left arm was hanging useless, but in his right hand was his gun and it was leveled at the brother that shot the man. He was firm, "Boys, the law says you have to stay in jail until Judge Farmer comes to town. As soon as he rules on this, you'll go free. From where I stood, it was self defense."

Walt said, "Tim, I'll watch these two, you go check on the man on the ground. And, somebody get me a doctor!"

The two brothers looked at each other and started to take a step farther out into Main Street. Walt said, "Hold it! There's another gun pointed at you. Don't you dare take another step!"

The brothers stared at the door of the restaurant and the double-barreled shot gun aimed at them. Judy was just inside the doorway. They didn't make another move. She was concerned about Walt, but knew there was more danger in trying to help him than in holding his prisoners for Tim to lock up.

Tim stood up and said, "Walt, he's dead. He's shot through the heart!"

Walt said, "Tim, take the brothers' guns and secure their hands. We'll have to keep 'em in jail 'til the judge comes next week."

Bill came out of the hotel, "Walt, I'll go get Doc Lewis. I'll be right back. Tim, as soon as you get these two in irons, help Judy get Walt into Myrt's room. It's the closest bed and the Doc can take care of him there."

Tim came up on the hotel porch and got Walt's extra set of hand-irons. He secured the brothers' hands and sat them down on the ground, back-to-back. Tim handed a gun to Lance and told him to sit on the top step and watch the brothers until he could get the sheriff into Myrt's room.

Judy put her gun down, standing it up in a corner by the front door. Then she and Tim got Walt to his feet and walked him to Myrt's room. She was asleep in her big chair. When they knocked and opened her door, she was instantly wide-awake. "You mean I missed the whole thing! Is the sheriff goin' to be all right? Has someone gone for Doc Lewis? Where's Mr. Jenkins?"

"Myrt, honey, that's a lot of questions. Tim has two brothers under arrest outside for killin' a man. We all believe it was self defense, so they'll prob'ly be set free as soon as the judge gets here. Mr. Jenkins has gone for the doctor, but we needed to get Walt to the nearest bed, so that's why we brought him to your room. Is that all right?"

"Lord, love 'im, Judy. Of course it's all right. He can stay here as long as he needs to. I can sleep in my big chair. Doctor Lewis is here, now. We should wait outside 'til the Doc tells us to come back in."

When Judy and Myrt left the hotel and went to the restaurant, Tim, Lance, and the two brothers were gone. The older man had gone with them, carrying three sets of guns, gun belts, and holsters. The undertaker had been summoned and he was giving instructions to some men who were carrying the dead man away. There was blood in the street where the man was shot, and blood on the porch where Walt was hit.

Tim locked up the two brothers without further incident. Then he left the jail and asked Lance to come with him to check on the sheriff. Judy saw them coming and went to meet Tim to ask, "Is it all right if I use a bucket of water to wash away the blood in the street and here on the porch?"

Lance spoke up, "If it's all right with Deputy Tim, I'll do that for you, Miss Judy."

Tim said, "I know who the witnesses are, including the sheriff, so I don't need to keep the area like it is. Yes, Lance, go ahead and wash it down. We don't want the people coming to supper to get upset at the sight of so much blood!"

"Thank you, Tim. That was my worry exactly. And, Lance, thank you for offerin' to do it for me."

"I'm glad to, Miss Judy!"

She watched as Lance went to fill a water bucket and carry it down to the dirt side street and throw it full force on the bloody mess. Although the roadbeds and streets in the city were dirt, blood didn't easily disappear in the hard packed earth.

He made three trips with buckets of water before he was satisfied that the blood was gone. Then, while Judy watched, he washed down the front porch.

She had to smile as she watched the older man stand a little straighter. He was proud that he was asked to help with the arrest of the brothers and then to collect and carry all of the guns to the jail.

Judy mumbled, "He's proud 'nough to bust! I'm so glad for him. Lance needs people to respect him for who he is. He'll get plenty of respect now!"

When Judy went into the restaurant her gun was gone. She went into the kitchen and saw that it was in its place in the cabinet under the reach through. Sylvia smiled, "I put it up for you. Yes. It's unloaded. The shells are behind it."

"When did you learn about guns?"

"My grandpa used to take me huntin' until he got too old. Then I went by myself. But, I didn't know what to think when you loaded it and went to help the sheriff. Isaac told me he heard you were an expert with guns!"

"Sylvia, honey, I do thank you. But, I'd just as soon you didn't tell people about me and guns. You know how people like to talk!"

"Don't you worry 'bout that. I won't tell anybody anything."

Judy finished helping with the supper crowd, ate quickly with Myrt, and filled a bowl with steaming chicken soup to take to Walt. When she went into the room, Myrt was there and the sheriff was asleep. Bill came to the door and motioned for Judy to come out to the lobby.

"Judy, the doctor got the bullet out. Walt went into shock afterwards, but he's all right now. He's been given some morphine to deal with the pain and to make him sleep. Myrt said she'll sit with him tonight, but if you want we can take turns tomorrow so she can rest. I've never asked about Walt's family. Tim doesn't know anything about them either. When Walt wakes up, we'll ask him if we should notify anyone."

Tim came to the restaurant for supper and to see Bill. He was seated at the sheriff's corner table and invited Tim to sit with him. After they ordered, Tim asked, "Will it be all right if old Lance spells me for a couple of hours twice-a-day until Walt gets back on his feet? I'll sleep nights at the jail, but if he could come over at ten o'clock each morning and stay until noon and again at three-thirty and stay until five-thirty in the evening, I'd appreciate it. The City Council will authorize us to pay him, or to pay you for his time. We'll do it however you want. There's no danger; the prisoners are locked up. I'll give them their meals so he'll have no direct contact with them. I know you have to ask Lance first."

Bill looked a little uncertain, but asked Sylvia to have Lance come to see them. She went into the kitchen and told the older man she would finish the dishes. "You go see why Mr. Jenkins and Deputy Tim want to talk to you."

The smile that broke across Lance's face was beautiful to see. If he could have stood any straighter, he would have. "Yes sir, Deputy Tim, I'll be proud to help you. That is, if it's all right with Mr. Jenkins?"

"Lance, its fine with me, but you must do exactly what Deputy Tim tells you. You're to have no contact with the prisoners. He'll explain all that to you."

Then Bill turned to the deputy, "Tim, when do you want him to start?"

"Tomorrow, but I want him to come with me to the jail after supper. It won't take long to explain what he's to do. Can he leave in a half-an-hour?"

Mr. Jenkins asked, "Lance, have you had supper?

"No sir, Mr. Jenkins, but it won't take me long to eat. I can be ready to go with him in a half-hour."

"Go clear it with Isaac and Sylvia. Get yourself a plate. Take your time eating. I'm sure Tim will wait for you. Maybe you both should have a second cup of coffee and a piece of Isaac's apple pie."

While Bill and Tim were arranging for the jail to be manned twenty-four hours a day by using Lance to fill in, Judy and Myrt were sitting with Walt. The doctor still had him sedated, but he did manage to stay awake long enough to have a bowl of chicken soup. After he ate, he dozed off again.

Judy didn't try to ask him about Jim Collins. She thought she should wait until Walt improved enough so he didn't have to use morphine. She decided to wait and see what would happen. "Well, the weekend's comin'. Maybe Mr. Collins will come by the restaurant. I'll send word to Ethan to keep Mary away from the hotel for the next two Sundays, until after the judge rules on the killin'."

Walt was continuing to improve and by Sunday he became the worst patient Myrt and Judy had ever seen. It was all they could do to make him stay still so his shoulder could heal properly.

For Sunday dinner, Judy filled a plate with pot roast and delivered it to him. The beef was fork-tender and baked with potatoes, carrots, cabbage, and onions. With that he had cornbread, coffee, and a big helping of warm blackberry cobbler. She added a small pitcher of cool, heavy cream to pour over the cobbler.

She asked, "When did Doc Lewis say you could get out of the room here and stir around?"

"He told me today that in another week I could do anything I felt like doing. That means I'll be up and around by the end of next week. If the Judge comes before then, Bill will bring him to the hotel to talk to me. How much do you want me to tell him about your part in it?"

"I want you to downplay my part of it. I don't want people talkin' about me and my knowin' my way around guns. Some people think it ain't fittin' for a woman to know how to use a gun. Say, I found out that Sylvia knows a lot about guns. Her grandpa taught her and took her huntin' with him."

Walt grinned mischievously, "That's good to know, Judy. Now I have two gun-toting women to back me up when I need them."

Judy laughed, "If you weren't hurtin' in your shoulder, I'd belt you one!"

She stayed with Walt until he finished eating, then she and Myrt left him to nap while they went to Sunday dinner. They sat at the corner table. When Judy looked up, she saw Mr. Collins seated at the table by the front window.

Sylvia came and took their orders. Myrt's eyes grew huge as she watched Judy excuse herself and walk over to the window table to speak to a strange man. Then she smiled knowingly as she saw that Judy was obviously attracted to the good-looking, dark-haired, dark-eyed, olive-complexioned man.

She chuckled, "Well, it's 'bout time our Judy girl got interested in a man. If I was forty-years younger and single, I'd be interested in this one, too."

Mr. Collins looked up as Judy approached his table. She greeted him warmly, "Hello, Mr. Collins, It's good to see you again."

"You know my name, but I don't know yours. Do you work here?"

"My name's Judy Smith, I'm the restaurant manager. I just don't have my apron on today."

"Oh, well, I like your restaurant very much. You have a good cook. I know 'bout cookin'! Thanks to your sheriff, I have a job at the boardin' house as cook, with some maintenance work on the side."

"I'm glad you've found work. I hope that means you plan to stay in Hazard, and I hope you join us for Sunday dinner every week!"

"Yes, I do plan to settle here as long as I can keep steady work. I heard that Sheriff Middleton was hurt in a shoot-out. Is he all right? He's a nice fellow and I hope he'll become a good friend."

"The sheriff's on the mend from a gunshot wound in his shoulder. Yes, he's a good man and a nice friend to have if you're on the right side of the law."

Jim Collins chuckled showing white, even teeth, "I certainly intend to stay on the right side of the law!"

Judy was a rosy pink from her collar to her eyebrows. She was embarrassed by allowing herself to notice so much and for being so attracted to Mr. Collins. She was almost stammering, "Mr. Collins, enjoy your meal, and please come back again."

Myrt hadn't missed a thing as she watched the budding romance unfold between Judy and the handsome newcomer. When Judy returned to their table, her rosy blush was not unnoticed either. Myrt exclaimed, "Lord, love you, child. I do believe you're gonna have yourself a beau! Well, it's 'bout time! Here's our sweet girl with our orders. I'm that hungry, I could eat a bear!"

They hadn't quite finished their meal when Judy watched Jim Collins push his chair back, getting ready to leave. He left a tip on the table for Sylvia. Then he put on his hat and heavy wool coat. When he reached the front door, he stopped and turned toward their table. He smiled at them, tipped his hat, and left.

Myrt grinned impishly, "Now, don't you worry a bit! He'll be back next Sunday, sure as shootin'!"

Judy's worried face was a puzzle to Myrt's keen eye. "What's the matter with you?"

"Myrt, honey, I don't really trust men any more. Ever since my girls' Pa deserted us and cost us our home out of pure meanness, I've not looked twice at any man. I don't understand why I'm attracted to Jim Collins. He told me he's got a job cookin' at the boardin' house. He likes cookin' and he works at fixin' things, like our Roy Jackson does here at the hotel."

"Judy, maybe time has healed some of the hurt you've had, and it's time for you to meet someone else. Why not wait and see what God has planned for you and this Mr. Collins?"

Judy was quiet for a minute, "You're right. I do believe God has a plan for me. I let Him lead me. My Pa had a vision that showed me with a new man who was a father to my girls. He saw us as a family. Pa said I had to trust that God was in my life and to let Him lead me in makin' right decisions. But, dear Lord, Myrt, sometimes it's so hard figurin' out what is the right decision!"

When Judy took Walt's supper to him later that evening, she told him about seeing Jim Collins again in the restaurant. Walt smiled, saying, "I hope he's working out well over at the boardinghouse. He's cooking and doing light maintenance work for them. Since I got shot, I've not been able to follow up on him. He told me that he's been in the army and that's where he learned to cook. I figured if he could cook for a bunch of soldiers, he could cook in the boardinghouse. His family's in Clay County. He wants to stay if he can steady work."

"Walt, I swear, you're as gossipy as a housewife. I can tell you were impressed by Jim Collins. To tell the truth, I am, too. I'd like to know him better."

Walt's eyebrows shot upward and he chuckled, "So that's how it is, is it? Well, I do think you'll like the man. Do you want me to check him out for you?"

Judy reddened. "No! I don't want you to check him out. I think he's been truthful to both of us so far. I think he'll take Sunday dinner here from now on. If he wants to know me better, I won't say 'no' to him."

Walt said, "Judy, there's no reason to get your hackles up. I hope you and Jim Collins do hit it off together. The good Lord knows you deserve a good man. Maybe he's the man for you. Only time will tell. Now, tell me, have you heard anything more about the man who was killed? Tim told me his name was Art Bailie and that his family was traveling west with a wagon, following the Kentucky River through Hazard."

"The talk around town is that the family asked for help in burying him. They took back the horse that was left in the Livery Stable. It does have what they call 'popped knees' and won't be strong enough to pull their wagon. The Bailie man did have a right to be mad at the Owens brothers. And, I hear he's got two brothers who are mad enough to hurt somebody. When Judge Farmer hears the case, I think he'll rule that it was self defense, but maybe he'll make 'em do right by the man's widow and give his money back so she can buy a good horse."

"Judy, I think you're right. When I talk with the Judge, I'll recommend that to happen. If his widow gets a good horse, the whole family can continue on their way, I don't want to see a full scale feud started over this."

Judge J.T Farmer arrived at the boardinghouse that Sunday evening. Bright and early on the next morning the Judge opened a formal Inquest Hearing on the killing of Arthur Bailie by Chad Owens, the oldest brother. Walt insisted that he felt well enough to attend the hearing and testify, but he had strict orders from the doctor to return to the hotel when it was over.

Bill and Judy went to the Inquest Hearing. As they walked across the dirt street, Judy asked, "Did you find anyone to notify when Walt got shot?"

"Tim didn't know of anyone to notify, and when I asked Walt later, he said he didn't want to bother anybody. So, I left it at that. Do you testify today?"

"I don't think so. Not unless they call on me. I think Walt's testimony will be enough. The only thing I can say is that the bullet that hit Walt was from the gun fired by the man who was killed. It was an accident because the man fired wild, hitting the sheriff. You see, all of our testimony will be the same."

Judy was right; she didn't have to testify. Walt, Tim, and Bill all had the same story. Lance was a potential witness, too, but he wasn't called on. There was only one member of the Bailie family there. He was one of the man's brothers and he sat all by himself in the courtroom.

Walt testified that the Owens brothers had, in fact, cheated Art Bailie by knowingly selling him a lame horse. He added, "Their criminal act of fraud caused the man's death. He leaves a widow and children who are stranded without a sound horse for their wagon. The court must decide how the widow and her family will be compensated for their loss."

Judge Farmer looked at the Prosecutor, who said nothing. Then he asked the sheriff, "What was wrong with the horse they sold to the victim?"

"Your Honor, the horse had severely popped knees, and from the scarring around its legs, it's been lame for some time. Before witnesses, they denied knowing the horse was lame when they sold it to Art Bailie. They were lying. They accused Art Bailie of having injured the animal himself. The man's family needs his money returned to them, and any additional compensation for their loss that the court deems is appropriate."

106

Judge J.T. Farmer couldn't hide the sudden anger that washed across his face. "Sheriff Middleton, I thank you for your additional testimony which sheds new light on how this tragic and unnecessary killing happened. Court is adjourned until tomorrow morning at nine o'clock, at which time I'll give my decision regarding the Inquest and address the question of compensation to the Bailie family."

Art Bailie's brother, Walt, Tim, Bill, and Judy were at the courthouse at nine o'clock the next morning. The Bailiff sang out, "All rise, The Honorable Judge J.T Farmer presiding."

The Judge came from a backroom and seated himself behind the elevated desk. Everyone in the courtroom sat down. After a quick glance around the court room the Judge said, "Will the defendants please rise."

The two brothers slowly got to their feet. Then a look akin to fear and disbelief washed over their faces as Judge Farmer scowled at them, "This case will not go to trial because Chad Owens shot Art Bailie in self defense. However, both of the defendants are culpable because their act of fraud caused a man's untimely death and undue hardship on his widow and her family."

The Judge cleared his throat and continued, "There's no need to have a trial over the charge of fraud because your guilt has been proven beyond any doubt. Therefore, Sheriff Middleton will ensure you return the money you received from Art Bailie to his widow. In addition, you will each pay a sum of one-hundred and fifty dollars over the next eighteen months to the sheriff. Mrs. Bailie is instructed to stay in contact with the sheriff so he can forward the monies to her."

Walt asked, "Your Honor, if it pleases the court, in the event the defendants don't comply with your order, what are the consequences for them?"

Judge Farmer's face became hard as granite, "Sheriff, in the event of any default on the part of Chad Owens and his brother on the terms just outlined by this court, you are instructed to arrest them for fraud, contempt of court, spitting on the sidewalk, and anything else you can think of! We'll see to it that they spend time in prison. Now, get them out of my sight!"

Walt and Tim escorted the two brothers back to the jail. From the paper poke filled with their personal belongings, he took out the forty dollars they received for the horse. He filled out a receipt for the money and placed it in the poke. Then he went to find Mrs. Bailie.

Because of the shooting and waiting for its outcome in court, Judy hadn't been to church or seen Mary for almost two weeks. She went to the Brownlett's early Sunday morning for church, but told Anne they wouldn't be staying for Sunday dinner. She told Mary, "We'll have dinner at the restaurant. There's someone I want you to meet. It's a man. His name's Jim Collins. He works as a cook and handyman at the boardinghouse. We have become friends."

Mary's eyes grew huge, "Ma, have you got a beau?"

Judy grew red in spite of herself, "No. I wouldn't call him a beau yet. I just met him recently. I do think he's very nice and I'll say he's my friend!"

"What does Myrt say about this?"

"Myrt thinks it's time for me to meet some nice man. I think I have."

"I promise I'll be nice to him, Ma. I won't embarrass you!"

Judy laughed and hugged her daughter. "You never embarrass me! I want you to know that I'll never make any serious decisions for our family without including you and Della. I need the two of you to help me think things through so I make the right choices!"

After church they rode to the restaurant. Myrt was sitting at their usual table in the corner. This time she had her back to the wall. As soon as they sat down, Sylvia came to take their orders. Judy and Myrt ordered Sunday dinner specials, while Mary ordered her usual. "Miss Sylvia, I'll have cured ham, eggs over easy, home fries, a biscuit, and a glass of milk. Is that all right?"

"That's just fine, honey!"

Jim Collins came in and seated himself at his usual table by the front window. Judy felt a glow of pleasure as she saw him turn to search the room for her. When their eyes met, he smiled and nodded to them. Sylvia came back to the dining room and went over to him to take his order. When she retreated to the kitchen, he got up and walked over to their table, "Well, now we have three lovely ladies. Judy, I know you, but who are these other two?"

"The lady smiling so beautifully in the corner is Myrt Baker. She lives here at the hotel. The other one is my older daughter, Mary."

He smiled and nodded to acknowledge Myrt. Then he chuckled and asked, "Mary, your Ma said you were the older daughter. What's your younger sister's name, or is there more than one?"

Mary blushed a rosy pink, "There's just one, her name's Della. She's away at school in Harlan County."

Judy spoke up very boldly, "This is a table for four; would you like to join us? We'd be delighted to have you."

There was only a slight hesitation on Jim Collins' part as he accepted their invitation. Myrt was grinning like a Cheshire cat. Mary was stunned, but smiled dutifully in order to please her mother.

He went back to his table and waited until Sylvia returned to the dining room. He signaled her and explained that he was joining the party in the corner. She quickly moved his coffee cup and water glass to the empty place next to Judy. "This is very nice of you. I'm so tired of eating alone!"

Judy was amazed at how easy it was to talk with Jim Collins. He was careful to include Mary and Myrt in their conversation. She found out quite a bit about him. He was in the Army for six years, and had never married. He enjoyed living where he worked at the boardinghouse. His Sundays were free. He liked to go riding on his day off and rented a horse from Raff's Livery Stable.

Judy said, "Mary and I go riding almost every Sunday. She has her own horse and mine is boarded at the Livery. We usually ride out along the North Fork Branch that flows into the Kentucky River. There's some real pretty country out there. Jim, would you like to go with us sometime?"

"If you're free to go next Sunday, I'd like to go with you. Depending on the weather, perhaps we can take a picnic basket for supper and eat by the river?"

Judy beamed her pleasure. "That would be lovely. We'll have Sunday dinner here. Our horses can be ready for us. We'll leave at about two o'clock. Mary, be sure to dress warm because it'll turn cold when the sun goes down."

Myrt was grinning. She was pleased that Judy had boldly taken charge of planning her first date with the handsome stranger. Mary was aghast over her mother's lack of feminine decorum. For a woman to ask a man to socially accompany her anywhere was just not done in polite society. Mary was grumbling, "Well, at least they won't be alone on this picnic. They included me."

Judy was ecstatic. She couldn't believe she had dared to be so bold as to ask a man to accompany them on a Sunday ride. And, he said "Yes!"

They finished their meal and Jim took his leave. He included Myrt and Mary in his sweeping glance as he said, "Goodbye, now. I'll see you all next Sunday. If the weather permits, we'll have our ride. Mary, keep your fingers crossed that it'll be warm 'nough and the sun will shine!"

They chorused three 'goodbyes' and watched him leave. Their eyes followed him until he was out of sight heading south on Main Street.

Mary frowned at her mother, "Ma, how could you ask a man to socially accompany you like that?"

Myrt said, "Lord love you, child, your Ma did exactly what she should've done. If you wait on a slow-witted man to do the askin', you may never get asked! Now you all have a good time next Sunday. When the day's over, you'll both know if you want to continue this romance or not."

Chapter Nine
WONDROUS LOVE

Sunday dawned beautifully with sunshine breaking through the morning fog. After breakfast Judy rode to the Brownlett's to attend church with Mary. She paused to stare upwards at the cloudless sky and exclaimed, "Oh, what a lovely day we'll have for our ride!"

After church, she and Mary left the Brownlett's and went to the restaurant. Jim Collins was seated with Myrt at their corner table.

When he saw them, Jim scraped his chair back and got to his feet. "Miss Judy and Miss Mary, here you are! We were waiting on you to order. We're having the Sunday dinner special, and here's Miss Sylvia, right on time!"

Myrt was grinning with delight all through the meal. Mary said little while her mother and Jim kept up a steady stream of conversation. They talked about anything and everything, including their jobs, cooking, cleaning, repairs, hunting, fishing, and family.

Myrt butted in to say, "Jim, Mary and her mother are going to Big Laurel in Harlan County to spend Christmas with her sister's family and her hundred- and-two year old father. Mary's sister, Della, will be there, too. If you're going to be here, maybe you and I can eat together? I truly do hate to eat alone!"

Jim didn't answer Myrt right away. Instead, he looked at Judy and asked, "How long will you and Mary be gone? Do you have someone to go with you? I've heard that the Harlan Trail can be very dangerous."

Judy's face was a puzzle. She didn't know what to say. Finally, she spoke, "Mary and I travel the Harlan Trail often and we've had no trouble with anyone or with wild animals. I always take my gun with me and I do know how to use it when it's necessary."

"Would you like for me to go with you?"

"I thank you for offerin'. But, no, not this time. My folks ain't expectin' anyone but us. I wouldn't want you to feel you were imposin' on them. I'll tell them about you and that you'll be coming with us next time."

Jim nodded in agreement, "Then it's settled. Myrt, you and I'll have Christmas dinner together here and the next time Judy and Mary go to Harlan County, I'll go along."

Mary's face was one of shocked disapproval! She didn't say a word, but she didn't have to. Judy's watchful eye didn't miss the displeasure that washed across Mary's face at the thought of Jim making an overnight trip with them.

Myrt was oblivious to Mary's rude reaction to Jim's offer to accompany them to Harlan County. She responded with joyful glee, "I'm so happy, I'll be with Jim. We'll be a family together for Christmas. Judy and Mary will be with their family. This couldn't have worked out better!"

The next two weeks passed quickly with Jim joining them for dinner each Sunday. Mary was slowly warming up to him. However, she still worried about what people would think and say about them, and the almost shameless way her mother was behaving toward this man. She made a mental promise to herself, "We'll be alone soon and I'll try to talk some sense into Ma."

Christmas came on Monday and Judy made plans for them to leave on Thursday morning before daylight. If all went well, they would arrive at Jonie's before dark on Friday. On Saturday they would deliver the Church's love offering to Miss Pettit and pick up Della. Then they would have time to relax and rest before celebrating Christmas Eve and Christmas Day with the family.

She said her goodbyes to Myrt, Mr. Jenkins, Lance, Isaac and Sylvia on Wednesday night. When she arrived the next morning at the livery for Curly and Ned, they had them ready and waiting for her. She quickly packed Ned for the journey and went to the Brownlett's.

Mary's little mare was saddled and ready to go. Ethan, Anne, and Mary were waiting on the front porch, along with the bulky love-offering for Pine Mountain School. Ethan helped with the final packing of Ned. Mary's packing sacks were slung over her little mare's back.

Ethan gave Judy a large, sealed, brown envelope that contained the cash-money donated by church members. She carefully put the envelope in her saddlebags. They left Hazard around six o'clock, a good two hours before dawn.

There was moisture hanging in the cold December air. The Harlan Trail was wet, but not muddy. Judy told Mary, "If the sun comes up when the fog lifts, the trail should become dry. I want to get to our stoppin' place 'round noon and then we'll have the special dinner that Sylvia packed for us."

The sun was directly overhead when they stopped to eat. Judy removed the chicken-fried steak sandwiches from their food pack. They didn't take time to build a fire, but ate quickly and drank water from their canteens. "Mary, honey, let's not dally because we want to get to the half way marker and make camp in time for me to gather the firewood we need afore it gets dark."

Mary had been waiting all day for a chance to talk seriously to her mother. She was deeply concerned about the budding romance between Judy and Jim. Instinctively, Mary had a personal distrust of the man, but she didn't know if she could trust her own instincts. She was nine years old and her sister was six when their father deserted them and unexpectedly sold their home. She remembered the hurt and sadness in her mother's eyes.

This caused her to be suspicious of strange men and to question their true intentions. Aside from that, Mary was jealous of the precious time she spent with her mother and didn't want to share that time with anyone else.

There was about an hour of daylight left when they reached the big rock overhang. While Judy gathered firewood, built a roaring fire, and prepared some of the glowing embers to warm up the container of beef stew, Mary was busy unpacking the camping gear they needed for sleeping on the ground. The rocks behind them reflected the warmth of the fire.

While they ate supper, Mary brought up the subject of Jim Collins. Judy was surprised that Mary was even thinking about him. She asked, "Why are you being suspicious of Jim? I thought you liked him and I know he likes you."

"Ma, I don't dislike him. I just don't trust him that completely, yet. Do you intend to marry him?"

"Honey, I just met him a little over a month ago. People don't usually marry someone they just met. We have to spend time together to really get to know each other. Besides that, he has to ask me first."

"Why did you invite him to come with us the next time we go to see Aunt Jonie and Grandpa Alex? This trip is the only time we get to really be alone together and I don't want anyone else to come with us!"

Judy turned her head to stir the fire and to hide the grin she needed to conceal from her daughter. She was pleased that Mary cared so much about her mother that she was jealous of Jim, but knew it would become a serious problem if they didn't talk about it.

"Honey you know that the next planned trip is in May when we come for Della's graduation. That's five months away and anything can happen. We need to enjoy this time we have together and postpone worrying. You'll be with me every time that I'll be with Jim so you can keep a watchful eye on us!"

"Oh, Ma, you are joshing me now! But you're right. Something may happen between now and next May that he wouldn't even want to come with us."

"You're not plannin' to do something mean to Jim, are you? I want you to still be the sweet young lady that he's used to. If it is God's plan for me to marry again, I believe Jim Collins is the one I would choose!"

"Ma, you're really serious about him. I can tell. I love you and, of course, I'll keep on being nice to him. What're you going to tell Grandpa Alex and Aunt Jonie? What're you going to tell Della?"

"I'll tell them the same thing that I just told you. I like the man and if things work out and I feel it's God's will, Jim will come with us to Della's graduation in May. As long as you're with us, we'll not be alone. You don't have to worry about that. Della will be with us when we go back. So you see, I'll have good, eagle-eyed chaperones with me comin' and going!"

Mary laughed out loud. "Yes, you will! We'll be watching and you'd both better behave yourselves!"

On that note the subject of Jim Collins ended and they began planning their overnight shopping trip to Harlan. It was eight o'clock when Judy banked the fire and they rolled in their blankets. They depended on the horses and Ned to sound the alarm if anyone or anything came near them. Judy said her prayers, closed her eyes and it was close to daylight when she woke the next morning.

While stirring the fire to get it going good, she woke Mary and hurried her to get dressed.

She said, "We'll have sandwiches for breakfast so we can be on our way in about a half-an-hour. While you get dressed, I'll saddle the horses and load the pack back on Ned. I'll put their nosebags on 'em while we eat and then we'll water 'em from the spring. As soon as we're ready we'll leave. It's cold. That's why I built up the fire, but we'll drown it good afore we leave."

Their luck was holding on the weather. Although there was scattered frost on both sides of the trail, the ground was dry. Judy really pushed them along and only stopped at noon to eat cold biscuits and dried beef jerky.

She reassured Mary, "Don't you worry. We'll have a proper supper waitin' for us at your Aunt Jonie's!"

It was dusk when they rode into Jonie's yard and started to dismount. As if by magic, Jonie and her family, all but Alex, descended the porch steps at the same time. Alex waited patiently while they all gathered around Judy and Mary and everyone was talking at once. There were hugs, joyful tears, and urging to hurry up and come in to supper.

Mary and all of her girl cousins hurried into the house. Judy stopped by her dad to give him a hug and a kiss. She asked, "Pa, are you feelin' all right?"

"Yeah, honey, as all right as an old man should feel! I just can't get up and down steps easy like I used to. So, when I don't have to go off the porch, I don't. Jonie or the young'ins do everything they can for me. Nowadays, I let 'em! It's so good to see you. Praise the Lord! I'm that pleased that you're looking so happy, and pretty as a picture. We'll have time to talk tomorrow. For now, you go get your fill of your sister's good cookin'!"

Enoch was still in the yard holding onto Curly, the little mare, and Ned. He handed all three of the reins to his sons and told them, "You boys take the animals to the barn. Unpack 'em and get 'em ready for the night. Leave the mule's pack-goods in the hayloft where nothing can bother them, but bring the rest of their stuff in the house."

Otis and Gib were already eyeing the gaily-wrapped Christmas gifts that were visible in the top of two of the canvas packing-sacks. They took their time unloading the animals and had grins of satisfaction on their faces as they worked because they had spotted two gifts with their names on them. Curly, Ned, and the little mare were munching oats from their nosebags while the boys rubbed them down. After they scattered fresh, clean bedding in their stalls, they removed their nosebags. Before leaving the tired animals, they spoke gently to them and gave each one a loving pat on the neck.

It was pitch-dark out when the two brothers came into the house. Judy and Mary were seated at the long family dining table with heaping plates of Jonie's good food in front of them. Jonie asked, "Are you two boys still hungry?"

"Yeah, Mam, what can we have?"

"Just fill yourselves another plate of whatever you want. I knew you were hungry again by the way you were looking at little Mary's plate!"

Both boys flushed red, but didn't hesitate to join Judy and Mary. Jonie beamed with pleasure. She loved to watch hungry people eat at her table.

She looked at Judy and Mary, "I know you're both worn out from two days in the saddle. Why don't we all go to bed early tonight? We have all day tomorrow to get ready for Christmas Eve, and we can catch up on all our happenings while we work."

Judy grinned. "Jonie, honey, it's so good to be here with you all, but Mary is about to lay her head down in her plate because she's so tired. So, let's do go to bed early. I have to go to Pine Mountain School in the mornin' to deliver their gifts from the Church and pick up Della. When we get back, I'll help you with the bakin' and cookin' to get ready for Christmas, and we'll talk."

Early the next morning, she and Mary were ready to leave right after breakfast. Alex was still asleep. While they ate, Jonie's sons saddled Curly and the little mare for them. They also helped Judy re-pack Ned with his bulky burden of gifts for the school. It was one of the shortest days of the year and the morning darkness was moisture-laden from the thick fog that rose off Little Greasy Creek. It didn't lighten up until almost nine o'clock.

Mary complained, "Ma, this is too creepy for anything. We can barely see the road. What if we meet up with a panther or a bear?"

"Honey, they can't see any farther than we can. We just have to be watchful and I've got my gun handy. Anyway, in this fog, I'll bet they're as afraid of us as we are of them and they'll run the other way if we do meet up with anything. Now, I don't want you to worry about the fog. Curly would sense anyone or anything close to us and give us plenty of warning."

"Ma, are you always so trusting of animals?"

"Yep, I trust animals a lot farther than I do some human bein's. The good Lord made animals honest by nature. Humans have free will and can make choices and often times their choices are pure evil."

Mary breathed a sigh of relief as the fog began to lift. Judy grinned, "Pa always said that if the fog lifts and the sun comes shining through right away, it will be a sunny day. If it hangs low and you don't see the sun, look for rain or snow. According to Pa's prediction guide, we'll have a nice sunny day!"

It was around ten o'clock when they reached the school office building. Mary scampered up the stone steps to the front door and walked in. She found Miss

Pettit at her desk with an open ledger book. She sprang to her feet, exclaiming, "Mary, child, it's so good to see you! Is your mother outside?"

She replied, "Yes, ma'am, Miss Pettit. She's waiting for you. She has old Ned and the church's love-offering for the school. Where is Mrs. Zande?"

Miss Pettit closed the ledger and crossed the room quickly to hug Mary. "Let's go see what all old Ned has on his back this time. Mrs. Zande is at Laurel House, but due to come back any minute. There's a young man, Tim Turner, working at the next building. Would you go there and get him for me. We need him to help bring the gifts inside."

"Miss Pettit, there's no need for that. I can help my mother bring the gifts in. They aren't heavy, just bulky. By that time Mrs. Zande may be here."

"That's sweet of you, Mary. We'll do as you suggest. Let's go see your mother and unpack poor Ned."

There were no handrails on the sides of the stone steps, but Mary gaily skipped all the way down to the roadway while Miss Pettit carefully descended behind her. When Miss Pettit reached the bottom step, she greeted Judy with outstretched arms, "Here's our Judy! It's so good to see you and our little Mary who isn't so little any more, but quite grown up. Let's see what you have brought us from Reverend Brownlett. Poor Ned doesn't look so woe-be-gone this time!"

Mary beamed her pleasure when Miss Pettit said she was "grown up."

Ned was quickly unpacked and the gifts were carefully placed on the bottom steps. Mary and Miss Pettit began to carry them up to the school office. When the last of the gifts were placed on-and-around the large desk, Judy retrieved the brown envelope from her saddlebags and gave it to Miss Pettit. With her receipt for the cash money carefully put away, Judy said, "We need to find Mrs. Zande and pick up Della. Are you planning on making a trip to Harlan like we did last year? If so, Mary, Della and I would like to go with you, but we'll stay overnight so we'll have more time to shop."

"Yes, Mr. Wilder and I will make the trip to Harlan on Tuesday for their Day-after-Christmas sale. Staying overnight will be a good experience for Mary and Della. But, we'll return home Tuesday evening."

With that settled, Judy and Mary rode to Laurel House. They went to the back of the large building, dismounted, and walked toward the door that opened near the large kitchen. Mrs. Zande saw them ride by and dismount. She burst through the back door with arms wide-open and a beautiful smile. "Judy, Mary! Oh, my dears! It's wonderful to see you. Della is waiting for you at the older girls' house. Mary, why don't you go and fetch her while your mother and I visit with each other?"

At first, Mrs. Zande didn't give Judy much chance to talk. She said, "You know that Della is due back at school on Wednesday, the third of January? She's still singing for our special programs. When she moves to Hazard I hope she continues to practice. I'll give her a note to take to her new music teacher."

"How is Della doing in her other studies?"

"Oh, Della is an excellent student in every subject. She's especially good in reading, English literature, history, and Reading Bible History. She's growing very tall for a girl. Her voice can be mistaken for an adult woman. That makes her a good oral reader. We call on her more than the other girls to read aloud."

Judy's face was a puzzle. She asked, "What's an oral reader?"

"Someone who's well voiced and able to read aloud, either to an individual or to a group of people. She reads aloud from the Bible during Sunday service in the Chapel. We're very proud of Della!"

"Has there been any more trouble from the Heltons?"

"No, not since Kathryn assured Mrs. Helton that the Northeastern Presbyterian Mission Board approved of Della's living here until she graduates. I don't think we'll hear from the Helton clan again."

Then Mrs. Zande laughed and said, "Della is so excited because she'll graduate from the sixth grade the third week of May. She's expecting you, Mary, and her whole family to be here!"

At that moment they saw Mary and Della coming around the bend in the road between the Chapel and Laurel House. They were riding the little mare. When Della spotted her mother, she quickly slid down off the horse and ran to greet Judy with a big hug and a wet sloppy kiss.

Mrs. Zande said, "I know you're in a hurry to get back and prepare for Christmas with your family. Give them our best wishes for a wonderful holiday. I'll walk with you to the office. I'm sure Kathryn needs help in making final preparations for our Christmas week here on campus."

Ethel Zande said goodbye as they crossed over the little footbridge spanning the spring-fed creek. Della and Mary began to 'girl talk' and that lasted all the way to Jonie's house. After greeting their cousins, they sat down at the long dining table and had a wonderful meal. Then Mary and Della joined the older girls in planning Christmas dinner with the grownups in the kitchen.

Everyone had a chore assigned to him. Jonie tried to allow each of her older daughters to help prepare their favorite dishes. The two boys were assigned the task of keeping the wood-box full and taking care of the animals. Alex and Enoch were to stay out of the way!

There was merry laughing and talking by every one. An equal amount of nonsense and fun along with some serious conversation took place. Then without warning someone started singing the familiar words to a favorite hymn. All conversation stopped while they all joined in to sing. Alex seated himself in one of the corners of the big room and thoroughly enjoyed the festivity.

The women folk worked on cooking and baking until dinnertime. Then it was Christmas Eve! Enoch said, "Otis and Gib are going with me to find our Christmas tree to put up and decorate tonight."

The three of them took their guns, a double-blade axe, and a twenty-five-foot piece of rope with them. They crossed Little Greasy Creek and walked part way up Alex's Branch toward the old family farm. Enoch cautioned them about going too far. He didn't want to get anywhere near Brother-in-law Rob's land.

They had many trees to choose from, including white pine, fir, cedar, ponderosa, and hemlock. They chose a perfectly shaped, five-foot-tall white pine. Gib chopped it down. Otis looped the rope around the lower branches so they could drag it without breaking any of its foliage.

When they entered their front yard, the younger girls shouted with glee as they ran to meet them. Enoch made the strong "X" shaped stand to securely fasten the tree in an upright position. Alta, the oldest girl, had the job of supervising the younger ones in decorating the tree. They cut into long strips a few sheets of brightly-colored construction paper and pages from an old Sears and Roebuck Summer catalogue. Then they made paper chains alternating the solid-color paper with the picture-pages of the catalogue.

Jonie popped corn on top of the kitchen stove and they all joined in making white, cloudlike chains to wrap around the tree on top of the paper chains. Jonie said, Judy, honey, we may not have the neatest tree around, but we know it's done from the heart of each one of the young'ins. That's what Christmas should be about. All our feelin's from the heart!"

There was more singing and story-telling until Dolly and baby Delphia were asleep on the floor near their mother. Then, Alex grew tired and announced that he was going to bed. Judy said, "Pa, can you stay up a little while longer?"

Jonie asked Alta and Mellie to round up the younger ones and get them into their pretty flour sack nightgowns. Gib and Otis didn't need any urging, but went on to bed. Della and Mary wanted to stay up until later, but Judy shooed them off, too. Mary knew why her mother wanted Grandpa Alex to wait awhile. She was going to tell him, Aunt Jonie, and Uncle Enoch about Jim Collins.

Jonie had arranged Alex's bedroom so that the two boys shared it with him. This worked out well. Both boys watched over their Grandpa. If Alex needed anything, Otis and Gib were there for him.

When the grownups were finally alone Judy asked, "Pa, is there anything that you need or want? The girls and I are going to Harlan with Miss Pettit and Mr. Wilder the day after Christmas. We're going to spend the night to have more time to shop. I wondered if there was anything that we could bring back for you."

Alex thought a minute, grinned and said, "Yeah, I'd like some soft leather shoes that I can wear just in the house. It's getting to be a real chore putting on hard shoes everyday. I wear a size ten. Get them as wide as you can."

"Pa, I'll be glad to. If the ones we find are too narrow, they can be stretched some on your iron shoe-last."

Judy decided she had stalled long enough. She took a deep breath and said, "I want you all to know that I've met a man that I like very much. His name is Jim Collins. He's a cook in the Hazard Boardinghouse. He's a hard worker, soft spoken, and seems to like me and Mary. I want to invite him to come with us in May to Della's graduation. I want you all to meet him."

Alex was the first to respond. "Honey, are you positive you know enough about him. Have you made him any promises about marrying him?"

"No, I've not known him long enough. My good friend, Sheriff Walt Middleton, has checked and says he's who he says he is. May is five months off. If we still like each other, he'll come to meet my family. I didn't want to show up here in May with a strange man without you knowing about him ahead of time."

"What does Mary think of him?"

"She wasn't too crazy about my having a beau. But, she admitted that the real reason was because he took away part of her time with me and she was jealous. She and I talked that out and she's all right about my seeing him now."

Alex said, "Honey, this falls within the vision I had for you and your girls. I saw a man who would be good to you and a father to Mary and Della. I didn't think it would take this long to come to pass. If you like this man and after you get to know him better, you still want to spend the rest of your life with him, I say go ahead. I believe my vision was God's plan for you."

Judy looked at Jonie and Enoch. "You haven't said anything. What do you think?"

Jonie winked mischievously at Enoch, and said, "I just wondered where you thought he was going to sleep?"

Enoch laughed out loud. "Mam, of course, he'll sleep in Grandpa Alex's room with Otis and Gib."

Judy breathed a sigh of relief. "Then it'll be all right if I invite him to Della's graduation? She'll be going to Hazard to live as soon as that's over."

"Jonie hugged her sister, "You silly goose, of course it's all right!" Now tell me about this family that Della's goin' to work for. I don't believe any family could be as nice as Mary's Reverend Brownlett and his wife."

"You're right. That's a worry. Their name is Cantrell. They're very rude people. However, Reverend Brownlett said he'd keep a watchful eye on Della. I exercise Curly by riding out past their farm twice a week. I'll be watchin', too."

Alex looked real concerned. "If they ain't what they're supposed to be, I know you'll deal with them in your own way. Just don't wait too long. Della must not be hurt by them. Young'ins carry hurts all their lives when they have a trust betrayed. That kind of hurt can cause them a lot of pain in just livin'."

"Don't worry, Pa, I'll keep a watchful eye on Della. Now you should go to bed. We all should. You know those young'ins will be up at the crack of dawn! And, we have a lot of cookin' yet to do for Christmas dinner."

Christmas day was a joy from the early hour that the children surrounded the tree to open gifts until the end of the day when they all ate a piece of Jonie's applesauce stack-cake and drank sweetened sassafras tea. A big surprise was a visit from Israel, Id, and Rhodie Miniard. Id came in the house calling out. "Christmas gift! I said it first and it's the rule that you owe me a gift. Aunt Judy, what're you gonna give me?"

Israel laughed at the puzzled look that washed over Judy's face. He assured her, "Don't worry, he's kiddin'. It's a new trick his men friends pull on their families. It don't mean a thing!"

Judy recovered quickly from her surprise at Id's presumptuousness and with a hearty laugh, she invited them in for a piece of Jonie's pumpkin pie and coffee. Id wasn't about to let it go that easily. He finished his piece of pie and then held out his empty saucer, saying, "Aunt Jonie, for my gift I'll take another piece of your pumpkin pie with a little of your heavy cream on it."

Jonnie grinned delightedly, "Id, honey, you eat all of my pie you want. It does my heart good when someone enjoys my cookin!"

After about an hour, Israel, Id and Rhodie excused themselves to return home. Before leaving, they invited Alex and all of the Lewis' to visit them. Judy said, "Della told me that you've been coming to the school to visit her. She's happy to know some more of her family. She'll graduate from the sixth grade in May and would like you all to come. Rhodie bring your young'ins, too. After her graduation, she's moving to Hazard with me and will work for a farm family."

Israel said, "We'll keep in touch with Jonie and go to see Della like we've been doin'. Have you heard her sing? She can tug at your heart and make you cry! We wouldn't miss her graduation for nothin'!"

After the Miniard's left, Judy asked Jonie about Rob and Becky. Jonie looked real sad as she explained, "I don't get to see them at all. Every once in a while I see one of their young'ins. The oldest ones are quite grown up. Rob has favored his sons over his girls. He believes women have no use for schoolin'. He says all a girl needs is to know how to work a farm and have young'ins. They tell me that Becky is never well. She doesn't go to town anymore. When Rob goes, he takes his oldest sons with him."

There was a deep sadness in Judy's voice, "I'm real angry with Rob over how he treated Pa when the home place was sold. I'm thankful that Pa has a good home with you and Enoch. When Mary and I come to visit, I'd love to see Becky, but I don't know what to do about Rob. When we come back in May, I may have time to ride up there to see them. For now, I'll just wait and see if anything changes."

Alex had retired long before the children went to bed. Jonie, Enoch and Judy relaxed by the flickering fire to talk about the day's events and their plans for the coming week. Enoch said, "I know you're going to town with the Pine Mountain School people in the mornin' and staying in Harlan overnight, but I'd like for you to go huntin' with me on Thursday. If we can get a turkey, and maybe a deer to put up, we'll have fresh meat for the first of the year."

Judy beamed her pleasure, "Jonie, do you mind if I leave you here to go huntin'? It's been years since I've hunted in my home mountains."

"No, honey, I don't care a bit. I'll be fine with all the young'ins. Pa's here and the boys are a big help. Alta and Clara will help with the little ones. Mary and Della can help me with the cookin' chores in the kitchen. I hope you all do bring home some fresh meat. You'll make me and Pa mighty happy!"

"I'll still have part of Thursday to visit with you and Della. Mary and I have to leave for Hazard early Friday morning. If the good Lord's willin', we'll get plenty of fresh meat for you."

When Judy went to bed that night, she was tired, but it was a happy tiredness. She loved being with her family. She could tell that her father was worried about her being so far away. She worried about it, too. Because of Alex's advanced age, it was uncertain if he would be able to enjoy another Christmas with them. She fell into a dreamless sleep and slept peacefully until the rooster crowed outside her window.

Judy, Della, and Mary met Miss Petit and Mr. Wilder just inside the gate at the school. They had the same plans as before: To stop at the boardinghouse at Putney for a quick early dinner and then go on to Harlan, expecting to get there by early afternoon. Mr. Wilder was out in front leading the pack mules. Judy and Miss Pettit rode side by side. The two sisters were last in their little caravan.

Mary and Della were riding double on the little mare, and they chattered all the way about the school clothes they would buy, including underclothes, stockings, and new shoes. And, maybe a new hat!

Miss Pettit told Judy that Della would need a white outfit, either a dress or a skirt and blouse, for her graduation. Her patent leather shoes would be fine. The school furnishes a large white satin hair ribbon for the girls. Judy, chuckled, "They'll be real pretty. What're the boys wearing?"

"They're asked to wear dark suits, either navy blue or black with white shirts. The school is providing them with black 'string' ties to wear."

Miss Pettit continued explaining about the graduation ceremony and the long-range plans for the school. "Our next project will be a wood frame building for a community hospital and clinic. It'll be available for our students and for people who live up in the remote mountain hollows."

"Where will you find a doctor and nurses who're willin' to work here?"

"Just as it is with our current teachers and some of the other school staff, they'll be retired missionaries from around the world. Mrs. Zande and I only have to ask the Mission Boards, both Presbyterian and Catholic, for help in locating staff and we find ourselves with several different applicants to choose from. God has a lot to do with our getting the best of committed people who want to work for and live with our mountain children."

Judy guessed that it was because everyone but Mr. Wilder was engaged in lively conversation that they seemed to arrive in Harlan in record time. They said their goodbyes to them in front of the A&P Super Market. Then, she and the girls walked to the boardinghouse to make arrangements to stay the night.

Mary complained, "Ma, why do we have to stay in the boardinghouse? Why can't we stay in the Harlan Hotel? I wouldn't be able to tell my friends at school that I stayed at a boardinghouse while shopping for clothes in Harlan!"

Della interrupted before Judy could answer Mary's question, "I think it'll be fun to stay at the boardinghouse. Anyway it'll be cheaper because it'll include our meals. At the hotel we'd have to pay extra for the meals, wouldn't we, Ma?"

Judy silently blessed Della for speaking up like that. "Yes, we would have to pay more for the room and the meals would not be cheap. There's no reason that you have to explain to anyone where you stayed. It's none of their business. I think we should go now to get something to eat. We ate dinner early and I know you're hungry. Would you like to get ice cream now?"

The frown on Mary's face vanished as if by magic. Both girls grinned and chorused, "Yeah, Ma, let's get ice cream!"

Judy said, "Okay, we'll go to Howard's Drug Store!"

They started their shopping at Newberry's and Scotts' Five and Dime stores. Mary and Della took their time to put together several attractive school outfits and then shopped for underwear. Judy didn't find what she was looking for in Newberry's or Scotts'. She walked up the slight rise in the street to Powers and Horton. In their window was a white eyelet dress cut in the princess fashion. "Oh," she exclaimed, "That dress will look beautiful on Della."

She turned around and went back down the little hill to Newberry's and met the girls. They paid for their selections and then all three of them went back up the hill to Powers and Horton. Judy pointed out the white eyelet dress that was displayed in the window, and asked, "Della, honey, do you like this dress? Miss Pettit told me to get an all white graduation dress for you."

Della squealed with delight. "Ma, it's so pretty. Can I try it on? Can I really have it? Oh, let's go in the store so I can try it on!"

Then a small frown clouded Della's face. "Wait, Ma, how much does it cost? Maybe I can help pay for it with money that I have saved from school."

Judy hugged her daughter. "I've already looked at the price tag and the dress is just right for you. Let's go in so you can try it on."

122

Della was outfitted with satiny soft step-ins and a white-satin princess-slip to wear underneath the dress. It was a perfect fit. She looked positively angelic in the pure white of the eyelet material. "Honey, you look beautiful! This will be your graduation dress. You mustn't wear it at all 'til May."

Della's eyes were shining with happy-tears as she retreated to the little fitting room to change back into her street clothes. Judy told the clerk she would take the dress and underclothes, and to wrap them up in a package suitable to transport by horseback.

Judy watched Mary's face turn into a pronounced scowl as she jealously watched her sister try on the lovely dress. She headed Mary off before she said something unkind about Della. "You'll graduate from High School in 1926. All of your classmates will wear the same color, too. Over your dress you'll wear a long black robe and a flat-topped cap that I heard someone call a mortar board. What do you think about that? And, honey, the good Lord willin', you'll be the first child in our family to ever graduate from high school!"

Mary's scowl disappeared and a radiant smile magically took its place. Her mother's words painted a word picture in her mind. She had seen a group of girls last May wearing caps and gowns. She asked, "Oh, Ma, do you really think that dream will come true for me? I do so want to keep going to school, but I keep thinking something bad will happen and I won't be able to."

Judy reassured her, "I think God has a plan for our lives. We don't know what it is. Only God knows that. We have to trust in Him and pray we make the right choices. It was trust in God and prayer that led us to Pine Mountain School. We were all together there and you got a good beginnin' in your schoolin'. I believe God led us to come to Hazard. Whatever happens in our life, your Grandpa Alex says it's God's will. We must trust Him to take care of our needs."

Della came skipping happily out of the fitting room and handed the dress and satin underwear to her mother. Mary hugged her little sister, mostly out of feelings of remorse for being so jealous just a few moments ago.

Then Judy found and bought a perfect pair of soft, leather house shoes, size ten-wide for Alex. When their shopping was done, the three of them went back to the boardinghouse. Although the short winter day was coming to a close and it was getting dark, they were in plenty of time for supper. They took their purchases to their room and the girls had a giggly good time trying on everything. Judy smiled as she watched her daughters behave like happy and loving sisters.

The next morning Judy was up at five o'clock and went to the livery stable to saddle Curly and the little mare. She brought them to the boardinghouse and tied them to the hitching rail. It was six by the time she had all of their packages tied together and slung over the backs of both mounts. Mary and Della dressed quickly and the three of them had a hasty breakfast before heading home.

Mary asked, "Ma, are you still going hunting with Uncle Enoch? We're going to get to Aunt Jonie's awful late."

"I plan to go with him. If we're lucky, we'll bring home a deer and one or two wild turkeys. But we do need to hurry. You know how short the days are and it will begin to get dark around five o'clock today."

Enoch was dressed for the hunt and waiting impatiently for Judy to arrive. She handed the shoes to her father and watched a big grin light up his face. It took her about ten minutes to change into a hunting outfit and a heavy split-tail topcoat. They each took extra shells with them. Enoch was mounted on a big roan named "Red" that carried his weight well. Judy was on Curly.

They were in luck! Enoch killed a young doe and Judy shot two wild turkeys. Enoch helped his sons butcher the deer while Jonie and Judy prepared the two turkeys. One was preserved in the smokehouse, and the other would be roasted for the Lewis family's New Year's Day dinner. Jonie and Enoch would take Della back to school two days later.

Judy and Mary gave Alex tearful hugs the night before and told him they wouldn't wake him when they left the next morning. It was long before daybreak when they said goodbye to Jonie and Enoch. Jonie handed up a heavy travel-sack of food to Judy, enough to last a good two days or more.

Mary looked back and waved. Judy looked straight ahead. She knew Jonie was crying, because she was, too. Then she shook off her tearful mood and smiled, "I've arranged for Pa and them to meet Jim in May. I sure hope they like him. He's everything my Robert wasn't."

They had good traveling weather. It was bone-chilling cold, but the trail stayed dry. When they arrived in Hazard, they stopped at the Brownlett's to let them know they were home and they would see them in Church the next day. Anne Brownlett was planning a big New Year's Day dinner for Monday and invited Judy to eat with them. She said, "I don't think I can. It's a big event for the restaurant and I'll feel better if I'm there to help Isaac and Sylvia. They handled Christmas by themselves and I need to give them a break."

Anne replied, "I understand. Ethan, do you think we can all stop at the Restaurant in the afternoon on New Year's Day for pie with Judy?"

"That's a great idea. Mary can be with her mother on New Year's and it'll get you out of the kitchen for a change!"

Judy said, "Its gettin' dark and I'd better be on my way. I'll see all of you on New Year's Day!"

When she arrived at the restaurant she was met with a smile and a hug from Mr. Jenkins. Lance helped her unload Curly and carried all the packages up to her room while she took Ned and Curly to the livery. As she prepared to leave, she patted Ned while Curly jealously nuzzled her shoulder. In return, she spoke softly to him and gave him a loving pat on his sleek neck.

When she returned to the hotel, Bill said, "I know you're tired from two days on the trail. You go on to bed and we'll talk in the morning."

"Is there something wrong?"

"No, there's not a thing wrong! It's just that you need to get some rest."

"I've got to say hello to Isaac and Sylvia and then I'll get some rest!"

Judy was pleased to see how neat and clean the restaurant was. She could hear Isaac and Sylvia laughing and talking while the two of them were cleaning up the dishes. Isaac was noisily scraping the pots and pans.

Judy thought back to how it was two years ago. Her talk with Isaac and help in setting him free from the influence of his evil brothers made a world of difference. She hoped that he and Sylvia would become romantically involved.

When they looked up and saw Judy standing there watching them, they both flushed red but Sylvia squealed her welcome and hugged her. Isaac found his voice, "Miss Judy, it's so good to see you home safe and sound!"

"I just got here and am ready to go to bed. I'll see you early in the morning. Everything looks fine. I couldn't go to bed without seeing both of you!"

Sylvia said, "Miss Judy, you go on now. We'll talk in the mornin'!"

Judy looked concerned. This was the second time in the last ten minutes that she had heard, "We'll talk in the morning!"

"Sylvia, is something wrong. I didn't see Myrt. Is she all right?"

"Yes, Myrt's fine. She goes to bed early since the days are so short and its pitch dark at eight o'clock. She'll be here to have breakfast with you same as usual. Stop your worryin' and go on to bed!"

Her bedtime prayers included heart-felt blessings for her father, Jonie and her family, Mary and little Della, her new-found closeness with Israel, Id and Rhodie Miniard, and the good friends at Pine Mountain School. Then she asked God to bless her budding relationship with Jim Collins.

Chapter Ten
DELLA'S GRADUATION

Judy woke the next morning before the alarm clock rang. She quickly said her morning prayers, ending them with "Thank You, dear God for this day and my job. Help me to always do my best and to please You. Amen."

She decided to let Mary sleep late, but would wake her in time for breakfast and to get ready for church. Tonight was New Year's Eve. Judy, Isaac and Sylvia would spend part of the evening preparing the New Year's Day menu. Judy wondered if she would see Jim Collins tomorrow. She mentally scolded herself, "Of course, you'll see him. He has nowhere else to go. He'll come and join Myrt and me, same as usual!"

After church, Judy joined the Brownlett's and Mary for Sunday dinner. Then she returned to the restaurant. At about five o'clock Myrt came to have supper with her. Mr. Jenkins ordered a plate brought to him so he could eat at the front desk. They had just placed their orders when the front door opened and Jim came in and joined them at their corner table.

He reached over and grabbed her hand. He was smiling as he exclaimed, "Judy, I'm so pleased that you're home safe and sound! You must tell me all about your trip. I want to order whatever the special is for the night. It's New Year's Eve and I want to spend the evening with you."

Myrt was grinning like a Cheshire cat. Judy was smiling up at him as she pulled her hand free and said, "I'll have the same as you're havin'. The roast beef sandwich with mashed potatoes and brown gravy. But, I do have to work tonight to get things ready for the morrow. Our special will be roast-pork-short-ribs and sauer kraut with all the trimmin's. This is our long-standin', traditional good-luck dinner for New Year's Day."

"You noticed that I have my cook's uniform on. I came dressed for work and thought I could help you get ready for tomorrow, if it's all right with you, Isaac, and Sylvia. They all looked at each other. Then Judy, in her sweetest voice, said, "We'll be happy to have you help us. Then we'll watch the New Year in together. But that'll put you on the street awful late. People do crazy things at midnight. They'll be shootin' off guns in celebration and can be dangerous."

"Don't worry. I'll take a back street to the boardinghouse. I'll be fine!"

Myrt finished with a big piece of pumpkin pie and coffee and retired early. She wished all of them a Happy New Year! After Judy and Jim finished their supper, they helped with the final clean-up chores and began to prepare vegetables for the next day. At a quarter to twelve, Sylvia closed down the kitchen and all four of them sat at the corner table having pie and coffee. They heard the big clock in the hotel lobby striking midnight when Jim got up and prepared to leave.

Isaac and Sylvia stood up very close together and without warning both men, as if on cue, embraced the two ladies and kissed them.

Sylvia and Judy were not as surprised as they pretended to be. Each of them returned their kiss by planting one on each of the two men's cheeks. With Happy New Year wishes still ringing in her ears, Judy said good night to Jim. Then she smiled as she watched Sylvia and Isaac leave together. They were holding hands like two teenagers!

Jim's and Judy's romance continued through the winter months. Every Sunday that was warm and dry enough for them to go riding, they did. Mary seldom went with them now. She was busy with her schoolwork and watching over the Brownlett children She stopped worrying about her mother being alone with Jim. The truth of the matter was that Judy wanted to ride out toward the Cantrell farm and used exercising Curly and her standing date with Jim as an excuse for keeping an eye on them.

She and Jim made plans for him to take off a few days from his job and accompany her and Mary to Della's graduation. The graduation ceremony was scheduled to be in the Zande Chapel at the School on Sunday, May 20, 1923. They planned to spend that night at Jonie's and begin the return trip to Hazard early the next morning.

The Farmer's Almanac had a saying about March: In like a lion out like a lamb. The lion-of-winter had roared all through February and was hanging on in Hazard until late March. There was deep snow early in the month and heavy frosts during the end. This made it hard on the farmers who wanted to plant potatoes and other root vegetables while the signs were below the knees.

The Cantrell family was no exception.

Not being able to plant early caused ugly moods to settle on Harvey Cantrell. He constantly scolded Sarah, his wife, over the least little thing he could find wrong. His two sons, Harvey, Jr. and Jimmy also bore the brunt of his foul moods. However, he doted on his girls, Lacey and Winnie. In his eyes, they did no wrong. They knew it, too. The girls constantly goaded their older brothers.

The Cantrell sisters were smart enough to know how to manipulate their parents and stay on the good side of their Pa. They only had to feed the chickens and gather the eggs each day. Yet, they pretended to be overworked and tired.

If Sarah asked her daughters to help with housework, Harvey scolded, "My girls have weak constitutions. Don't you go piling work on them! There's nothin' wrong with you. You tend to your job in the house and the boys will help me with the outside work. I'll be glad when we get that mountain girl in May. She'll do work inside and out. I don't want you to go coddlin' her. She's just another mouth to feed and I'm goin' to get my due from her!"

Sarah was already feeling sorry for the young girl who was coming to live and work on their farm. She didn't dare cross her husband. He had never struck her, but he threatened her with beatings. The boys did all he asked of them, but didn't hide the way they felt about working the farm with their father. They talked with her and each other about finding work in timber at one of the mountain based sawmills. She knew it was just a matter of time before her oldest son would walk away from his home and family. She couldn't blame him, but knew it would put a larger burden on Jimmy and the new girl, Della.

Outwardly, nothing changed at the Cantrell farm that Judy could see. Both boys were seen working outside all winter long. The time was drawing near that they would make the trip to Big Laurel and Pine Mountain School. Jim showed his excitement about meeting Judy's family. He made it no secret that he was Judy's beau and very serious about his feelings of love for her.

Myrt enjoyed overseeing the growing love affair. He was mindful of her feelings and catered to her. He knew how much Myrt's friendship meant to Judy.

Walt and Mr. Jenkins felt more than a little uneasy about how swift the Judy and Jim love affair had taken root and grown. The sheriff felt protective toward Judy and without her knowing, he did check out Jim's background and found nothing wrong. She had no idea that Walt and Mr. Jenkins had discussed her relationship with Jim Collins at length. Both of them were relieved that he had nothing in his background that confirmed their suspicions

Mr. Jenkins told the sheriff, "I know that Judy's in love with Jim Collins, but he is just too oily for me. Compliments roll off his tongue like he practices in front of a mirror!"

Walt laughed, "Bill, I swear, I think you're jealous, or else you're afraid she'll get married and move away, and you'll lose her. Which is it?"

"Maybe it's a little of both. Judy has been with me going on three years and is like a daughter to me. I know how badly she was hurt by her first husband and I don't want to see it happen again!"

Walt asked, "Did you know he's going with her to little Della's graduation? I understand from Judy it's so he can meet her family. If all goes as they plan, she expects him to ask her to marry him right after they get back, if not before. So, we might as well get used to them being a couple!"

Bill said, "I'm planning on going to Florida when Judy gets back. If my brother's still agreeable, I may retire next year and live there. I want to see how hot it gets later in the year. Walt, I know your four years as sheriff are almost up. What are your plans? Are you going to seek another four-year term?"

"No, I don't think so. It seems that one term is all sheriffs serve in Hazard and Perry County. I got shot once and I don't want to press my luck. I plan to head west and find some free land to homestead. The Bailie family was heading toward the Dakotas and Montana where there's supposed to be free range for herds of cattle and free land."

"That's all well and good. Have you given any thought to finding yourself a wife? You'll have a hard time making it on a homestead without a good woman to share your life and help you with the work."

Walt laughed, "You know if I had my druthers about a wife, she would be just like our Judy, only younger!"

During the first week in May, Judy received a letter from Miss Petit that explained how the graduation ceremony would take place. All the family members that planned to attend would need to be in the Chapel by ten o'clock. Della had a central part in the program and would be singing two hymns. Judy felt a warm rush of pride surge through her because of her youngest daughter.

She, Mary, and Jim planned to leave early in the morning on Thursday, the seventeenth of May. This gave them all day Saturday to visit with family before going to the school the next morning. Jonie was preparing a celebration dinner for Della early Sunday afternoon. They would leave the next morning for the return trip home.

Alex, Jonie, and Enoch were anxious to meet Jim Collins. Alex said, "If it's God's will, this man will be the one to spend his life with Judy. I pray that she's makin' the right choice. We have to believe that the Lord is leadin' her on the right path. I know she trusts in God to show her the right way."

They were lucky. The weather on the third weekend in May was perfect. The Harlan trail was overgrown with lush underbrush in some parts, but was well marked by frequent use. Jim was afraid of getting lost. Some parts of the trail were weird looking to him because of the strange, large rock-outcroppings. He asked, "Don't you and Mary feel scared to be near these huge rocks that jut up out of the ground and the ones that come right out of the side of the mountain?"

Judy and Mary both laughed out loud. Judy reassured him, "No, because we've traveled this trail many times. We're used to the way the big rocks look. They're even larger when you get near Pine Mountain School."

"Well, if you don't mind when we camp at night, I want my back against the rock backdrop. I want to be able to see what might be coming at me."

Mary spoke up, "You don't have to worry about that either. Ma depends on the animals to let us know if anything or anyone is nearby. She trusts them with her life, but she always sleeps with her gun and it's loaded!"

At first it amused Judy that Jim showed fear of what to him was the unknown. It brought back memories of how her girls' father, Robert, had been afraid from cowardice. Jim wasn't acting like a coward. She knew from their Sunday afternoon rides that he always carried a hunting rifle on his saddle. She had never seen him use it, but at least he did own a gun.

The trip into the tall mountains on the Harlan Trail was a pleasure outing for the three travelers. The heavy growth of wilderness that they passed through provided a pristine habitat for every kind of wild game. It was a hunter's paradise.

The lush conditions of the foliage and wild flowers brightened their way and when they stopped for meals, the perfumed air was intoxicating.

The music of song birds was all around them. The wild grape and honeysuckle vines seemed to dance on both sides of the trail and over the mountain sides in wild abandon. Many different shades of pink and snowy white blossoms adorned not just the different wild fruit trees but also the mountain laurel, dogwood, redbud, and the thorny locusts.

Judy smiled in pure pleasure. She lifted her head high and breathed in the rare mountain air. Her heart was about to burst as she recalled the happy days of working her farm, living off the land, and hunting in these mountains that were still full of lovely sights, sounds and aromas.

They arrived at Jonie's well before dark on Friday. When Alex and the family came out on the porch and into the yard to greet the travelers, they welcomed Jim as though he were a long lost relative! In fact, they were so enthusiastic in their greetings that he was so embarrassed he was speechless. Judy grinned. For the first time she saw the oily voiced Jim at a loss for words.

After everyone was introduced and felt at ease, Jim delighted all of them with his honesty. He chuckled good-naturedly, and said, "I hope you all don't expect me to remember who you said you are. It's going to take me a while to match faces with the proper names! Alex, sir, it's a real pleasure to meet you!"

Upon arrival, Judy had climbed up the porch steps to hug and kiss her father's cheek. She noticed that Alex looked almost frail compared to his normally robust constitution. Judy decided it was probably due to the lack of physical exercise since arthritis had crippled his knees and hips.

Jonie and her family all looked well. The house was filled with wonderful smells from the kitchen. Jim took a deep breath and said, "Judy, I see what you mean about wonderful mountain cooking. Just the smells of Jonie's cooking sets my mouth to watering!"

Jonie's face beamed her pleasure from Jim's compliment and she ushered them all into the house to eat supper. Jim wondered how there could be room to seat everyone, but when he saw the long wooden table, he understood. Tonight, Enoch sat at the head of the table, Jonie at the other end, and the rest of the family lined both sides. They barely had elbow room, but they all did fit!

Judy took a moment to drink in the joy she felt at that moment. She was with her father whom she adored. Jonie, and her family were very dear to her heart. Mary was with her tonight and after her graduation on Sunday she would have Della with her in Hazard. Her family had welcomed Jim with open arms and she was now more determined than ever to live the rest of her life with this man. All she had to do was to wait until he asked her to marry him!

Saturday dawned with a beautiful sunrise and white, fleecy clouds in the sky. Judy and Jonie spent most of the day cooking and baking. The front and back doors were open to catch cross breezes to cool off the hot kitchen. After the boys finished their chores, they joined Alex, Enoch, and Jim on the front porch to listen to the men talk. All of the girl cousins were engaged in play with their dolls in a make-believe playhouse in the shade of a big oak tree behind the house.

Every once in a while, Mary and Alta went in the house to offer to help in the kitchen. Mary was anxious to see the cake that was being made for Della's celebration. Her Aunt Jonie loved to make the six-layer applesauce stack-cake, and had one already made in the metal pie safe. Mary watched with some envy as her Ma filled a large oblong pan with yellow cake dough. When the cake was done and cooled, Judy beat egg whites and used a special sugar to make white icing to cover the top. Then she beat a cocoa mixture until it was thick like fudge and spelled Della's name on the cake. Mary approached her mother, "Ma, you've never made such a cake for me. Will you make one for me like that when I graduate from High School?"

"Of course I will, honey. Now I want this cake to be a surprise for Della. You have to promise you'll keep my secret. You mustn't tell her!"

Mary found her smile and promised.

Sunday morning dawned with just a little fog rising up off of Little Greasy Creek. The whole family, except for Alex, Alta, and the youngest girls was ready to leave by eight o'clock. As they mounted their horses, the Miniard's, including Israel, Id, Rhodie, and their two oldest girls, Pauline and Katherine, came to accompany them. Israel said, "We've been waiting for today! Della asked us to come to watch her graduate and we promised her we would. We saw Bish and Sadie last week and told them we were plannin' to go to Della's graduation. They said that some of them might come, too. Said they hadn't seen any of Judy's family for a long time"

They arrived at the school and rode to Laurel House to dismount. Two young boys appeared and took the reins of their horses to lead them to the barn a short distance away. Then, Judy and her family walked up the slight hill and around the bend to the Chapel.

Della and her class mates were gathered in the front yard of the Chapel. They were all dressed alike. Della was a picture of sweetness in her white eyelet dress. There was a large white satin ribbon in her long, curly, black hair. The way it sat on the crown of her head, Judy thought it looked like an angel's halo on her younger daughter. Jim nodded his approval when Judy pointed out which of the girls was Della. Mary didn't say a word.

The graduates lined up and marched by twos into the chapel and down the long, center aisle to stand in a double line facing the congregation. As Della's family entered the front door of the chapel, two younger students, a boy and a girl, handed them mimeographed programs. Judy immediately looked for Della's name. Mary elbowed her mother, and pointed to the Graduation Ceremony Section of the program. In an audible stage whisper, Mary exclaimed, "Ma, I didn't know Della was going to sing. She's listed as the lead singer for two songs. Did you know about this?"

Judy shushed Mary, "Yes, Miss Pettit told me in her letter."

They were seated about half-way down and near the center aisle of the Sanctuary. Judy looked for her sister, Sadie, but didn't see any of the Boggs' family. Somehow, she hadn't really expected them to come. Then she became aware of the Miniard's moving over to let someone sit down and looked back at them. She was pleased to see two of the Boggs boys being seated. There were so many of the brothers it was hard to tell them apart. She guessed the two young men were Art and Freeland.

Miss Petit and Mrs. Zande accompanied the graduating class to the front of the Chapel. After they each took turns welcoming the various families and making complimentary remarks about each individual student, Mrs. Zande introduced Della as their leader in singing the hymn "Fairest Lord Jesus."

Della came forward and stood ramrod straight with her chin lifted high. Her voice was sweet and pure with the mountain twang that was now uniquely hers. She sang the first verse all the way through by herself.

Fairest Lord Jesus, Ruler of all nature,
O thou of God and man the Son,
Thee will I cherish, Thee will I honor,
Thou my soul's glory, joy, and crown.

When she was ready for the second verse, Mrs. Zande signaled for everyone to join her in singing the rest of the hymn.

Fair are the meadows, fairer still the woodlands,
Robed in the blooming garb of spring:
Jesus is fairer, Jesus is purer,
Who makes the woeful heart to sing.

Fair is the sunshine, fairer still the moonlight,
And all the twinkling, starry host:
Jesus shines brighter, Jesus shines purer,
Than all the angels heav'n can boast.

Judy remembered all the words to the old hymn because they sang it often on Sunday mornings and for Vespers at night. She loved this hymn because she thought it told the story of Jesus best. It told of the beauty of the earth in all its natural glory and related it to the Lord Jesus' purity and grace.

Each one of the graduates recited either a poem or a short essay.

They closed the ceremony with Della singing "Once to Every Man and Nation." As she sang the students marched slowly by Miss Pettit who handed them their rolled up and beribboned diplomas. Each of the graduates shook hands with Miss Pettit, turned and flashed a big smile at the audience. Most of them waved to their family and then joined them in the pews.

Judy found it hard to not sing along with Della. This old hymn spoke of character, honesty, love of God, and His constant protective love for his people:

Once to every man and nation comes the moment to decide,
In the strife of truth with falsehood for the good or evil side;
Some great cause, God's new messiah, offering each the bloom or blight,
And the choice goes by forever twix that darkness and that light.

By the light of burning martyrs, Jesus' bleeding feet I track,
Toiling up new Calvaries ever with the cross that turns not back;
New occasions teach new duties, time makes ancient good uncouth;
They must upward still and onward, who would keep abreast of truth.

Though the cause of evil prosper, yet tis truth alone is strong.
Truth forever on the scaffold, wrong forever on the throne.
Yet that scaffold sways the future, and behind the dim unknown.
Standeth God within the shadow keeping watch above his own.

When the last lingering notes were done, Della marched over to Miss Pettit and received her beribboned diploma. She flashed a big smile at the audience and walked toward her large family gathering. Della hesitated just a moment when she saw the strange man seated next to her mother.

Family members moved over to allow Della to sit next to Judy. Filled with both excitement and mixed emotions with the realization that her years at Pine Mountain School were over, Della didn't hear a word that Miss Pettit said in her closing remarks and her heartfelt words of good luck to the graduates.

Then it was over and the students and their families slowly filed out of the Chapel to spill over the grassy, sloping ground. The children and their families clumped together in tight little units. Della's eyes grew huge as she realized that she had the largest delegation of family members. Her attention was drawn to the man seated next to Judy and to the two Boggs brothers. She was too young when she last saw her Bish and Sadie to remember their family.

First, Judy said, "Della, this is my good friend who came with us from Hazard to be here for your graduation. His name is Jim Collins."

Mary, with an almost wicked grin, blurted out, "Della, he's Ma's beau!"

Jim looked uneasy, but Della smiled her sweetest and offered her hand to him. As she took his outstretched hand in hers, she didn't miss the action of her mother elbowing Mary, shushing her.

Then Judy turned toward the two brothers and was embarrassed because she didn't know their names. Israel sensed the reason for her hesitation and skillfully filled in with the introductions. He said, "Della, these are your cousins, Freeland or 'Frillin' and Floyd Boggs, two of Bish and Sadie's boys. I told them about your graduation and I'm so glad they could come."

Della extended her hand and nodded to them, "I'm so pleased to meet you and I thank you for coming today."

Judy restrained herself from hugging the young men. It was more than six years since she had seen Sadie's family. She didn't have to worry. After the introductions, there were hugs all around, including the two Boggs boys.

Jonie extended invitations to everyone to come to her house to share Sunday dinner with them and celebrate Della's Graduation Day. All but the Boggs brothers accepted. They excused themselves, with Freeland saying, "Ma will have dinner waitin' for us, so we'd better be headin' toward home. It's a ways up the trail to Turkey Fork. Cousin Della, we're glad we came today. When you come here from Hazard, do you stay with Aunt Jonie and Uncle Enoch?"

"Yes, we do stay with them. We'll be coming back for Christmas."

"I'll tell Ma and Pa and we hope to see you all then."

After saying goodbye to the two Boggs brothers, Judy asked Della if she wanted to change her dress before they left. She said she did, and asked them to wait for her while she gathered the rest of her belongings. "Mary, will you come with me? Don't you worry, Ma, I'll hurry the fastest that I can!"

As soon as they were out of earshot of the others, Della asked, "When did Ma get a beau? Do you like him? Are they serious about each other?"

"Whoa, slow down!" Mary exclaimed, "How many questions was that?"

Della was impatient with her older sister who was enjoying her role as informant. She was delighted that she knew something so important long before Della had a clue about what was going on with their mother.

Mary said, "They've known each other about six months. I didn't like him at first because I didn't want some man hurting Ma and us again. Yes, Ma's serious. She really likes him and is expecting him to propose to marry her any time now. I like him now for Ma's sake. I want her to be happy."

"What does he do for work? Is he a farmer?"

"No, he's a cook for the boardinghouse in Hazard. They met because he doesn't cook on weekends and comes to Ma's restaurant for Sunday dinner. He and Ma go riding together on Sundays and I go with them sometimes. We always go riding out toward that Cantrell farm where you're going to work. I don't like them. Are you still going to work there?"

"Yes, I gave my word to Miss Pettit that I'd work for them and go to school with you. She talked to me about living according to God's plan for me. I don't rightly understand how she knows about God's plans for people, but she seems to believe this is the right thing for me to do right now."

Mary hugged Della and said, "If they don't treat you right, you tell me or Ma. It's going to be about three months before school starts. That's a long time. They're supposed to bring you to church, but they miss coming themselves most of the time. Ma says we have to pray for them and trust God to watch over us."

Della finished changing into a school outfit and lovingly put away the white, eyelet dress and satin hair-bow. She packed the rest of her belongings in two travel-sacks. Then with a last look around at the room that had been her home for four years, she and Mary hurried to rejoin her mother. Everyone was mounted and waiting. She slung her travel-sacks over the little mare's back and they both climbed up with Mary in the saddle and Della hanging on behind.

Jonie was beaming as she looked around the long dining table that was loaded with mountain cooking and counted seventeen people. Besides herself, Enoch, and Alex, there were Israel, Id, and Rhodie Miniard and two of their girls. There were Judy, Jim Collins, Mary, and Della. Then there were their children, Alta, Clara, Mellie, Dolly, and little Delphia. Their boys, Gib and Otis had volunteered to put up the horses while everyone else ate. Otis laughed, "See, brother, by being last we can eat all we want and no one counts how many seconds we take!"

Shortly after they finished dinner, including a piece of Della's special white-iced cake, the Miniard's departed for home. Judy and her family spent the better part of the afternoon and evening talking about old times, telling favorite stories, singing, and getting better acquainted with Jim Collins.

Alex's face was a puzzle, but his eyes told her he needed to talk with her. She couldn't tell how her father was feeling about Jim. She was determined to talk to him alone before she left the next morning. Alex must have had the same plan! After everyone was asleep, Judy went outside. Alex sat in his rocking chair near the far edge of the porch. Judy picked up a straight, cane-bottomed chair and carried it over next to him. She asked, "Pa, couldn't you sleep, either?"

"No, honey, I hoped you'd come outside to talk about your Mr. Jim."

"Pa, I really like him. I think he likes me, too. He's been nothing but nice to Mary and today he was the same with Della. If he asks me, and I think he will, I intend to marry him. This seems to be a fulfillment of the vision you had of me with a man who would take care of me and my girls. Are you okay with that?"

"My only worry comes from my love for you, honey. I watched him as he looked around at Jonie's and Enoch's home. He spent a long time inside her pantry room. I got the feelin' he was countin' the jars."

Judy laughed, "Pa, he's a cook! It's only natural for him to be interested in any kind of food, including Jonie's cannin' jars."

"No, it was something else. It was a look in his eyes. I can't quite explain it, but it was a look you would see on a wise ol' schemin' fox. Just be careful. Don't give him complete control over your money, your girls, or your life."

"Pa, I expect that he'll work with me at the hotel and in the restaurant if we do get married. Mary is staying on her job with the Brownlett's and Della will be with that Cantrell family that I'm not sure about yet. I thought that if we do set a date, it'll be in the early fall, say September or October."

"Where would you have the weddin'?"

"Probably in Reverend Brownlett's church, there in Hazard."

"Just so long as you watch out for his wantin' to own you and all you have. You know I've lived a long time and know when there's questions 'bout a man's true feelin's when he's tryin' to hide them. Their eyes give them away every time. Pay attention to his eyes and to the messages they send!"

"Pa, I'll remember what you've said tonight. But, you must know that the most important thing is for you to give us your blessing for this marriage?"

"Yes, honey, I do give you my blessing. May God bless you and hold you in His hands. Keep your faith strong. Live 'cording to Jesus' teachin's, and God will lead you in makin' the right decisions for you and your family."

Judy kissed her father lovingly on the cheek, and said, "Pa, I love you with all my heart. Take care of yourself. Let me know if you need anything. Now, we'd both better get to sleep. I need to get an early start in the mornin'!"

It took a while for Judy to drift off to sleep. She mulled over in her mind all that her father had said. It hadn't occurred to her that Jim might be overly possessive of her and the girls. Her last waking thought was, "a little bit of that wasn't such a bad thing. She wanted him to love her, but she would be watchful just as her father had warned."

Saying goodbye to her father and the rest of her family was always hard for Judy. This time it seemed more so. Jim was his usual delightful self and his almost syrupy sweet voice with its Syrian accent pleased Jonie, Enoch, and their children. However, Alex was strangely reserved in bidding his farewell to Jim. Judy was watchful as her father extended his right hand to Jim. When he closed his left over both of their hands she watched to see if his lips moved. They didn't! She turned away to hide her smile of relief. To her, this was proof that Alex had accepted Jim at face value.

Elihu (Hugh) Boggs - father of Bish Boggs

Bish Boggs and five sons - (front) Alex, Bish, Art - (back) Hugh, Jim, Floyd

Chapter Eleven
THE CANTRELLS

Della was tearful for the first mile or so as she left Pine Mountain School and the comfortable life she had known for so long. She was leaving all that was familiar with sadness, but she was able to replace those feelings with the anticipation of living in Hazard. She and Mary kept up a lively conversation about work, school, clothes, and boys!

The trip to Hazard by horseback on the rugged mountain trail was a memorable one. It was the end of May and springtime warm during the day, but cold at night. The heavy foliage was of every shade of green, and the fresh air was fragrant with sweet wild blossoms and pungent pine.

In Hazard, they first dropped Mary off at the Brownlett's. When they reached Main Street, Jim said goodbye and left them to go to the boardinghouse. Della and Judy were finally alone. At the hotel they placed the travel-sacks on the front porch. Della stayed on the porch while Judy went to the livery. As they moved everything upstairs to their bedroom, Della was full of questions about Jim and her intentions as far as marriage was concerned. Judy tried to reassure her, "Della, honey, before I make any decisions that affect us as a family, I'll listen to all you and Mary have to say about it."

Then for the first time, Della showed her anxiety about the work-study job on the Cantrell family farm. "Ma, will I see you every week? I want to spend Sundays with you, but will Mr. Collins always be with us when we're together? What if I need to talk to you, but can't because he's there. How will I be able to be alone with you?"

"Honey, that's easy to answer. Yes. We'll spend our Sundays together. If you need to talk to me alone, just ask me to come up to my room with you. We will then be alone in my hotel room and you can tell me anything you want. How do you feel about that?"

"That'll work out fine. I'm so afraid I won't be able to get along in my job with the Cantrells like Mary does with the Brownlett's. I want you to believe in me. I'll always do my best to please them. Ma, if it doesn't work out for me it won't be my fault. What will I do if it doesn't work out? Will I be able to live with you? What if you marry Mr. Collins, will I still be able to live with you? Would he let me live with you?"

Judy was shocked at how insecure Della was feeling. She did her best to reassure her. "Honey, I know you'll do your best. You always do! If it doesn't work out for whatever reason, of course you'll live with me at the hotel. No one has to give me permission to take care of you. You're my daughter. I love you and Mary more than anything else in the world. No man will ever change that! Now, stop worrying. You only have a few days left to be with me afore you're to go to the Cantrell's. Let's make the best of them!"

Della smiled through welling tears. She hugged her mother so tightly that Judy cried, "Hey, honey, I can't breathe!

They both laughed as they made their last trip to move the packing-sacks to the upstairs bedroom. They greeted Mr. Jenkins. He had waved to them as they carried in their travel-sacks, Then he came from out behind the front desk to give each a hug. He said, "Judy, honey, Myrt had something go wrong with her heart while you were gone. She's better now, but is in bed. Sylvia has been watching over her and taking a tray to her room three times a day. Each time she does, she stays and makes sure Myrt's eating. The doctor says it's just her age, but that she can get better with bed rest. As soon as you're settled, go to see her."

Judy exclaimed, "No, Bill, I'll go to see her right now! Della, do you want to come with me?"

"Yes, I want to see Myrt. She's my friend, too!"

It was a shock to see Myrt lying so listless in bed. However, she brightened immediately upon seeing Judy and Della. "Oh, the Good Lord will love you both! Hey, I'll get well for sure with you here with me. Oh, Lordy! Oh, how I missed you, Judy, honey! Dellie, you look beautiful!"

Della grinned in spite of herself. No one had called her Dellie before Myrt started calling her that. She decided she liked it. She leaned over the bed to hug Myrt and kiss her cheek. Judy did likewise, but continued to sit on the bed, holding and caressing the older woman's hand.

Myrt said, "You've just got here from two long days on the trail. Now you go get settled in. After you eat supper have Sylvia give you my tray and both of you come and stay with me while I eat. Okay? I want to hear all about Jim meetin' your family and Dellie's graduation!"

The next three days were pleasant and passed all too quickly. Della helped her mother in the kitchen preparing meals. She also helped Sylvia clear tables and wash dishes. Sylvia joked, "Della, honey, if that other job doesn't work out, we'll see about you getting a permanent one right here with us!"

On Friday, June 1, 1923, riding double on Curly, Judy took Della out to the Cantrell farm. When they arrived, Sarah Cantrell didn't make an appearance. Harvey Cantrell came from out of the barn. He had a scowl on his face. "I expected this girl yesterday. The first day of the month is already half gone. If I'm gonna feed her and pay her for a full month, she'll owe me a full month."

With a nod of his head in Judy's direction, he dismissed her as though she had already left. He fixed his gaze on Della, saying, "I fixed up a room for you in the hayloft of the barn. It's all ready. Get your stuff off the horse and come on with me."

Judy turned in the saddle while dancing Curly sideways away from Harvey Cantrell so she could whisper to Della. "You don't have to stay. I don't like it. Say the word. I'll take you back to the hotel. What do you want to do?"

Della whispered back, "Ma, I'll stay for now. Sleeping in the barn gets me away from him and his family. Let me try it for a month."

Then louder so Harvey could hear, she said, "Come and get me on Sunday like you promised."

Harvey Cantrell turned his attention back to Judy. "No, she owes me a day for comin' so late this mornin'. There'll be no Sunday off this week."

Judy's eyes narrowed as she looked at the rude man in disgust. Della poked her mother in the back, "Ma, its okay. It'll give me more time to get settled in and learn what all he wants me to do. Now you'd better leave. I'll be as good at this as Mary is. You'll see!"

Harvey didn't have a clue as to how dangerous Judy was when she was angry, and she was more than angry at the moment. Reluctantly she gave in to her daughter's pleading. After Della slid off of Curly, Judy handed down two packing sacks to her

Della looked questioningly at her mother. Then she understood why Judy had kept back two of the cloth bags. One contained her new white eyelet graduation dress, silk petticoat, and satin bow. The second one held her better shoes, the trinket box containing her money, and other prized possessions. Della nodded, and said. "Its okay, Ma, I'll see you a week from Sunday!"

Judy kept looking back as she rode away from the Cantrell farm. Della and Harvey Cantrell had disappeared inside the large barn. She was mentally beating herself up for allowing Della to stay with the rude man. And where was Mrs. Cantrell? The fact that she wasn't anywhere to be seen gave Judy even more cause to worry about her daughter.

Judy was grumbling under her breath, "Della wants me to give her a month to prove she's as good a worker as Mary. Being with that family's got nothing to do with how good a worker she is. Nothin' is going to please or be good enough to suit him. I doubt he ever intended to pay her a penny! Well, I'm only goin' to give her a week from Sunday to try to make this placement work. Mr. Harvey Cantrell better watch out how he treats my Della!"

Della glanced backwards and saw her Mother's face as she rode away. She started to wave, but thought better of it. With her face set in a rock hard look of determination, Della followed Harvey inside the huge barn and liked what she saw. It was well kept and very clean. There were cows, horses, goats, and sheep in separate stalls or pens. Chickens of all kinds and colors roamed freely over the floor of the large barn. She looked and didn't see a hen house. There were ducks, geese, and turkeys scratching for food outside of the building.

Della asked, "Mr. Cantrell, I don't see a hen house. Where do the chickens roost at night and lay their eggs?"

"I don't have time to answer a lot of questions from you. Just be quiet and listen. You'll learn all you need to know!"

Della bit her tongue to keep from giving him a retort in return.

He pointed up a short ladder to one of the four different hay lofts. "Your bed is up there. There's a wood box for you to keep your stuff put up. Wear your oldest clothes to work in. This is a workin' farm and only my girls will ever be dressed up on a week-day. The boys are older and do all the heavy work.

After you put away your stuff, come on into the house and my wife will tell you what she wants you to do. After that, I'll show you what you're to do outside. The one thing I won't tolerate is dawdlin' time away or talkin' out of turn to me. I want the work done my way and no questions are allowed. Do you understand me so far?"

"Yes sir, Mr. Cantrell, I understand. I'll come in the house in just a few minutes. Please tell Mrs. Cantrell that I'll be right there."

Harvey finally got a pleasant look on his surly face. "Well, at least you have some manners and are showing' good sense!"

He turned and walked quickly to the back of the farm house and banged shut the heavy, home-made screen door behind him.

Della waited until Harvey disappeared inside. She climbed the short ladder to see for the first time the space that was to be all hers. Two big bales of hay were pushed together to form a bed. They had a faded feed-sack quilt thrown over them. Another folded-up quilt was placed at the foot of the makeshift bed. There was an open wooden box to one side of the room. "So this is what he meant for me to use to put my clothes in. There's no way to keep spiders and bugs out of my things. I'll find something later to use as a lid."

There was a chipped and cracked ceramic pitcher and a bowl for her to use to wash her face and hands. On the wall by an open window she saw a water dipper hanging by its long handle from a large nail. On the floor under the dipper was an empty, galvanized water bucket.

For the first time, Della grumbled under her breath, "I'm always hungry and there's no place to keep or save any food away from the mice or bugs. I've got a feeling that he's going to watch every bite I take. I can't abide being hungry all the time. I'll find a way to hide stuff that I can eat late at night."

The back door to the house banged shut. She hurried down the short ladder and ran out of the open barn door. Harvey was walking fast toward her with a deep scowl on his face. When he saw Della running toward him, he stopped and scolded, "I told you I won't tolerate dawdlin' time away. You've already lost a good half a day of work-time. Get in the house now. Mrs. Cantrell is waitin' for you!"

The fact that the surly man didn't call his wife by her given name wasn't lost on Della. As she hurried into the house, she silently prayed, "Dear Lord, what have I gotten myself into with this family? Please help me through this day and the coming week. I promise you that I'll do the best I can to please everyone. Lead me in Thy ways and keep me safe. Amen."

When Della stepped through the doorway, she found that it was an enclosed back porch. It took only a quick moment for her to absorb what she was seeing. The space was used for a clothes washroom. Two galvanized washtubs stood ready to be filled with water on heavy, wooden benches. A wider than normal and much-used washboard for scrubbing clothes was hanging on the wall above one of the tubs. There was a large three-legged kettle for boiling clothes by the other wall. It was made of copper and the inside was shiny clean, but the outside of it was blackened with soot from hanging over an open fire. A shelf attached to the wall held yellow, home-made lye soap for the wash water and a box of store-bought bluing for use in the rinse water.

Just as quickly, she thought, "This is Friday. It's not a wash day. It's going to be either cleaning or baking for the weekend."

When she stepped into the large farm kitchen, her mouth instantly watered from the fragrant cooking aromas. It took her eyes a moment to adjust from the outside light to the dim interior. There was a large wood-burning stove that had a reservoir for keeping water hot or warm all the time. A warming closet above the stove kept prepared food warm until eaten.

There were built-in cabinets with doors on them. They had them in Pine Mountain School's kitchen, but she had never seen any in a family home before. Three large covered barrels stood against the far wall. She guessed that flour, sugar, and corn meal were stored in them.

A long dining table with benches and a few chairs took up most of the middle of the kitchen. Counting her, there were seven people to make room for and there was plenty of it around this table. She knew it was close to noon now and her stomach was already growling, wanting food.

Sarah Cantrell stepped through the doorway from the large farm pantry room that was next to the kitchen. She wasn't smiling when she said, "Mr. Cantrell was just now tellin' me that you are prone to dawdlin' time away. You took too long putting your clothes into a box and coming to the house to begin your chores. We won't have you wastin' any time. When I tell you to do something, it must be done as fast as you can or Mr. Cantrell will be very angry and you will be punished. Do you understand me?"

Della swallowed hard, and said in a strained, frightened voice, "Yes Ma'am, Mrs. Cantrell."

"Good!"

The woman turned and walked toward the room she had just left and motioned for Della to follow her. There were some filled canning jars on the floor, a bench for standing on to reach the top shelves, and a cleaning cloth.

"I want you to dust all the jars and shelves in this room. Keep like vegetables together. Be careful to not break anything. It takes a lot of hard work to put up all the food our family needs each harvest time. I'm gettin' this room ready for this year's cannin', dryin', and storin'."

"Will anyone be helping me?"

"No. This is your work. Mr. Cantrell won't allow any questions. If you want to eat today, get busy."

Della pressed her lips together in a firm line. She gave no response to the cruel-sounding woman. It was a large room, but she thought she could do the dusting in record time. The one thing that Della knew she was good at was working fast and she was always careful.

She began making her imaginary cake by dividing the shelves of canned food into layers. There were three walls of shelves that reached from the floor to just below the ceiling. Each wall would be two layers of her cake. She grinned and thought, "When I get this done, I'll imagine that I've made one of Aunt Jonie's applesauce stack-cakes."

As she worked, she softly hummed one of her favorite old English folk songs, "John Riley." She started at the bottom of the wall of shelves. After carefully placing all the glass canning jars of food on the wooden floor, she wiped the shelf clean. Then one at a time, she dusted the jars and placed them back in order on the shelf. Della repeated this routine with each shelf until she completed five of the shelves. Then it became too hard to lift each jar higher than her head. She left a shelf of jars on the floor and cleaned by standing on the bench and moving the jars down to the empty shelf. She did this for the last three shelves and then it was simple to dust the jars and move them up one shelf at a time. With one wall done, Della gave a big sigh of satisfaction, saying out loud, "Two layers of my cake are done. I wonder when Mrs. Cantrell is going to cook dinner. I'm starving!'

Della gave herself a break to find a drink of water, the outhouse, and a clock. She wanted to find out what time it was. It seemed like it had to be early afternoon. She walked through the kitchen and out to the clothes washroom to find the water bucket with a long-handled dipper in it. She drank greedily. After her second dipper full, she replaced it on the wall.

She walked back into the kitchen and found no clock there. Then she walked to the door of the formal parlor and saw a mantel clock. It was almost three o'clock. No wonder she was hungry! She turned around to go back into the kitchen. She needed to find the outhouse. Then she came face to face with Harvey Cantrell. Della jumped in alarm in spite of herself. This man scared her.

"What're you doing in here? You're not to leave your job 'til it's done."

"I'm sorry Mr. Cantrell. I was thirsty and got a drink. Now I'm going outside to the outhouse if you will kindly tell me where it is."

"I'll show you where it's at. It's back behind the barn where the pig pens are. Now you show me how much cleanin' you've got done. I told you I won't tolerate any dawdlin' to waste time!"

She walked across the kitchen to the pantry room and stood silently while he inspected the first wall of shelves. "This is fine. You should be done by suppertime."

Della was shocked. "Did I miss dinner?"

"No. We don't eat dinner. This is a workin' farm and we eat two meals a day. Breakfast at seven o'clock after the mornin' chores are done. Supper is at seven o'clock at night, before the evening chores are done. We don't have time to be cookin' and cleanin' up three times a day! Don't worry, you'll get used to it."

"Don't bother about showing me where the outhouse is, I'll find it if it's beside the pig pens. I'll hurry back so I can finish the pantry cleanin'. Where's Mrs. Cantrell? Where are your girls and boys?"

"They took the wagon into Hazard to do some store shoppin' and to get a load of seed and feed. They'll be home soon."

"Thank you, Mr. Cantrell."

She left him standing in the back door watching her make her way around the big barn. It was obvious she was getting close to the pig pens from the smells. The outhouse was a "three holer." It was clean inside. She was happy that the use of lime was adequate to mask the odors.

This was the first time Harvey Cantrell had spoken civilly to her. Maybe there was hope for this job after all! His revelation that they only ate twice a day, twelve hours apart was appalling to a growing girl. She grumbled to herself, "I'll bet you money his children snack during the day. I bet they're all eating in town. It's not natural to work like this and not eat three times a day!"

Della was almost done with the third wall, when she heard doors slam and footsteps coming through the house. First to come near her were the two girls. She remembered their names were Winnie and Lacey, but she didn't know which was which. They were both older than her. She smiled at them and said, "Hello." They just stood there in the doorway and stared at her. Then without saying a word, they lifted their noses high in the air and turned away.

Next to come near her was the oldest boy, Harvey, Jr., the 19 year old. She smiled at him and said, "Hello." He gave her a sloppy salute, grunted something and left.

The last of the children finally came to the doorway. He was Jimmy, 17 years old. Again, she smiled and said, "Hello." Jimmy responded with a smile and asked,

"How are you doin'? It looks like you've got a lot done today. Your name is Della, ain't it? I'm glad you're here!"

Della responded to the kindness in his voice. "Thank you, Jimmy."

It had been at least two hours since Della had hummed as she worked. It was hard to work while her stomach complained because it was empty. Finally she heard food-preparation noises coming from the kitchen. Pots and pans were being placed on the stove. She heard an armload of chopped firewood drop into the large wood box. Then she smelled potatoes frying along with cured ham.

She finished the last shelf of jars and sat down on the bench to rest a minute and to look at all she had done. It would have been a major job for a grown up. Della had just turned thirteen in April. She picked up the soiled dust cloth and got to her feet just as Sarah Cantrell came into the pantry.

"Well," she said, "It took you all day, didn't it. You'll have to learn to work faster if we're going to get all the work done around here. Go on out and wash up. I've got some work for you to do in the kitchen until supper's ready. We'll eat at seven o'clock. It's almost six o'clock now, so you have another hour. After we eat there'll be chores to do 'til dark. I'll let you know what yours are after we have supper and the kitchen's cleaned up. Run along now. Remember no dawdlin'!"

Della was tired of hearing that word. She silently turned and walked out the back door. Against the back of the house was another bench with a large galvanized pan and a bucket of cold water. She emptied the pan and poured in some fresh water. She didn't see anything to use for a wash rag or a towel. Picking up the sliver of yellow, homemade lye soap she lathered up her hands and with her eyes closed tightly, rubbed her face with it. Then she splashed water on her face to get the soap off. She reached down and turned her long skirt over to the underside and rubbed her eyes dry before she opened them.

Della talked to herself, "Well, that's not such a bad idea. I'll just dry my face and hands on my underskirt. I'll have to take a small piece of soap with me when I go to bed tonight, but thank goodness I do have some of my own towels in my box in the barn!"

When she went back in the kitchen, Mrs. Cantrell motioned for her to sit down at the long table. "I want you to help me get ready for the morrow. I've put together a good mess of shucky beans to soak overnight. I want you to take them off the strings, look 'em, break 'em up, and wash 'em. Then put water over top of 'em and cover 'em. We'll set the pot on the back of the stove. They'll be ready to cook for tomorrow's supper. You do know how to do all that don't you?"

"Yes Ma'am, Mrs. Cantrell."

It was a welcome chore. At least she could do it sitting down. It was all she could do to keep from yawning and to keep her eyes open. She silently prayed, "Dear Lord, help me to get through this day. I'm so hungry and sleepy I can't help closing my eyes. If I do, I'll get in big trouble. Please, give my mind something to do so I'll stay awake!"

Jimmy came in the back door stomping his feet. The noise jarred her sleepiness away. She was wide awake. His mother asked, "Did you get everything done? Did you remember to feed the goats? You're inside awful early! Supper will be ready in about a half-an-hour."

"Yeah, Ma, I fed the goats. I got all my chores done. Maybe I could help Della finish these beans. Do you mind if I do that?"

"Yeah, if you really want to help her, you can. She looks like she's about to go to sleep sittin' up. If she does, she won't get any supper!"

Jimmy laughed good-naturedly, "Della, Ma ain't as fierce as she sounds. You have to get to know her. She works hard, too. Really too hard! So just relax while you break up the beans. If you don't watch what you're doing you can cut your fingers on the hard, bean-shells. With me helpin' you, we'll get them in the soakin' pot in plenty of time for supper!"

Della's shining eyes reflected her gratitude to the young man. As long as they were all mean to her, she was okay. She could handle that, but the minute someone was nice to her she was close to tears.

She kept her head down so he couldn't see her welling eyes and concentrated on breaking and looking through the dried beans. The two of them made quick work of the job and they both grinned as Jimmy put the lid on the big pot and shoved it to the back of the stove, under the warming closet.

Della heard the front door slam and stomping feet as the two girls came in complaining that they were starved. Their mother asked, "Did you feed the chickens like I asked you to? You know they won't lay good if they ain't fed regular, mornin' and night. We need eggs for us to eat and to sell on Saturday at the Farmers' Market!"

One of the girls answered her mother, "Yeah, Ma, we hear you. We fed 'em! Lacey just dumped out two big piles of corn instead of scatterin' it like you told her. Tell her again. Make her do it right!"

Della's eyes grew huge. She wondered how come the girls got away with talking back to their mother. The girl that spoke up to complain about her sister had to be Winnie. The other one who was too lazy to scatter the chicken feed was Lacey. Now she knew who was who!

Mr. Cantrell and Harvey, Jr. came in the back door together. They all began to sit down at the long table at the same time. Della waited to see where they wanted her to sit. Mr. Cantrell was at the head of the table, and his wife was at the opposite end. The two girls sat opposite each other, one on each side of their father. The boys sat opposite each other, too. Della was relieved when Jimmy motioned for her to sit next to him.

They didn't say a blessing for the food, but began to pass the bowls around the table. They were filling their plates with fried ham and potatoes; two kinds of baked bread, a biscuit pone and cornbread. Mrs. Cantrell had warmed up leftover home-canned green beans seasoned with salted pork fatback.

By the time the bowls of food got to Jimmy and then to her, there wasn't much left. Under the watchful eye of his father, Jimmy cut the last piece of ham in two and shared it with her. She had just enough potatoes, green beans, and cornbread. The food tasted heavenly.

Then she noticed that there wasn't anything on the table to drink. She was accustomed to having a water glass by her plate. It wasn't hard to figure out that they didn't drink with the meal so there wouldn't be any glasses to wash. "Well," Della talked silently to herself, "That's all right. I'll get myself a good drink after supper!"

There wasn't anything that could be called a dessert. As soon as they finished eating everyone scraped their chairs back and got up from the table. The men folks went out the back door. Winnie and Lacey went out the front door. Mrs. Cantrell and Della looked at each other and both grinned in spite of themselves. "I guess you and me will do the dishes and tidy up the kitchen. Della, you clear the table while I get the warm water ready to wash the dishes. You can begin to wash the dishes while I put the food away and get scraps ready for Jimmy to slop the hogs."

Della was an expert at clearing tables and doing dishes. That had been one of her often-recurring assigned-jobs at Pine Mountain School. Sarah Cantrell brought a large aluminum bucket into the kitchen to use for the food scraps.

"I'm heatin' up a kettle of corn meal mush to add to the scrap bucket for the hogs. We've found that's the best way to fatten a hog. They can eat their weight in the stuff!"

They made quick work of cleaning the kitchen. Sarah laid the fire in the big cook stove so that all she had to do was light a match to start cooking breakfast. She put oats in a kettle ready for water to be added. Then Della watched as Sarah put coffee in the top and water in the bottom of the coffee pot. She said, "Della, I've got enough bread made for breakfast. We have to get an early start for the Farmers' Market in the mornin', so we'll have some more of the ham along with eggs and gravy. That won't take too long. On Sundays, I usually fix our homemade sausage and hotcakes for everyone."

"What time do you want me to get up in the morning?"

"You should be up, dressed, and ready to work by six. It's daylight early, so you'll hear the rooster crow, tellin' you to get up, if you ain't up already. Then you come on over to the kitchen to help me get breakfast ready."

"Yes Ma'am, Mrs. Cantrell."

When she went out the back door and started for the barn, she saw Mr. Cantrell coming from the directions of the pig pens. She looked up and saw that the sun was low in the sky, ready to drop behind the mountain. It was beginning to get dark. Harvey Cantrell called to her, "Della, take a lantern off the back porch and some matches from the kitchen. You'll need a light when you go to the barn. Just be sure you blow it out before you go to bed."

"Yes Sir, Mr. Cantrell."

She waited to be told if she had anything more to do that night. Thankfully, everyone left her alone. She took some matches from the kitchen and picked up one of the lanterns off the back porch. She checked it to make sure it had coal oil in it. She was satisfied that she would be all right now and slowly walked to the barn. She climbed up the short ladder and lit the lantern. She picked up the empty water bucket and made a quick trip to the well. Then she sat by the small window to watch the stars as they began to peep out one at a time. When it became fully dark, she blew out the lantern and got ready for bed.

Della's prayers were short on this first night at the Cantrell's. She felt as if she had been praying all day. Still gazing out her window at the lovely night sky, she talked to God, "Thank you dear God for listening to me today. I know I wouldn't have been able to last through this first day without your help. Please speak to the hearts of Sarah and Harvey Cantrell. They showed me they can be civil. Something evil must have happened to them to make them sound so mean to people. Help them to learn how to soften their hearts toward others. Keep me safe and help me through tomorrow. Bless Ma, Mary, Aunt Jonie, Uncle Enoch, and all of my family and friends in the Pine Mountains. Amen."

Judy had worried about Della all day and now that it was night, she told Myrt, "Well, I guess she has made it through this first day. If it had been too bad for her, she would have walked all the way to the hotel. Jim and I will ride out that way on Sunday and check on her."

Myrt was already in bed and obviously very sleepy. The doctor gave her some medicine that did that to her. Judy wanted to sit with her each night until she did go to sleep. Myrt protested that she didn't need to do that but Judy knew that she was secretly happy to have the company. She was worried about her dear friend. In less than a week, Myrt's health had failed to the point that she was severely weakened and very pale.

Mr. Jenkins volunteered to sit with Myrt part of the time. Sylvia took turns with Judy. The only time she was alone in her room was from about midnight until four in the morning.

Between worrying about Myrt's illness and Della's beginning the new job, Judy was stressed almost to the breaking point. She knew she wouldn't see Jim again until Sunday. After she said her prayers and climbed in between the cool, white sheets, she turned her thoughts to Jim, and began planning their Sunday together. The next thing she knew the alarm clock was sounding off.

Della was wide awake at first light. She guessed it was about six o'clock. She was fully dressed before the rooster crowed. She left the lantern safely hanging on a nail and hurriedly walked to the house. When she opened the back door, she found Sarah already preparing the large farm breakfast. She asked Della to peel and slice the home-grown potatoes and fry them in the large cast iron skillet that was getting hot on the stove.

Della made sure she ate a good breakfast now that she knew it would be twelve hours before she would eat again. Harvey and the boys loaded the wagon with surplus produce, and even included some of the filled jars from the pantry.

The Farmers' Market was already busy with customers who were there early so they could make their purchases before the produce was picked over. This was the first time Della had experienced being a part of such an exciting event. It was better than Fair Day at Pine Mountain School. She couldn't wait to tell Ma and Mary about it.

There was only one thing that marred the fun of Farmers' Market for Della. The two Cantrell sisters did not hide the fact they thought they were much better than "the mountain girl." When they were alone with her and out of earshot of the rest of the family, they made a point of calling her that.

She decided she would ignore them.

Sunday morning began very pleasantly. While Harvey and the boys took care of the outside morning chores, she helped Sarah prepare the sausage and pancake breakfast. She placed two full bowls of sweet creamery butter on the table along with a big glass pitcher of warm maple syrup.

When they all gathered at the table Lacey began to whine to her father that the hired-help shouldn't eat with the family. She talked about Della as if she wasn't there. "The mountain girl is hired-help ain't she? Why's she eatin' with us? If she was hired-help for a town family, she wouldn't eat at their table. Our friends say it ain't fittin' to eat with the hired-help!"

Harvey and Sarah looked at Della and frowned. Then Sarah asked, "Della, would you mind waitin' until we've finished breakfast and then you can eat at the table alone. After you eat you can help me clean up. Please leave the table now. You can wait out back until I call you."

Della swallowed the large lump in her throat and with eyes welling with tears, said, "Yes Ma'am, Mrs. Cantrell."

It seemed like an hour had passed before she was called to come back into the kitchen.

She looked at the table and saw that all of the sausage was gone. Sarah was making extra pancakes because the family ate all she prepared earlier. Mrs. Cantrell saw the look of dismay on Della's face and became angry. She was scolding as she said, "Lacey and Winnie are right. You have no business expectin' us to treat you the same as family. From now on you'll wait and be satisfied with whatever's left. Eat your pancakes while they're hot. I'm goin' out to the barn to check on something. When you finish eatin', clear the table and start the dishes. I'll be right back."

As the back door banged behind her, Jimmy stuck his head around the corner from the parlor. In a stage whisper, he said, "Della, I left you a piece of sausage in the warming closet. Hurry up and eat it before Ma gets back!"

"Thank you, Jimmy. I'm beholding to you!"

Sarah was mumbling to herself, "The nerve of that mountain girl thinkin' she's better than us! Nobody can say that my girls have to take a back seat to anyone. Well, we'll just see."

The angry woman climbed the short ladder and stepped into Della's room in the hay loft. She carefully lifted out all of her Della's clothing and examined each garment. Then she placed each item back in the box hoping it was just like it was before. Della didn't seem to have any money. She grumbled to herself, "Maybe she keeps her money under her clothes. Why would she tell my girls she has more money than they do? Their father will decide if they need more spendin' money. I'll have to watch what our mountain girl spends."

Della finished eating breakfast and was almost through with the dishes by the time Sarah banged the back door behind her. Sarah had begun to like Della until her daughters poisoned her mind with their lies. Now, she was scheming on her own to cause their "hired help" pain and discomfort.

Della had dried the last of the dishes, when Sarah turned to her and said, "Well, that took you long enough! Today's Sunday, but don't think 'bout goin' to church. You owe us a full day for bein' late last Friday. Now, tomorrow's washday. I want you to lay the fire under the big copper kettle so it's ready to light in the morning. Then carry water from the well and fill the kettle a little over half full. Tie a piece of cheesecloth over the top to keep bugs and leaves out of the water. Then, carry water and fill the rinsing tub on the back porch about two-thirds full. Fill up the reservoir in the cook stove so we'll have hot water for the wash tub. You do understand what I want you to do, don't you?"

"Yes Ma'am, Mrs. Cantrell."

Della was drawing the tenth load of water when she overheard Harvey, Jr., ask his mother, "Why's the girl drawing and packing tomorrow's wash water? You know Pa gave me and Jimmy that job. I think it's too heavy a job for a girl younger than our sisters. You'd never ask them to do that!"

"You just mind your own business, Harvey Jr., our little mountain-help was braggin' to your sisters that she's better than they are."

"Ma, do you really believe that? I've watched her. She works hard and is trying to please you and Pa. My sisters are lyin' to you because they're jealous!"

That business at the breakfast table was a rotten thing for them to do about Della eatin' with us. They're my sisters, but they made me ashamed of them!"

"Are you saying your Pa and I did the wrong thing in askin' Della to wait outside and eat later?"

"That's exactly what I'm saying. You let those spoiled girls get away with murder! If they were to do a real day's work like you expect from a thirteen year old, it'd kill 'em! I know Della would never say it, but, yeah, your little, mountain hired-help is head and shoulders better than our Lacey and Winnie!"

The young man's father came up behind him and heard almost all that he said about his sisters. "Well, that beats it all! I'm hearin' my son turnin' 'gainst his own flesh and blood to side with the hired-help. I wouldn't have agreed to have her here if I'd known it was goin' to cause a split in my family over how she's treated."

"Then treat her fair and don't believe everything my sisters say. In your heart you know they're lying about Della."

"I don't know any such thing!"

"Then ask them when she said it? Then ask Della if she said it. I've never seen them even speak to her. They think they're too good! If you know what's good for you and this family, you'll get to the bottom of this right now before Lacey and Winnie get us all in trouble for mistreating a nice young girl."

Harvey's face was beet red. He yelled at his oldest son, "If you have such a low regard for your family, you can just leave!"

The young man's face paled and his eyes grew huge. "Pa, I hadn't decided about leavin' afore this, but now I have. You decided it for me. I'll be gone afore the end of the week. I have a good job for the askin' and a place to stay. You and Ma won't have to worry 'bout me. Take my advice and put my two lazy sisters to work!"

Della stood still. She was holding a bucket of water ready to pour it into the rinsing tub, She had no choice but to listen, She didn't know that Harvey, Jr., even knew she was alive and here he was taking up for her.

She was panic stricken as she silently prayed, "Dear Jesus, I need your help. How shall I act when I come face to face with any of the Cantrell family now that I know those two girls have lied about me and their folks believed them? Lord, like his older brother, I feel sure that Jimmy didn't believe them either. He left me the piece of sausage so I wouldn't be too hungry all day. Ma is coming out here today to check on me. What am I going to tell her? Help me to act like everything's fine. I can't give up on this job after just three days."

Della finished pouring the bucket of water into the tub and walked back to the well to draw another load. She watched silently as Harvey Cantrell and his oldest son walked to the barn together. It was plain to see from their body language that they were both terribly angry. She turned toward the house and saw

Sarah Cantrell watching her. It took all of her will power to smile at the hateful woman. But she did it! Sarah turned angrily and went back into the house.

Della guessed that it was close to noon when she finished the first major chore. All the wash water was drawn and ready in the big copper kettle, the rinsing tub, and the reservoir on the stove.

She put the water bucket under the outside bench and went in the house to find Sarah to ask what she should do next. A big pile of dirty clothes were in the middle of the washroom floor. Sarah called to her from the kitchen. "Don't just stand there! Separate the clothes; the whites from the colors; the work clothes from the dress-up. After you empty the pockets, examine each garment to see if it needs mending. If it does, put it in a separate pile. We don't sew a stitch on Sunday, but you'll mend everything in the morning afore we start the wash."

"Yes Ma'am, Mrs. Cantrell."

Della finished separating the dirty clothes and made neat piles of each bunch in the washroom and stepped outside to look at the sky. From the position of the sun, she guessed it was about two o'clock.. She was tired now and thirsty. As she stepped over to the water bucket to get a drink, she saw her mother and the man, Jim, riding into the barnyard. Mary wasn't with them.

She didn't know what to do! If she ran to meet them, she could get into trouble with the Cantrells, but if she didn't, her mother would know something was bad wrong. Della decided she would walk slowly out to meet them. Judy dismounted and walked quickly to her daughter and hugged her. Della didn't have to say anything. Judy could tell immediately that something was bad wrong. She didn't mince words, but asked her, "I can tell this isn't going to work for you. Do you want to get your clothes and come with us now?"

"No, Ma, I still want to stay the week at least. Except for their sons, they're meaner than any people I've ever met besides the Heltons. Next Sunday come and get me to stay the day with you. I can't face the Brownlett's and let Mary know I can't make a job work out like she did. I just can't!

Sarah saw Judy and Jim riding in, and deliberately stayed in the house. Harvey came out of the barn, but Harvey, Jr. stayed in the doorway to watch. Jim was a stranger. Harvey reached up and offered to shake hands. To Judy he gave a little nod, but no smile and no greeting.

To Della he scolded, you've got work to do, say goodbye and get back in the house. She answered him dutifully, "Yes, sir, Mr. Cantrell."

Then she turned back to her mother, "Ma, come for me early next Sunday so I can go to church with you, Mary and the Reverend Brownlett's! I've got to go now."

"Della, honey, we'll be here Sunday about eight o'clock. You be ready!"

Judy was seething inside as she turned to face Harvey with narrowed eyes. For Della's sake she didn't rake him over hot coals, but she was sorely tempted.

Today, she didn't touch him. However, Jim spoke up on Della's behalf. In his oily tongue and with a slight accent, he looked into Harvey's eyes and said, "You know Della just turned thirteen in April. I went to her graduation at the Pine Mountain Settlement School. She was honored there for her school work and for working her way through boarding school. You're lucky to have such a hard-working young lady placed with you. But, treat her fairly!"

Jim was smiling as he talked, but there was an obvious warning in his tone and in his eyes. Judy remounted Curly, nodded to Harvey, and led the way out of the barnyard.

With Harvey, Jr. trailing behind him, Harvey walked quickly to the house. Just inside the kitchen he caught up with Della and roughly grabbed her by the arm, "Girl, what did you tell them? Who is that man? What's Reverend Brownlett's girl, Mary, to you?"

Della pulled away from the angry man and backed up against the wall with both hands tight against it to brace herself. She was near the cook stove and Harvey saw her eying the long, black poker that was near her outstretched hand. He wasn't a total fool. This girl was ready to defend herself. He calmed his face, and asked his questions again.

Della, I'm not goin' to hurt you. Just tell me who the man is, and how do you come to know Brownlett's older daughter?

She still didn't trust this man to not harm her physically. She answered in a strained voice, "His name's Jim Collins. He and my mother are expecting to be married soon. You met Mary before. She isn't Reverend Brownlett's daughter, she's my older sister. She's workin' for him just like I'm workin' for you!"

"Nobody told me you had all of these relatives here in Hazard. What does your mother do? Where does this Jim Collins work?"

"My mother manages the Hazard Hotel Restaurant. Mr. Collins is the cook and handyman for the Hazard boardinghouse."

"Well, you take a breather now. Go to your room in the barn. We'll come and get you when it's time to cook supper."

Harvey Jr., had a tough time keeping a straight face. He almost laughed out loud. On his way out to the pigpens, well out of earshot of his father, he talked to himself, "It's hard to admit my father's a bully and a coward. It's not just the mountain girl he has to worry about now, but her whole family and the Reverend Brownlett. Good for Della! He won't dare lay a hand on her, but he and Ma will figure out mean things to do to her just to get even."

Without knowing why, Harvey Cantrell felt like he had been tricked. He thought he was getting a hired-girl that he could treat anyway he wanted, and that he could get as much work out of as possible. Instead he had a hired-girl who had people looking out for her. He vowed to get even with all of them!

Della helped with the preparation of supper, but was required to wait out back until the family ate. Again, all the meat was gone by the time they called her in to eat. Jimmy winked at her as he went out the back door. She smiled and nodded. This was his signal that he had left her something in the warming closet. Sarah banged the door shut as she went out the back to sit on the bench.

Della was left alone. She looked in the warming closet and found a small pork chop. There were more shucky beans, fried potatoes, and biscuit pone. There was nothing you could call a dessert. She ate all she could, but wished there was more meat. To make sure Jimmy wouldn't get into trouble, she carefully hid the small pork chop bone deep in the scrap bucket. Again, there was nothing on the table to drink.

She left the kitchen as it was and went outside to the water bucket to get a drink. After her second dipper full of water, she turned to go back in the house. Sarah was right in her face, scolding. "What are you doing out here? Get back in there and start clearing off the table."

"I'm sorry, Mrs. Cantrell, but I had to get a drink of water. There was nothing to drink in the kitchen."

"Don't leave the house again until the kitchen is cleaned. I'll fix the corn meal mush for the hogs. You can go to your room in the barn when your work is done. Tomorrow is washday. Get up early so we can get started before breakfast. Wear your oldest work clothes."

Every day the next week was similar to the first three days. Work from dawn to dusk and less and less to eat. Jimmy wasn't able to hide some meat for her at every meal. The only sure protein she ate was in beans of some kind.

Early Friday morning, while clearing the breakfast table, Della heard Harvey cursing, ranting and carrying on in such a manner that she was afraid. She shrank back against the wall as Jimmy came running into the house, banging the back door. His father came after him, his face contorted in fury. He screamed his son's name, "Jimmy! You turn around and look at me!"

The young man stopped short, turned around, and faced his father. "You knew he was leaving didn't you, boy? Do you know where he went? He didn't take a horse, so he's walkin'. When did he leave? Answer me, boy, or I'll whale the tar out of you, so help me!"

"Pa, Harvey, Jr. left about midnight last night. He said he was going to a place called Pathfork to work at a lumber company's sawmill. I don't know where that is. I think it's in the Pine Mountains in Harlan County. He said he wasn't comin' back! He said you told him to leave and not come back! Did you tell him that, Pa?"

Harvey leaned forward and slapped Jimmy hard across the face. He stormed at him, "How dare you question me? I'm your father! What happened between me and your brother is none of your business!"

He turned to go back outside and saw Della pressed tight against the kitchen wall. With a face etched in fury, he shook his fist at her, "This is your fault! You better stay out of my way today!"

Then he was gone. Jimmy sank down on the bench at the long table and put his head in his hands. Della didn't know what to do or say. She silently began to do the breakfast dishes. Jimmy was still sitting at the table when she quietly went out the back door and around the house to find Mrs. Cantrell.

The next morning was Farmers' Market Day. With his older brother not there to help, Della was told to take the older boy's place and help Jimmy load the wagon with produce. The young man tried to make sure Della didn't have to lift the heaviest of the baskets, but she still struggled to hand up the other baskets.

Lacey and Winnie still did little or nothing that was of real help with the farm work. Feeding the chickens and gathering eggs was all they were required to do and they didn't volunteer for anything else. They had yet to have a conversation with Della, but pretended she talked to them and said outrageous things about herself and them.

The sisters tried to get their father to give them more money to spend, saying that Della bragged that she had more money than they did. Harvey was too much of a skinflint with money to fall for that. "Ma knows that Della has no money here with her, so you girls don't have to worry about that. No. You'll get no more money and that's final!"

Della was marking time, waiting until Eight o'clock tomorrow morning. Sunday was her day off and that was when her mother was coming to get her. She would be so happy to get away from the Cantrells for one whole day!

However, that night when Della left to go to the barn to go to bed, Harvey stepped around the back of the house and confronted her. He scared her so that her heart skipped a beat. "When your Ma comes in the mornin', tell her that you can't go with her. Since my oldest son's left, you'll have to fill in for him and help Jimmy slop the hogs and feed all the rest of the animals. You'll be busy all day here on the farm. You tell her that. Don't expect to get any Sundays off all summer unless my son comes back home!"

Della's eyes welled with tears in spite of her resolve to not let this man get the best of her. She swallowed hard and responded to him in her usual way, "Yes, Sir, Mr. Cantrell."

Chapter Twelve
A RECKONING FOR THE CANTRELLS

In her makeshift bed in the hayloft, Della was beside herself to know what to do. Could she endure another week with this family? Harvey, Jr. wasn't coming back. Who could blame him? How was she going to get more food to eat? Jimmy was being watched closely and wouldn't always be able to slip her any of the supper meat. She could tell from how her underclothes fit that she had lost weight in just ten days. The heavy work she was required to do, eating just two meals a day, and their shorting her on the meat portion was making her ill.

Della dutifully said her prayers, but it was hard to ask God to bless any of the Cantrells except for their two sons. Again, she asked God to soften their hearts and help them to be more forgiving to others.

Sunday dawned with a beautiful pink and blue sky. She dressed quickly and went to the house to begin preparing breakfast. Sarah was busily frying their homemade savory sage sausage. She was heating another big iron skillet to make the pancakes. Della began to set the table. She missed the oldest boy each time set out six places instead of the usual seven. When Sarah started serving up the pancakes, she motioned for Della to leave.

With welling tears, she quietly went out the back door to sit on the bench. She had learned to get a good drink before eating. To take her mind off her hunger, she started to hum. Not wanting the family to hear her, she walked about fifty feet away and sat on the ground under a huge oak tree. Della's voice was clear and sweet with her Pine Mountain twang as she closed her eyes and sang her favorite old English ballad, "John Riley."

> On walking out one summer morning,
> To take the cool and pleasant air,
> I spied a fair and most beautiful damsel;
> Her cheeks were like some lily fair.
>
> Then I went up to her a-sayin',
> "Would you like to be a sailor's wife?"
> "O no, O no," she quickly answered,
> "My mind is to live a single life."
>
> I said, "Fair maid, what makes you differ,
> From all the rest of woman-kind?
> You are too fair, you are too handsome,
> To marry you I would incline."
> "Kind sir, kind sir, I could have married

Some two or three long years ago,
All to a man whom they call John Riley,
He was the cause of my overthrow."

"Oh leave off thinkin' of John Riley,
Come go with me to some distant shore;
We'll sail over to old Pennsylvania
Where John Riley lives forevermore."

"I'll not leave off thinkin' of John Riley,
Nor go with you to some distant shore;
My mind is with him. I'll not forsake him,
Though his face I may never see no more."

Then I walked up to her sweet kisses,
The kisses she gave were one, two, and three,
Sayin', "I'm the man whom they call John Riley,
And I've just returned to marry thee."

Della kept her eyes closed a few moments longer savoring the last few words of the song. When she heard a movement near her, she opened her eyes to see Sarah scowling at her. "Don't you have anything better to do? Get in the house now and eat. You've got to help Jimmy. You've got a lot of work to do!"

This time Della was silent as she got to her feet and walked into the house. She looked out the back and saw that Sarah had sat down under the old oak tree, leaned back and closed her eyes. Making Della wait to eat, gave the cruel woman a welcome chance to rest until she heard noises from the kitchen that signaled when Della started to clear the table.

Jimmy had left her a good sized piece of sausage, but there were only three small pancakes on a plate. She checked and there was no more batter in the mixing bowl. She used sparingly of the butter, but was generous with the now cooled maple syrup. Della was sick hungry and had to choke the cold pancakes down, but she was grateful for the tasty sausage.

She was chewing the last of the sausage when she heard Sarah bang the back door. The last morsel of pancake was on her fork and she quickly put it in her mouth and began to chew. Sarah looked at her suspiciously, but didn't say a word. Della began clearing the table.

Jimmy came to get her to help him with the livestock feeding. He did all of the heavy lifting that was involved with feeding, but she had to draw and carry water around behind the barn for the pigs. Then she drew and carried water to the horse and cow watering troughs. She lost track of time. It had to be late in the day.

She was heart sick as she realized her mother had come and she hadn't got to see her! She said aloud, "Oh, I must have been out behind the barn feeding the pigs with Jimmy when she came. Dear Lord, what am I going to do?"

After church was over Judy waited until everyone greeted the minister and left. She stayed behind to talk with Reverend Brownlett. He was all smiles as he walked up to her, but the smile vanished when he saw her face. He asked, I know Mary was here, she's expecting to go to dinner with you and Mr. Collins, but where's Della? I am most anxious to hear about her treatment by the Cantrells. I understand from the gossips that their oldest boy wasn't with them at Farmers' Market on Saturday, and were told by Jimmy that his brother had left home after an argument with their father."

"I don't know anything about that, but I do know they aren't treating Della fair. I went to get her for church this morning and Harvey Cantrell wouldn't let me see her. Something's wrong. I would be forever grateful if you went with me later this afternoon and insist on seeing her."

"Come by the house about one-thirty. Bring Mr. Collins, too, if you want. It wouldn't hurt to bring Mary. Sometimes children can talk with each other when grownups can't."

It was two o'clock that afternoon when Reverend Brownlett, Judy, Jim and Mary rode into the Cantrell's barnyard and dismounted. Mary saw Della just inside the barn pitching new straw into the stalls.

"Ma, I see Della in the barn, I'm going to go talk to her!"

When Mary walked into the huge building, she saw Jimmy Cantrell pushing a heavily loaded wheelbarrow of straw toward the back door.

She called to her sister. Della looked up and gave a squeal of delight. She dropped the pitchfork and ran to Mary. They hugged each other like they would never let go. Mary said, "Ma, Jim Collins, and Reverend Brownlett are all here to see about you. Mr. Cantrell wouldn't let us see you this morning."

Jimmy was down at the far end of the building and out of earshot. He had a big smile on his face and waved a greeting to Mary. Della had tears in her eyes. In a thin little voice, choked with emotion, she said, "Jimmy is the only one that's good to me. If it wasn't for him I would have starved to death. They are deliberately shorting me on food. They said I told their girls that I was better than them and was richer. They both lied. They haven't spoken to me once since I've been here. I'm not allowed to eat with the family and by the time they're done, there's no meat left for me. Jimmy slips and gives me part of his meat when he can. Mary, I don't know what to do. Can you tell Ma, but not get me in any more trouble. He hasn't struck me, but he scares me to death."

"I see that Mr. Cantrell is talking with Mr. Jim and Reverend Brownlett. Stay here and I'll go talk to Ma, alone. Wait about five minutes and ask Jimmy to come with you to where I am. I'll tell Ma all you told me and then leave it up to her how she wants to deal with it. Will you be all right for now?"

"Yes. Tell Ma to bring me something to hide in my room so I can eat it at night before I go to bed. I'm getting sick from not eating enough. Mary, they only eat twice a day!"

"What? Bless the good Lord, how have you managed to live like this?"

She didn't wait for a reply from Della, but walked over to her mother and told her everything her sister had said. Judy's face contorted in fury, then relaxed in a frozen smile, with narrowed eyes. She looked toward the house and saw the two Cantrell sisters standing in the front yard watching the drama unfolding before them. They were smiling, smirking, and elbowing each other.

Judy walked over to them and grabbed their right hands in hers. They tried to pull away, but couldn't break the contact. She said, "What pretty young ladies you both are. It's Lacey and Winnie, isn't it? What do you use to wash your hair? It is so shiny I bet you use rain water and castile soap don't you?"

She turned loose of their hands and managed to touch their hair, one after the other. Her lips were moving, but making no sound. Then she said, "You know, when girls have hair as pretty as you do, it means they're good girls and always can be trusted. Bad girls who cannot be trusted don't have pretty hair. In fact I've known some really untruthful and untrustworthy girls who lose their hair altogether. The only way to make it grow back is to make their wrongs right. But you don't have to worry about anything like that, do you?"

With that done, she went over to see what the men were talking about. Mr. Cantrell was looking terribly uncomfortable. He scowled visibly when Jimmy and Della came out of the barn and Della ran to her mother.

Judy caught Della in her arms and hugged her tight. Reverend Brownlett extended his hand to her, patted her shoulder and said, "Mr. Cantrell has promised you'll be in church with all of them next Sunday. The morning chores will be done before church and then you'll spend the afternoon with your mother. You'll have dinner and supper in the restaurant. Then, you're to come back in time to do the evening chores before bed. Is that all right?"

"Yes Sir, Reverend Brownlett!"

Judy said, "Honey, we must go now so you can finish what you were doing. Jimmy it's good to see you. Mr. Cantrell, give your wife my best. We'll see you next Sunday, if not before."

With that thinly-veiled parting threat, Judy, Jim, Mary, and the Reverend rode out of the Cantrell barnyard.

Della and Jimmy finished feeding and bedding down all the livestock shortly after supper. Harvey only had to tend to the milking. The two Cantrell sisters did nothing after they scattered a scant amount of chicken feed around in the yard. Jimmy had managed to hide a piece of pork roast in the warming closet to go along with home grown canned green beans cooked on fatback, fried sweet potatoes, and biscuit pone. Since Della had been there she hadn't seen any sign of a sweet pie, cake, or fruit. At least, tonight she felt almost satisfied with her meal.

Inside the house, Jimmy was getting ready for bed. His mother reminded him that he and Della hadn't carried in the wash water today, so they had to get up extra early to draw the water and get ready. "You should be done with that before breakfast so we can get an early start again."

"Did you tell Della to get up extra early?"

"No. She knows its wash day so she better get up when she's supposed to. If she don't she'll be sorry. She made your Pa look bad today in front of the Reverend. She'll get no special treatment from us."

Sarah got up out of her chair and went into the sisters' bedroom. She found them brushing their hair. While she stood in the doorway watching them they both stopped at the same time and examined their hairbrushes. She asked them, "What's the matter, what are you looking for?"

"We're losing some of our hair with every brush stroke. Ma, look at this! What do you think is wrong?"

Sarah examined their hairbrushes and saw a little wad of hair on each one. She laughed and hugged each girl, "You silly gooses! Everyone loses some hair every day. Your hair's beautiful. Don't worry. Now get to bed. It's gettin' late and tomorrow's wash day!"

Lacey spoke up, "We don't have to help with that. The mountain girl's supposed to do all of the clothes by herself. Pa said so today after her folks left."

"Okay, but you girls are going to have to start helpin' out more since your older brother has left. Jimmy and Della can't keep doin' it all."

Winnie pouted, "Pa said all we had to do was the chickens just like we've been doing. He's still mad at the mountain girl. She's a braggart and says mean things about us all the time. She needs to know her place!"

"I'll talk to your Pa about it. Now go to bed!"

Jimmy got up even earlier the next morning and went out to the barn to wake Della. She was just waking up when she saw his head come up over the hayloft floor. Alarmed by his presence, she asked "What's wrong?"

"Nothing's wrong. Ma wants you to get up extra early to get the wash water ready before breakfast; she didn't tell you on purpose to get you in trouble. Don't mention that I told you anything, but come on out as soon as you can."

With that he was gone. She knew he had gone all the way to the back door and come around the barn to pretend that he had been to the outhouse.

Della's hands trembled in spite of her resolve to not let any of the Cantrells get the best of her. She decided she was just hungry. She also decided that the best thing for her to do was to hurry so she could eat sooner.

She and Jimmy had the big copper kettle filled and the fire was laid, ready to be lit. Della drew the water and Jimmy carried it. He filled the reservoir on the cook stove. Then he filled the rinse tub.

Della went to sit under the big oak tree. Jimmy went in to eat breakfast.

The two sisters had just come out of their bedroom and their hair was in a huge tangle. He looked at them and started to laugh. "You two must have had nightmares all night from the looks of you!"

Lacey looked at Winnie. Winnie looked at her sister. "Oh." They said in unison, "Look at you!"

They both retreated back to their bedrooms. When they looked in the mirror they were horror stricken. Then they looked at the beds. On their pillows were little gobs of loose ringlets of hair.

Their mother followed after them into their bedroom. She laughed at them, saying, "I told you last night that everyone loses some hair every day. Now brush your hair and come on to breakfast."

Lacey raced to the door to close it, and turned to her sister. She said, "We both know what's going on here. The mountain girl's mother told us that if we told lies and were dishonest our hair would fall out!"

Winnie responded in a panic, "You're younger than me. Do you really believe that's what's happenin' to us? If it's true, then we have to own up to lyin' about that Della or we'll lose all our hair!"

Lacey said, "Maybe Ma's right. Let's wait and see if we lose any more hair. If we admit to lyin' Pa's going to be awful mad. He may start makin' us help Jimmy. All of this is that mountain girl's fault!"

Sarah was amused by her daughters' fear of losing their hair. She was sure their feeling of horror was because they just hadn't noticed daily normal hair loss. She dismissed their concerns as of no importance.

Jimmy came outside to tell Della to go in to eat breakfast. His mother walked past her to sit on the bench. There were scrambled eggs on her plate and cream gravy in the big iron skillet. She had a choice of biscuit pone or cornbread. There was no meat on the table, as usual. She looked in the warming closet and retrieved the small pork chop that Jimmy had hid for her.

She wolfed down the pork chop while she worried that Sarah would walk back in the house and catch her eating meat. Then she relaxed and put a big spoon full of the cream gravy over a piece of cornbread and mashed it up. The eggs, gravy and cornbread made a good breakfast. She was more satisfied than usual and began to clear the table. Sarah came in and glared at her. "Well, you sure took your time this mornin'! Start the dishes while I gather all the dirty clothes. Then you sort out the pile and start washing the white clothes. Jimmy's already feedin'. The milkin' was done afore breakfast. So, if we hurry, we'll get a good jump on the day!"

162

Della was happy to respond, "Yes, Ma'am, Mrs. Cantrell."

By being alone to begin the dishes, she could eat some more of the gravy and cornbread as she worked. She just had to be sure that Sarah Cantrell didn't catch her chewing!

The two Cantrell sisters finished their easy chore of feeding the chickens and gathering the eggs. They hurried back in the house, and spent the better part of the day before a mirror with a hair brush. Their dismay grew greater as more and more gobs of bright shiny hair came loose as they brushed.

The next day was Tuesday, the twelfth of June. Della was feeling sorry for herself. She couldn't help it. She was mumbling as she waited under the big oak for the family to finish breakfast, "If I make it until Friday, Harvey Cantrell will owe me for two weeks of work. In my heart I know that if I don't stay the whole month, he won't pay me anything. I have to stick it out! I want to get paid! Maybe Ma will ride out tomorrow and bring me some snacking food to hide in my room. All I need is enough to eat so I don't always feel starved!"

Judy did ride out the next day and brought a dress for Della. Wrapped up in the material were pieces of bread, cookies, and dried beef strips. Harvey watched with a scowl on his face as Judy handed her the dress. Her mother said, "Honey, I'll stay here while you take it up to your room. Put it away neat and then come back so I can say goodbye."

Harvey scolded, "We have too much work to do for you to come botherin' Della in the middle of the week!"

"Oh, I can tell that you folks stay busy all the time. You have one of the best workin' farms that I've seen in a long time. You make me a little jealous because I once had a farm pretty much like this one. I cleared the new ground myself and had over forty acres under plow. Here comes Della now. Good day to you Mr. Cantrell. Della, I'll say goodbye, honey. Remember to be ready for church early Sunday mornin'!"

Judy was satisfied. Della didn't look quite so peaked. Mr. Cantrell knew that she would be checking on him twice a week. As she rode away from the farm, she smiled and muttered under her breath, "I wonder how the Cantrell sisters are dealing with their hair problem?"

The next two days passed by quickly. When she wasn't hungry all the time, she could concentrate on her work and play her games to make them easier.

Something was wrong with the two evil sisters. They were acting strange. For the last two days they both had head scarves wrapped around their heads like turbans. It was too hot to wrap up your head. Saturday came and they all went to the Farmers' Market again. Sarah told the girls to take off the head scarves, wash their hair, and tie it back with ribbons. Her eyes grew huge when she saw the way their hair had thinned out. "What have you silly girls been doing that's makin' your hair fall out?"

Winnie paled, but Lacey toughed it out. How did her mother know they had done something if what the mountain girl's mother wasn't right?"

Lacey said, "Ma, we want to go to church tomorrow. Will you take us? We'll get up extra early so we can feed the chickens afore we go."

Sarah was dumbfounded. She usually had to make the girls go to church with her. "Sure, we'll go. Della is going with her mother and you two can go with me. Your Pa and Jimmy can take care of the livestock while we're gone."

The next morning, Judy was in the barnyard at eight o'clock. Della was delighted when she saw that her mother rented a little midnight black mare for her to ride. "Ma, she's a beauty! The saddle is perfect! Can I have her to ride each time you come to get me? I'll help you pay for her."

Judy grinned with pleasure. Now her youngest daughter was behaving normally. For the first time in over two weeks, Della was allowing herself to relax and be happy.

When they arrived at the church, they were surprised to see Sarah Cantrell and her two daughters pull their wagon up to the hitching rail. The girls had their normally very thick beautiful hair tied back in a skinny pony tail. Judy guessed why the girls were in church. Something told her they wanted to get their thick hair back!

After the services were over, the Cantrell sisters told their mother they wanted to talk to Reverend Brownlett and asked her to wait in the wagon for them. Sarah was mystified, but reluctantly agreed to wait for them.

They hung back behind the rest of the congregation so they would come out last. Winnie pushed Lacey out in front of her so it would be natural for the older sister to do the talking. Reverend Brownlett turned a puzzled face toward the two girls, "Yes? Girls it's good to see you here. Now, what can I do for you?"

"Reverend, we, that is, me and my sister, we've done something bad wrong and we need to know how to make it right."

"Girls, I'm sorry to hear that, but I'm glad you have made this decision. Let's go over there to sit on the bench and you tell me about it. I know your mother's waiting. Is this something you don't want to talk about in front of her?"

"We know we'll have to tell her and Pa later on. We know our Pa is going to be awful mad at us, but now we need some advice on how to make what we did right!"

"Before you begin, tell me what happened that caused you to suddenly have a change of heart and decide to do the right thing?"

Winnie blurted out without warning, "Our hair started to fall out!"

Lacey viciously elbowed her in the ribs. "Hush, Winnie, we agreed that I would be the one to talk to the Reverend."

By now Reverend Brownlett was giving them his full attention. He saw Sarah get down off the wagon and start toward them. He waved to her, motioning for her to stay back.

Lacey began: "You know we have the mountain girl stayin' and workin' at our farm? We don't like her cause she can work harder and faster than we ever could. Pa and Ma were beginnin' to like her when she first came. We decided to tell Ma and Pa that Della was braggin' that she's better than we are. That she was richer than we are. That she had lots more money than we do. When we told them that we didn't want Della eatin' with the family, that it wasn't fittin' for hired-help to eat at the table with us, they agreed and made her wait until we finished the meal. Winnie and I made sure we ate all the meat so Della wouldn't get enough to eat. We thought she'd give up and leave, but she didn't!"

Both girls had tears in their eyes as Lacey reluctantly related to the Minister the appalling story of how their evil actions had caused their folks to give in to their own evil natures and torment an innocent child.

Lacey continued, "Pa makes Della do twice as much work now that our older brother's left home. Ma makes her do almost all of the inside house work, even to drawing and carrying the water for wash day. Jimmy works with her. We think he likes Della."

Reverend Brownlett said, "Let me get something straight before you go any farther. You made this decision to set things right because your hair started to fall out? Is this true?"

Both girls flushed a deep red and nodded, "Yes. Someone told us that when you lie and are dishonest before God, your hair will begin to fall out. That you have to set things right to stop it from happening and to save your hair."

It was clear to Ethan Brownlett that these two evil girls were only confessing their sins in an effort to save their hair. It had nothing to do with any Christian feelings or remorse for the pain and suffering they had inflicted on Della. He felt a terrible anger toward these two children, but even more so toward their parents. How could they torment a child? Not only did they deliberately starve her, but they had piled an impossible burden of work onto her shoulders.

"You know in your hearts that now since you have confessed that your hair will stop falling out. But, you have to take this one step farther. I will come with you right now and the three of us will talk with your brother, Jimmy, and your parents. I'll be with you the whole time, so you don't have to be afraid. You go on home with your mother, I'll stop by my house for a minute and then I'll follow you home."

Ethan walked over to the wagon with Lacey and Winnie. He told Sarah that he was coming out to see them as soon as he stopped by his house. "You go on now. I'll follow in about a half-an-hour."

Sarah's eyes grew huge, but she was silent until Reverend Brownlett was out of earshot. Then she turned on her girls in a cold rage. "What have you done? Have you disgraced our family in some way? Why is the Reverend coming so fast to see us? Has this got something to do with that miserable mountain girl?"

Lacey braved her mother's wrath, "Ma, we promised to not talk about it until the Reverend was with us."

Sarah restrained herself from striking her daughter. Her worry now was how Harvey was going to react and if she was finally in danger of the beating he always threatened. Whatever it was, it was better that they had a witness like the Reverend. They had lost their oldest son. She didn't want to lose Jimmy, too.

Ethan stopped at his house and asked Anne to forego Sunday dinner and go with him out to the Cantrell Farm. He told her, "Let's take the children to the Hazard Restaurant and ask Mary and Judy to watch them for us. This is an emergency and it concerns Della!"

Quickly, Anne donned her Sunday hat and they put the children in the buggy and drove to the Restaurant. Judy, Mary, and Della were alarmed at the urgency with which Ethan and Anne arrived and left, leaving their children to eat dinner with them. Anne said, "Make sure you save us some food. We'll be starved when we get back!"

All of fifteen minutes had passed when they left the city and were on the back road to the Cantrell farm. Sarah and the girls would barely have time to summon Harvey and Jimmy to tell them he was coming to visit right now.

Sarah was beside herself by the time they pulled into the yard. Jimmy came running to unhitch the horse and lead him into the barn. One look at his mother told him that something terrible was about to happen. Both of his sisters were pale and trembling. He watched as his father came from behind the barn. He walked toward them and with each step he had a premonition of trouble. None of them, neither his wife, nor his children were acting normal.

He scolded, "Woman get in the house now. What are you just standin' here for anyway?"

Lacey spoke up, "Pa, the Reverend's coming to see us. He's on his way, now. We need to wait here for him."

"What are you talkin' about, girl? I'm not waitin' out in the sun for nobody, much less a useless preacher!"

Sarah finally found her voice, "Yes, Harvey, you will. We all will. The girls have done something wrong and were afraid to tell us, alone. I don't know what it is. They talked to the Reverend and he's comin' on account of them."

Harvey turned to his daughters. "You both know you don't have to be afraid of your Pa! Whatever it is that you think you did wrong we'll work it out. Oh, here he comes now. He's got his wife with him!"

Reverend Brownlett had briefly told Anne what the girls had done and how badly Della had been treated by the Cantrells. She was as appalled as Ethan had been. When he helped Anne down out of the buggy, Sarah suggested they all go to the benches under the shade trees in the front yard. Jimmy offered to put their horse in the shade, too.

After they were all seated and Jimmy had rejoined them, Reverend Brownlett turned to Lacey and asked, "Do you want to do the talking to your folks, or shall I talk for you?"

Lacey paled, ignored her mother and looking directly into her father's eyes, bravely began to speak, "Pa. you know you agreed to have the mountain girl stay with us and work for us. We don't like her because she can work harder and faster than we ever could. You and Ma were beginnin' to like her when she first came here. Winnie and I decided to tell you and Ma that Della was braggin' that she's better than we are. That she was richer than we are. That she had more money than we do. When we told you those things, we lied.

We told you that we didn't want Della eatin' at the table with us, that it wasn't fittin' for the hired-help to eat at the table with the family. You both agreed with us and made her wait until we finished the meal. Winnie and I made sure we ate all the meat on the table so Della wouldn't get enough to eat. We thought she would give up and leave if she was hungry all the time. But she didn't. What we did was bad, but you and Ma treated her even worse!"

Harvey was red from the collar of his shirt to his eyebrows! For once in his life he was speechless. When he collected his raging thoughts, he turned toward Ethan and Anne, "Well, what do you want me to do about this. For some reason my girls are saying they lied about our hired-help. She's all right. Nobody's hurt her. Maybe she did get a little hungry, but we'll take care of that. Now, I want to know why my girls all of a sudden got a guilty conscience over nothin' more than a complainin' mountain girl."

Winnie blurted, "Pa, we tried to tell Ma something was wrong for the last three days and she just laughed at us. We had to admit we lied about Della. She has never said anything to us. We caused you to not let her eat with our family and you went along with our starvin' her. We had to make things right to keep the rest of our hair from fallin' out!"

"What on earth are you talkin' about?"

"We know our hair was fallin' out. Just look at us! Pa, you'll begin to lose your hair, too, if you don't 'fess up to how mean you've been to Della!"

"Don't any of you say another word! Get in the house, now! Jimmy, go get the Reverend's buggy. He's leavin'."

Harvey didn't speak as he watched his wife and daughters slowly walk into the house. Jimmy left to go to the barn and get the horse and buggy.

A soon as everyone was out of earshot, Reverend faced Harvey with raw rage on his face. "Mr. Cantrell, I vouched personally for you when I helped arrange for that young child to work for you. She was to be treated as one of your family. Obviously, you don't know how to treat your family, or to raise Christian children. The only reason your girls confessed to lying and causing all of this pain and suffering for an innocent young girl was because they believed their lies were causing their hair to fall out!"

"What are you going to do? Is Della comin' back or not?. I promise she'll get enough to eat, but she'll have to give me my due when it comes to the work that has to be done. My oldest boy left home over a week ago. Della had to take his place and do his chores along with Jimmy."

"You're standing there telling me that you expect a child, barely thirteen years old to do the heavy-lifting and work of a grown man! Mr. Cantrell you haven't shown the least bit of remorse over how your wife and daughters have treated this child. I shall pray for your souls and your redemption. If Della comes back to work for you, it'll be her decision. Her mother will hear all that has transpired here today. You don't know who Della's mother is, do you? Miss Pettit at Pine Mountain School told me that Judy Turner-Smith beats every man in three mountain counties at all of the turkey shoots. You've picked the wrong woman to cross by mistreating her daughter. May God forgive me for how I'm thinking about you and what you've done to the child! You'll be lucky if Judy Turner-Smith doesn't shoot you!"

Harvey was thunderstruck. He stood motionless with his jaw dropped and his eyes huge.

Ethan had spoken with all the emotion he could muster. He curtly nodded to Harvey and quickly climbed in the buggy next to Anne. He didn't look back as he urged the horse to a brisk trot.

Chapter Thirteen
JOYS AND SORROWS

Della was thoroughly enjoying her Sunday with her mother and sister. After church they went to the restaurant to eat dinner. Myrt didn't join them because she was still not feeling well enough to leave her room. When Jim came through the front door to join them, Sylvia handed out four menus.

Della was hungrily eyeing the plates of the other customers when Judy said, "Honey, you can order anything you want"

"Ma, I'll have whatever you're having. I'm so hungry! If I want, can I have seconds? What can I have for dessert? I've not had any fruit, cake or pie since I've been with the Cantrells. Did you know they only eat twice a day and always run out of meat so I don't get any unless Jimmy sneaks me some."

"Why do they just eat twice a day? Are they that hard up for food? Are they that poor?"

"No, there's plenty of food, but Mr. Cantrell says there is too much work to be done to waste time eating at dinnertime and doing dishes. So they just eat breakfast and supper. I never get enough to keep from feeling starved. I have to wait twelve hours before I can eat again! And, Ma, you can't drink anything at the table. They don't want to dirty up glasses and make more dishwashing. If I go out back to get a drink before I finish the dishes and cleaning up the kitchen, Mrs. Cantrell yells at me. She told me to not come outside until my work's all done."

"Do you want to quit? You don't have to work for them, you know."

"There's thirty days in this month. And I am just now past the half way mark. I know that if I don't stay the whole month, Mr. Cantrell won't pay me anything. I'm doing a man's work because I'm taking his oldest son's place. He ran away, but he's nineteen years old and a man. I don't blame him one bit. His father is the meanest man I ever saw. They are pure evil, both him and Mrs. Cantrell. I think they've even got the Heltons beat!"

"I'm not going to have you going hungry to the point you feel like you're starving! Why do you feel like you have to make this money so much that you're willing to work for them at all?"

Before answering her mother's question, she looked at Mary. Although her older sister had said nothing the whole time while Della was talking, the younger sister was hurt by the superior smirk on Mary's face.

Della said, "I don't want anyone to tell me I failed at this job. Even if it's not my fault and they treat me mean and unfair, I don't want to let them get the best of me! God promises to take care of me. Ma, am I right about that? When I pray, I ask Him to help me to get through just one more day. So far, he answers my prayer. I know Mary is treated like one of the family by Reverend Brownlett and his wife. Mary, all of the Cantrells thought you were their older daughter and they

169

had no idea you were my sister and just worked for them. He was in a rage when he found out. Although he's threatened me, he's never hit me!"

Judy looked at Mary. She had seen the same smirk on her older daughter's face that had hurt Della. Her question to Mary was right to the point. "Mary, what do you think Della should do? What would you have done if the Brownlett's had mistreated you the way the Cantrells have mistreated Della?"

Mary drew a deep breath and said, "Ma, I wouldn't have stayed one more day, much less two whole weeks just for money. If I'd had to, I would've walked all the way back to Pine Mountain School to tell you. I know you wouldn't have made me go back to Hazard."

Judy said, "You see, honey, even Mary believes that you're not to blame because the Cantrells are the way they are. Now, what're you going to do? You have to decide. But, before we make any big decisions, let's order. I'm going to have the roast beef and mashed potatoes with brown gravy. Yes, you can have seconds if you want, and a big dish of blackberry cobbler with heavy cream."

Mary ordered her usual breakfast for dinner.

Judy was heart sick as she watched Della wolf down the food and then ask for another plate of the same. The big bowl of cobbler was gone quickly and Della finished off her second glass of sweet milk.

They were still at the table when Reverend Brownlett and Anne paid them a surprise visit.

Judy asked Della and Mary to take a food tray to Myrt and sit with her while she ate. They were delighted to spend some time with the older lady. When the two girls were out of earshot, Ethan and Anne related to Judy all that had happened, starting with Lacey and Winnie finally telling the truth because they were afraid if they kept lying, all their hair would fall out.

Judy couldn't help it. She turned her head away so she could grin at the thought of the two mean sister's fear of losing their looks.

She asked, "Did they show any remorse about mistreating' Della?"

"None at all, and neither did their father. Their mother stayed out of sight. I think she was in the house the whole time. Harvey admitted that he had made Della shoulder the chores of their oldest son who has permanently left the home. Their other son, Jimmy, will be eighteen in about six months and I suspect he'll do the same thing. With parents like that, who could blame him?"

"How did you leave Mr. Cantrell? Was he angry? He has no reason to be angry, but my experience has been that people like them always get angry and are only sorry if they get caught!"

The Reverend finally grinned, and said, "Judy, you are taking this a lot calmer than I did. I had to ask God to forgive me for my thoughts about that family. You don't seem surprised by all this."

"Well, I'm not. Della had just finished tellin' me, Jim and Mary about how they've mistreated her and starved her. She told me about the oldest boy leavin' and how she had to do all of his chores. Jimmy has been slippin' meat to her each day when he could. If he hadn't done that, I think Della would have become seriously ill. He's a good young man."

The Reverend's face grew serious again. "Kathryn Pettit told me about your reputation with a gun. She told me about your winning all the turkey shoots competing with men. I have to tell you that I was so angry with Harvey Cantrell that I told him when you found out he had been forcing a thirteen year old girl to do the lifting and carrying of a grown man, you were liable to shoot him!"

Judy didn't hide her grin this time. "Ethan, what did he say?"

"He didn't say anything. He got pale as a ghost and his jaw dropped. I left him that way. I got in my buggy with Anne and we left. I doubt we ever see them in my church again."

Then he continued, "I'm so sorry this happened to Della. It's going to be hard for her to trust in the goodness that's in most people. What is she going to do? I'll go out and get her personal belongings if she decides to not go back. I'll also ask him to pay her for the time she's already worked this month. I think I can shame him into doing that."

Anne had let Ethan do all the talking, but Judy had noted that she had nodded in agreement to everything he said until he volunteered to go back for Della's belongings. Judy understood Anne's fear of what could happen if Ethan faced Harvey Cantrell again.

After giving it some thought, Judy said, "Ethan, I think you and Anne have been involved all that you should be. People like Harvey Cantrell become like cornered animals when they get caught like this. He could harm you. He won't harm me. I believe that he'll take you at your word. He's afraid I'll really come out there and shoot him."

She could tell from their faces that Ethan and Anne were relieved that she was going to handle the situation herself. Their children were already in the buggy and waiting. They excused themselves, leaving Judy and Jim to discuss what they should do if Della insisted on returning to the Cantrell farm.

Jim asked, "Why are you leavin' it up to her to decide. Just tell Della she ain't goin' back."

Judy frowned, "No. That's not the right thing to do. If I order her to quit, she'll always wonder if she could have handled it by herself. If she decides on her own to quit, then she'll feel she made the right decision and won't feel like she failed. Della has a good head on her shoulders. She survived two weeks when 'most any other child her age would've come cryin' to me after three days. I'm fiercely proud of her. I don't know if I would've had that much endurance!"

Jim smiled and wisely agreed with her.

Mary and Della came back to join them at the table.

Mary asked why the Brownlett's had come by and then left so quickly. Judy told them about the two Cantrell sisters confessing their lies to him after church today and that he had ridden out to their home with them to talk to their folks. He thought it was important to come to see us because he wanted to tell me what he'd found out. He was surprised that Della had already told us most of it.

Then Judy asked Della, "Now we need to decide what you're to do 'bout this. If you want to quit, you can work here in the restaurant and make more money than you ever could on that farm. Don't you worry 'bout them gettin' the best of you. That's neither here nor there. No one has to put up with people like them, not when they have other options. You do. Sylvia would love to have you work with her. When school starts, you can earn money by workin' part time."

Della had a huge frown on her face. She asked, "Ma, All my stuff's out there. How'll I get it from them? He's liable to keep it just to be mean!"

Judy smiled, "Honey, I don't think you have to worry about that. I'll go with you to get your stuff. Jim, will you go with us?"

"I sure will. I want to be there when he loses his good worker and has to face you. I sure didn't know you knew anything about guns. What a surprise!"

Judy turned back to Della, "Honey, is it settled then? We'll go right now. Then we'll come back and plan for your startin' to work with Sylvia."

"Shouldn't we ask Sylvia first?"

"Well here she is, I'll ask her now."

Sylvia's face was a puzzle. "Ask me what?"

Judy grinned and asked. "Della wants to come and work with you in the kitchen and dining room. Is that okay with you?"

"Oh, my, yes! Honey, I would be so proud to work with you!"

Della was beaming, she was so pleased. Tears were on her cheeks. She exclaimed, "Oh, let's do leave right now. Ma, I'll be so happy if I never see that farm again! What about Jimmy, though? He's been so good to me. His father will make him do all of my work, too!"

"Jimmy is almost eighteen. He can do the same thing his older brother did. I'm sure he can get a job away from home. We can't worry about him, honey. If you're ready, we'll leave now. Mary, we'll drop you off at Reverend Brownlett's on the way. Is that okay with you?"

"Yeah, Ma, that's fine."

With a huge sigh of relief now that Della made her decision, the three of them rode out of Hazard on the road to the Cantrell farm. Harvey saw them coming. He came to the barnyard to greet them. Now that he had been warned, he was eying the hunting rifle that was on Judy's saddle.

Judy spoke first. "Mr. Cantrell, Della has decided she has to quit workin' for you. She needs to go to her room in the barn and pack up her belongin's. You can go ahead and figure how much she's earned so you can pay her now for the two weeks she's been with you."

I don't figure I owe her anything. She's slept under my roof, ate my food, and lived free for two weeks."

"I think you had better do some serious figurin'. How much were you plannin' on paying her at the end of the month, or were you aimin' to cheat her all the way around. I know you've been shortin' her on food. She has lost weight to the point of being sick. You've worked her like a grown man for the last week. She's earned a man's wage. Now I want a figure from you and I'll decide if it's fair or not. I'm warnin' you to not be foolish."

Judy reached down and placed her hand on her rifle. She was talking in a calm voice, but her eyes were narrowed as she stared at Harvey. He visibly paled. He took a small notepad and pencil out of the top of his bib overalls and began to write down some figures. He heard Judy tapping the wooden stock of her rifle with her fingers. The sound was intimidating and it was hard for him to concentrate on his figures.

Finally, just as Della was coming out of the barn carrying two packing-sacks, he looked up and said, "I was going to give her two dollars a week. That would have been eight dollars for the month. Now I'll give her three dollars because she's quitting afore a month is up."

"That's not enough. You'll have to pay a man to take her place and that will be at least a dollar a day. I think you'd better refigure her wages."

"She's just a young girl. She's not worth a man's wage!"

Della positioned herself behind Curly. Jim's horse sidestepped away from Della. Judy sensed her fear and with a voice cold as ice, said, "You need to refigure her fair wages. I'm not waitin' much longer."

Sarah came out of the house to stand next to Harvey. She had been watching and was surprised that her husband was even agreeing to pay the girl anything. Judy looked at the woman with contempt in her eyes. From Sarah's body language, Judy guessed that they had both schemed to work Della all summer for no wages.

Judy's fingers stopped tapping the wooden stock of her gun and her hand closed tightly around it. Finally, he said, "All right, I'll pay her seven dollars."

"No. You'll pay her seven for the week she took your son's place and worked like a man. Then you'll pay her three for the days she worked afore your son left. That's ten dollars you owe her. The starving and overwork you piled upon her deserves a severe penalty for both of you, but we'll let God take care of that 'because the Bible says, vengeance is mine, saith the Lord."

Then she turned slightly in the saddle to speak to Della. "Does that sound about right to you? Is it enough? He hasn't got enough money to pay you for what you've put up with from both of them."

Harvey reached into another pocket in his bib overalls and pulled out a leather pouch. Carefully he counted out ten dollars and handed it to Judy. She refused to take it. "No. You hand it to Della. It's her money."

His face was red from his collar to his eyebrows as he handed the wad of bills to Della. She was almost afraid to take the money, but she did.

Judy was curt in her manner and cold as ice toward the Cantrells as she said, "When you see any of us anywhere, I suggest you cross the street to keep from meetin' us face to face. You got off easy today! Our business is done here. I bid you good day, sir!"

All three horses turned away at the same time. In leaving, they put their horses to a fast trot and didn't look back.

They stopped at the Brownlett's to let them know that Della would be living at the hotel and working there. Mary, Ethan, and Anne were so happy for her, they invited them in for some refreshments to celebrate. Judy begged off with a promise that they would have dinner with them next Sunday. Their invitation also included Jim. When they reached Main Street, Jim left them to go to the boardinghouse.

Della's happy excitement was contagious. When they arrived back at the hotel, Sylvia, Isaac, and Myrt all wanted to do something special to celebrate. Judy said, "I know what we'll do. Mr. Jenkins' chair has casters on it. We'll get another chair for the front desk and wheel Myrt into the dining room. That way we can all have supper together!"

This was the first time Myrt had left her room for some time. Judy was concerned because her friend was so weak. Myrt's health was going downhill so fast it was heartbreaking. She had lived at the hotel now for almost two years. Although she corresponded with them, her daughter's family hadn't made the trip from Big Laurel to Hazard to visit since she sold her farm. Mr. Jenkins, Judy, Sylvia, Isaac, and Sheriff Walt Middleton acted as her immediate family.

Bill welcomed Della to the Hotel and was in complete agreement that she could stay there and work with Sylvia in the kitchen and dining room. Judy related the story of Della's stay with the Cantrells to Bill, Sylvia, Isaac, and the sheriff. They were all incensed by the way she'd been abused. The sheriff wanted to know if Judy wanted to press charges against them. She didn't. "I don't think we'll hear any more from them. You might look in on them once in a while to be sure they haven't harmed their son, Jimmy. He was kind to Della and slipped food to her when there was danger of his father and mother finding out. I don't want anything bad to happen to him."

Walt agreed to do that. Then he became serious, "Judy, I'm not planning on running for another term as sheriff. Next year in November a new man will be elected. I'm planning to follow in the path west that the Bailie family took. I know it's just the middle of June, but time passes pretty fast. I've told my plans to Bill, but I wanted you to know, too."

Judy's eyes grew huge. She had come to rely on Walt as a best friend. The thought of him not being there in her life, upset her. He laughed and said, "Hey, now. Don't go and get all sentimental on me. Sheriffs only last four years here in Hazard and Perry County. I've had a hankering to go west for a long time. I liked the Bailie family and have kept in contact with them because of the money I sent to Mrs. Bailie from the Owens brothers. She and her family have become my friends. If I find them, I'll know someone and maybe I'll settle down near them."

Judy smiled and said, "When you leave, you'll write to me and Bill and let us know where you are and how you're making out, won't you?"

"Sure I will. Who knows, maybe you'll go west some day!"

"Not that far west, I won't! If I go west, it'll be back to Harlan County, Little Greasy Creek, and Alex's Branch."

The following Sunday, Jim came to the restaurant to have dinner. He was waited on by Sylvia, but saw Della working with Isaac by filling food orders as they came to them. He asked Judy, "How's Della working out? Is she learning the restaurant business quickly enough to suit Isaac and Sylvia?"

"She didn't have to learn. Her jobs at school prepared her for work like this. When she goes back to school in September, we'll miss her."

"I'd say she's one lucky girl."

"Della makes her own luck. She does her best at everything she tries to do. I think that in the future whoever gives her a job will be getting a worker who will more than earn their pay."

"Where's Mary today?"

"She's helping Reverend Brownlett with a special 'dinner on the grounds' meeting this afternoon."

"Are we going for our Sunday ride today?"

"Yes. Right after we finish dinner we're going down along the Kentucky River. It's not too far. I don't want to see the Cantrell farm again."

Judy noticed that Jim was flushing red off and on like something bad was bothering him. At first she said nothing about it, but when they came to the trail that followed the river, she asked, "Is something wrong?"

"No, I just want to ask you a very serious question."

"Oh, well go ahead and ask me. I think we know each other well enough by now that you should feel you can ask me anything you want to."

Jim stopped his horse, dismounted, and tied the reins to a tree. Judy followed suit and they both sat down on the grassy bank and watched the water for a few moments. Finally he found his voice. "You know that I've got special feelings for you. I went with you to meet your family and to Della's graduation. I think your

175

girls like me. You don't have to answer right away. What I'm trying to say is that I love you and want to marry you."

Judy smiled at him with a merry twinkle in her eye as she teased, "That's not a question. Now what did you want to ask me?"

Jim laughed out loud, "Judy Turner-Smith will you marry me?"

"Yes, Jim Collins, I'll marry you."

He pulled her to her feet and took her in his arms. Judy was ecstatic. It had been so long since she felt true love in her heart. After their first long, passionate kiss, they sat on the grassy river bank and made plans for a wedding.

Judy said, "We should wait to be married in the fall after both of my girls are in school. A trip to Big Laurel to see my family would be nice and can be our wedding trip. I would like to be married the first Saturday in October. I've got a little calendar in my saddlebag. I'll get it."

When she came back, she sat by him and squirmed around until she was leaning into his shoulder as she looked at the months of 1923. "Oh, she said, the first Saturday in October is on the sixth."

"Do we have to wait that long?"

"Yes. Maybe we should even wait until after the first of the year and get married in the spring of 1924."

"No." Jim said, "I want to get married right away. We'll set the wedding date for October sixth if that's what you want. We'll take a whole week off so we can spend two days at your sister's. We can go to Harlan while we're there."

Judy thought about it for a few minutes and said, "Jim, you'll only be taking five days off from work, but I'll be taking six. It'll be Friday the twelfth when we get back to Hazard. You don't have to be to work until that Monday, but I have to be at work the next morning. Since we're planning this far ahead I'm sure it'll be all right with Mr. Jenkins. Sylvia and Isaac, with Della there, can take care of the restaurant just fine."

"After we're married, will you still be able to stay at the boardinghouse during the week?"

"I don't know about that yet. I have to get up at three o'clock in the morning to get breakfast for the men who leave for work around four o'clock. After seven o'clock, unless there's something that needs fixing, I'm free until time to cook supper. My boss and his wife just snack for dinner."

Judy laughed, "We sure are two peas in a pod. How romantic is it to be planning so seriously right now? We sound like we're planning a business deal! We've plenty of time to figure out all of this later. Right now, I'm so happy and I love you so much. My Pa's vision for us is coming true. To me, that means this is God's plan for us."

"Jim laughed and said, "I don't know about it being God's plan. Sometimes I wonder if He's still on speaking terms with me. I do know it's been my own plan for some time now to ask you to be my wife. I love you, honey. You've made me so happy!"

The reality of the moment caused a glorious feeling to come over both of them. Jim jumped to his feet, caught both of her hands in his and pulled her up into his arms. Then to the music of his humming a slow love song, they waltzed together on that grassy bank by the Kentucky River, just east of Hazard.

Judy waited until Sunday after church to tell Mary and Della that Jim had proposed and she had accepted. They were on the way to the restaurant. Mary and Della were riding double on the little mare.

She said, "Let's stop here under the willow trees a few minutes. I have something I want to tell you before we get to the restaurant. Last Sunday while we were out riding Jim asked me to marry him. I said, yes!"

Judy had dismounted and was holding on to Curly's reins while looking up at her daughters. Both girls sucked in their breath at the same time. Mary let the air out of her lungs first. Della was turning blue and still holding. Then both of them caught some air and exclaimed, "Oh. Ma, that's wonderful! When, where, and will we be with you at your wedding?"

In unison, they both slid off the little mare and grabbed their mother in a big hug. Judy was thunderstruck by their reaction. "Are you both okay with this? I didn't know whether or not you liked Jim."

Mary spoke up, "Ma, we like him, don't we Della?"

Della nodded in the affirmative, and said, "Even if we didn't like him, if he makes you happy, then we're happy, too."

Judy had happy tears in her eyes, "Thank the good Lord for two of the sweetest girls any mother could wish for!"

Mary asked, "Now that you've said you're going to marry him, when and where is the wedding going to be?"

"We are planning it for the sixth of October. I want to be married in Reverend Brownlett's church and you'll both be there with me. I'll need you two to help me pick out a dress to wear and to make plans. Will you help me?"

Della, ever the practical one, asked, "How much money can we spend?"

Judy laughed, "Mary knows how stingy I am. We'll shop around and get the best prices we can find!"

All three remounted and put their horses at a swift trot as they hurried to meet Jim. They would have dinner with him and Myrt, if she was up to it.

Mary and Della kept up a steady stream of chatter. Judy was deep in thought. It was near the end of June. Bill had planned a summer trip to visit his brother in Florida. He wanted to go when it would be hot and during what his brother called the stormy season. She would be in charge of the hotel again. Isaac and Sylvia would handle the restaurant. Della would be there to help them. School started by the second Monday in September. The wedding would be just four weeks after that. Judy's mind was reeling, "Lordy, I've got to write all this down. I'll make a list of what I have to do over the next three months. I'll pray that God will see me through this."

The summer seemed to float by like a hazy dream. Bill left in time to spend the fourth of July with his family. It was hot in Hazard, Judy wondered how much hotter it would be in Florida. Only she knew that Bill was planning to retire to Florida if he felt like he could stand their summer weather.

While Judy was counting the days until October, Della was counting time until school would start. The Cantrell sisters were both older than her and would be at least one and two grades ahead. She hoped she wouldn't see them, but if she did, she would follow their lead and speak to them or ignore them. Mary was a year older than Lacy and a grade ahead. She wondered if Mary would stick up for her if she needed her.

While Judy and Della were deeply involved in their thoughts and plans, Mary was looking forward to a real shopping spree. She loved to walk through downtown Hazard and window-shop. There was a store that had beautiful wedding gowns in their window display. She imagined her mother in the one that had a dropped waistline. The skirt was floor length and had eight gores. On the mannequin's head was a little wisp of a white veil. There was no price tag in sight. Mary wasn't brave enough to enter the store and ask the price. She'd tell her mother about it and hope that she'd agree to come to the store to look.

Labor Day Monday was on the third of September and school started for Mary and Della on Wednesday the fifth. It was just for a half day so they could register and receive class schedules for Junior High and High School students.

There were a lot of children for the seventh and eighth grades. Judy went with Della. Mary was familiar with everything and managed on her own. She would be sixteen in November and felt quite grown up.

There was an assembly at the end of the morning that brought all the children together. Della looked around and didn't see the Cantrell girls anywhere. She thought mean thoughts about their father, "I'll bet they're being made to do everything I was doing and Mr. Cantrell won't allow them to come to school!"

Mary's classes were in an entirely different building. She walked over there to wait for her. She saw a girl in a turban-like hat that was standing with her back to everyone, but was obviously waiting for someone, too. Della spoke to another girl who was standing alone and they struck up a conversation about their classes and teachers.

It wasn't long before she saw Mary coming to meet her. Something was wrong because Mary looked like she was ready to burst into tears. Next to her was Winnie Cantrell. She was wearing a turban-like hat, too. Mary came to walk with Della and Winnie went to Lacey to walk with her.

Della didn't have to ask Mary what was wrong because the instant Winnie saw her she said as loud as she could so everyone could hear, "Well, here are the two mountain girls. It's good you have each other to walk with and talk to because no one else will want to do either!"

Della was red from her collar to her eyebrows, but her eyes narrowed to mere slits as she turned the tables on the evil sisters. She replied just as loud to Winnie, "You haven't learned manners yet have you? Is your hair still falling out because you lie and are rude? Is that why you're wearing turbans? Take your hats off and show us your hair!"

The other students started to laugh and chant, "Show us your hair! Show us your hair! Show us your hair!"

The two Cantrell sisters were mortified. They started to run away from the crowd of chanting students. Mr. Cantrell drove his wagon close by to pick them up. He heard the chanting, but didn't understand what the students were saying. The girls clambered aboard and urged him to hurry up and leave.

Mary looked at Della in disbelief. "Why did you say what you did to that mean girl? She had me so rattled, I couldn't think of a thing to say back to her. In a few more minutes I would have been crying and that would have been awful."

"Those are the evil Cantrell sisters that lied about me and caused all my trouble with their folks. I know they worried about losing their hair because they lied and weren't honest. They did begin to lose their hair. I don't know how much, but they're wearing those hats today to hide it. You'll know what to say the next time they call you a mountain girl. Every girl here is a mountain girl. Hazard's in the mountains, but maybe they won't give us any more trouble!"

After the first week at school, Della was settled in. She learned her way around enough to find her classes, knew all of her teachers' names, and made friends with several other girls. She worked three hours each day after school and eight hours on Saturday. Della earned more than she could have on the farm.

Her prayers at night had changed from asking God to help her to make it through one more day to thanking Him for showing her His plan for her life.

Mr. Jenkins returned from Florida. He reported to Judy that it was hotter in Florida mostly because of the humidity. However, his brother had ways of cooling the air. Sometime over the next year he would think about retiring.

Myrt continued to fail in health. She had to be waited on at meal times, when retiring at night, and helped out of bed in the morning. Judy made sure she had all of the help she needed.

Judy asked Bill and Walt if they knew where she could borrow a real wheel chair so they could take Myrt to her wedding at the church. They assured her they would borrow one either from the hospital or from the funeral home.

The first Saturday in October was fast approaching. She and Jim only spent time together on the weekends. Judy said, "We barely see each other now. Do you think it'll be much different after we're married?"

"We're still going to be workin'; me at the boardinghouse and you here at the hotel. Honey, we'll be together more than you think. Everything's going to work out just fine. Don't worry your pretty head about that!"

Mary was disappointed because her mother shied away from a traditional wedding gown. "Honey, I've been married afore. All I want this time is a pretty dress. I want you and Della to each have a pretty new dress, too. They'll be your Sunday dresses after the wedding."

Mary enjoyed helping her mother choose her lovely satin underclothes, white silk stockings, and white patent leather shoes. They went to the Hazard Jewelry Store and Judy chose a lovely white-gold lady's wrist watch.

Della practiced working on her mother's long-thick black-curly hair. She experimented with using a hairdresser's 'rat' to make a full, rolled-back bang that covered most of Judy's forehead. She had a perfectly formed widow's peak, but when Della finished dressing her hair on her wedding day, it couldn't be seen. Then she pulled the hair back on each side of her mother's face and tied it so that two ringlets of hair cascaded down to just above her shoulders. She achieved the look she wanted by using the white satin bow she wore for her graduation.

When they arrived at the church at ten o'clock most of the people were there. Jim was dressed in a new black suit, white shirt and a black string tie. He was standing near the altar beside Reverend Brownlett. Bill Jenkins and Sheriff Walt were standing next to Jim. Walt was Jim's best man. Isaac and Sylvia came in the front door wheeling Myrt in the borrowed wheel chair.

Mary and Della preceded their mother to the front of the church. They turned around to face the front to watch as Judy walked down the center aisle. She was lovely and radiantly happy!

When the brief ceremony was over Judy turned around and saw Isaac and Sylvia. In a panic, she asked Bill, "Who's at the hotel and the restaurant? How could you all leave at the same time?"

Bill laughed, "You tell her Sylvia!"

Sylvia flushed red, "Don't you say a word. We put a big sign on the door of the hotel and restaurant saying, 'Closed-gone to Judy's and Jim's wedding. You're invited to the reception at the restaurant at eleven o'clock.' I think you'll find a lot of people there when we get back."

Judy, Jim, Della, and Mary led the wedding procession, riding their horses that the girls had decorated with two white ribbons on each side of their halters by their ears. Curly knew something important had happened and he pranced like a show horse all the way through Hazard to the livery stable. Raff warmly greeted

Judy and Della as he took their horses. He offered his congratulations and, in return, was invited to the reception.

Judy looked around the room and her heart swelled with emotion to the bursting point. She had made so many good friends. She thought of Myrt as a surrogate mother. Mr. Jenkins was like a father to her, Walt like a brother. Isaac and Sylvia were like her children, although they were too old to be. Even old Lance was a true friend. A lot of the business people of Hazard were there. The entire Brownlett family came, too. Mary and Della helped Isaac and Sylvia serve refreshments to all of their guests.

Three church members who played the fiddle, guitar, and banjo provided the music for dancing. Tables were pushed together to make room in the middle of the dining room. Jim and Judy were the first couple on the dance floor. He made a big show of twirling her around a few times and then surprised every one by doing a solo dance that was just stomping his feet to the beat of the music. He beamed his satisfaction when he received a round of applause from the guests.

The ladies in the crowd asked Judy to throw her bouquet. A younger, very slim, blonde lady caught it and almost swooned with emotion. Her escort was congratulated on his expected soon-to-be marriage to the bouquet catcher.

There were several gaily wrapped gifts and envelopes for the bride placed on the table in the corner. Sylvia seated Myrt at the gift table and she watched with glee as Judy opened the cards and gift packages. Anne Brownlett volunteered to keep a record of each gift and the giver.

Judy lost count of the amount of money that was in the cards and envelopes. Judy glanced up and her eyes met Jim's. She knew that he wasn't missing any of the money gifts and was mentally keeping track. She dismissed the little nagging worry that crept into her mind and concentrated on opening the gifts. The packages held a conglomeration of items, including various kinds of linens, dishes, vases, figurines, pots, pans, and a journal book.

The party for Judy and Jim lasted until almost four o'clock. There had been so much food served as refreshments, that Isaac said, "I doubt we have any supper crowd tonight. They've already been here and ate."

Myrt spoke up, "I'm here yet and I'll be hungry again by six o'clock!"

Isaac laughed, "Myrt you ain't part of the supper crowd, you're family!"

Bill said, "There'll be at least a dozen of us here anyway. This is a wonderful day. I wish the best for Judy and Jim. You're going on your trip tomorrow. May God bless you and keep you safe until you're home again!"

It was hard saying goodbye to Myrt. Judy worried that something would happen to her while she was gone. The jolly old lady shushed Judy's worries about her by saying. "God is looking out for me just like he always has. Didn't He send me to you so you could take care of me?"

Judy hugged her and said, "I won't wake you in the morning, Jim and I want to leave about daylight. The days are getting' shorter now and we want to be at my sister's house afore dark day after tomorrow."

The two newlyweds spent their first night together as man and wife in the Hazard Hotel. Jim was loving and charming. Judy was deeply in love with him and he knew it. Somehow, he was being too charming and was coming across as pretending when he declared his deep, abiding love for her.

Judy mentally scolded herself for being too suspicious. "Jim is probably just as nervous and unsure of himself as I am. Dear Lord, after living with the snake that Robert Smith turned out to be, it's hard not to be suspicious of any man. Forgive me. I love Jim. I took him today as my husband, for better or for worse. That was my vow. Help me to never break that vow."

Judy and Jim were awake well before dawn. Sylvia and Isaac had put together a food bag filled to the brim with delicious leftovers from yesterday's party. Della and Myrt were sleeping when they went to the Livery and mounted the horses. Judy had reserved old Ned again. They rode around to the front of the hotel and quickly packed their supplies and travel sacks on his back.

Bill, Sylvia, and Isaac stood on the large hotel porch and waved until they turned the first corner. Within minutes they were on the Harlan Trail. Judy looked at her new wrist watch and saw that it was a little before seven. They had a good start and she hoped they would have a dry trail all the way to Jonie's.

They arrived on the second day near dusk, and it was a celebration all over again. Jonie had invited the Miniards to eat with them. Alex extended his hand to Jim in welcome. Jim, in turn, put his arm around Alex. Enoch laughed, and said, "You've chosen one of the finest women I've ever known as your wife. Take good care of her or you'll answer to me and the old man over there!"

Jim was startled, and then laughed along with Enoch, "I have every intention of taking good care of Judy, and she's gonna take good care of me!"

Jonie made the supper a festive occasion. The laughing, singing, story telling, and good conversation was enjoyed by everyone. When it grew late and time for Israel and his family to leave, there were hugs all around. For Jim it wasn't nearly as special an event as it was for Judy.

They rested the next day and visited with the family. On Wednesday they left after breakfast to go to Harlan. As they neared the entry to the school, they ran into Miss Petit and Mr. Wilder. They were leading two mules to carry the supplies they would buy in Harlan. Judy spoke up, "Miss Kathryn Pettit, Hank Wilder, this is Jim Collins, my new husband as of last Saturday!"

Mss Pettit exclaimed, "Oh! My dear Judy, Congratulations! And congratulations to you too, Mr. Collins! It's a pleasure to meet you."

Mr. Wilder extended his hand to Jim. "I'm very pleased to meet you."

Judy said, "We're going to Harlan, too. We would like your company."

Hank Wilder nodded his agreement while Miss Pettit laughed merrily, "By all means, my dear Judy. It would please us greatly to have your company! I see you don't have poor Ned with you this time."

"He's at my sister's gettin' his rest. We have to return to Hazard tomorrow. The good Lord willing, we'll be back to spend Christmas with my father and the rest of my family."

"Tell me about Mary and Della. I had a very disturbing letter from Ethan telling me about the Cantrells and what a disappointment they turned out to be. Tell me more about them and what is Della doing besides going to school?"

Judy told Mr. Wilder and Miss Pettit the whole story of Della's bad experience with the Cantrell family. With a lot of pride in her voice, she told her how Della had fitted in perfectly as a food server, kitchen helper, and waitress. "She's doing well in school, too. We're so proud of her!"

Miss Pettit turned toward Jim, "Mr. Collins, what do you do when you aren't taking your bride on a wedding trip?"

Jim blushed red, "I'm a cook, Ma'am. I work at the Hazard Boardinghouse. We're both real good in a kitchen!"

"That is just lovely. Judy, dear, I'm so happy for you. So now your name will be Judy Turner-Collins."

"I think I'll be happier if people know me as Mrs. Jim Collins."

They stopped to eat at the Putney Boardinghouse; Jim couldn't help but compare it to the one where he worked. He whispered, "I don't want to hurt anyone's feelings, but my boardinghouse is cleaner and my cookin's better!"

Judy shushed him, "Well! I didn't know you were noticin' such things. What do you think of my restaurant? Does it meet your approval?"

"Your restaurant is A-1! It would pass any inspection test!"

Judy laughed, "Thank you, kind sir!"

There wasn't much time for shopping while they were in Harlan. Judy was most interested in going to Powers and Horton to find herself two pairs of shoes. She needed one pair for work and one pair for dress. She told Jim, "If you need shoes, this store has the best line of good ones that I've seen."

Judy and Jim had made their purchases and left the store when they came face to face with Loretta Helton. The woman stopped and stared at Judy, and then Jim. Judy smiled and said, "Mrs. Helton, this is my husband, Mr. Jim Collins. He's from Hazard. Jim this is Mrs. Loretta Helton from Big Laurel."

Jim smiled, tipped his hat, and said, "I'm pleased to meet you, Ma'am."

Loretta Helton hesitated at first. Then she felt forced to acknowledge both of them. She nodded a greeting to Judy, and smiled at Jim, saying, "Pleased to make your 'quaintance. I have shoppin' to do. Good day to you!"

Judy didn't explain anything about the Heltons to Jim. She was pleased that she had forced the woman to be civil. She pointed up the street and said, "We have some time left before we have to meet Miss Pettit and Mr. Wilder, so let's walk down to the end of the block to the Drug Store for ice cream.

They finished their ice cream and walked back toward the A&P Store. Long before they got there, Judy saw Miss Pettit and Mrs. Helton. They seemed to be laughing and talking normally. Judy guessed everything was all right between them, but she would never let down her guard to trust any Helton.

Judy told Jim they should stay on their side of the street while the two women talked with each other and wait until Mr. Wilder came with the pack animals. They didn't have long to wait. Loretta Helton went into the A&P Store just as Mr. Wilder came from the back of the store with the loaded mules. It was about two o'clock. They were in a hurry to leave Harlan. They knew they couldn't get to the school before dark, and it got cold when the sun went down.

They said goodbye to Miss Pettit and Mr. Wilder at the entrance to the school. Judy and Jim both urged their horses to a brisk trot. Suddenly they were both starving and knew that Jonie was saving supper for them.

They left the next morning before daylight. Jim was in a happy mood and tried to sing one of the songs they both knew. With his accent, the meaning of the words seemed to change, causing Judy to laugh right out loud. His happy mood lasted for the whole trip home. The trail was dry and the dense mountain foliage was near its peak in fall colors. The air was crisp and smelled vaguely of wood smoke from the scattered cabins along the trail.

They arrived in Hazard at dusk. Jim went with Judy to the hotel. He didn't have to be at work until Sunday night, but Judy had to work the next day.

The newly-weds were welcomed back with hugs and kisses on the cheek. Sylvia took their orders for supper and disappeared into the kitchen. When she came back, Judy asked about Myrt. Sylvia said that Myrt had supper in her room tonight. "She's still feelin' poorly. I'm worried about her."

When Sylvia brought their food, she was obviously nervous about something. She finally sat down at their table. "Miss Judy, Isaac asked me to marry him. I said yes. We set the date for Saturday May 31, 1924. We'll want to take that weekend off. Will that be all right with you?"

Judy was delighted. She mentally counted the months until May. She got to her feet and pulled Sylvia up, too. She hugged and kissed her in glee. "Honey, that's a good seven months away. That gives us plenty of time to plan."

She asked Isaac to come out to the dining room. The big man blushed red as he approached their table. She hugged him, "Oh, I'm so happy for you both. Did you tell Myrt? She's a hopeless romantic and will be so pleased!"

Sylvia, in a small hesitant little voice asked, "Miss Judy, what about being able to take that weekend off for the wedding? Will we be able to plan on that? If we can't both be off at the same time, I don't know what to do."

Judy looked at Jim. He didn't say anything, but he was grinning. She asked, "Honey, will you be able to fill in for them on that weekend? It's Memorial Day on that Friday. So we may not be too busy."

"I'll be happy to fill in, that is, if Isaac will trust me with his kitchen!"

Judy was beaming, "Then that's settled! You can begin to plan for your weddin', but you have to keep me and Myrt informed as you go along!"

After they ate supper, Jim went on up to their room while Judy stopped to see Myrt. She was propped up on pillows in bed, but she wasn't asleep. When Judy knocked on her door and walked in, she was instantly wide awake and grinning. "Lordy, honey, but it's good to see you. Where's that new husband of yours? You shouldn't oughta let him out of your sight."

"He's gone on up to the room. We're both tuckered out from two days on the trail, but I had to see you afore going to bed. Besides, I have great news! Isaac proposed to Sylvia and they want to get married next year on May thirty-first. I've been hoping this would happen. They're both good people and deserve to be happy. Now, how are you? Sylvia said you've been feelin' poorly."

"Oh, I'm doing as well as can be 'spected for an old woman. I'll be much better now that I've got 'nother wedding to look forward to. I can't wait 'til tomorrow to tell both of them how happy I am for them!"

Judy kissed her on the cheek, tucked her covers up under her chin, and said good night. "I'll see you in the mornin' and we'll have breakfast together."

Morning came earlier, or so it seemed. Judy's feet hit the floor as the clock sounded off at four o'clock. Jim was sound asleep. She didn't want to wake him so she got dressed by the low-glow from the outside streetlight.

When she got downstairs, she was pleased to find there wasn't much for her to do because Sylvia and Isaac had done an excellent job of helpin' out the morrow. She made coffee and put water on for the grits and oats. Then she brought the eggs, bacon, sausage, steak, and ham out of the cold storage locker. She was peeling potatoes for the home fries when Sylvia and Isaac came to work at five. Sylvia protested, "Miss Judy, you didn't have to do all of this. I should've come in earlier. We won't have much of a breakfast crowd 'til well after six."

"That's okay, honey, you can take over peelin' potatoes for me while I have a cup of that coffee. I want you to tell me where you and Isaac plan to live after you're married."

"His younger sister who's been livin' with his folks is leavin' to get married 'bout the same time we are. We'll prob'bly live with them for a while and work the farm. That's a while off yet and anything can happen. We'll always be willin' to help out here when you need us."

"What about Isaac's two brothers that are in prison? They'll be gettin' out next year and will come back here."

185

"Ma and Pa Blevins had his sister write to them and tell them that they won't be welcome here anymore. Isaac says he doesn't expect any trouble out of them. I'm not so sure, but we'll see."

Della came to work at eight o'clock. She greeted Judy with a tight hug and a kiss on the cheek. Sylvia told her to have breakfast with her mother and then she could put on her apron.

Jim showed up at before nine o'clock and joined them at the corner table. Della finished breakfast as he sat down. She excused herself to go to work.

Sylvia checked on Myrt at nine o'clock and found her struggling to get dressed. She wanted to have breakfast in the dining room. Sylvia fastened Myrt's dress in the back and, with a button hook, helped her put on her high-top shoes.

"Why don't you wear your low-cut house shoes to go from your room to the restaurant? No one'll know the difference under your long skirt."

"Lord love you child, but you're wrong 'bout that! I'd know, and I know it ain't fittin'!"

Myrt leaned on Sylvia's arm and used her walking stick to travel to the corner table in the dining room. She joined Jim and Judy. Although she had eaten breakfast, Judy ordered more coffee and a sweet roll. Della took their orders.

Without any hesitation, Myrt sang Della's praises. She still insisted on calling her by the nickname she had given her, "Dellie is a mighty fine young waitress and kitchen helper. She's been so good to me. Both she and Sylvia have me so spoiled that I figure I'm ruined!"

They all laughed when Judy assured Myrt she was already ruined.

When they were the only customers there, Myrt insisted on both Isaac and Sylvia coming out to see her so she could extend her congratulations to them. Isaac had to be urged to come, but Sylvia was laughing as she tugged at his arm. They both stood in front of the older woman as she fixed a stern eye on them. "Now, I want both of you to know that you're part of my family. When you get married, don't you dare to forget that. Don't you forget 'bout me!"

Sylvia laughed and hugged Myrt, kissing her on the cheek. "The good Lord knows that we'll never forget you! You're our family, too!"

Bill left Lance to cover the front desk so he could join them for breakfast and extend his congratulations to Isaac and Sylvia. Isaac asked Jim to come into the kitchen with him; he wanted to show him something different about the huge Majestic stove. When Jim left the table, Myrt asked Judy for a glass of cold buttermilk. "Sure, honey, I'll get you some. Do you want anything else?"

"I'd like some buttered toast."

"Okay, comin' right up with buttermilk and buttered toast!"

As soon as Judy was out of earshot, Myrt turned to Bill and said, "I needed to talk to you without anyone else hearin' us. I want you to ask one of your lawyer friends to come and see me next week so I can make out a legal Will. You and Sheriff Walt can be my two witnesses. No one else is to know."

"Yes, Myrt, I'll let you know when they can come to see you. Do you have the details written down or will you need to tell them what you want done?"

"I'll tell them what I want done. You'll have to 'range it so no one knows what I'm doing!"

"Trust me. Sheriff Walt and I will know how to do that."

Bill saw Judy and Jim coming back to the table and changed the subject, "Did you know that the sheriff's planning to leave Hazard and go west?"

"When's he supposed to do that?

"He can't leave 'til after the election in November next year and the new sheriff's sworn in. So it'll probably be sometime after January in 1926."

"That means we'll have a new sheriff. You know that old people don't like changes in their life. Oh, I'll miss Sheriff Walt. He's been my good friend!"

True to his word, Bill arranged for Arthur Babcock, a lawyer friend, to come to the hotel on Tuesday and meet with Myrt in her room. She deliberately ate a late breakfast and told Sylvia to bring her dinner tray around two o'clock. Bill chose the dinner hour for the time of her appointment, because Judy and Sylvia would be too busy to be nosy.

The attorney only needed a few minutes to write down the pertinent details of Myrt's wishes. He said he would fill in the rest of the legal verbiage that was required by law. Mr. Babcock assured her when it was ready for signatures it would be binding. She would have a copy, he would keep a copy for his files, and a copy would be legally recorded at the court house.

It was a week later that Bill made the follow-up appointment for Mr. Babcock and Walt to come to the hotel during the noon hour and meet with him in Myrt's room. Again, Judy and Sylvia were too busy to be a problem.

All three copies of the Will needed to be signed. After Mr. Babcock read the contents aloud, Myrt signed first, and then Bill and Walt signed as her witnesses. Mr. Babcock took the original with him to be legally recorded, kept a copy for his permanent files, and gave the third copy to Myrt.

After the three men left her apartment and went to the restaurant for dinner, if she had been able, Myrt would have gleefully danced a jig!

Chapter Fourteen

WEDDING BELLS FOR SYLVIA AND ISSAC

It was a Saturday evening and Myrt had been in her room all day. Thanksgiving had come and gone, Christmas was just around the corner, and Myrt couldn't have been happier. She had helped to celebrate Judy's and Jim's wedding in October and now she had Sylvia's and Isaac's May wedding to look forward to. With the legalities of her Will taken care of, she relaxed in the knowledge that her exact wishes would be carried out by Mr. Jenkins.

Health-wise, she knew it was just old age creeping up on her. She chuckled to herself and said aloud, "I thank God that my mind ain't as old as the rest of me! I do thank You, Lord, for every day of my life on this earth that I'm living here in the hotel where people that I love take care of me."

There was a knock on her door and Sylvia stuck her head in to ask if she wanted a tray or to come to the dining room for supper. Myrt grinned and said, "I'm feelin' so good I'll come out there to eat. Yes, I'll put on my house shoes so you won't have to use the button hook. I'm already dressed so we can go now."

Sylvia laughed, "You're impossible, you know. I love you, silly goose that you are. We all love you! Judy and Jim are sitting at your favorite table."

Leaning on Sylvia's arm, Myrt made her way slowly to the dining room. When she sat down, Judy greeted her with a hug and a kiss on the cheek. Then she and Jim continued discussing their Christmas trip to Big Laurel. Jim wanted just the two of them to go, but Judy insisted that the girls would go with them.

Myrt always expressed her opinion bidden or unbidden. She instantly silenced Jim, "Leave the girls here? What a mean idea. Christmas is for lovin' the Lord Jesus with your family. Their grandpa is a hundred and three years old. Perish the thought! Now since that's settled, let's order. I'm starvin'!"

Jim had a huge frown on his face, but bit his tongue. He was wise enough to know when he was beaten. He ate in stony silence. When Myrt left the table to return to her room he asked in a furious voice, "Why do we let that old woman tell us what we should do? I can't stand havin' her always buttin' into our business. And you let her think its okay for her to tell us what to do!"

"It's okay for her to give her opinion. She's usually right. You're mad 'cause she agreed with me this time. Just wait, some day I'll be the one that's wrong and she'll agree with you. Then you'll like her buttin' into our business!"

Jim laughed and mellowed instantly. Judy laughed, but took his quick temper seriously. It was a side of him that he managed to hide during the months of courtship. A thought went flashing through her mind of her brother Rob and his Becky. Rob's wise young wife said you had to overlook 'courtin' lies.'

Mary and Della looked forward to their annual Christmas trip and had no idea that Jim didn't want them along. They enjoyed Christmas at Jonie's and the sharing of their family's tradition of special foods, singing, and story telling.

Again, they all wanted to take advantage of the after-Christmas sales in Harlan. This year Jonie and Mellie wanted to go, too. Then Israel, Id, and Rhodie asked to join them. A caravan of nine riders left before daylight on Friday.

They were so early that Judy wondered if they would meet Miss Pettit and Mr. Wilder. It was about eight-thirty when they reached the school and there was no sign of them. Judy said, "If they're going, we'll see them in Harlan."

The road from the school to the beginning of the Laden Trail had been widened and graveled. Judy learned that the School used donation money to finance the construction of this road and that it was completed now all the way to the top of the tall mountain. It was rumored that the missionaries spent a hundred thousand dollars on the Laden Trail. They were waiting for the Kentucky Commonwealth or some Federal grant money to extend the road to Putney.

The improved road helped to cut the travel time, but when they arrived at Putney, instead of stopping, they ate while staying in the saddle and rode on. It was one o'clock when they arrived in town. They split up to shop and agreed to meet later at Creech's Drug Store for ice cream.

With Jim tagging along, Judy, Mary and Della went to the ten cent stores for school clothes. Then they went to Watson's for heavy coats and hats. Judy bought a few things for herself. Jim didn't buy anything. When she went to Powers and Horton's, he groused about how much money she was spending. She was glad that the girls were in the shoe department and out of earshot.

Judy said, "Don't you worry about me spending my money. Mary and Della both have money from their work and we save all year to come to the after Thanksgiving and Christmas sales both here in Harlan and in Hazard. The girls look forward to this and so do I. They're not wasting a penny. We're saving a lot of my hard earned money."

"I think you're forgetting that we're married now and all the money this family makes is our hard earned money!"

Judy's eyes grew huge and then narrowed. "Oh, when did we decide the girls' money and my money was our money? I've not heard you talk about your money as our money! I don't want to talk about this now and spoil the day for the girls, but we'll talk about it again as soon as we're alone."

The day wasn't spoiled for Mary and Della, but it was for Judy. The thought flashed through her mind again of her brother Rob and his 'courtin' lies.' She remembered, too, Alex's concern about Jim having a jealous side where others were concerned, but it never occurred to her that he would lay claim to all of her money. He talked like he meant to claim Mary's and Della's money, too. She was determined to not allow that to happen. Jim would never know how much money she had. No one knew and she wanted to keep it that way.

Jonie, Mellie, and Rhodie shopped at Scott's Ten Cent Store. Jonie bought school clothes for Mellie and the other children. Rhodie bought school outfits for Pauline, Katherine, and their brothers and sisters. Israel and Id shopped at the McComb supply company for farm tools and parts to fix a busted wagon. Some of the repair parts had to be ordered. Most of their purchases were put in large paper 'pokes' that would fit in their travel-sacks. Israel said he would come back later on to get the other farm tools, hardware, and repair parts.

Just as they were leaving for home, they saw Miss Petit and Mr. Wilder at the A & P. Judy and the girls crossed the street at the intersection to greet them. Miss Pettit said, "We won't be ready to go for another hour at least. I see you have some of the Lewis' and the Miniard's with you. You must have left extra early this morning. I'm sorry we didn't catch up with you!"

Judy said. "I'm glad we did get to see you. Give our love to Mrs. Zande. We probably won't be able to come back to visit for a long time, maybe not 'til next Christmas. We're leavin' now. We don't want to be too late gettin' back."

Judy, Mary, and Della said their goodbyes. They filled their travel-sacks with their purchases and slung them over the horses' backs, tied them securely, mounted, and started on the road toward Putney.

Jim and Judy weren't completely alone until they arrived back in Hazard. Judy was building a gnawing resentment toward Jim because she understood he claimed that all money, including Della's and Mary's, was under his control

It was Friday night when he brought up the subject of their money again. Judy was tired from having been three days traveling if you counted the Harlan trip and only wanted to sleep. When he insisted they had to talk about money, she asked. "Have you been worryin' about money ever since we were in Harlan?"

"Yes. Money's a serious subject with me. I want to know how much we have and how much you think we can save between us say over the next six months. I don't want to live like this much longer. I want us to be together. I want us to buy our own restaurant and work together to manage it. The girls can quit school and help us. If its family operated, we won't have to hire any extra help. I want you to agree with my plan for us to be a workin' family!"

Judy listened to all he said. She was too tired and sleepy to argue about anything. So she just nodded, and said, "It all sounds good. We'll begin to plan on having our own place tomorrow. Now, I have to get up at five. You can sleep in tomorrow. I can't. Go to sleep!"

Judy's eyes closed. She heard him grumbling something about women. She woke up just enough to say a silent prayer of thankfulness that they had made the trip over the mountains safely. She thought of her father and her sister Jonie and her family with love in her heart. The next thing she knew, the Big Ben was sounding off for five o'clock.

She shut off the alarm and checked to make sure Jim was still asleep. He gave a big snort and a heavy snore to signal that he hadn't heard the alarm clock. She silently walked over to her dresser, quietly opened the bottom drawer and took out some white satin material. She then gathered together a needle, some straight pins, thimble, white thread, a yard of store-bought white lace, and a small scissors. Then she put all of the items into a paper poke that she took with her downstairs to the restaurant.

She went immediately to the Majestic stove and prepared the kettles, skillets, and various food items for the beginning of breakfast. Sylvia wasn't due until six. She had a half an hour. She began making a lady's money-sack. She cut out the material in the traditional, rectangular pattern. Then she cut out the long ties that would reach around her waist. It was about five minutes to six when she finished cutting out the pattern. She quickly put everything back in the poke and tucked it away on the shelf under the reach-through, behind the gun.

They went to church on Sunday and then spent time with Mary and Della until it was time for Jim to go back to work at the boardinghouse. Judy had purposely given him no opportunity to talk to her alone except when they were in bed. Then she complained of being too tired and having to get up at five the next morning to go to work. The subject of money never came up.

Each morning she spent about an hour making her new lady's money- sack. It had to be well made and strong enough to keep its contents secure. When it was finished she waited until she locked up that night before retrieving the sack from its hiding place on the kitchen shelf behind the gun.

She crossed the lobby, said goodnight to Bill, and went upstairs to her room. With the window shades pulled down, she undressed to her petticoat and untied the belt to her old money-sack. While sitting on the bed, she emptied its contents into her lap. She counted her loose change, then the paper bills. She had almost five hundred dollars. Then she looked at her little yellow bankbook.

Judy never spent any money that she didn't have to. What with so little expense while working and living at the hotel, she had saved a tidy sum. When she added that to the proceeds from the sale of her farm, savings from her job at Pine Mountain School and the reward money she received from Walt, the balance in the savings account was now over four-thousand five-hundred dollars. At the beginning of the New Year she planned to add the next five-hundred dollars to reach her goal of five thousand dollars.

She was mumbling. "I'll go to the bank tomorrow and see about openin' a second savin's account. If I can do that, I'll put four-hundred dollars in it and keep my other money separate. My new money-sack will be for my first account book and some secret foldin' money. I'll wear it under my petticoat. My other money and the new account book will be in the old money-sack that I wear under my clothes over my petticoat. No one will know I've got two!"

She had to worry about Jim finding her money-sacks. The only times she took them off were when they made love, when she took a bath, and when she changed her clothes. There was no way to keep her second money-sack secret from him if he became suspicious and searched their room.

The next day while at the bank, she asked if there was a way that people could keep important papers in the bank's safe. The bank clerk was very happy to tell her they had safe deposit boxes for rent.

"How do they work?"

"You pay two dollars a year to rent a box. You're given a key to the box and we have a key, too. It takes your key and our key turning at the same time to open your box. You can't open it without our key and we can't open it without your key. So, you see? What you put in your box is your secret."

"Am I alone with the box when I put something in it?"

"Yes. You go in the little room over there by the big safe. You close the door and no one will bother you. When you're done, just come out and give me the box. Again, we have to use both keys to put it back in the safe."

"I want to rent a box in my name only."

"That'll be fine. Just fill out this card with your name, address, and the name of the person you wish to be your beneficiary."

"What's a beneficiary?"

"In the case of your death, your beneficiary is the person you want to have the contents of your safe deposit box. Your putting their name on the card gives us the authority to allow them to open the box and remove the contents."

Judy sat down at the long table in the small room and filled out the little white index card. After some thought, she chose Mary for her beneficiary. Della would be the most practical one, but Mary was older. It would be some time before she would trust Jim enough to give him a free hand with her precious money. Then Judy grinned, "Well, anyway, I don't plan on dyin' anytime soon!"

She gave the index card and two dollars to the bank teller. Her box number was 717. Under her breath she said, "That's easy to remember. My birthday is July the seventeenth! I'll think of my birthday and I'll think of 717."

Together they unlocked the little door to box No. 717. Judy took the long narrow box into the little room and shut the door. She lifted her skirts and removed her new money-sack. She looked at the contents and made sure that it contained her first savings account book and one hundred dollars. Then she folded the money-sack to fit perfectly, put it in the box, and shut the lid.

The bank teller gave her a shiny brass key. It had Yale 0717 stamped on it. She thanked him and left the bank.

Across the street was a jewelry store. She went in and looked at gold chains suitable to use with a pendant. She chose a lovely cameo brooch with a large pin across the back. Then she asked the manager if there was some way she could place her key on the back of the brooch and put both on a gold chain. He fitted what he called a 'slide' to the key so it would lay flat. Then he did the same thing to make a pendant out of the brooch. She bought a long heavy gold chain with a strong safety catch. Then she put the chain over her head and looked in the mirror. Satisfied that the pendant effect hid her key from sight, she paid the jeweler seventeen dollars and said, "You don't have to wrap anything. I'm goin' to wear them home. This is a Christmas present I'm buyin' for myself!"

She brazenly lied to Sylvia who noticed the pendant right away. "My Pa had an old key bronzed to look like shiny new brass and had it attached to the cameo brooch. I bought the long chain so I can wear it around my neck. He said he wanted to be the key to my heart."

Sylvia was impressed, "That is so sweet! I bet your sister helped him. I can't believe a man over a hundred years old still thinks of loving things to do. How are you going to wear that and cook? The steam will damage the brooch."

"Oh, I'll wear it under my dress while I'm helpin' in the kitchen. You don't have to worry. It's from my father and I'll guard this with my life!"

To keep her key hidden from Jim, when she had to remove the chain and pendant, she placed them carefully in her trinket box on top of her dresser. She decided it was best to hide them in plain sight. She was right. Jim didn't give women's foolishness and trinket boxes a second thought.

New Year's Day came and went. Jim had four days off over the holiday, but Judy stayed busy in the restaurant. It was the next Sunday before Jim finally asked her about how much money they had between them.

He said he had about six hundred dollars. She figured he was hedging just like she was and probably had twice that much. When he looked at her figures and saw that she had a savings and some extra cash, he was pleased. Well we have almost a thousand dollars. I figure we need about two-thousand to open our own restaurant. What do you think?"

"I think we should just keep savin' like we're doin' and see where we are by this time next year. We need to buy a place. I don't want to have to pay rent. After we find what we want, we'll need start-up money. Don't you think that we should have everything perfect from the beginnin'? You do, don't you?"

Jim reverted to his oily, accented sweetness that she now mistrusted. "Yes, I do. Honey, you've made me so happy. You're thinkin' like I am. Now you see why I was sayin' our money. Let's talk to the girls and see if they want to be a part of our family business. I'll bet they both will want to work with us!"

Judy didn't agree entirely. She countered his plan by remindin' him that the girls were still in school. She said, "Mary has another year to go to finish high school. Della has four. I want them to have good educations. They'll be more valuable as workers, but we'll cross that bridge when we come to it."

Now that she had her money safely hidden away from Jim, Judy could concentrate on Sylvia and Isaac. She talked with the sheriff about Isaac's two brothers who were due to be released from the LaGrange prison early in 1924. Judy was afraid that if they just showed up unexpectedly with nowhere to stay, they would cause trouble again for Isaac and his folks

Walt said he would look into it for Judy. It was the third week of March that the sheriff came by to talk to Isaac. "Your brothers will be released from prison the first week of April. Have they contacted you about a place to live?"

"Yes. They had somebody write a letter for them. They want money for a grubstake to go out west. Sylvia and I don't have much saved, but we'll give them what we can. They need good horses and a pack mule for supplies. I don't know how much all that'll cost, but it'll be worth it to have them leave."

Walt thought for a long minute, "I have some discretionary money. I'll talk to Raff at the livery and see what we can do that way. Maybe we can scare up some wedding present money to use, too!"

Sylvia talked to Judy about her worries over Isaac's two brothers being released from prison. She and Isaac were going to try to get together two horses, a mule, and a grubstake of supplies and money for them so they would leave. She was fighting back tears when she exclaimed, "If they do go out west somewhere, I hope they find a place to stay and never come back!"

"Are they offering to leave on their own if they get a good grubstake?"

"Yes. Sheriff Walt said that somebody at the prison told them they'd served their time and could live anywhere they wanted. They came up with the idea of movin' out west. We got a letter askin' for money so they could leave, but they didn't say how much it would take. I got the feeling that whatever we come up with, it won't be enough!"

"Are you afraid they'll get Isaac in trouble by forcin' him to help them gather up supplies and money to leave and go west?"

"He told me they got him in serious trouble afore. He's talked with Sheriff Walt about their wantin' money and he's tryin' to help Isaac to come up with 'nough to make sure they leave Kentucky altogether."

"Let me talk to Walt about this. I wouldn't say anything about it to anyone else. Let's keep it between you, me, the sheriff and Isaac. Don't even involve Isaac's folks. It'll just worry them. They'll have to know when the two brothers get out of prison. Let's hope they only have to say goodbye to them!"

Sylvia hugged Judy. "You make me feel like everything's goin' to be all right. God bless you for helpin' us!"

The first week of April was coming to a close. Walt told Judy that the Blevins brothers were scheduled to be released from LaGrange Prison on

Monday, the eighth. "LaGrange is one of Kentucky's oldest prisons. It's near the Ohio River a little east of Louisville. I'm sure they don't want to go back there. The prison will give them each a change of clothes and ten dollars. If no one meets them, they'll have to walk or hitch a ride to Hazard."

Judy said, "Walt, everyone involved would be a lot less nervous if they could be met somehow so they wouldn't come to Hazard. Could we manage to buy two horses and a mule to give to them along with enough money for a grubstake? They'd be a lot farther along toward going out west if they left from Louisville. How much money do you think it would take?"

"I need to talk with Raff at the Livery and see what it'll cost to get two good horses, a pack mule, and what new rigging they'll need. Isaac may have kept their old riding gear out at their family farm, but if it hasn't been oiled regular it'll be ruined. I'll ask him to bring their hunting rifles to me to check out. If I need to, I'll take their guns to the gunsmith and get them in good working order. Anything they'll need that we can take to them will save money later on. I think a hundred dollars each should be enough to buy their supplies.

I'll call the warden to let him know it'll be me that meets them. He won't let them out of the prison gate until he talks with me. I'll take some extra money with me in case I need it to satisfy them. If I have to, I'm also going to put the fear of God into them so they won't ever come near Isaac again!"

"Will you get into trouble with anyone by doing this on your own?"

"No, I won't get into trouble. I'm the sheriff and I do whatever I need to keep the citizens of Perry County safe. But, I have to know how much money Isaac and Sylvia can afford to spend on buying off his brothers. I won't take all of their savings, but they have to pay something for their own peace of mind."

Judy was deep in thought for a moment. Then she said, "Whatever amount they come up with I'll match. Sylvia, Isaac, and Jim mustn't ever know I put any of my money into buying off these two troublemakers."

"How can you match that much money without Jim knowing you used some of your money for something?"

"I've hid some of my money from him. We've not been married long enough for me to trust him completely. He knows nothing about the reward money you gave me and of my savings from working at Pine Mountain School."

"Where did you hide it?"

"I've got my saving account book locked away in a box at the bank. I made Mary my beneficiary in case something happens to me. I thought that was the best thing for me to do. I trusted my first husband and he betrayed me and his children in a most evil way. When we've been married a year, I may trust him enough. Then, again, I may never completely trust him!"

"Judy, what you've just told me will never be repeated unless something should happen, and I'm still here. When I leave in early 1926, you may want to confide in whoever will be the new sheriff."

Raff Pennington made the sheriff a good deal on two young horses and a good mule. When Walt asked Isaac about the condition of the leather on his brothers' riding gear, he admitted it hadn't been cared for properly.

Walt told Raff they would need new riding gear for both horses and also new pack-rigging for the mule. He asked Raff to add the saddles and everything else two people would need for long-distance travel in all kinds of weather. Walt used his discretionary money to pay for it.

Isaac told the sheriff that between them they had saved almost three hundred dollars. Walt told Isaac that he would need one-hundred dollars from him. Isaac protested, "My brothers won't take just fifty dollars each."

The sheriff told him that some friends who wanted to remain unknown had given him enough money so that when he put it with their hundred dollars there was enough for his brothers to leave from the LaGrange Prison gate and head west. "I'm going to meet them, myself. They'll have two good horses, a pack mule, and all the rigging they need for long distance travel. I'll give them about two hundred dollars for a grubstake. That's more than most families have when they leave to go west to stake out a homestead."

Isaac said, "Sheriff, I don't know what to say. I had no idea we had friends like that. You know who they are, of course. So, do thank them for us! I can't wait to tell Sylvia! We were on the verge of postponin' the weddin' 'cause we thought this was going to take every penny we had and all we could borrow."

Walt exclaimed, "Oh, no you don't! The wedding must go on. People have made special preparations and expect a wedding!"

Walt left on Wednesday by horseback to make the long trip to LaGrange Prison. He followed the Kentucky River towpath until he came to a major cross road that led to Lexington. On the other side of Lexington, he took the road that led northwest through Louisville, and then about another thirty miles northeast to the prison. He was leading the two young horses and the pack mule.

A smile played on Walt's lips as he thought of Judy's fear of his buying Ned for the Blevins Brothers and his assuring her that he didn't buy her favorite!

On Monday morning, he met the warden and arranged to meet the two brothers at 2:00 o'clock that afternoon when they came through the prison gate. Walt saw them before they saw him. They were walking briskly, grinning, and talking loud to each other. When they saw Walt waiting for them they stopped and stared, "Sheriff Middleton, what're you doing here? We ain't done nothing!"

"I know you boys haven't done anything wrong. I spoke to the warden and he gave you both a good report. What I'm here for is to act in place of your brother, Isaac. He received a letter from you saying you wanted to travel west to settle on land out there, but that you needed horses and a grubstake. The animals I have here are for both of you and here are the three Bills of Sale showing your ownership. He furnished you with the rigging you'll need for travel."

Both men stood still with their mouths open, staring at him as if they were in a trance. Then Josh found his voice. "You came all this way to bring us these horses and a mule and you say we own 'em. You know we can't read too good. Who signed the Bills of Sale?"

"Raff Pennington. All three animals were bought from his Livery."

Gabe spoke up, talking to his brother, "Josh, we still need money for a grubstake. We have to live while we travel out west."

Josh asked, "Was Isaac able to send us any money?"

"He sent some. He was afraid it wouldn't be enough. How much do you boys think you'll need?

Josh looked at his brother, "I don't know. Well, Gabe, do you think we could get by on about a hundred and fifty dollars?"

"Yes we probably could, but I doubt Isaac was able to raise that much money and pay for these animals, too."

Walt was beaming his pleasure, "Boys, your brother really loves the two of you! He used his savings and, I think he borrowed some so he was able to send you two hundred dollars for a grubstake."

Gabe grew suspicious and asked, "What does Isaac want from us? Do we have to pay him back, and if we do, how soon?"

"That's up to you. He didn't tell me to ask for anything from you except that when you get settled on your own land in the Dakotas or Montana to let him know where you are and how he can get in touch with you. Everything is here that you need so that you can head west from right here outside these prison gates. You're free men and can do whatever you want with your lives from here on. So, good luck to both of you!"

Walt mounted his horse and started to ride back toward Louisville. He looked back and saw that the two brothers had recovered from their shock and they were riding after him at a brisk trot while leading the pack mule. When they caught up with him, they asked about the names of the horses and the mule.

Walt said, "They're young, I don't think they have names yet. You can give them whatever names you like and that way they'll really belong to you."

Gabe asked, "Do you mind if we ride along with you 'til we get to the crossroad that'll take us to the Ohio River ferryboat to cross over to Indiana. That's the way we planned to go. We think that the country stores in Indiana will be cheaper than the stores in Louisville. It's still early so I think we'll be able to buy some supplies afore dark. It's sure good to have our old huntin' rifles. They're in good shape, too. When you get to Hazard, be sure to tell Isaac that we do thank him for all he's done for us. He's a good brother to us; much better than we deserve. We'll send him letters along to let him know where we are."

The three of them were silent, each deep in their own thoughts until they reached the center of Louisville. Walt turned in his saddle to shake hands with both of them. The crossroads where they parted company was wide. For several blocks in each direction, it was lined with shops and stores. The brothers turned northwest and Walt figured they were an hour's ride from the Ohio River ferry.

He wanted to find a hotel or boardinghouse so he could spend the night in Louisville. He located a livery stable and arranged for the care of his horse. He asked the man for the name of a good place to spend the night and to eat supper.

He directed Walt to a hotel near a major race track. He was surprised by how nice the hotel was, and how crowded it was with people for that part of the city. There was a mixture of horse drawn buggies and wagons, and the pesky automobiles. He hoped the noisy things never caught on. He grumbled, "Give me a good horse any day. You can't make a friend out of one of those contraptions."

He went inside and registered for the night. When he told the desk clerk that he was going out for a while and would be back later, he watched as the man placed his room key in the cubby hole on the back wall.

Walt wanted to make sure the brothers did get on the ferry and cross the river into Indiana. They were about a half-an-hour ahead of him by now, but he could ride to the river's edge and make sure they were gone. He mumbled under his breath. "When I strike out on my journey west, I'll know where to stay in Louisville and how to cross the Ohio River to Indiana."

Walt sat on his horse and watched the ferry pull away from the shore. He saw the two brothers with their horses and pack mule standing at the boat rail looking toward the Indiana shore line. He stayed well back behind some trees so he was out of sight if they should look back. He didn't have to worry. Their eyes were glued to the far side of the wide river.

Satisfied, he headed back to the hotel and the restaurant to have a good supper. Early the next morning after a big breakfast, he was on his way home.

Walt followed the road through Lexington and on to the Kentucky River. He took a ferry across the river and followed along the towpath through the mountains. He was satisfied that they had done the right thing regarding Isaac's brothers. With a new start in life they just might make it fine out west. He deliberately had not told them about Isaac and Sylvia getting married. When they wrote their first letter, Isaac could tell them about that when he answered them.

Judy and Della were full of plans for the wedding. When Mary was with them on Sunday, they plotted and planned even more. Bill was leaving in another week for Florida and would be gone a month, but would be back in plenty of time to fulfill his role of walking Sylvia down the aisle to give her away.

The only one grumbling about the time they were spending on Isaac and Sylvia was Jim. He groused, "You'd think they were kinfolks the way you carry on. They just work here. You're the boss of them. Why don't you act like it?"

"They mean more to me than just hired-help. They're like family and I'll keep treating them like I always have. I owe them both a lot. You need to treat people nice. Remember the old saying, *to have a friend, you have to be a friend!*"

On the day of the wedding, Judy, Mary, Della, and Myrt were dressed in new silk dresses, hats, and gloves. Bill was elegant in his three piece suit, cummerbund, and tall silk-embellished hat.

Jim didn't attend the wedding. He had a good excuse. He was cooking for Isaac. Della only stayed for the ceremony and then hurried back to help him.

The newlyweds' reception was in the social room of the church. Mary and Judy, with Anne's help, served food and drinks to all the guests. As Sylvia opened the gifts, Anne kept the registry for her. Then they said goodbye and left in a gaily decorated wagon. Neither of them would say where they were going.

Chapter Fifteen
MYRT'S LEGACY

May 31, 1924 was a happy day for Isaac and Sylvia. Their friends couldn't have been more supportive. Even the sheriff couldn't stop grinning. He cornered Judy and said, "We'll never tell Isaac how much we spent to get his brothers out of their lives. He and Sylvia both work hard. They deserve to have some happiness. Deputy Tim is holding down the fort for me, so I think I'll have supper with you at the restaurant. You said that Jim's cooking tonight. I've never tasted his cooking!"

Judy laughed, "I don't think any of us have, except Della. She's worked with him almost all day. Maybe after everyone is served she can join us."

Bill asked Lance to watch the front desk of the hotel and to come for him if anyone wanted a room. The corner table wasn't big enough for all of them so they put another three tables together in the center of the room. Bill said, "This celebration is in honor of our absent newlyweds. God bless them!"

Bill and Walt carried on a lively conversation while Myrt, Judy, Mary, and the Brownlett's gave Della their orders. Jim's 'special' was roast chicken with sides of cornbread dressing and chicken and dumplings as the entrée. His other sides were a spicy potato salad, turnip greens, and a cooked medley of peas, carrots, and cauliflower. Also, he offered a dinner roll, biscuits, or cornbread.

Della took their orders and retreated to the kitchen. Judy's keen ears picked up that Jim was complaining again about wasting time on a wedding. She frowned in spite of her resolve to not let him upset this day. When Della brought their food, she was not her usually smiling self. Judy knew that Jim was making her young daughter uncomfortable because of his bad mood.

Jim was an inconsiderate grouse, but he could sure cook! The rising aromas from the steaming plates were irresistible. Bill, Walt, and Ethan dug right in and their facial expressions gave testimony to the quality of the food. Walt said, "No wonder the folks at the boardinghouse don't want him to ever leave. Everything on my plate is delicious. Judy, Jim could give Isaac some pointers."

Bill and Ethan nodded their complete agreement.

Judy had to agree with them that Jim was an excellent cook.

For dessert they had a choice of cake, pie, or cobbler. After they finished eating, Judy went to the kitchen and asked Jim to come out to the dining room. He asked her to give him a minute to change to a clean apron.

When he presented himself at their table, the three men all started to talk at the same time. Then Walt spoke for all of them, "We've just had the best meal we've ever had. I know you were a cook in the army. Your good cooking would make one want to join up! Everyone really enjoyed your special tonight! "

Jim had the good grace to blush and say, "Well, thank you, sheriff, for those kind words. I put my heart into my cooking, and I'm glad you all liked it."

Everyone at the table nodded their heads in agreement. When Jim retreated back to the kitchen, Della came to their table and was smiling. Judy knew their complimenting Jim's cooking had at least lightened his mood.

Myrt struggled to her feet. She supported her weight by holding onto the top of the table. She was beaming at all of them when she spoke to Della. She used the nick name she had created for her, and said, "Dellie, Lord love you child! Sit yourself down here a minute. I want to say something to you all"

Myrt's eyes began to brim with tears as she began to speak from her heart. "All of you've become my family. You've given this old woman so much pleasure these last few years. I know that you've gone out of your way to 'clude me in the joys and sorrows of your own lives, and I just want you to know how much love I have in my heart for all of you."

With that said, Myrt fell back into her chair. Judy was instantly on her feet and at Myrt's side. She asked, "Are you all right, honey?"

"Of course I'm all right! I got to say what I wanted to say, but I just can't stand up for any length of time. My legs give out and I sit down, hard!"

Judy laughed and kissed her cheek. Della asked, "Miss Myrt, can I go back to work now?"

"The Lord love you, Dellie! Yes, go on back to work, child."

Everyone was reluctant to let the day end. Walt scrapped his chair back from the table, saying, "I'd better get over to the office and let Tim come to eat his supper. I'll tell him to order Jim's special."

The Brownletts and Mary said their goodbyes and left. Bill asked Judy to walk with him to the hotel lobby so he could discuss something with her. She told him to go ahead and she would be right behind him. "I'll be there as soon as I tell Jim that I'll be back in a few minutes to help him clean up."

When Judy went to the kitchen to speak to Jim, he complained, "It's about time you paid some attention to me and your job. I've been working here all day. I told Della she could leave, but I want you to help me prepare for the morning breakfast crowd. How long will you be this time?"

"I don't know. Mr. Jenkins, who is my boss, wants to talk to me. I'll be back as soon as I can."

"Oh! So, go on! Don't keep the man waiting. Just hurry back as soon as you can. I need help here and I want to rest awhile before bed tonight."

Judy was angry with Jim for having a grumpy attitude. She mumbled, "He volunteered to cook so the weddin' could take place as planned. No one forced him. We could have closed for the day. He's goin' to get paid for two days. I wonder what Bill wants to talk to me about. I hope nothin's wrong!"

When she walked into the lobby, she noticed that Lance was gone. Bill got up from behind the desk and walked over to one of the big overstuffed chairs and sat down. Judy pulled a straight chair over near him, sat down and waited for him to begin. He came right to the point, "You know that my brother's asked me several times to move to Florida to be near him. He asked me again on this trip and I'm seriously considering it. If I do make this move, I'll need to sell the hotel and restaurant. I figure that'll take a good year or more unless I get real lucky."

"Bill, if you sell out and move to Florida, will I ever see you again? You've been so good to me. I don't know what I would have done without you. Do you really have to move to Florida? You can sell out, but can't you just retire and still live here?"

"You know that I don't have any real family here. I need to be with relatives who'll take care of me later on. My brother is fifteen years younger than I am and I hope will outlive me by a lot of years. If I'm going to make such a move I should do it while I still have my health. Anyway, it's not going to happen for at least another year."

Judy was silent for a few moments, then her eyes widened in alarm. She exclaimed, "It just hit me! You and Walt are both talking about leaving Hazard. You're going to the deep-south and he's heading out to the far west. My two best friends in the world are leavin' me at the same time!"

Bill said, "We're making plans. Nothing's solid yet. Anyway, 1926 is a long way off. Let's just wait and see how things work out. I heard what Jim said to you earlier about wanting you to clean up for him. I don't want you taking any guff off of him. He's lucky to have you. I remember when Isaac was acting the oaf and you set him straight. See if you can't do the same for Mr. Jim!"

Judy couldn't help the warm smile she gave to her good friend. "Don't worry about Jim. He's a real good cook, but I guess a temperamental one. So far I've been able to josh him out of his bad moods. He'll be here 'til about seven tomorrow night and then he'll go back to the boardinghouse."

Judy changed the subject to say, "I'm real worried about Myrt. Have you noticed that she seems to be expecting to die soon? I'd hate it if something happened to her."

"Yes. I've noticed it and I feel the same way you do. I think what Myrt is trying to tell us is that she isn't afraid of dying and that she wants to prepare us for whenever it happens. She's a good friend to all of us. Let's just hope for the best and enjoy the time we have together. Enough of this kind of talk! Go and try to placate your grumpy old husband!"

"What does placate mean?"

It means to make a man happy enough to change his grumpy mood!"

Judy laughed and exclaimed, "Oh! Bill, if you ain't the wise one!"

She hurried back to the kitchen and took over for Jim. She told him to go ahead up to their room and she would be up as soon as she was done.

"What did Mr. Jenkins want with you?"

"He wanted to tell me about his trip to Florida and his plans to retire down there in a year or so. I'll tell you more about it later, if you're still awake."

It was almost nine o'clock when she locked up and went upstairs. Jim was wide awake. Her news that the hotel and restaurant might be for sale had him excited and scheming. "Do you think he'd separate them? How much do you think he'd want for the restaurant? I really like that kitchen. Let's save every penny so we might have a chance to work a deal with the old man."

"We might offer to rent the restaurant from the new owner, but I doubt there's any way to separate the two in a real estate deal. I don't think it would be legal. Anyway, it's late and I have to get up at four o'clock. You don't have to come down until around six o'clock. It's Sunday, so there's not much of a breakfast crowd. It gets real busy for the Sunday-dinner folks though."

Jim was definitely in a much better mood with the prospects of them getting their own restaurant within a year or so. When he began to snore, Judy sat up in bed and looked at him. The street light at the corner gave enough light for her to see him plainly. He had gone to sleep with a dreamy smile on his face. She grinned, slid out of bed, and dropped to her knees for her prayers. Tonight she had some special things to talk over with God.

She prayed, "Thank you God for this special day. Bless Isaac and Sylvia and their marriage. Take care of Bill and Walt as they plan to leave to begin new lives far away. Please take special care of dear Myrt. If she's right and it is her time to leave us and be with you, hold her in your loving arms and let her passing be a painless one. Bless my Pa and all of my family. Bless Della and Mary. Give a special blessing to Reverend Brownlett and his family. Bless Jim and help him to control his temper and be happy with what we have. Lead me to make the right decisions as I try to follow Your plan for me. In Jesus' name. Amen."

Tonight's prayer was longer than usual, but it was important that she included God in everything that touched her life and that of her family and friends. Jim's moods and temper-fits worried her more than she wanted to admit. So far he hadn't been violent in any way, but she was fearful that he was capable of becoming a danger to her and to her girls.

Sunday passed without incident. Judy didn't take Curly out to exercise as was her custom because Jim was working in Isaac's place and she and Della were filling in for Sylvia. Bill used his front desk chair to wheel Myrt into the dining room for all three meals. Judy tried to sit with her while she ate. Each time she returned to the kitchen, Jim grumbled at her for wasting time on that old woman. Each time she joshed him out of his bad temper.

Judy noticed that Della had as little contact as possible with Jim.

Della didn't want to cause her mother to worry, but if she could have, she would have avoided all contact with him. After she hooked her food orders onto the rotating wheel just inside the reach-through window and received her filled orders from Jim, she silently picked up the plates to serve the diners. Unless there were special instructions from the customer about the food preparation, she didn't talk to him at all.

Judy was ashamed to say she was relieved when eight o'clock came and Jim left for the boardinghouse. She wouldn't see him again until Friday evening. Jim, on the other hand, was full of dreams and schemes on how they might end up owning the restaurant free and clear. He had held back about twelve hundred dollars in a savings account that Judy didn't know about. He guessed she had done the same with some money. If she had even a thousand all together they might get a loan and buy the whole building.

He grumbled, "She has to stop taking so much time and trouble helpin' other people like that old woman, Sylvia, and Isaac. Instead, if she spent all that wasted time trying to help us get ahead, we'd be better off. And, she spoils those two girls. They're makin' money and by rights it belongs to me and our family. I've got to take over managin' the money. After all, I've got more than she does! Come next Friday, so help me God, I'll change things!"

The next morning Isaac and Sylvia were on time. Judy smiled while watching them show a new tenderness toward each other as they all worked together that Monday morning.

At about nine o'clock, Bill knocked on Myrt's door ready to wheel her to the restaurant for breakfast. When she didn't answer, he opened her door and was instantly alarmed because she seemed to be disoriented. He left her and went to find Judy. By the time they returned she was sitting on the side of her bed. When she saw them, she said, "Something's wrong with me. I'm going to need help in gettin' dressed. I think I'd better sit in my chair and have Sylvia bring me a tray. Bill, you'd better call the doctor to come to see me this mornin'!"

They assured her they would take care of her. Bill left to call the doctor. Judy went to tell Sylvia that Myrt would need a breakfast tray, and then she went back to help her to wash up, and with getting dressed.

The doctor came at around eleven o'clock. Judy and Bill both waited while he examined Myrt. When he came out to the lobby, he said, "I'm afraid she's having episodes of mental confusion due to hardening of the arteries. Someone should keep a close eye on her. She could have a fatal stroke at any time. However, she's just ornery enough to go on doing whatever she takes a mind to. That's all right. Her fine attitude is helping her to deal with this. I think that in the long run, she'll live a lot longer than other folks who give up and die."

Myrt had her breakfast and dinner in her room, but insisted on going with Judy to the restaurant for supper. They ate together, talking and laughing. Myrt seemed to be her old self again.

On Tuesday morning, June 3, 1924, Judy found that Myrt had died in her sleep during the night. She was devastated. Her comfort came from knowing that God had answered her prayer and had taken Myrt in His loving arms and led her away from this life peacefully and painlessly.

Judy, Bill, Walt, and Sylvia met later that afternoon in the hotel lobby to plan for Myrt's memorial and burial. Bill enlisted the Hazard Funeral Home to handle the arrangements. He told Judy to take Sylvia with her to pick out a nice coffin for Myrt. Then he said, "Take the clothes you think she'd want to be buried in. I think she'd like the new dress she wore for Sylvia's wedding. Don't worry about the expense. She asked me to see that she was put away nice.

I'll come down to the undertakers later to see about the grave, headstone, and whatever else they offer to make the memorial service extra nice. I sent Lance to let Walt and Reverend Brownlett know. We'll want Ethan to preach the funeral. I have to send a telegram to her daughter as soon as I know when we'll have the memorial service."

Judy was puzzled, but touched by the time and effort that Bill was devoting to Myrt's final affairs. He was showing a deep affection for the older woman. The funeral would be on Monday, June 9 at eleven a.m., with burial taking place immediately afterwards.

Early Wednesday morning, Bill sent a telegram to Gertrude and Roger Burnett in Big Laurel. They would have four days to prepare themselves and make the journey to Hazard.

When they arrived in Hazard on late Saturday afternoon, they went straight to the Hazard Hotel to see Mr. Jenkins. He was very considerate and gracious, inviting them to stay at the hotel as his guests. He said, "After you're settled in, come to the restaurant to have supper with us. We'll wait for you."

When they presented themselves in the hotel lobby, he led them into the restaurant dining room. Judy, Jim, and Walt were already seated at the large round table in the corner. When all six of them were seated, Bill introduced the Burnett's to Jim and Walt.

After Della took their orders, Gertrude looked at Bill and asked, "Is there going to be a wake for my mother tonight and tomorrow night?

Bill answered, "Yes. It's tonight from six to nine o'clock, and tomorrow from four until nine o'clock at the funeral home. It's on High Street. We'll walk over there after supper. Myrt was a good friend to a lot of people and we all wish to join you as part of her family to greet people. Is that all right with you?"

Gertrude smiled through tears, "Oh, my, yes! We'll be so grateful. We are the only members of the family that could come from Big Laurel and I didn't know how we were goin' to be able to take care of everything."

Bill smiled with compassion in his eyes, "Myrt's funeral is Monday at eleven o'clock at the church. You'll meet Reverend Ethan Brownlett at the wake tonight. He was a good friend to your mother. He'll preach her funeral."

Roger looked at Bill and asked, "How long do you think we'll need to stay in Hazard. I know you've invited us to stay at the hotel as your guests, but we can't keep taking advantage of you."

"Let's wait until after the funeral on Monday to discuss that. It's going to be hard on everyone just to get through these next two days."

Judy had remained silent during the conversation between Bill and the Burnett's. She was startled when Jim turned to her and said, "I've got some work that needs to be done. I've got to go."

Then he left the restaurant.

The next two days seemed endless to Judy. Her grief over Myrt's passing was hard to endure. Jim's grousing over the amount of time she was wasting 'on that old woman' only made matters worse. Mr. Jenkins couldn't help noticing Jim's lack of consideration for everyone's feelings where Myrt was concerned. For the time being he chose to ignore Jim's moods.

Bill ordered two mourning-wreathes; one each for the hotel and restaurant doors. There were signs next to them to let people know they were closed for Myrtle Baker's funeral.

Then he said, "My plan is that after the burial we'll come back to the restaurant just to get a snack. I'm sure we can scare up enough meat and bread to make sandwiches. Then we'll open the hotel doors at three o'clock and the restaurant for supper customers at five. Judy, do you think we can manage that?"

"I'm sure we can. I've always got some extra dishes made and stored in the cooler just for emergencies. We'll be fine."

The church was only about a quarter full. Myrt had outlived most of her friends from her younger days. Judy had remembered the beautiful rose garden that had been so lovingly tended on Myrt's farm, and she ordered a 'blanket' of red, white, and yellow roses to be placed on the coffin.

Reverend Brownlett gave a fitting eulogy that was a celebration of life for Myrt. It ended with a well-known poem entitled 'Crossing the Bar.' After the service was over, most of the people who were there accompanied the hearse to the Hazard Hillside Cemetery. It was just a few blocks from the church.

When they returned to the hotel it was about two o'clock in the afternoon. They found Jim sitting on the porch steps in front of the hotel. He had used the panic bar on the inside of the door to get outside on the porch, but when he tried to go back inside, the door automatically locked. Judy braced herself for an angry outburst from Jim, but he controlled himself in front of Mr. Jenkins and the sheriff. Judy unlocked the restaurant and asked everyone to come in and be seated. "I'll have sandwiches, potato salad, and a relish tray together in just a few minutes. There'll be coffee and lemonade, too."

Gertrude, Sylvia, and Isaac followed Judy to the kitchen to help. Jim stayed in his chair and began an idle conversation with Bill, Walt, and Roger Burnett. Bill and Walt were still thinking about the funeral service. Each had a role to play now that it was over in executing Myrt's Will.

Bill asked Roger Burnett how long he and his wife planned to stay in Hazard. Roger said, "I'm not sure how much time we'll need to take care of Mom Baker's personal affairs. I think my wife needs to just relax tonight and we'll worry about that tomorrow.

"That sounds like a good plan. There's no need to rush things. I'll be at the front desk in the morning. Why don't you come to see me after you've had your breakfast?"

"Mr. Jenkins, I want to thank you for all you did for Mom Baker. We weren't in a position to take care of her like we should have. She had some good friends here and I can tell you all cared about her. We'll do what you asked about seeing you in the morning."

The ladies made a big production of setting up a buffet-style array of food. They had ham, roast beef, and chicken salad sandwiches. Judy had whipped up a creamy dip with chopped green onions to use with the large relish tray. She watched and listened to Myrt's family and friends as they visited with each other and enjoyed each other's company.

Judy firmly believed that loved ones who passed over were never really that far away. She imagined that Myrt was sitting at her favorite table in the corner. If she was there, Myrt was smiling her approval!

Just as Bill had requested, the next morning at about ten o'clock the Burnett's came to the front desk to talk with him. He asked them to sit on the large overstuffed divan over against the far wall, and then he settled himself into one of the chairs facing them. He directed his attention to Gertrude. His voice was compassionate as he began, "I don't know if you knew that your mother left a detailed and legal Will."

Gertrude exclaimed, "My goodness, no! We had no idea. What all is involved? What do we have to do? If Ma had unpaid bills, we're good for them."

Roger interrupted, "Mr. Jenkins, we expected to be responsible for some of Mom Baker's last expenses. I was surprised that you had gone ahead and made all the necessary arrangements. The undertaker told me that you signed for everything in your own name. Why did you do that? It'll take us some time to pay you back for all of your expense, but you will be paid."

Bill held up his hands to stop Roger before he said any more. "I'm sorry that you were worrying about that. There was no need. I didn't feel it was fitting to talk about money before your mother was buried."

Gertrude asked, "What did Ma put in her Will? What should we be doing about her Will?"

Bill looked at both of them, "Myrt named me as executor of her Will. The sheriff and I were her witnesses. Her attorney is Arthur Babcock. He drew up the legal document and it was recorded by the Perry County Court Clerk. I'll ask Mr. Babcock and the sheriff, to meet us here at three o'clock tomorrow afternoon. The other people she has named should be here, too."

Roger asked again, "What about your expenses from the funeral arrangements and her other final expenses? How will we pay for them?"

Bill looked at Gertrude, "Your mother had a paid up five-hundred dollar 'Burial' insurance policy for more than twenty years. That paid for the funeral with money left over. Like I said, don't worry about the expenses. Mr. Babcock will read her Will tomorrow afternoon for all to hear Myrt's wishes. Do you want to go through your mother's personal possessions?"

"Yes. I wasn't sure which one was her room or which floor it was on. Can I keep the key? It may take me a while to look at everything."

"I have the key right here. You may keep it as long as you need to."

He showed them to Myrt's room, turned to Gertrude and said, "Your mother would wish for you to have any of her personal belongings that you want. Take all the time you need to decide. "

Promptly, the next day at three o'clock, Mr. Babcock, Bill, Walt, Judy, Sylvia, Isaac, Lance, and the Burnett's assembled together in the restaurant dining room. There were signs on the hotel and restaurant doors saying they were closed for a meeting.

Mr. Babcock wasted no time. After he called the roll of participants and was satisfied that everyone was present that were named in the Will, he proceeded to read it in its entirety.

Myrt instructed Bill as her executor to use the paid up insurance policy to pay her final expenses. Then she listed by name and the amounts they were inheriting from her estate the following people:

My daughter, Gertrude and her husband, Roger	$ 500.00
William Jenkins for acting as my executor	50.00
Walter Middleton, Sheriff and good friend	50.00
Sylvia and Isaac Blevins, caretakers and good friends	300.00
Lance Middleton, good friend	50.00

After all final expenses, including any medical and legal expenses, have been paid and the people named in this my final Will and Testament have received their designated amounts of money, I do bequeath the balance of my estate to Judy Smith-Collins, caretaker and good friend."

Bill looked around the table at everyone. Gertrude and Roger were stunned. Sylvia and Isaac were equally stunned. Judy was sitting with both hands locked together on top of the table and appeared to be in a trance. Her jaw had dropped and her mouth was still open.

The attorney addressed Gertrude and Roger, "Your mother wanted you to have any of her personal possessions that you choose. After you make your choices, she also wanted Sylvia Blevins and Judy Smith-Collins to receive whatever they choose of her possessions. Then, whatever is left that needs to be disposed of she wishes it to be donated to Reverend Brownlett's church.

The Will and Final Testament of Myrtle Baker will be filed as is required by law with the court to be probated. Do I hear any objections to Mr. Jenkins proceeding to follow Myrtle Baker's last wishes?"

Gertrude struggled to find her voice. With eyes brimming with tears, she said, "I had no idea Ma made such detailed 'rangements. The good friends that she named showed her love and friendship when she needed it more than at any other time in her life. I thank you from the bottom of my heart for makin' my mother's last years on earth so lovin'. Mr. Jenkins, please do follow her wishes just as she has outlined them. Is there anything that Roger and I need to do?"

"No, everything is taken care of for you. Myrt, God rest her soul, wanted it that way. You should go through her things again and make sure you have taken all you want for yourself. You can be with Judy and Sylvia when they make their choices. I know she wanted each of you to have some of her treasured possessions to remember her by."

The attorney turned to Judy and said, "After all the disbursements are made from Mrs. Baker's estate by Mr. Jenkins, the remaining funds will be issued to you. It's up to the court as to when the monies may be disbursed. The Will is very clear as to her wishes. I don't believe probate will take very long."

Bill asked, "Arthur do you have some business cards that you can give to each of the people here? If they have questions, they can contact you."

Arthur Babcock nodded in agreement and searched through the papers in his satchel to find the cards and then handed them out to everyone.

He stood up to leave, "If no one has any questions, I'll go now. You know how to contact me. It was nice meeting all of you."

As soon as he was gone, everyone started talking at once. Bill rapped on his desk top and said, "I think all of you want to know the approximate amount of Myrt's Estate. After everything's settled and the court and other legal fees are paid,

I figure there'll be between nine-hundred to a thousand dollars left. That money will go to Judy. This was Myrt's wish."

Gertrude looked at Judy, got up from her chair, and walked over to her. She was smiling through tears as they embraced. Then she said, "Judy, you couldn't have been kinder to my mother if you'd been my sister. When she sold the farm we told her to use the money to live here at the hotel like she wanted and where you'd take care of her. I know that Sylvia loved her, too. I'm happy that Ma was able to name all of you in her Will. I still don't know how she was able to live so well and still have money left over. Ma was amazin'!"

Bill was smiling, too, and said, "I think Miss Myrt raised an amazing daughter.

Chapter Sixteen
SMILING THROUGH TEARS

The Burnetts left on Friday morning. Bill, Judy, and Sylvia stood on the porch, seeing them off. Gertrude and Roger had stayed a full week at the Hazard Hotel. As they parted company, Bill assured them that as soon as Myrt's funds were legally released from Probate he would send Gertrude a bank check. "You can cash the check at the Harlan County Savings and Loan. It'll be a lot of money to carry with you. I suggest that you place it in a savings account at the bank. That'll be the safest place for you to keep the money for now."

Gertrude and Roger Burnett mounted their horses and looked at Bill. Roger said, "Mr. Jenkins, I don't know how to ever thank you 'nough for your kindness. We'd like to hear from you now and then. Judy, when you come to visit your Pa maybe you can see us, too. Sylvia, say goodbye to Isaac for us. We want to hear from both of you. Goodbye, for now."

They turned their horses, and leading their pack mule, began the long journey back to Big Laurel.

That evening after cleaning up the kitchen at the boardinghouse, Jim returned to the hotel. As he climbed the front steps he found Lance busy sweeping off the double porches. He looked up as Jim smiled a greeting at him. Mr. Jenkins nodded to him as he climbed the stairs to their room. Judy was still working and wouldn't get off until late. He lay down on the bed and dozed off. When he woke up the sun was setting behind the mountains.

Judy was in the kitchen by the pass-through when she saw Jim come in. Walt was finishing his pie and coffee, sitting at the corner table. He nodded to Jim and stood up, ready to leave. Jim seated himself close to the kitchen. Judy brought out two steaming cups of coffee for the two of them. "I thought you were late getting' home, but Lance said you were already here. Where've you been?"

"I've been here a while. I went to sleep. I wanted to come down and have coffee with you. Can I have a piece of pie with the coffee?"

"Sure you can, honey! Do you want apple or blackberry?"

"Blackberry sounds real good. Everything tastes better when somebody else does the cookin'!"

Judy smiled at his attempt to be jolly. It finally dawned on him that no one had actually spoken to him, except Judy. He frowned, nodding toward the front door, "I see you still have those ugly mourning-wreathes up. That old woman is dead and long buried, why don't you take them down now?"

"We all decided to leave them up another week. Her family just left this mornin'. Our displaying the mourning wreathes for another week is a way to honor Myrt. She was a good friend to all of us."

"What did she ever do besides meddle in everybody's business?"

Judy looked at him and couldn't hide her disgust. "Well, for one thing she may have given us the money we need to get our own restaurant."

Jim almost spilled his coffee. He exclaimed, "What?! That old woman had money? Why didn't you tell me? How'd she give you any money" She must've left a Will!"

"Yes. She did leave a Will. Mr. Jenkins is the executor. He and the sheriff were her witnesses and her lawyer, Mr. Babcock, recorded it for her with the Perry County Clerk of Courts. So, it's all legal."

"Did she leave money to anyone else? Her family can contest it in court, and they will, you know."

"No, you're wrong. They're not contestin' any of it. She left money to her daughter, to the sheriff, to Lance, to Sylvia and Isaac, and to me."

"How much did you get?"

"I won't know until after probate, but Bill guesses it will be around a thousand dollars."

"You say she left money to Sylvia and Isaac; why do you suppose she didn't leave the money to both you and me?"

"I don't know. Let's just be grateful she thought enough of me to provide the means for us to own our own restaurant!"

"I'm sorry for what I said about her mourning wreathes. Since she gave you money, I don't care if you leave them up all month!"

Judy was appalled by Jim's crassness. All he was thinking about was the money. From the way he was talking, it appeared he was glad Myrt was dead. She stood up with her coffee cup to go back to the kitchen.

Jim was startled, "Hey! Where're you going? Sit back down and let's talk about this some more."

"I have to finish gettin' ready for the morrow. We can talk upstairs."

When Judy came out of the kitchen at around nine o'clock Jim was gone.

She grumbled under her breath, "I'm glad I didn't tell him about my other money. I had to tell him about Myrt's legacy because that'll be public through the court. I'll find out tonight how much money he really has. If we both save like we plan, I think we can make a deal with Bill to buy both the hotel and the restaurant using just the money that Jim knows about."

Jim was so excited about the prospect of Judy getting her hands on an additional thousand dollars to put with their money that he didn't remember that he had lied to her about his own savings. When he let his secret out of the bag to her, she didn't act surprised at all. Together they figured they would have more than three-thousand dollars by the time Bill was ready to sell the property.

Jim grabbed Judy up in his arms and swung her around and around. He was laughing and practically dancing a jig and forcing her to dance with him. His happiness was infectious. She was caught up in it and relaxed for the first time in a long while. Her guard was down, but not to the point where she was willing to divulge the amount of her own secret savings account.

Finally, she said, "Honey, you don't have to work tomorrow, but I do. Why don't you spend the day figuring what it'll cost to upgrade the hotel like you want it to be and to build a second sleeping room on the first floor using some of the unused storage space? We could have two full-time renters stay here and use the restaurant for their meals. I think there's a real market for that."

The next three months passed quickly. It was September. Della was fourteen and in the eighth grade. Mary would be seventeen in November and was in her junior year at Hazard High School. Della was still working weekends in the restaurant. Mary knew she had less than two more years with the Brownlett's. She didn't want to be a waitress in a restaurant. Both sisters saved their money and kept it secure in their lady's money-sack they wore under their clothes.

It was in early November, 1924 when Judy realized that something was not right with her and she might be pregnant. When the thought hit her she was in a daze the rest of the day. She said nothing to Jim because she didn't know how to tell him. She decided she had to talk this over with God and then she would know what to do. She waited until she heard Jim begin to snore. Then she slid out of bed, sank down on her knees, and prayed, "Dear Lord what if I'm really going to bear a child. I'm forty years old and my youngest daughter is fourteen. What will people think? What will Jim think? Dear God is this your plan for me? My Pa's vision was that I would have a new man and live in a new town. He said he couldn't tell who the man was. That was because he hadn't met Jim yet. Jim is so full of himself planning for our own restaurant that he may be angry at the prospect of our having a child."

She paused in her prayer, to think about how to tell Jim. Then she continued, "I will trust you, dear Lord, to show me the way about this. Whatever happens, I know I'll love this child. Thank you for keepin' me in your loving arms. Lead me to make the right decisions for my girls. Bless Pa, my family, and my friends. I'll give you all the praise! In Jesus' name I pray. Amen."

Judy decided that she would wait to tell Jim until they were with her Pa and sister Jonie's family for Christmas. If he chose to be angry about it, she wouldn't be alone with him. After she told him, she would tell the girls. She expected Mary to be embarrassed about it. She thought that while Della would be happy to have a little brother or sister, she would be the one to worry because she felt her Ma was old. She did the numbers and figured her baby would be born sometime during the early part of May, 1925.

Thanksgiving came and went. Judy was wracked with the 'morning sickness.' She held off questioning looks from Sylvia and Isaac, telling them she must have caught a flu bug from someone. One of their older and wiser customers advised her to make ginger root tea and sip it lukewarm. Someone else told her to keep a lemon close by to suck on when she felt sick.

Judy tried both and decided the lemon worked best. When it was time to make the Christmas trip she was over that phase of her pregnancy.

Because all of her skirts were gathered full at the waist, she wasn't showing, but she was getting thick around the middle. She complained that she had to cut down on eating because she was getting fat. Judy laughed out loud when Jim agreed with her.

On Thursday, the day after Christmas, while in Harlan on their annual shopping trip, besides buying shoes for herself and the girls at Powers and Horton's, she found just what she needed in their women's sizes; larger-sized gathered-skirts with matching smock-like tops. She confided to the clerk that she was 'expecting' and needed something dressy for church. The nice middle-aged lady brought out a navy wrap-around adjustable skirt, a creamy-white sateen middy blouse with smocking across the yoke and side slits for comfort. To top it off, was a matching boxy open-front navy jacket. She told Judy the material was a combination of cotton and wool. It would have to be dry-cleaned.

Judy said, "I have to be practical, but if I only wear it to church on Sunday that shouldn't be a problem. Don't you think?"

The clerk knew she had a sale, and her response was positive, "You're right, and it suits you just fine. The deep-blue material brings out the blue-green color of your eyes and the creamy-white of the middy accents the blue. It's a beautiful outfit and you'll be able to wear it right up to your time!"

Judy knew the elegant outfit would be expensive, but she plunged on with shopping for herself. She told the clerk, "Now, I need underclothes. I want cotton, but expandable either with elastic or by pattern design."

The underclothes she bought were the fanciest she had ever owned or even seen before. Every piece that she chose was pure white.

Next, she asked for a full-cut coat with a split up the back to accommodate riding a horse. The one she chose was made of soft, brown leather and lined with cloth of the same color.

She wasn't prepared for the final store bill. With the shoes for the girls and then adding her special purchases, the cost was more than forty-two dollars. Judy told the clerk she needed to use one of their fitting rooms for a minute. The wise sales lady smiled, "I understand perfectly. You take all the time you need."

She went into the little room and pulled tight the heavy curtain. Then she pulled up her skirt and took fifty dollars out of her lady's money-sack. She put the money in her small purse that she carried while shopping. She paid the clerk and asked for shopping sacks that would fit over the back of a horse.

The clerk very carefully packed all of her purchases as she asked. She left them at the store and brought Curly to the front hitching rail. Then she slung the packing sacks over his back and secured them with rawhide cord that wrapped around under his belly.

It hadn't been that long since she was last in Harlan. It was amazing the number of automobiles that were now clogging the narrow streets of town. Curly didn't shy away from the noisy things unless some showoff blew the silly-sounding horn, 'OOOGA!' and startled him. She grumbled, "There should be a law against people blowing their horns in town! If they keep this up, pretty soon there won't be any hitching rails for people's horses and wagons."

Jim had been window shopping, killing time until the girls and Judy were through and they could start back to big Laurel. When he saw all the packages slung across Curly's back, he yelled, "What'd you do, buy out the store? You know we gotta save if we're gonna get our own place. Whatever you got, we don't need so you take it back right now!"

Judy's face was red from her collar to her eyebrows, but she held her ground. "Jim, honey, I need everything I bought and it's not wasting money. We only get here once a year and it's just smart to take advantage of sales."

"I don't know what all that is, but I bet it cost over twenty dollars."

Judy smiled sweetly at the angry man and lied, by omission. "I know you'll be happy about the good bargains I found. I'll tell you all about them when we get back to Jonie's place."

When they got back across the mountain, it was after dark, but not late. The daylight hours in late December were only about eight-hours long. Alex was sitting in his rocking chair by the blazing fire. He had a small quilt wrapped around his shoulders and another over his knees. Judy pulled her chair over to sit by him. Jim was in the kitchen helping Jonie get supper on the table. She was too sweet to tell him he was in her way and she wished he'd leave!

Alex smiled at his daughter, and said, "Well, when are you going to tell me about my new grand baby?"

Judy was shocked, "How'd you know?"

"When you get as old as I am, honey, you read the signs and you know a lot of things people don't give you credit for. You have a happy look in your eyes. It's the look that women get when they're bringing new life into the world. I think God has a lot to do with it. It's a new soul and he helps mightily with its creation. I'm so happy for you!"

"Pa, you're just amazin'!"

"Honey, there's another kind of look in your eyes when you are with Jim. You're not completely happy. I've had another vision and it's disturbin' to this old man. I see Jim perfectly this time as the man in your life. That's mostly 'cause I know him now. But he's an angry soul and I think unpredic'able. He's a danger to himself, to you, and to the girls. Be careful after the baby comes. I'm guessin' you'll be due sometime in May."

"Pa, I thank you for tellin' me your vision. I'll be watchful, and you're right. It's going to be sometime in May."

Jim came into the room at that moment. "What's going to be in May? What're you talking about?"

Judy smiled at him and said, "Pa's guessed that we're having a baby and it'll be born sometime in May."

Jim's jaw dropped. "You're not serious. How can we take care of a baby with both of us workin'?"

"The good Lord will make a way for us to take care of all that. I'm not worried. Let's wait 'til the time comes and see how things work out."

Jonie came up behind Jim in time to hear what he said. She pushed past him and grabbed Judy in a tight bear hug and exclaimed, "Judy, honey, I heard Jim say you're gonna have a baby. Good glory and praise be! I'm so happy for you! When do you think you'll deliver?"

"I just told Pa that it'll be sometime in May."

Mary and Della were listening to the grownups making all the noise in the room with the big stone fireplace. Mary frowned. She turned to her sister and said, "Ma can't be having a baby now. She's too old, I'm too old! How will I face my friends if I've got a brand new baby that's with Ma? I'll have to take care of it sometimes and people will think its mine!"

Della was all smiles, she scolded, "Mary, you silly goose. Nobody's gonna think it's yours. They'll know its Ma's and our new brother or sister. I think it's just great! She said it can be born in May. School will be out in May and we can take turns helping to take care of the baby."

Everyone was thrilled at the prospect of a new little life in the family except Jim and Mary. Both of them groused all evening while the others were in a celebration mood. Jonie baked her favorite cake. The applesauce stack-cake had six layers and by slicing thin portions, everyone got a piece. The grownups, including Mary, Otis and Gib had coffee, while the younger children had sweet milk and buttermilk with their cake.

Judy wasn't worrying too much about Jim's attitude because of the baby coming. It would be his first child, but her fourth. Little Stella died when she was about 18 months old. Judy took comfort in thinking that the new baby was God's way of giving her another child to love in place of Stella.

When they arrived back in Hazard, Judy told Mr. Jenkins about the baby. He was delighted. I'll be its grandpa here in Hazard! We'll use Myrt's old room for you when the time comes so you won't be running up and down steps.

Sylvia and Isaac congratulated Judy and Jim. They were shocked at Jim's reaction. He mumbled something under his breath and walked away.

Isaac asked, "What's the matter with him?"

Judy said, "Don't pay him any mind. He's in one of his moods."

Sylvia winked at Judy. "I bet I know what it is. He thinks the baby will cost him a lot of money!"

Judy laughed, "You must know him pretty good. I didn't know other people knew how Jim likes to squeeze a penny!"

Bill had a good time fixing up Myrt's old room for Judy to use. At the end of March he found and bought a cradle that would be all right to use until the baby was about six weeks old. They would use the same dresser and chest of drawers that was already there, but he bought a small table and put it in the room. He laughed and told Judy she needed an 'operating' table for bathing and diapering his new grandbaby.

Judy teased Bill, "For someone who's never had any children, you sure know a lot about babies!"

"Remember, I'm the oldest of my brothers and sisters. I learned a lot from watching my Ma and Pa. While they worked in the fields, I took care of the younger ones. I'm leaving to see my brother in Florida the first of April. Don't you let anything happen until I come back. Tell the Doctor I said so!"

Judy thought that the time would drag during the last six weeks of her pregnancy, but instead it went racing by. Bill made his trip to Florida and returned. The girls were excited about Easter and new Sunday clothes. She went shopping with them, but while they looked at dresses, she shopped for baby clothes and a larger baby bed. The bed came on the next Monday and the delivery men put it upstairs in her room and assembled it for her.

Sylvia and Anne surprised her with a baby shower. Ladies from the church brought a complete layette, receiving blankets and three dozen diapers. There was bedding to fit the cradle, and also some for the larger baby bed.

Jim looked over all the baby stuff Judy had assembled in the downstairs room. He turned to her and smiled, "Honey, I'm beginning to believe we're really having a baby. Look at all this stuff. We got it free. I didn't know you had so many women friends. I don't have any men friends to speak of. The men at the boardinghouse like my cookin', but none act like a friend."

"You know, I've told you before that to have a friend, you have to be a friend. You have to like people and always treat 'em as you would like to be treated by others. My Pa calls that the Bible's golden rule."

"I'll never be able to do that like you do. I don't trust people 'nough to let them get to know me too much. I'll be nice enough when I want them to be customers or buy something, but I don't want people meddlin' in my business!"

"Then, I guess you and I'll just keep on being the way we are. I'm not going to change my ways and you won't change yours. Anyway, we make a good team. The baby will be here in the next two weeks. School is out in the middle of May and Della will be here to help me with the baby. Sylvia and Isaac are capable of running the restaurant without me for the ten days the doctor says I have to stay in bed or take it easy."

On May 8, 1925, Judy delivered a healthy baby boy. He weighed eight pounds and three ounces and was twenty-one inches long. He had a lot of black hair and the blue eyes of a new-born. They named him Luther Justin Collins.

Judy was thankful that it was an easy birthing. Because of her age, she had been afraid she would have a difficult time or the baby wouldn't be healthy. Jim was ecstatic! He had a son! He had been so sure that Judy would have another girl. He forgot all about how much money this baby would cost him. At that moment he would have bought little Luther the moon!

Judy was happier than she had been in a long time. During the ten days she was recuperating, she taught Della how to take care of baby Luther.

Sylvia and Isaac did a super job of taking care of the restaurant. They only had to consult with Judy about supplies and menu ideas. Judy suspected Sylvia invented questions to ask so she could come and play with the baby. Jim broke his custom of not appearing at the hotel except at weekends, and came by almost every evening to be with Judy and his son. He was so proud!

Judy was amused when Jim began to use a pet name for baby Luther. In his Syrian accent and sweet oily way of talking he called the baby his little Lu-tee. When he talked loving baby talk to him it was almost in a sing-song chant. He repeated over and over, "Baby Lu-tee; baby Lu-tee; my baby Lu-tee!"

On the first of July, Bill told Judy he was placing the hotel building on the market. He said, "I have made up my mind that next spring is the time for me to make the move to Florida. I'd like you to be able to stay on as Restaurant Manager for the new owners."

"Bill, do you have a price in mind that you'll ask for your hotel?"

"I have to get an appraisal of the property first. After that, the bank will help me find a buyer and arrange for financing if it's necessary."

"What all are you selling? Will you sell all the furnishings? The kitchen equipment and dining room furnishings will be included in the sale, won't they?"

"My idea is to sell the hotel and restaurant business property in an 'as is' real estate deal. All taxes are up to date. I suppose the business name would stay the same. It's been the Hazard Hotel and Restaurant for a long time."

"Will you let me know as soon as you decide on a price. I'd like to have a 'first right of refusal' in making an offer on the property."

Bill's eyes grew huge, he was almost stammering, "Why, Judy, honey, where would you get that kind of money?'

Judy laughed. "I'm not saying I can raise the kind of money you may be asking for everything, but Jim and I did pool our savings and we have more than we thought possible. Even my girls have some savings from working since they were twelve years old. If we do anything at all it'll be a family effort. Anyway, I like to dream about owning our own place and business!"

Judy talked to Della about the possibility of them owning their own restaurant and asked her how she felt about helping financially and by working in a family owned place.

"Ma, I would love that. I'm fifteen now and if I'm able to get straight A's in school and still work at least twenty hours a week for you, I think I can be a partner with you and 'Daddy' Jim. That is, if he'll let me without always fussing and complaining about everything."

Judy was surprised that Della had called him 'Daddy Jim.' She saw her mother's look of surprise and said, "Well I have to call him something, don't I. Do you think he'll mind?"

"Honey, I think that's nice, but let's see his reaction first. Don't you think his moods are better now since your little brother's here?"

"Yes. He's better, but you never know when he's going to get in a bad mood again. I hate having to always be on guard against him."

Judy cautioned Della, saying, "Let's not say anything to Mary or Jim about our plans 'til we know what we have to do financially to make it happen. Mary told me she doesn't want to ever be a waitress. So, I can't count on her for sure about any of the work that might need to be done. Jim gets too excited over every little thing. If it should be out of the question entirely, then if he doesn't know anything about it to start with, he won't be upset."

Della was surprised and very pleased that her mother confided in her about the plan to own a family business. It made her feel very grown up. She was sensitive enough to realize that her years at Pine Mountain School, both with her mother and then alone, had given her a maturity way beyond her young age. It made her wonder about Mary and her attitude about family and sharing any responsibility. She decided that her older sister had been sheltered completely from unpleasantness by her mother and then by the Brownlett's while she had been almost completely on her own the last three years.

Della had worked to pay her own way through school at Pine Mountain and managed to save almost fifty dollars after all her school expenses were paid. This was a lot of money for a twelve year old girl. Then she had endured the stress of dealing with the evilness of Dora Mae Helton and her mother, Loretta.

If it hadn't been for the forthrightness of Miss Pettit in dealing with the Heltons, and the gentle loyalty and friendship from Mrs. Zande, she didn't know what she would've done. One thing she did know was that if it hadn't been for the goodness of the two missionaries, she would've had to leave school and walked to Aunt Jonie's. Then she would've had to write her mother to come and get her. That would have been awful. Della shuddered with such thoughts.

While recounting all the bad things that happened she included the two weeks she endured with the wicked Cantrells. She really thought that Mary and her mother would blame her for failing to keep that job, but they believed in her and literally rescued her from the evil couple and their daughters.

She remembered that the Cantrell's younger son, Jimmy, dropped out of school and disappeared like his older brother. He was good to her. She hoped he was safely away from his family. She liked to imagine that he joined his brother working at a saw mill.

Della found herself enjoying an impish grin. In her young heart, she rejoiced silently, while her thoughts rambled on, "I did it all by myself! Ma and Grandpa Alex told me to talk everything over with God. I did what they said. I took my problems to Him and left them there. He took care of me. Yes, He did!"

It was two weeks later that Bill met with Judy secretly and told her the bank's appraisal had come back. He said that he thought the amount quoted was too low. He explained that the appraiser had taken into consideration that the entire section of town that included the hotel was in a potential flood zone. The Kentucky River and the two other forks of the river formed a triangle around the town. There had been a serious flood in 1913 and the water had reached to the top step to the porch, but stopped short of reaching the lobby of the hotel.

He said, "The price they've set is three-thousand five-hundred dollars with warnings to the bank about the possibility of flooding. This alone discouraged the bank from offering to issue a mortgage to a prospective buyer. What do you think about this?"

"I didn't know about the flood threat. No one has said anything to me about a flood in 1913. I remember there was a bad flood in Harlan at that time. It actually washed some houses away. It was awful!"

Bill said, "I'm going to go in and talk to my friend at the bank tomorrow. After I see him, I'll tell you what he says. Then I'll give you my price for the property on an 'as is' basis."

Judy didn't say anything to anyone about what Bill told her. She had a restless night, tossing and turning while thinking about the likelihood that they could actually afford to buy the hotel building.

The next day, Bill asked Judy to come to see him. The first thing she asked was about the bank and what they said. "Well, they just repeated what the appraiser said yesterday. They said they couldn't approve using any bank funds for a mortgage. My banker friend advised me to take a note on the side if I found a reliable buyer, and they couldn't come up with the full price up front. My friend advised me that if I was determined to sell, I should price it below the appraised value and include everything like I said I would on an 'as is' basis."

"What will your price be, then?"

"I'm going to advertise it at three-thousand two-hundred dollars."

"Will you wait until I talk with Jim and the girls to see how much we have between us and I'll let you know what we can do. Like I said, if we can do this, it'll be a family business with all of us pitchin' in to make it work."

Judy left baby Luther with Della that afternoon and went to the boardinghouse to talk with Jim. They went out on the wrap-around front porch and sat in the swing. Quickly, Judy explained to Jim the terms under which Bill would sell the hotel property. He was excited, but also cautious. "What is the least amount you think he'll take? You know we have about three-thousand dollars between us. But, we'd also need start-up money."

"I told you that he was advised to consider taking a side note for some of the purchase price. We can talk about all this if you come to the hotel after you get off work tonight. I'm keepin' you from your job. I don't want to get you in trouble with your boss. Can you come to see me when you get done tonight?"

"Yes. I'll be there about nine o'clock. Okay?"

"That's fine."

That night Judy and Jim talked and made a joint decision to pool their money and make Bill an offer. They had three-thousand dollars between them if Judy counted Myrt's legacy. By the time Bill was ready to leave Hazard, the money should be there. Judy wanted to hold back five-hundred dollars of their joint funds to use as start up money. In order to do that she figured they could offer a side note to Bill that would be payable monthly.

He wanted Judy to give Isaac notice that he was losing his job, Jim intended to take over the cooking for the restaurant. He said that Sylvia could stay on until school was out. To save money, Jim wanted Della and Mary to be full-time waitresses and kitchen helpers.

Judy said, "Bill isn't going to move until next fall or even next spring. We'll wait 'til he's close to leaving afore we make decisions. I know you want to take over everything yesterday, but it can't work that way. We have to wait on the court to release the money that Myrt left to me. We don't even know for sure how much it'll be. Bill guessed it would be around a thousand dollars."

Jim grumbled, "I know you're right, but I don't have to like it. Who would've thought that old woman had that kind of money and that she would give it to you. I'm grateful, of course. If I'd known this was going to happen, I think I would've been nicer to her. I'm sorry now that I wasn't."

"I'm glad you realize that now. Sometimes we all need new lessons in life on how to treat people."

Jim stood up, hugged Judy, and kissed her goodnight. "Honey, I have to go. Kiss little Lu-tee for me. My Big Ben alarm sounds off at three o'clock and the men are ready for breakfast by four or five. I pack their lunch buckets for them, too. Then they leave to go to work, some to the local coal mines and some to cut timber or to jobs at the saw mills. I'm sure glad I'm a cook!"

Judy felt a little guilty about holding back her other savings. She would rather pay interest on a side note than let Jim use all of her money. No matter how closely they planned, she knew they would need to pay out some serious chunks of money, and probably long before they showed a monthly profit.

Regardless of how Jim felt about it, Della and Mary were going to finish school. She grumbled, "I've a feeling that I'm going to have a fight on my hands with him about my girls. They both help when they can with baby Luther. Della works weekends in the restaurant. Mary has her job with the Brownlett's and I know they're countin' on her stayin' with them 'til she graduates next year."

The next day Judy told Bill that she and Jim wanted to buy his hotel building. She told him, "Whenever you're ready to move to Florida we'll have the money for you."

Bill's face was a study. "Judy, I don't want to ask you where you got so much money. I know that you're depending on Myrt's legacy to help raise the three-thousand two-hundred dollars you and Jim will need. The only thing that worries me about this is that I know you can't get flood insurance. The last big one was in 1913 and we're due for another one anytime. If it's a bad one, you could lose all your money. I don't want that to happen to you. Would you agree to continue our agreement that if I find a cash buyer, I'm to give you 'first right of refusal?' That way, you're free to change your mind."

"I'm perfectly agreeable to do that. You told me before that you planned to make this move in early 1926. Is that still your plan?"

"It will be more like March or April, next year."

"You know that I'm having mixed feelin's about this, don't you? You've been like a father to me. I think you're my best friend. When you do move, I'm going to feel lost without you. I don't want you to dare forget me!"

"There's no way that I could ever forget you. Do you want to tell me how you and Jim plan to raise the money you need to take over the hotel and restaurant? You know that I have to ask."

"Bill, I've not told Jim everything about my money. Walt and Deputy Tim know about my getting a reward for the capture of two 'wanted' men over two years ago. I've got some savings from working both at Pine Mountain School and from working here. That money is in a separate savings account and I keep the little yellow account book in a safe-box at the bank. Mary knows about it because I made her the beneficiary should anything happen to me."

"Judy, you know I'll never tell anyone what you're telling me now."

"Jim doesn't know about that money, but I don't need to use it for the hotel; at least, not yet. Jim has over twelve hundred dollars to put with the thousand or so that I have in another savings account that he does know about. When the court releases Myrt's money to me, I figure that'll be enough to put us over the sale price. We'll need some 'seed' money to use for startin' out, but I figure we'll save enough between now and then to be all right."

"You'll be all right. You have a good head for business. I'm not surprised that you're protecting yourself by not telling your husband everything about money. I get the feeling that he wants to always be the boss, including trying to control the lives of Mary and Della. I know you well enough to see that he won't be allowed to do that. Mary's so close to finishing school that she'll be fine. Della is a hard worker; it'd be a shame if she didn't finish high school, too."

"The good Lord willin', both girls will finish school. I'll see to that. My Pa's visions have shown Mary finishing school. Jim wants them both to quit right now and work full time to bring in more money. I've said no. Mary still works for the Brownlett's. Della helps me care for the baby and waits on tables, too. She makes all A's in school. Her teacher says she's real good in arithmetic. I'm so proud of her!"

Bill grinned and nodded in agreement. "You know, Judy, I've noticed that Mary has a little jealous streak in her. It's important that you give Della a lot of credit and praise, but spread it over both girls. Mary's older, but she can be hurt if she feels you're making a difference between them. Listen to me! I sound like their grandpa or something! You and your family have been the closest thing to a real family to me that I've ever had, so you have to forgive me!"

Judy was silent for a few moments as she digested what Bill was saying. She had to agree with him that she had been slighting Mary in favor of Della. She said, "I'll have to watch myself where Mary's concerned. There's nothing to forgive. Instead, I have to thank you. This weekend, I'll do something special for her and include Della to help in the planning for it."

Judy was relieved when Jim begged off from going to church, saying he was tired and wanted to just nap and read all afternoon. Sylvia gleefully volunteered to watch baby Luther during the Sunday afternoon slow time.

She and Della were free to plan an outing that included just the three of them. Judy confided in Anne that they had a picnic planned and wanted Mary to go with them. Anne was pleased that Mary would be with her mother all Sunday afternoon. So, immediately after church, they told Mary they'd packed a big picnic basket and were going to ride across town to the banks of the Kentucky River. "There are a few tables and benches set up under three big oak trees that's a perfect picnic spot. While we're there I want you both to plan to take a whole day next Saturday to go shopping with me. It's Hazard's School Daze Sale. Della, you're growing out of everything. Mary, this is your last year. I want you to plan for at least three special outfits for school and a new Sunday-best dress."

Mary was noticeably agitated when she said, "Ma, one of my teachers told the graduating class that after Easter next year there'll be a special dance held. It's called the Senior Prom. She thought it would be in April or early May. All the girls will need to either buy, or have made by a dressmaker, an evening gown and wear matching shoes for dancing. We're supposed to begin to plan our dates right after Christmas. I need to make friends with a boy, any boy, so I'll get asked to be his date. If I can't get a date for the Senior Prom, I'll just die!"

Della asked, "Did she have any pictures from other years to show the kind of evenin' gown you're expected to wear?"

"Yes, she did. Most of the pictures showed them to be full skirted with a low neckline, and a matching wrap or cape for over the shoulders. But some of them were slim-line cut to make the girl look slender and taller. I think that's the style I need. Every boy I meet will think I'm too short and they're too tall!"

Judy showed full sympathy for Mary's concern. She asked, "What about the dancing shoes you said you need. Can they have a heel on them that's an inch and a half high? That would add some inches and give a longer line to your evening gown. When we go shoppin' why don't we go ahead and buy a pair of nice high heels so you'll get used to wearin' them? If we get the shoes first, then you can take your time to shop for the dress you want. I'll bet if we add the inch and a half we're talking about, you'll look just right for the dance!"

Della, ever practical, asked, "What else do you need for when you graduate next year?"

"This teacher was really nice to warn us about all the expense we have to prepare for just because we're seniors. We have to get pictures made as a class and by ourselves. We need to buy a class ring that we can keep forever. There's printing charges for invitations with little cards to go with them that have our names on them in old English cursor writing. The invitations come with matching envelopes. Then we have to wear rented graduation caps and gowns. She told us to count on all of that to add up to about twenty dollars."

Della got up and walked quickly over to Mary to give her an excited bear hug. "You know I'll help you pay for everything that you need. You want to look as good as any of the other girls. The only thing to worry about, though, is we can't let Daddy Jim know how much it's going to cost!"

Judy and Mary both laughed. Then Mary became serious. "There's just one girl at school who puts on silly airs and brags about how much money her family spends on her. I'm sure you've guessed that it's Winnie Cantrell."

Della was very solemn when she said, "I know that Jimmy's gone. I hope he's with his older brother. But, I bet you money those lazy girls still don't do anything but feed the chickens and gather the eggs. Their father has probably found someone else to do all the other work that his sons did and pays them next to nothing. The last time I saw Winnie and Lacey, their hair looked normal. You know, they thought that because they lied about me they would lose all their hair. Their guilty consciences caused them to start to lose big gobs of it. They both confessed to their folks and I swear I think their hair started to grow back."

Judy listened to Della and smiled. She didn't say a word about her role in the Cantrell sisters believing their lying and dishonest would make them go bald. She knew that as soon as they confessed and changed their ways somewhat, their hair would grow back.

The Sunday outing and the pleasant hours under the big oak trees on the Kentucky River bank passed by all too quickly, but it helped to restore Judy's sense of wellbeing. Della and Mary were chattering happily all the way back to the hotel about school, clothes, and boys.

When they arrived at the hotel, Baby Luther was sitting with his father on the front steps. Jim was laughing and playing 'horsey' with his son. The baby was a-straddle of his foot and crowing and laughing while being bounced up and down. Jim was in a jovial mood. He called out to them before they could dismount, "Well, did you have a good time on your picnic?"

Judy said, "Yes. We did. Are you hungry? If you want we could have an early supper. Then, I'll take Mary home to the Brownlett's. I've got to help in the kitchen for the Sunday supper crowd."

Jim said, "I'm ready to eat. Mary, Dellie, how about you?"

Della was taken by surprise by Jim using Myrt's pet name for her, but didn't let on. Usually he didn't call her by any real name. She was just 'girl' or 'hey, you' when he wanted her to do something for him.

The next Saturday was a fun day as they shopped during Hazard's Back-to-School sales. Della bought new underclothes and four school outfits. After she chose a new basic wardrobe of school clothes, Mary found a darling pair of sandal-strap high heels in a black patent-leather. She assured Judy that black would go with any color evening gown she decided on. A serious look washed across her young face, and she said, "Ma, I don't want to be foolish. The new dress I buy to wear to the Senior Prom will be one that I'll wear to church on Sunday and to other places where I'll need to dress-up."

After the expense of getting Mary and Della ready for school was out of the way, Judy also bought winter-weight clothes for baby Luther. Jim's favorite past-time was sitting on the front steps with his son and in his sing-song Syrian oily tones use baby talk to the darling little curly-headed, black-haired, brown-eyed boy. Even in late October, Jim dressed Luther in warm clothes and the two of them would sit outside until wind or rain chased them indoors.

Chapter Seventeen
NEW DOORS OPEN

The election had come and gone. Lester Cornett was the new Perry County Sheriff who would be installed in Walt's office in late January. Tim was notified officially that the new Sheriff would install a young man named Lloyd Campbell as his own hand-picked deputy. Tim would be out of a job.

Walt was making plans to leave Hazard by the end of March, 1926 to join up with the Bailie family in Western South Dakota. He was surprised when Deputy Tim asked if he could go with him. Although Tim was younger, the two men were excited about becoming partners. Both wanted to either raise cows and horses or run a large farm.

By the time Jim and Judy were planning their annual Christmas trip to Big Laurel, little Luther was crawling and pulling himself up to tables and chairs.

Jim went out on the Saturday before Christmas and bought a baby 'bouncing' swing set and a special kind of stroller that when you removed the handle, the baby could push himself all around the room. He told Judy the two items were pre-Christmas gifts. He hastened to add, "They didn't cost hardly anything. Besides, my Lu-tee needs his exercise!"

They left on Tuesday because Christmas was on Friday this year. This was the second year that Ethan had failed to send wrapped Christmas gifts to Miss Pettit at the school. He explained that the members decided it was too much trouble to buy gifts, wrap them, and ask someone to deliver them. Instead, they collected money and sent it by mail well ahead of time so the missionaries could use it to buy needed items for the school and for the children.

Judy planned to make their annual trip to Harlan to take advantage of after Christmas sales on Saturday and start back for Hazard on Sunday. Jim grumbled, "For once I'd like to spend an extra day with your folks so we're not so rushed and tired."

"We can if you make the arrangements with the boardinghouse. You wouldn't be back to work 'til Tuesday. Do you want to do that?"

"Yes. I do. When we're working for ourselves we may not be able to take a Christmas trip."

Judy's eyes narrowed in anger, as she scolded him, "Pa, will be a 105 years old next year. As long as he's alive, I 'tend to make the trip every Christmas. You never know when it may be the last time I'll get to be with him."

Jim said with sarcasm in his voice, "Now, Judy, you know that everybody dies sooner or later. Your Pa will live or die no matter whether you travel to see him or not. I'm not going to argue over something this silly. We'll decide what you'll do when the time comes!"

Judy said nothing, and let her anger pass.

It was Baby Luther's first long trip. Judy fashioned a sling carrier for him that fitted over one of her shoulders and under one arm. It was long enough to allow his little bottom to rest comfortably on the saddle. Jim soon learned how to use it so Luther could ride with him. He kidded Judy about making an Indian papoose out of little Lu-tee.

They arrived at Jonie's on Christmas Eve. Judy was saddened to find Alex feeling poorly. He perked up when he saw his visitors, saying, "I must have a bit of the flu that's going 'round. I'm all right now."

Judy hugged her father close, and in the rush and bustle of Christmas she forgot her worries about Jim.

On Saturday after Christmas, they made their usual trip to Harlan. Jim carried baby Luther in the sling and tagged along everywhere Judy went. Finally she told the girls to go on to Powers and Horton by themselves and look in their Better Dresses Department to see if they had an evening gown like Mary wanted. With Jim out of earshot, she said "Mary, you should ask for Sybil. She's the clerk that helped me last year."

Mary asked, "Ma, how much should I spend?"

"A gown like that will probably cost between ten and twelve dollars. If you find what you want, send Della to get me."

When Della didn't come to find her, Judy knew that Mary didn't see anything she liked. They would buy the Prom dress in Hazard, or find a Simplicity dress pattern that suited her, buy the material, and have it made by a dressmaker. The extra day they spent in at Jonie's was used for sleeping late the next morning and relaxing all day long. Judy admitted it was a blessing to have the extra day. On all their other trips, they always got back from Harlan one day after Christmas and then had to leave way before daylight the next morning.

Judy was happy that she was able to sit and visit with Alex. Mary and Della both doted on their grandfather and stayed near him listening to his stories most of the day. Baby Luther spent the better part of the day on Alex's lap. When he got fussy and began to rub his nose with his little fist, Judy knew it was time to put him down for a nap.

Their Aunt Jonie made a huge dinner for all of them. The children's favorite was her slick dumplings and creamy cooked chicken. Jim wanted to know how she got her chicken stock to have such a strong and delicious flavor. Judy said, "Jonie and I make chicken and dumplings just alike. When I make them for the restaurant I have people coming from miles around just to order them from the special menu."

"You've never had chicken and dumplings on the menu when I've been there on Saturday or Sunday."

"That's because I never make them on the weekend. Chicken and dumplings is a week-day dish."

Jim continued, "Jonie, they're sure good enough to be a weekend special. I'd take them over roast beef any time."

Everyone laughed when Jonie grinned and said, "You're sayin' that 'cause you've not tasted my roast beef and seen that I make it so tender you can break it apart with a fork!"

Jim chuckled good naturedly, "Well then, Jonie, you're going to have to show me how to do that, too. Next Christmas I'll spend most of my time in your kitchen watching you cook."

Judy smiled, but felt a pang in her heart. It was Jim's Syrian charm that she had fallen in love with. She missed that side of him more than anything. He could turn it on and off at will. His moodiness, grumbling, and anger were the real Jim that she and the girls saw the most. He had changed for the better since Luther was born, but she knew in her heart that it wouldn't last.

When they arrived back in Hazard Jim went straight to the boardinghouse. Mary was very tired and glad to be home with the Brownlett's. Judy and Della wouldn't admit it, but they were both glad to be going on to the hotel alone. All they wanted to do was to unpack, take the animals back to the livery, and then relax for the rest of the evening. They set the alarm for five because they both had to be at work by six o'clock the next morning.

New Year's Day came and went. It was now well over six months since Myrt's Will had been filed with Probate Court. Bill received word from Mr. Babcock on Monday, January 18, 1926 that the funds had been released by the court and could now be disbursed. When Bill went to the lawyer's office, Mr. Babcock said, "All of Mrs. Baker's funds are here except for my legal fees. I deducted them first. You don't owe me anything more. I'll depend on you as her Executor to send the monies due them to the heirs of her estate."

Bill said, "You don't have to worry. I'll mail the Burnett's bank draft to them tomorrow morning. All the other heirs are here in Hazard. I'll ask them to come to see me and give them their money one at a time."

Lance, Isaac and Sylvia received their money that same day. Walt came the next morning to receive his money. Bill deducted the fifty dollars due to him from what was left. Since the Burial Fund Insurance Policy had more than paid all of the funeral costs, Myrt had no other unpaid expenses. It didn't take long for Bill to figure out what was left over and then he asked Judy to come to see him.

Isaac and Sylvia had told Judy they received their money, so she was expecting to hear from Bill the next morning. There was a big smile on his face when she pulled a chair over to sit next to him.

He asked, "Do you want me to show you the receipts I've received from the heirs as I disbursed their monies to them, or will you take my word for it when I say this is all that's left of Myrt's legacy? You know that you're to receive all that's left over."

"Bill, you know that I'll take your word anytime!"

He started counting out paper money, laying the bills one at a time in a stack on the front desk. He counted to one-thousand and kept on going, Judy's eyes grew huge. The final count was thirteen-hundred and fifty-four dollars.

"Bill, are you sure about this amount?"

"Yes. I think everyone forgot about the five hundred dollar Burial Fund insurance policy that Myrt had paid up long ago. So, you were right when you said you and Jim would have enough money between you to buy my hotel."

"I'm having trouble believing all this money came from Myrt. I miss her every day. She was closer to me than my own mother ever was."

Bill nodded in agreement, "I miss her, too. The best thing we ever did was to prepare that sleeping room for her right here by the lobby. We used it when Walt was shot, and again when little Luther was born."

Judy gathered up the stack of bills and carefully placed all of the money in a large brown envelope that Bill gave her. She asked, "Have you got a date in mind for when you want to close the deal and transfer your deed?"

"I've been in touch with my brother and we've decided the best time for me to arrive in Florida is around the middle of March. So, you and I should finalize everything between us by the first. That gives you and Jim two months to get your money together, and then we'll meet at the bank to sign the papers."

When Judy left Bill she was trembling with excitement. She went upstairs to her room to put more than thirteen-hundred dollars in her lady's money-sack. She then sat on the bed and hugged herself. Would anyone ever believe that she could own this huge building? Before she left the room, she slid to her knees to thank God for guiding her to make right decisions, for her father's visions, and for His unfolding plan for her!

She decided to wait until Jim was off work Friday night to tell him that she received the money from Myrt's legacy. Judy had a bad feeling about what Jim might do as soon as he knew they had enough money to buy the hotel. She worried that he might want to quit his job right away. He had talked about letting Isaac go and taking over the cooking in the restaurant himself.

However, Isaac worked for Bill and until both parties signed the papers that closed the deal, Jim had no authority or say in the matter. Isaac and Sylvia needed their jobs. Judy felt a need to protect them from Jim.

Friday came and Jim arrived at the hotel just as Judy was locking up for the night. She waited until they went upstairs to their room to tell him they now had enough money to buy the Hazard Hotel. His eyes grew huge and then narrowed. "When did Mr. Jenkins give you the money?"

"Yesterday afternoon."

"Why did you wait 'til now to tell me?"

"I thought it was best to wait 'til we could be together for the weekend so we can plan for our new business together."

"What did you do with the money? Where is it?"

"I have it with me. Do you want to see it and count it?"

"Yeah, I do."

Judy went to her dresser, pulled open the drawer that held her underclothes and removed the large stack of bills. She was all smiles as she handed the money to him.

Jim started counting. When he got to a thousand, his eyes grew huge again. He looked at the small stack of money that was still there to be counted. He kept on going until he reached thirteen-hundred and fifty-four dollars. He whooped, jumped up, grabbed Judy and swung her around.

She shushed him. "Della and little Luther are asleep next door, and we don't want to wake them."

He fingered the large stack of money while reaching for a piece of paper to write on. When he added Judy's eight hundred in savings to Myrt's money and then added his own thirteen hundred, he came up with a sum of thirty-four-hundred and fifty dollars.

He exclaimed, "Oh boy! Honey, we won't need to borrow any seed money. If we don't sign papers until March, we'll both have more savings to add to it and that should be plenty to use for startin' out!"

Judy said, "We'll have plenty of time to plan. Why don't you come down early and have breakfast with me in the morning?"

"No, I want to sleep in. Let's have dinner together, instead."

Jim went right to sleep. Judy listened for his first soft snores. As soon as she knew he was asleep, she slid out of bed to her knees for her bedtime prayers.

The new sheriff was sworn in on January 27, 1926. He and his new deputy moved into Walt's office as he and Deputy Tim moved out and checked into the boardinghouse.

Les Cornett was from Buckhorn. He asked Walt to work with him for pay for the next six weeks to help him until he became more familiar with the area surrounding the city and everything he was expected to do. Walt readily agreed since six weeks would bring him and Tim closer to their departure date.

Walt brought Sheriff Les Cornett and his Deputy, Lloyd Campbell to the restaurant to meet Bill and Judy. They were impressed with the two men. Les was very tall and slightly balding. Judy guessed he was in his early forties. Lloyd was about twenty-five, shorter and a little too heavy.

Les set up a monthly arrangement with them for the jail. He and the deputy would take their meals with Judy every day. If there were one or more prisoners in the jail they would let her know ahead of time so extra meals would be delivered on time. They asked her to keep a running tab for the jail. Les would issue her a bank draft for the total the first of each month.

Bill nodded his agreement to the arrangement and Judy did, too. They shook hands to seal the deal.

When Les and Lloyd left to go back to the jail, Bill excused himself and went over to the Hotel's front desk. Walt stayed behind and had another cup of coffee and a piece of Judy's apple pie. It was apparent that Walt wanted to talk somewhat privately with her.

She brought her own cup of steaming coffee and two flaky biscuits. Walt watched as she added two teaspoons of sugar to her coffee; broke open the two biscuits and layered them in the cup of hot coffee. She pushed them down firmly with her spoon and let them set for a few minutes.

Judy noticed the bemused look on Walt's face and explained, "I'm making coffeecake. Wait a few minutes and you'll see what I mean."

Walt enjoyed his pie while they both sipped on their coffee. He was very serious as he talked to her about Les Cornett. "He's a good man. I believe he's honest, almost to a fault. He's determined to enforce the law as it stands in the statutes, and not bend any rules regardless of circumstances. This may get him into trouble with some of the citizens of Perry County."

"Did you tell him anything about me?"

"Yes, I did. I told him how you've helped me more than once. He knew the name Judy Turner-Smith, from talk regarding the turkey-shoots where you competed against men. He's impressed. I think he'll be a good friend to you."

"Did Bill tell you that we're buying the hotel?"

"What!!?"

"Yes. We've made a verbal deal to buy it, as is, and sign papers in late February or early March. He's retiring and moving to Florida to live near his younger brother."

"Then Bill, Tim, and I will leave Hazard at close to the same time."

"I'm afraid so, you and Tim are heading northwest and Bill's going south. I do want you to keep in touch with me. Bill's promised that he'll write from time to time."

"I promise I'll do that, too. You know, I've been in touch with the Bailie family for some two years now in order to send Mrs. Art Bailie the judgment money for the killing of her husband by Chad Owens. Her brother-in-law invited me to come and claim some of the free grazing-land that's still available. They're on the far, western side of South Dakota. That's the main reason I'm going, but who knows where Tim and I may end up?"

Walt was watching as Judy sprinkled more sugar on the soaked biscuits in her coffee cup. She laughed, "I told you I was making coffeecake. Now I'll eat the biscuits with a spoon. It's as good as any other coffee or teacake."

The time seemed to fly by until it was late February. Bill had all the legal papers drawn up including the preparation of the deed to reflect his transferring ownership from himself to Jim and Judy Collins. They all three met at the bank on Friday, February 26, 1926 and signed the paperwork to close the deal. Judy and Jim paid three-thousand two-hundred dollars in cash. Bill owned the property free and clear of any mortgage and he promptly deposited the money into his savings account.

When they returned to the hotel, Jim asked Bill how long he intended to stay and use his room. Judy tried to shush him, saying, "Bill you're welcome to stay at the hotel as long as you need to."

Bill frowned at first, and then smiling, addressed his answer to Judy, "I'm already packing. I bought a wagon and a team from Raff Pennington to use for my move. Of course, I'll pay the day-rate for each night I stay at the hotel. I'll pay for my meals at the restaurant, too. I don't expect anything for free!"

Judy's eyes were brimming. She couldn't help it. When she needed a job in the worst way, Bill had been there for her. He taught her how to run the hotel, how to order supplies, and how to keep the hotel in good financial condition. Bill had been the best friend anyone could ever have.

Jim pressed on with his questions. "When are you planning to start out for Florida? Will you need Lance or someone else to help you with the heavy lifting? I'm giving Isaac notice, so he'll be available part of the time."

This time, Bill wouldn't be pressured. Again, he addressed his answer to Judy. "Walt or Tim will help me, I'm sure. I think I'll plan for Monday, March seventeenth. I know Walt and Tim are leaving the following Monday, on March twenty-ninth. Judy, I'd like to say goodbye to everyone before we leave."

She grinned impishly, "Bill, that's a great idea. We'll have a grand party on Sunday, the sixteenth and invite everyone to come and say goodbye to you, Walt, and Tim. Don't worry, Jim and I will pay for the party!"

All of a sudden Jim had a coughing fit. Judy thought he was going to choke. She couldn't keep from grinning as she winked at Bill. He pounded Jim on the back, "Jim, are you all right? The three of us will plan the party and I'll ask Sylvia and Isaac to help, too. I don't know if you read the fine print on the papers you and Judy signed, but I do have thirty days to actually turn the property over to you. Of course, I won't take that long, and I'll do what I said I would about paying to stay a few more days."

Jim had the good grace to blush red from embarrassment. He had been too excited at the time to really read what he was signing. When he looked at Judy and saw budding disgust for him in her eyes he quickly turned on his Syrian, oily charm. "Now Bill, you know Judy told you to stay as long as you want. We're going to really miss you. No one could ever have a better friend than you have been to both of us. I've got a lot to learn about running a hotel and I intend to ask you a lot of questions between now and March seventeenth!"

When Jim left them to go back to the boardinghouse, Bill went to the front desk and Judy went to the kitchen. She found Isaac and Sylvia upset over news they had just received from his younger sister who was living with his folks. She was there seated in the dining room, and had just told them that she was now ready to be married. It was the first time Judy had met her. She had seen her in church a few times. The young woman was very nervous as she continued, "The man I'm marrying has a farm near Buckhorn. That's where I'll be living."

"What do Ma and Pa say about your leaving?"

"They hate to see me go, but know I have to. They like the man I'm marrying' and I think you will, too."

"Do they have anyone else who can stay with them?"

"No, and really, they need to have a man stay with them who can work the farm. It's good land. There's about eighty acres. They made a good living on it and raised all of us kids. I'm the last one to leave home. We heard from my two brothers who went out west. They're working on a horse ranch and like it fine. They always did hate farming!"

"Tell Ma and Pa we'll be over to see them next week. You said your wedding's in March; what day?"

"It's on Saturday, March twentieth. I hope you and Sylvia can come."

"Where's it going to be?"

"The only preacher we know is Ethan Brownlett. He said he would marry us. He's known Ma and Pa a lot of years."

"When I come to see them next week, we'll talk about everything. Sis, I'm really happy for you!"

"Thanks Isaac. Of the three boys in our family, you've been the best!"

After his sister left, Isaac walked into the dining room and sat down. He looked at Sylvia. She pulled a chair over next to him and put her hand on his arm. "Don't worry so. God will make a way for everything to work out. I wouldn't mind livin' on that farm. It's beautiful in the highlands east of Hazard. There's a lot of high ground there that's level land."

"You mean you would want to live there?"

"If we need to. Someone has to take care of your folks in their old age. Remember Miss Myrt? She grew old on her farm and had no one to look to but us here at the hotel. God leads us to know and do the right thing. Anyway, let's wait 'til you go talk to them next week."

Sylvia looked at Judy and said, "If I can, I'll go with you."

Judy said, "Of course you can. The way we have to work, you seldom get a day off together. Della will be here right after school to help out. For the dinner crowd, Lance and I will take care of the kitchen and the dining room. You two go and do what you have to do!"

Judy's brain was in a whirl. If it worked out that Isaac and Sylvia could take over his family farm, and own it, they wouldn't need to keep their jobs. Myrt left them three hundred dollars and if they put that with their savings, it was more than enough for start-up money to buy equipment and stock. Maybe she could talk Bill into staying longer than the seventeenth so that Jim could take possession just as they moved to the farm. Wouldn't that be wonderful! It had to be God's plan for Isaac and Sylvia.

All that Judy had to do was ask. Bill agreed to postpone leaving until the twenty-second if it would help keep Jim from hurting the feelings of Isaac and Sylvia. He confided his misgivings about Jim to Judy, "You know I believe there's a mean streak in him. He was looking forward to giving Isaac notice, and almost with no warning. That's mean! I'm afraid for you and the girls if you get on the bad side of him. You've got to be careful."

"Bill, I'm afraid you may be right. The signs are there that he has two sides to his character. His moods and anger can be turned on and off at will. I think I'm a victim of 'courtin' lies."

What do you mean?"

"My sister-in-law, Becky Turner, told me that when a man's courtin' for a wife, he'll say anything that makes him look like something he's not. He'll pretend to be a nice, honest, hard-workin', and lovin' man 'til after the weddin'. Then his true self shows up!"

Bill laughed, "It sounds like she has all of us men figured out about right! But, I plead not guilty for myself."

Before Isaac and Sylvia left to visit his folks, Judy talked to them about living on the farm and caring for his parents in their last years. "Try to make a deal with them. In exchange for taking care of them for life, you want them to make you a legal deed to all of their property. Then, if they'll do that, ask Mr. Babcock to draw up the deed for signatures and then record it for you all legal and proper. If your folks are fair, they won't hesitate to do this for you."

"I'm afraid they'll think I'm a bad son to them."

Judy reassured him. "Isaac, you've given them no trouble. You've shown over the years that you love and care about them. It was your older brothers who gave them trouble and went to prison. They're way out west somewhere and show no interest in helping to care for their Ma and Pa. Your younger sister said she's done all she can for them and is moving to Buckhorn. You go ahead and do what I said. I believe you'll be surprised at how relieved you'll make them. When they agree to this, they'll have nothing more to worry about."

When they returned that evening, Sylvia grabbed Judy and hugged her. Isaac was all smiles. He said, "Miss Judy, it went just like you said it would. They want

Mr. Babcock to come out to the farm as soon as he can to begin to draw up a proper deed. We may have to meet with him, too."

Sylvia literally squealed, "Can you believe it? We own a farm. A farm so beautiful it takes my breath away."

Then a worried frown washed across her face, "But, Judy, what about you? You're going to need me to help you, at least for a while."

"You let me worry 'bout that. The important thing is for you two to get settled. You know that we'll buy eggs all year around from you, and when the harvest comes in, we'll want some of your surplus for the restaurant, too!"

Jim didn't say anything negative to Bill when he said he wasn't leaving until the twenty-second. However, he groused about it all weekend.

Sylvia, Della, Mary, and Judy spent a lot of time planning and gathering the supplies and favors they needed for the farewell party. Judy enlisted the help of Sheriff Les to extend invitations to various businesses, and other government, social, and religious leaders throughout Perry County.

They prepared for a hundred people, but were not surprised when a lot more showed up. It wasn't meant to be, but it turned out to be more of an open-house affair than a regular party. People came, greeted the three men, had some refreshments, and left. If everyone had stayed, there wouldn't have been room for them. Even so, many of the guests ended up in the hotel lobby. It was too cold for them to sit on the porches.

Everything was ready for Bill to leave on the twenty-second. He had been pleasantly surprised when his younger brother showed up on the twentieth to ride back to Florida with him in the wagon.

Jim had been speechless when Isaac gave him notice on the same day that Bill departed. He frowned, and demanded, "What're you going to do? Where did you get a job?' When are you leaving your job here?"

Isaac smiled and said, "Today's my last day. I now own a large farm over east of Hazard. Sylvia and I are going to be farmers!"

Jim almost snarled, "You mean Sylvia's leavin', too?"

"She can't very well work here and help me run a farm. She did tell Miss Judy she'll stay 'til you get somebody to take her place."

"You mean Judy knew you were leavin'?"

Isaac was smart enough to know Jim wanted to blame somebody for his being unpleasantly surprised. So, he said, "Miss Judy knew I've been thinkin' about leavin' ever since you all bought the hotel, but she didn't know it would be today. I knew you'd want to do the cookin' yourself. When we can, we'll come for Sunday supper and bring my Ma and Pa. We're going to miss little Luther!"

Judy arranged Sylvia's schedule so that she was only working part time. She rode in at seven o'clock and helped in the kitchen as well as waited on tables for breakfast and dinner. When Della arrived home from school she handled the supper crowd, and Sylvia went home to the farm.

Della was the one who found a replacement for Sylvia. She told her friends at school that the Hazard Hotel Restaurant was looking for a waitress. One of her good friends had an older sister who had restaurant experience and needed a job. Judy told Della to have her come to see her as soon as she could.

A neatly dressed and attractive young woman named Betty Lou Partin showed up the very next day. Judy asked her to work with Della to take orders and serve the food. Betty Lou was hired.

Sylvia asked Judy how much longer she should stay on the job.

"Can you stay until the end of the week to train Betty Lou for kitchen work, busing tables, washin' dishes, and waitin' tables?"

"I'll be happy to. Isaac's spending most of his time right now planning how we can build the place up so that it's like it was when he was a boy."

"Do you have your deed? Is it really your farm now?"

"Yes. They put the deed in both our names: Isaac and Sylvia Blevins. We have our own copy and Mr. Babcock recorded an original with the County Clerk of Courts. You see, I'm learnin' about these things! Isaac wants me to learn all I can. He said if he could, he'd send me to college! Can you imagine that?"

"Yes. I can. Isaac's a smart man!"

Walt and Tim left the next weekend. They bought their team and a wagon from Raff's Livery. Judy liked Sheriff Les, but it was with a heavy heart that she waved goodbye to Walt and Tim. She felt like the door to another chapter in her life had snapped shut!

Judy was glad Mary's graduation from High School and all the festivities surrounding it was giving her enough to think about so that she didn't dwell too long on the heartbreak of losing two best friends at the same time.

Chapter Eighteen
A TURN FOR THE WORSE

The transition of ownership of the hotel went smoothly. Judy took over the front desk just like she had each time Bill went on one of his Florida trips. It was a perfect occupation for her now because Luther was walking, getting under foot, and into everything. Everyone was excited when he began to talk. 'Shoe' was the first understandable word that little Lu-tee said.

Sylvia and Della baby-sat with Luther off and on until now. For the first time, Judy had a chance to really get to know her son. She splurged and bought a second-hand baby bed and play pen to keep in the hotel lobby so she had more control over his fits of exploration. Luther had plenty of toddler-aged toys, including building blocks and miniature logs to build forts and such. She purposely didn't buy him noise-making toys.

A short trip to the Hazard Public Library paid big dividends. She checked out colorful picture-books to read to Luther and some fourth-grade level books for her. When she put him in the play-pen or in bed for a nap, the sound of her voice reading the stories was the perfect way to put her energetic son to sleep.

Judy's new responsibilities were exciting and she enjoyed playing with Luther. Jim was too wound up to relax and enjoy his role as cook and master of his world in the restaurant. He found it was hard to prepare all of the different dishes offered in the menu.

Even with one the two other people besides Lance to help him with basic meal preparation, Jim was constantly calling on Betty Lou to do additional chores that were really his responsibility. She complained to Judy that she couldn't watch the front door and be in t he kitchen helping Jim at the same time! Jim was very hard to work with and his fits of anger were worse than Isaac's had ever been. Betty Lou was on the verge of quitting most of the time.

Judy offered to help him at peak times during the day if Lance could watch the front desk and Luther for her. It got to be a routine. She put Luther down for a nap around two o'clock every day. Then Lance would come over to sit behind the front desk while she spent about two hours helping Jim prepare for the supper crowd. She and Betty Lou worked well together. Both of them were fast and efficient. Jim began to calm down and turned on his Syrian charm again. Betty Lou told Judy, "It's amazing! He's like a different person."

By the time Judy was ready to return to the front desk, Della was usually home from school. She was near the end of her freshman year and if she had homework, Judy told her to complete it each day before going to work.

Mary's orders were in for her class ring, Senior Yearbook, pictures, and invitations. She found the perfect evening gown for her Senior Prom and a young man named Larry Ricketts asked her to be his date. She was ecstatic!

Because she was living with the Brownlett's, Jim didn't see any of the essentials Mary was buying for graduation. Judy used her hidden money to pay for the gown. She arranged for Mary to get her hair done in a bee-hive up-do at a ladies' hair salon. Mary felt and looked elegant!

Anne told Judy later that when Larry Ricketts came for Mary, she helped him pin his flower corsage on her shoulder. It matched the dress perfectly. She laughed, and said. "The high heels and the up-do made Mary almost as tall as her date. Your daughter almost floated out of the house and down the street."

Mary's graduation ceremony was on Saturday, May 22, 1926 at ten o'clock. It was being held in the Hazard High School Gymnasium. Judy planned to attend the ceremony and take Luther with her. Lance was watching the front desk. She and Luther were ready to go when Jim came storming over to the Lobby, "You can't go! I need you! It's silly for you to want to go. She's going to graduate whether or not you're there. I'll take Lu-tee's play pen over to the kitchen. You can watch him while you work."

Judy was exasperated with him. If he had known her better, he would have been worried when her eyes narrowed. It took all of her willpower, but she appeared calm and her voice was firm as she told him, "I wouldn't miss Mary's graduation for all the tea in China! She's worked hard for this. Della's missing it so I can go. You have two people to help you. As soon as I get back, I'll help, too. But, for now, I'm going to the High School!"

Jim watched with his mouth open as they went through the front doors and down the steps. Lance had seen and heard it all. Jim was grumbling as he went back to the kitchen, "She'll be sorry she talked to me like that in front of old Lance! Wait 'til she gets home. It's a silly graduation; just a silly graduation!"

Judy was so upset with her husband that she was trembling. A day of celebration and joy had been ruined for her. But, she didn't want it ruined for Mary. With great determination she put on a happy face. With a prayer on her lips giving thanks to God for leading them to this day of achievement, her spirits soared. In three more years Della would graduate. She was so proud of her girls! She hugged her son close to her heart and prayed that she could provide for him the same as she had for Mary and Della.

Mary's graduation and the confrontation she had with Jim marked the beginning of her falling out of love with Luther's father. He showed by his actions and words that there wasn't any real love for her or her girls in his heart. He loved his son, yes. Luther was part of him, but when he looked at her, Della, and Mary, he didn't see a family, but just dollar-signs. He felt he owned them and they owed him their money, time, and literally their lives.

It was May and a long time before she would see Alex again. She needed him. She needed to know if he had seen another vision. She needed his advice. The temptation to use her father's powers was strong, but she resisted that. Her promise to Alex and to God that she would not use them for personal gain was always uppermost in her mind.

Judy went to her room to be alone. She dropped to her knees and bowed her head. "Dear Lord," she prayed, "Help me to get through this hard time with Jim. Touch his heart and lift his spirits. Help him to conquer his moodiness and anger. Lead me to make the right decisions. Bless my Mary and Della. Keep them safe. I'll give you all the praise. In Jesus' name. Amen.

It was mid-afternoon. She asked Lance to continue to watch the front desk, but to come for her if he needed to check guests in or out. Della was helping Betty Lou in the dining room, but came to help her mother wrestle the folded up playpen through the doors and into the kitchen. While Judy was putting Luther down for his nap, Della and Betty Lou were getting the tables set for the supper crowd.

As Judy put on her large 'granny' apron that covered her good dress, front and back. Jim scolded, "Well, it's about time! I need potatoes peeled. I want you to peel enough to make mashed potatoes for tonight and to use tomorrow."

Judy cautioned, "They'll turn dark. You can't use them later."

"Yes. I can. We can soak them in salt water. They'll keep their color, even overnight. I learned that in the army."

"Okay. If you say so, but that I want to see!"

While Jim stood there frowning at her, she pulled a burlap bag of potatoes to the center of the kitchen. Then she filled a dishpan with potatoes to put on her lap. She started to use a potato peeler, but Jim handed her a long-pointed, razor-sharp paring knife. "Here, use this, you can peel 'em faster. We don't have all day! When you get done, you'll need to peel some apples for pies."

Judy finished peeling the potatoes. Washed them and put half of them on to boil and Jim covered the other half with cold water and added salt. She pulled a bushel basket of red apples over next to her chair, and using the same dishpan, filled it about half full to put in her lap. She held the knife in her hand, pointing downward, as she reached for the dishpan.

Suddenly, Jim yelled, "You don't have enough apples! Let me get some more for you. He hit her arm just right to plunge the sharp paring knife through all of the material of her apron, dress, and underclothes into the back of her leg just under her knee. The knife went all the way in up to the hilt. It severed the deep vein and blood began to spurt everywhere. Judy was afraid to remove the knife. She grabbed a dishtowel and, using pressure around the knife and the wound, tried to stop the bleeding. It didn't work.

She yelled for Della and Betty Lou, "Go get the doctor for me, quick. If I don't get this to stop, I could bleed to death!"

Della came running into the kitchen. Jim yelled at Betty Lou's back as she ran out the front door to get the doctor. "You come right back. You hear!"

Then he turned back to Judy. "Let me make a tourniquet out of a large dishtowel. Let me tie it above your knee. I'll use a wooden spoon to twist it tight. That should slow the bleeding."

Della knocked Jim's hand away, "That won't work, her clothes are in the way!"

Sheriff Les was coming in as Betty Lou ran out. He called after her, "What's going on?"

"Miss Judy got cut real bad. I'm going for the doctor!"

Les went quickly to the kitchen and found Judy slumped forward in her chair. He was alarmed by the amount of blood on the floor and the cabinets.

"How on earth did she manage to cut herself in the back of her leg?"

Jim paled and stammered an answer, "I was reaching around her to get more apples for her and I must have jostled her arm. It was an accident."

"Jostled, you say! Why, mister, it would take a deliberate hard blow to drive any knife into someone that deep. You must have tripped or something and didn't realize it."

Jim grabbed on to the sheriff's suggestion. "Yes. I must have tripped. It was an accident."

"Della, you're right, you can't get a tourniquet on her leg with these clothes in the way. We can't take a chance on removing the knife, either. Get me a pair of sharp scissors. I've got to cut her dress and apron up the side to get to her leg. With that done, Les took the dish towel and wooden spoon and repositioned it well above Judy's knee. "We can't keep it tight too long. You have to loosen it about every ten minutes. We don't want her to lose that leg."

He looked at Judy's pale face and realized she had gone into shock. "Jim, we have to lay her down. Go next door to the hotel and get some pillows and two blankets or quilts."

He did as the sheriff asked, but started up the stairs. Lance asked what was wrong. When Jim told him, he quickly opened the door to the sleeping room, "This will be faster. Don't you let anything happen to Miss Judy!"

Betty Lou was back with the doctor. He took one look and said, "It's good you didn't pull the knife out. It's blocking the bleed from a deep vein. We'll have to operate to repair the damage. I'm moving her to the hospital now."

Jim looked at Betty Lou. Who's going to help me and take care of Lu-tee? Can you stay here for the next few days?"

"I'll stay as long as you and Judy need me, but I can't afford to pay the nightly room-rates."

"No. There'll be no charge. You'll be doing us a kindness, There'll be no charge at all!"

"I'll go home and get some clothes after work, but I'll come back to spend the night."

Without saying a word to Jim, Della went with her mother in the ambulance. Judy was in surgery more than four hours. Finally, the doctor came out, and failing to find Jim, spoke to Della. "We had to tie off the deep vein in two places. I believe the smaller veins will take over the larger vein's job and provide sufficient circulation to and from the heart. This procedure is so new that results are unpredictable. She'll need to stay here in the hospital for four or five more days so we can watch her. There's always danger of infection and gangrene when a main artery is tied off like this."

"Do you think she'll be all right?"

"Yes. The surgery went well. Your mother's a strong woman. However, prayer wouldn't hurt and may do her a world of good!"

"When she does go home, how do we take care of her?"

"I'll go over all of that when the time comes. But, in preparation, you must have her bed where there are no steps to climb. A wheel chair will help, too. Until the wound heals and the smaller veins begin to take over like I said, she'll need to stay off that leg completely."

Della nodded in agreement to everything the doctor said. She went to Judy's room to check on her and found her still asleep. Taking advantage of that, she walked the few blocks to the Brownlett's to let Mary know about the accident. Ethan and Mary walked back to the hospital with her and stayed until Judy woke up.

Ethan told Mary to stay the night with her mother and not worry about them. He asked Della if she had eaten anything. "No, I've been here at the hospital with Ma. I'm starved!"

"Why don't you go home then and come back early tomorrow morning. There's just two more days of school this year and I'll get your report card for you. When you get here tomorrow, Mary can come home. I'll get the word out, putting your mother's name on our Prayer Warriors' list of people who are in need of a lot of prayer. Don't you girls worry now, everything's going to work out just fine."

Della left to go home and when she arrived, Betty Lou, Lance, and Jim were anxiously waiting for word from the hospital. Della told them what the Doctor said. Betty Lou said she would make up the sleeping room for Judy to use. Jim said he would buy or rent a wheel chair.

After Della ate her late supper, Jim asked, "What about school. I don't think you should go anymore."

"I won't go anymore this year. Reverend Brownlett's talking to them for me and getting my final grades. I'll be a sophomore next year. Ma will be well and I'll go back in the fall."

When Della arrived at the hospital, Mary was eager to leave. "It was a terribly long night. Will you be here all day?" How will you get your dinner? You know

I'm out of school completely, why don't I bring you something to eat? If Ma's okay, we'll go outside and sit on one of the benches while you eat."

Della hugged her sister, "I'll really appreciate that!"

Mary had been gone about ten minutes when Sheriff Les came to see Judy. "I want to talk to your mother alone for a few minutes."

Della looked at Judy. She nodded at Della, "Honey, why don't you go see if there's a place in the hospital where you can buy a dinner? Mary may not be able to bring you any food tomorrow."

As soon as Della left the room, the sheriff sat down by Judy's bed and opened a small notebook. "I need to hear from you what happened yesterday. The explanation your husband gave me didn't make sense."

Judy thought about it a few seconds and then said, "I came home from going to Mary's graduation at the high school. Jim had been upset because I insisted on going to the ceremony. He asked me to help him with the supper crowd and to prepare for Sunday dinner, too. Lance was watching the front desk for me. To help Jim, I peeled about a half a bushel of potatoes and started on the apples. When I started to lift the pan of apples into my lap, Jim yelled at me that I didn't have enough apples in the pan. Somehow he hit my arm and the knife went into my leg. I'm sure it was an accident."

"Was the knife that sharp? Would just a bump on the arm drive it in as far as it could go?"

"I don't know. It happened so fast. There was blood everywhere. I think I must have passed out. That's not like me to do that."

"You went into shock. When someone loses that much blood that fast, it's to be expected."

Judy thought a few moments, and said, "I have to believe that it was an accident. To think otherwise would make it impossible to live with Jim. We just began to operate the hotel as a family. Do you see what I mean?"

"Yes. But, in my report of the incident, I'll label it suspicion of assault with a deadly weapon, but no charges filed. If anything else happens, we'll have an official record on file. I'm just telling you to be careful in the future."

"I appreciate your concern. I'll be careful 'cause I have my two girls and the baby to worry about."

"Sheriff Walt told me how you helped him when he had some pretty serious trouble over the last four years. He's a good man and he cares about you. I don't want anything bad to happen to you. Let me know if you need me."

After the sheriff left, Judy did some serious thinking about the situation she was in. What if Jim did intend to make her cut herself. The very thought of that made her tremble. "If I really believed he was capable of that, I couldn't go to sleep at night. Dear Lord, I wish I could talk with Pa!"

Judy was still in the hospital five days later. Della stayed with her every day and Mary stayed at night. Jim didn't come to see her at all. He told Della to tell Judy that he couldn't get away during the day and was too tired at night. Della couldn't hide her anger at her stepfather. "Ma, he's not that tired. He plays a game of 'five hundred rummy' with Betty Lou every night. He told me it helped him to relax so he could sleep better."

"Don't worry about it. Right now it's better that I don't see him. He may be feelin' guilty. He caused me to almost kill myself."

"He's scolding me for spending all day with you. I told him you had to have someone with you all the time. Mary stays at night and can sleep in the big chair next to your bed. You can't walk and can't straighten your leg all the way to sit up in bed. You have to have someone stay with you."

Della was having a hard time controlling her anger. She continued, "He wanted to know if you were going to be a cripple. I told him the doctor said that with exercise you will make a full recovery, but it'll take time. He did seem relieved to hear that."

Judy patted her hand. "Now, you stop worryin'. I'm better and anxious to go home. Is Luther being taken good care of? I'm anxious to see him!"

"Yes he's fine. I'd bring him to visit you, but the hospital won't let me."

Judy was in the hospital ten days. She came home by ambulance. Then she was wheeled up the steps using a wheel chair. Sheriff Les arranged to be there when she arrived home. He wanted to observe how Jim greeted his wife after not seeing her for so long. Evidently the sheriff was aware that Jim hadn't visited her at all.

Jim wasn't stupid. He knew the sheriff seriously suspected that Judy's self-inflected wound was no accident but a deliberate action on his part. This knowledge made him self-conscious with the sheriff looking on. He kissed Judy's cheek and welcomed her home by wheeling her into the sleeping-room. Les followed behind him and observed Jim making a big deal out of telling her it had been fixed up just for her. The sheriff nodded to Judy and left.

After Les left, Jim relaxed and became all business. He began giving orders, "Dellie, you go to the kitchen and help Betty Lou. She has Lu-tee there with her. Tell Lance to stay at the front desk for now. I want to stay with your mother a few minutes."

When they were alone, Jim turned on the oily Syrian charm that by now was turning Judy completely off. "How're you feeling? Can you straighten your leg yet? Can you get out of bed by yourself? If you need someone to stay with you all the time, I'll ask Sylvia to come and stay with you during the day. Dellie can sleep in here with you at night."

Judy tried to answer all of his questions in order. She smiled and said, "Jim, that's a lot of questions. I'm feeling pretty good. No, I'm not supposed to try to straighten my leg just yet. All the stitches have been removed, but there's still some danger of infection. The doctor told me that I'll have an ugly scar, but it will remind me of how lucky I am that I didn't bleed to death. And, no, I can't get out of bed by myself, but I want you to buy me a pair of crutches for later on when I can. Did anyone tell Sylvia what happened?"

"I'll get you the crutches today. When you can use them instead of the wheelchair you should be able to take over the front desk again so that Lance can help me more. No, I don't think Sylvia and Isaac know you had an accident. They live too far away. Do you want her to stay with you a few days?"

"I would like to see her. She may volunteer to stay with me, but if she can't because of the farm work, I'll understand. Della and Mary know where the farm is, maybe they can ride out there to tell her, or Reverend Brownlett would do it if he was asked."

"What about the front desk? Do you think you can take it over again anytime soon?"

"Who's been orderin' supplies and doing the state record keepin'?"

"No one has yet. Lance didn't know about any of that. I didn't either. He kept a lot of notes of day-to-day stuff so you can catch it up."

Judy looked at him with new eyes. She knew that the love in her heart for him was fast slipping away. His show of concern when she came home was just 'gingerbread' on the outside and hid how he really felt.

Sylvia came two days later. She found Judy behind the front desk with Luther next to her in his playpen. She noted the pair of crutches in easy reach and standing against the wall behind her. Her sweet smiling face showed only true concern, but her words displayed a fierce anger toward Jim for what had happened. "Reverend Brownlett told me how you managed to cut yourself so bad that you almost bled to death. I know if a knife goes in that deep, it had help! And, I know it wasn't you that helped it."

Judy's eyes brimmed. She was near tears. She asked, "Sylvia, I know how much work it takes to run a farm, but could Isaac spare you to stay with me for the next two days?"

"Don't give it a thought. Isaac has practically ordered me to stay with you. He knows I'll spend nights here in your room. It's Myrt's old room. Wasn't it good that you and Bill fixed up that room for her?"

Judy assured her, "I just need someone else here as I try to take some steps without using the crutches."

"I understand perfectly. I'll stay three days. Then, we'll see."

Sylvia stayed four days. By the end of the third day, Judy was walking with a slightly-bent knee that protected the injury, but caused a very noticeable limp. The chair behind the front desk was an arm chair, so she had something to push up with and didn't use the crutches at all.

On the fourth day, Judy was close to tears again when Sylvia left to go home. She asked, "Do you and Isaac ever come into town for the Saturday morning Farmers' Market sales?"

"We're just getting our flock of chickens together. At first we hardly had enough eggs for ourselves. Now, we have enough to sell to the restaurant if we can bring them in every-other Saturday. That'll give me an excuse to come to see you and checkup on things."

It was only a week later that Anne came to see her. She was shocked to see how much weight Judy had lost. "You're supposed to gain weight when you can't exercise and here you are looking like a teenage girl again. It's not fair!"

"I think it's the worry over so much to do and how hard it is for me to move around to get it done. Sylvia stayed with me last week and helped me with learning to walk without the crutches. That helped a lot. I hated using crutches! How are you and Ethan? Thank him for me for taking the message to Sylvia."

"He was glad to do it. We've missed you at church. Mary keeps us informed about you when she spends Sundays here."

"How much longer will you and Ethan need Mary to live with you?"

"That's what I wanted to talk to you about. Our children are now old enough to take care of themselves. I'm sure the older ones would tell you they are quite grown up. They love Mary as though she was their real sister and I know she loves them. She's a high school graduate now and has made some comments about wanting to get a job at Newberry's Five and Dime Store. She thinks she would make a good salesgirl."

"What do you and Ethan want her to do?"

"We thought you would want her to live here at the hotel with you and Della. Maybe she and Della could share one room. How do you feel about her moving in here with you?"

"If you think you can do without her, I think it's the perfect time for her to live with me and Della. When will you tell her?"

We'll tell her tonight after we break the news to the children. I thought we should plan on her moving this next Sunday. I want to have a party for her on Saturday afternoon. If we come to get you in the buggy, could you manage to come? You can use either your crutches or the wheelchair."

"I will plan to come. It'll be like old times! I can't believe my little Mary is all grown up. Tell Ethan that I'm so proud that you and he are my friends. Mary is free to do whatever she wants. Jim is going to be angry when she tells us she wants to work somewhere other than here at the hotel. When that happens, I want Ethan to be with her. Jim won't be so mean about it if Ethan is here, too."

"Ethan and I have the suspicion that Jim isn't as sweet and caring as he pretends to be. I'm sorry you feel that Mary would need protecting. If he makes it too uncomfortable for her, she always has her room at our house."

On Saturday afternoon, Lance took over the front desk while Judy and Luther attended Mary's farewell party. Jim was adamant about Della having to stay behind to help him prepare for the supper crowd.

The Brownlett's had invited Mary's closest friends from their church and school, including Larry Ricketts, her Prom date. She received several lovely gifts from her friends and a twenty dollar bill from Ethan and Anne.

That evening Anne helped Mary to pack. She said a tearful goodbye to the children and Anne the next morning. The Brownlett's had been Mary's 'family' all the time she was in school in Hazard…from the seventh grade until she graduated from High School.

Ethan drove her to the hotel the next morning. He helped her to put all of her packing bundles on the front porch. Lance had been warned that Mary was coming to stay and would share Della's room. He was waiting by the door when they drove up and as fast as Ethan put the bundles on the porch Lance disappeared with them, taking them up the stairs.

Della caught a glimpse of the horse and buggy and burst through the dining room doors to the lobby to hug her sister. "Do you need help in unpacking?"

Mary was still wiping tears, but managed to say, "No, I'll do it myself. That way I'll know where everything is. But, thanks for asking."

Judy and Mary said goodbye to Ethan, thanking him for bringing her. He tipped his hat as he was leaving, "Mary, let us know if you need anything, you hear? We're going to miss you terribly, honey."

He saw that tears were starting to flow again and made a hasty departure.

Judy said, "Come now, let's be happy! You'll see the Brownlett's at church on Sunday. Anne and Ethan will probably still bring all the children here for Sunday supper. I hear that you want to work at Newberry's, downtown!"

"Mrs. Brownlett told you, didn't she? Yes. I do, and I've talked to them. They took my application. I'm supposed to go back today to see if I got the job. The opening they have is in what they call the notions department."

Judy's broad grin signaled her approval. "Honey, that's the department that has all the patterns, bolts of material, buttons, needles, thread, and all the stuff people need to make clothes, quilts, and other things for the home. You'll learn a lot working there. It's a good job for you. I'll be waitin' to hear!"

"You're not mad at me for not working at the hotel?"

"No. You're the one who has to make that choice. If it shouldn't work out, you know you have a job waitin' here. Think of it as a back-up plan. We'll need you to help out some. You'll have one or two days off each week from the store. For any work you do in the kitchen, dining room, or here in the hotel, you'll get extra pay for it, of course."

Jim had come into the lobby behind Mary just in time to hear part of what Judy was saying. Anger flared in his eyes, "Mary, you just got here and already you're thinking of not working for the family? Judy, I heard you going along with her on that idea. Where's she planning to work? She's not staying here for free if she's not willing to work with her family!"

"Jim, she just got here. Calm down. We can talk about this after she gets unpacked and settled. Now we have to stop talking to each other like Mary's not here. You ask her where she's hoping to get a job."

"I don't care where she wants to work. She's not twenty-one. She has to do what we say until then. I say she works with me in the kitchen."

Judy's eyes narrowed. The frown on her forehead should have been a warning to Jim, but he was enraged and beyond any reasonable thought.

She ignored Jim, "Mary, honey, your things are already upstairs. Go ahead and get unpacked and settled. Come back down at noon and we'll have dinner together, okay?"

With a terrified look at Jim, Mary fled up the stairs, grateful to get away from him. She looked back briefly and saw her mother limping to go around behind the front desk. Mary knew Mr. Jenkins used to keep a gun in a drawer under the desk. She felt like she could shoot the angry man herself!

Judy had no intention of shooting him. But mindful of what Sheriff Les had told her, she was taking precautions. Jim would never hurt her again if she could help it.

Chapter Nineteen
A MATTER OF SELF DEFENSE

It took a while for Jim to settle down. Judy stayed behind the front desk until Mary came downstairs to have dinner with her. She asked Lance to take her place while she and Mary went to the dining room. They sat at their usual table in the corner. Betty Lou came from out of the kitchen and took their orders. They both decided on the daily special. Judy laughed, "You mean you're not orderin' ham and eggs, your usual?"

"Ma, it's good to hear you laugh. I believe it's the first time since the accident that you've actually laughed. No, I'm not ordering my usual. Today I want to try the daily special."

Judy and Mary were about to order a dessert when Sheriff Les came through the door. He tipped his hat and asked if he could join them. Jim looked through the serving-window and saw Les sit down with Judy and Mary. He frowned, but said nothing.

Les gave Betty Lou his order and another one to go for the deputy. She said she would wait until he was ready to leave so it would stay warm. He thanked her. Judy asked Les if he had met her daughter, Mary. He nodded his head at her and said, "I've seen you, but I didn't know your name or that you were Judy's daughter. It's a pleasure to meet you."

Mary said, "It's my pleasure. I've been living with and working for Reverend Brownlett's family while going to school. I graduated just before Ma got hurt. I'm living here now. If I'm lucky, I'll get a job at Newberry's. I put my application in and they told me to come back today."

"Well, Mary, I wish you the best of luck! What time were you supposed to go there to see about the job?"

"They said between two and three o'clock."

Judy looked at the clock on the wall, "Honey, it's after one now. Do you want to get ready? I'll be fine. If I need help going back to the front desk, I'll ask Sheriff Les to lend me his arm!"

Mary scraped her chair back and left the dining room.

Les nodded toward Mary's retreating back and said, "She's a nice young lady. You must be very proud. Della is also very sweet. Where is she today?"

"She's working in the kitchen helpin' Jim prepare for the supper crowd. I think she's makin' cakes and pies."

"How old is she? That's hard work for one so young. Where did she learn to work in a kitchen and cook like that?"

"Della just turned sixteen; Mary will be nineteen in November. They both attended Pine Mountain Settlement School in Harlan County for six years. The school teaches children how to work at all sorts of jobs in addition to getting a good education. I'm very proud of them!"

I have to ask, "Are you all right? Both you and Mary seemed a little on edge just now. Has anything else happened?"

"When Mary came here to live this mornin', Jim found out she wasn't going to work here with us, and that she was tryin' to get a salesclerk job at Newberry's. He made a real scene. But, hopefully, he's over being angry 'bout it. If I feel I need help, I'll send Della to get you. Will that be all right?"

"Absolutely, and I'll come as fast as I can. Don't let him hurt you again."

While preparing vegetables for the evening crowd, Della noticed that her stepfather kept checking on something going on in the dining room. Finally, she said she was taking a break to eat her dinner. She filled her own plate with the daily special, poured herself a glass of milk, picked up a dinner roll, and went into the dining room. As soon as she saw her mother talking with the sheriff, she know what Jim had been so concerned about.

Les was just finishing his meal when Della came to their table and sat down. He said, "We were just talking about you and how hard you work. Your mother's very proud of you!"

Judy stood up. "I've got to get back to the front desk to relieve Lance or Jim will be yelling at all of us soon."

Les stood up and offered Judy his arm. No matter how hard she tried to not limp, she couldn't help it. Her leg wasn't strong enough yet for her to straighten it all the way.

When she walked through the lobby doors, Lance hurried away to return to the kitchen. He talked over his shoulder to Judy and the sheriff, "Mr. Jim will be fussing at me for being late!"

Mary got the job at Newberry's and would be the only salesclerk in the Notions Department. In her interview she demonstrated that she knew how to measure yards of cloth off the big bolts and could use the large scissors to cut in a straight line. It seemed that Mr. Alfred Stewart, the manager, was of the opinion that if she knew that much then she must have known what all the rest of the sewing supplies were for.

Mary found the notions department fascinating. It wouldn't take her long to know all about the merchandise. The store was fairly new, less than ten years old. It was clean and her department was filled with goods to sell that had that wonderful 'new' smell she loved. She was hugging herself all the way home!

The summer passed quickly. Della was preparing to begin her sophomore year. Judy gave her the extra money she needed and trusted her to take good advantage of the Back-to-School sales. Della was a good shopper and did a better job of finding bargains than her mother. She had grown two inches taller and the sleeves of last year's winter coat were way too short. The best buy she found was marked down from seven to five dollars. She came to the hotel to tell Judy she needed more money to buy the coat. Jim came through the double doors from the restaurant just in time to hear her say a coat cost five dollars. He grumbled at both of them, grousing because she didn't just quit school and work full time with him. He yelled, "You don't need high school to be a waitress! You can buy a second hand coat! If there's no high school then there's no waste of money on silly new clothes!"

Della ignored his outburst by turning away and leaving to go back to the store for the coat. Judy stayed at the front desk and ignored him, too. She learned that if one tried to use logic and reason with Jim, he just got angrier and would work himself into such a state of fury that he was scary.

Mary's job was her dream come true. In a few short weeks, she learned enough about the different sewing notions to answer almost any question. She was getting many repeat customers that included both the younger and older housewives. Her department was showing almost double its usual sales income.

Out of curiosity Mr. Stewart spent some time watching Mary wait on customers. He noted that she called most of them by name, and spent a little extra time asking questions to be sure they were buying the correct merchandise. When she received their money, she rang up the sale on the store's new National Cash Register machine, and counted out their change with a sweet smile. She ended each sale by saying, "Thank you and come back soon to shop at Newberry's."

On her next payday, when Mr. Stewart gave Mary her small white pay envelope, he took time to explain the writing on the back. "I've included a bonus in today's pay based on your volume of sales. I've enclosed a note in each clerk's pay envelope that explains that the store will begin to give bonuses based on their sales volume. You've increased your sales by a good margin and this is reflected by the amount of your bonus. Thank you for your good work!"

Mary stood for a moment with her mouth open. Then she recovered her wits, and said, "I do thank you, Mr. Stewart."

Mary couldn't wait for lunch time to open her envelope to see if all the money he talked about was really there. One of Della's gifts to celebrate Mary's new job was a miner's lunch bucket for her to use. Today, she picked it up by its wire bail and walked to the large Court House. There were young oaks growing there that gave a little shade and park benches to sit on. She sat down to eat her sandwich and smiled when she saw that Della had given her an apple and some sugar wafers. Drinking water and a small tin cup were in the bottom compartment of the lunch bucket.

Before taking her first bite, Mary opened her pay envelope and slid the pay slip, bills and change into her hand. The salary she was supposed to receive for five days a week, ten hours a day at a dollar and twenty cents a day, was six dollars. The pay slip indicated she had been given a raise of ten cents a day. The bonus based on her sales volume was an added amount of a dollar and seventy-five cents. She had a total of eight dollars and twenty-five cents! She sucked her breath in and exclaimed, "Wow! I'm rich!"

Luther was now almost a year and a half old. His baby fat was disappearing and he was growing tall and slim. He was talking more in sentences and beginning to tie them together to make paragraphs. Between Judy and Jim it was hard to give him all the attention he needed. Jim was seldom able to keep his Lu-tee with him for longer than an hour or so at a time. Judy was tied to the front desk from seven in the morning until eleven at night, but she kept Luther with her most of the time. It was hard to find enough interesting things for the active little boy to do to keep him occupied.

Judy and Jim hadn't slept together in the same room since the knife accident. She still couldn't climb the stairs, but was well enough to be by herself at night. Della and Mary were sharing one room on the second floor.

Both sisters were happy working at jobs they liked and enjoyed. They were taking their mother's advice and both were saving money. Judy cautioned them, "Don't let anyone know what you have. You can call it 'mad' money or savings 'for-a-rainy-day' money. Keep your money in your lady's money-sack and tied around your waist, under your clothes. If people know you have money, they'll begin to scheme on how to take it away from you!"

Every day Sheriff Les came for his noon meal at the same time that Judy had Lance take over the front desk so she could go to dinner. Jim could see them laughing and talking while seated at their regular table in the corner. Betty Lou waited on them and treated them special. Jim was sure Les came at the same time everyday to check up on him. The thought that Judy was helping the sheriff to spy on him infuriated Jim, but he didn't dare do anything about it.

It was the third week of October, and the mountains around Hazard were at the peak of autumn colors. Ethan came by on Saturday morning and invited Judy to bring Luther and go with him and Anne out to see Isaac and Sylvia. He said, "If it's not raining, it'll be a beautiful drive. Anne told me you stay cooped up here in the hotel all the time, and I agree that you have got to get out into the fresh air once in awhile. Will you be able to walk, or do we need to use the wheel chair on steps?"

"I've been walking on my own. If I hang on to the handrails, I can go up and down steps now. God has answered my prayers and I'm almost back to normal. I'll see if Mary wants to go with us. She could ride Curly."

Ethan's eyes widened, "Judy I forgot about Curly. Who's been exercising him for you?"

"Raff's oldest boy, Tom, takes him out for walks and runs about three times a week. Curly's grown fat and lazy! I've missed my long talks with him!"

Over Jim's loud protests, Mary, Luther, and Judy went for the Sunday drive with Ethan and Anne. Isaac and Sylvia had done wonders with the farm over the last few months. Isaac let Judy lean on his strong arm as he showed her his large patches of winter turnip and mustard greens. He had a large field of winter wheat that was almost ready for harvest.

Altogether they were away from the hotel about three hours. When they returned, Jim didn't say a word while the Brownlett's were there. They stayed until Mary returned from taking Curly back to the Livery. Judy smiled and said, "Ethan, this is almost like old times. We've missed you and Anne. I'm going to try to ride Curly next week. If I can, Luther and I will come to church next Sunday. Mary helps Jim to prepare the Sunday dinner menu and she can't get away, but I'll ask Lance to take my place for a little while on Sunday mornin'."

Ethan and Anne said their goodbyes and left. Jim was standing out of sight by the dining room window watching them leave. When they were out of earshot, he came storming out of the front door onto the porch, "It's about time you got back! You and that girl of yours act like you have nothing to do but try to be in high society. Lance is still at the front desk. Go in the kitchen and help me get the supper menu ready."

"Jim, I'm going to my room and change. Then, if Lance can stay at the front desk for another hour, I'll come to help you for a little while,"

His face was beet red as he raged, "You'll stay as long as I need you to!"

Judy said nothing. Maybe by the time she changed, he would be calmed down. She thought of what Sheriff Les had told her about letting him know if she needed him. She decided that if Jim continued to be unreasonable and dangerous like he was right now, she would send Mary or Della to get Les or the deputy.

It wasn't very late when Judy went into the kitchen. Jim was at the large meat chopping block preparing baby-back spare-ribs for roasting. He had a large meat cleaver in his hand and was cutting through the rib bones, shortening them and placing them in a long narrow baking pan. He had cut enough of the ribs to size to almost fill the pan. A kettle of his special recipe barbecue sauce was next to the pan of rib bones.

Jim came down on the spare ribs with the meat cleaver with a viciousness that drove the cleaver deep in the soft wood of the chopping block. He barked at Judy, "Get your apron on and begin to peel the pan of apples that's on the counter. Della, you finish chopping up the lettuce and make the big bowl full of tossed salad. Mary, you take care of any customers in the dining room. All of you lazy fluff-headed females, I said to move!"

No one had seen or heard Les come into the dining room and seat himself at the corner table. He was early tonight, but it was October and the days were getting shorter. He figured by the time he ate, it would be almost dark. He wanted to take Lloyd his supper and go home.

Judy walked to the counter and stood there for a minute. She leaned over to look on the shelf, behind the three stacks of dish washing cloths and towels, and saw the brown wooden stock of her gun. It was still there. Since the knife accident, she hadn't checked on it. That was five months ago! She hoped Sylvia had kept it loaded and that it was clean enough to fire if she needed it.

Judy pulled a chair over to the counter and set the pan of apples in her lap ready to begin peeling them. Jim yelled at her, as he gave another vicious whack with the cleaver. Again it was stuck deep in the chopping block. "What are you doing way over there? Come over here by me."

Judy was as calm as she could be under the circumstances as she tried to reason with him, "I need to be able to pull myself up out of the chair. I want to stay here and use the counter top to ----

That was as far as she got. Les pushed open the kitchen door just in time to see Jim lunge at Judy with the meat cleaver raised up above his head. Judy reacted quickly, but she barely had time to retrieve her gun and raise it slightly. She fired and Jim was hit in the side close to his waist. Les was in the middle of drawing his gun, but it had barely cleared the holster.

Judy and Della screamed over and over, "Oh, my God! Oh, my God!"

Les bent over Jim who was writhing in agony on the floor. He saw that Les was there and he screamed, "My wife shot me! Do something about it!"

The sheriff had no sympathy for Jim. He growled, "Be quiet, man. If she hadn't been able to get to her gun, I would have shot you myself! She was forced to defend herself against you!"

Lance came running over at the sound of the gunshot. The sheriff told him to go back to the front desk and call for an ambulance for Jim. Lance hesitated, "Is Miss Judy all right? Did he hurt her again?"

Judy reassured him, "I'm all right Lance, go call an ambulance."

"Les, use these dish towels to try to get the bleeding stopped. Oh, my God! Jim, talk to me!"

The deputy came running into the restaurant. He had heard the shot, but had a hard time deciding where the sound came from. The sheriff told him, "An ambulance is on the way. Judy shot Jim. I saw it happen and it was self defense. He tried to kill her with a meat cleaver. If she hadn't shot him, I would've had to, myself. When the ambulance gets here, you need to ride along. He's under arrest for assault with intent to kill. Inform the hospital staff that he's to be restrained."

Les bent over Jim as he slipped into unconsciousness. Judy was heart broken. Della was crying, saying, over and over, "Ma, he was going to kill you! He was going to kill you. He tried to kill you! I saw him! Oh, my God!"

After the ambulance crew carried Jim out to transport him to the hospital, it was Les who had the presence of mind to turn the large 'open' sign over and close the dining room to the public.

Judy was still sitting in her chair. She hadn't been able to move. But now she slowly got up and handed her gun to the sheriff. She was moving like she was in a daze, "I think you need to take this with you, don't you? Les, what am I going to do? Della, are you all right?"

"Yes, Ma I'm here. I'm all right."

"Where's Mary?"

Mary came over to the reach-through and said, "Ma, I don't want to come in there. I'm out here, but I don't want to come in there!"

"Honey, go stay at the front desk and make sure Luther's all right."

Then she asked Della, "Do you want to stay with me or go with Mary?"

"I'll stay with you. We need to put all this food away or it'll ruin."

Judy asked, "Les, what do you want me to do now? Do I need to go with you over to the jail? Am I under arrest? I do believe that if I hadn't had that gun close by, he would have killed me with that cleaver. Something is bad wrong with his head. He's not been acting normal now for over a year. I don't think where I shot him is fatal. When he gets well, he can't come back here to the hotel. We will never live together again."

Les had nothing but sympathy in his eyes as he let her ramble on. Then he said, "Judy, you don't have to do anything. You are the victim here. You acted in self defense. There'll be no charges filed against you, but there will be against him. He will be restricted from seeing or bothering you again. For your own protection, you need to file for a divorce."

"He has some of his money invested in the hotel. I'll have to use Mr. Babcock as my attorney to file for the divorce and to settle with Jim as far as his share of the hotel is concerned. I won't go to the hospital. I can't. Will you let me know how Jim is?"

"Yes. I'll go there now. One of us needs to stay at the jail. I'll let you know in the morning. I'd better go."

Les left abruptly. Judy sat down hard in the chair. She watched as Della finished putting all the perishable food in the big cooler. Della used a big bucket of soapy water and dish towels to mop up the pool of blood on the kitchen floor. They left everything else as it was and locked up.

Lance was still sitting behind the front desk. Judy told him to put a 'closed' sign on the front door. She told him, "We're going to be closed for the next two days."

"What about me, Miss Judy? I think I should be here in case you need anything done or bought here in town."

"Lance, that's real thoughtful. I do need you to get word to Betty Lou. Tell her to come back to work on Wednesday."

"Miss Judy, I'm real sorry all this happened. Mr. Jim didn't treat anyone nice but Betty Lou, and that's because she did everything he asked her to without any questions. He just liked to bully me because he knew he could! Oh, and don't you worry, I'll lock up when I leave."

Mary was still up when they went upstairs. Luther was sound asleep in his baby bed. The two sisters slept with their mother that night. Judy didn't get on her knees, but she silently prayed, "Dear Lord God, why is life so hard. I freely made the choice to marry Jim. It was clearly a wrong choice, but I have my sweet son. I wouldn't have him if I hadn't married his father.

Thank you for sending Les when you did. He witnessed the shooting and knew it was self defense. If I hadn't had my gun there on the shelf, I would be dead now. The way Jim had the cleaver raised above his head shows that he meant to bury it in my head. I wanted to talk with my Pa to ask his advice, but You protected me. Bless my three children. Help me to continue to provide for them. Bless my family and my friends. I'll give you all the praise. Amen."

Both Della and Mary had drifted off into troubled sleep. There would be many bad dreams about today. The day itself was a nightmare. It started out so nice for her, Mary, and Luther with the ride to visit Isaac and Sylvia. That made her think; she would send Lance tomorrow to let them know what has happened.

Another silent prayer was said, "Dear Lord, Don't let Jim die. Touch his heart and lead him to see that he was wrong in how he treated people and how he treated me and my girls. I'll never live with him again, but I can't find it in my heart to hate him. There's something bad wrong with his head and how he thought about money and women. Thank You for being here with me. I really need You more than ever. Amen."

Judy went to sleep in the wee hours of the morning. She didn't set the alarm clock, but was awake anyway at six o'clock. She quietly slipped out of bed and walked around to the other side to wake Mary. "What do you want to do about work today? If you take the day off, you need to let Mr. Stewart know. Let's be quiet so Della can sleep late. I'll get Luther up and feed him breakfast. When you're ready, come down to the kitchen and we'll eat together."

It was broad daylight that Monday morning, but the overcast sky made the dining room darker than usual even when she turned on the overhead lights

Luther finished his breakfast and sat at a table playing with ABC blocks. Mary peeped through the swinging doors of the kitchen; she saw that everything looked normal, and then came in and sat down. She looked at her mother, "Ma, I didn't think I could ever come in here again. But I can. I know you did what you had to do. If he had hit you with that cleaver he would've killed you! I don't know how you grabbed your gun. Thank God you did!"

Judy hugged Mary tight against her heart. "Honey, we're going to be all right. We're still a family and we have little Luther to think of. Today will give the three of us a chance to plan how we're going to run this hotel without Jim. I think we can still do it with me doing the cookin'."

"Will I have to quit my job at Newberry's?"

"I don't think so. I still have Betty Lou to help out in the kitchen and in the dinin' room. Della can help after school and on weekends. Lance does a real good job sitting behind the front desk. At his age, it's a perfect job for him. The other people will keep on doing the housekeepin' and maintenance work. I think it'll work out very well."

Mary's eyes brimmed with tears, but she quickly brushed them aside and with an impish grin, said, "Well, at least there won't be any yelling to worry about except little Luther's!"

Judy smiled in spite of herself. At that moment the sun came out from behind a cloud and filled the dining room with a warm, glowing light.

Chapter Twenty
ALEX'S NEW VISION

Hazard's population grew faster than builders could construct new housing to accommodate the booming coal mining industry and logging companies. The boardinghouse was filled to capacity and the spill-over kept the hotel close to full-occupancy through the work-week.

Judy gave the miners and loggers breaks on room rates and on the daily specials in the restaurant. Lance was perfect for the front desk job. He called the working men by their first names and asked about their wives and children. Sometimes, when she wasn't needed in the kitchen or dining room, Mary would sit next to Lance and help with greeting new arrivals. She often took over the desk while he was on a break or attended to other hotel duties.

Judy, Betty Lou and Della were the restaurant crew. Judy did the cooking. The salad and dessert lady continued to keep up with that chore. Betty Lou did a lot of the basic work, including preparing vegetables side dishes and fruit for pies. Judy couldn't look at apples without shuddering from remembering that it was while she was peeling apples both times that Jim had tried to hurt her.

Jim was in the hospital over a month. When he was well enough to leave the facility, the doctor told him he would not make a full recovery because the bullet nicked his liver and caused permanent damage. Les was there when the doctor released Jim and lodged him in jail to await trial. The grand jury indicted him on the charge of assault with intent to kill.

Judy asked about Jim's medical bill. Les told her that Jim was under arrest all the time he was in the hospital and prisoner bills were paid by the county. He said, "You know when he comes to trial, you'll have to appear and testify against him, and so will Della. How do you feel about that?"

Judy asked, "Is there any way I can avoid that happening? Della still has nightmares about it. I hate the idea of her re-living it by testifying in court."

"We can offer him a deal. I think the prosecutor will go along with dropping the charges if he agrees to leave Perry County and not return for a set number of years. Part of the deal can be that he's not to have any contact with you, your daughters, or his son. If he violates the agreement, he forfeits his rights and will go to prison to serve the maximum sentence under the charges."

"What's the maximum sentence for assault with intent to kill?"

"Ten to twenty-five years."

"What does that mean?"

"It means that with good behavior, he can be paroled in ten years. If parole isn't granted, he goes before the parole board about every three years until he's released or until the whole twenty-five years are served."

Judy said, "If this is explained to him that way, I'm sure he'll take the deal. Let me talk to Della about it. I want her to feel right about doin' this. Mary didn't actually see it happen. She probably wouldn't have to testify at all. I'll let you know tomorrow. Is that all right?"

"Yes. That's fine. If you want my advice, I would say to offer him the deal I just talked about. It would be hard on both you and Della to have to face him and re-live the whole thing all over again. This way none of you will have to ever see him again, and that's best."

"Les, I put up two-thirds of the money for the hotel and Jim put up the rest. He's going to want his money back. Do you think my lawyer, Mr. Babcock, can handle that for me?"

"That's what he's for. Let him handle it."

When Judy explained to Della and Mary about what it would mean if Jim took the deal Les had outlined to her, they both were in favor of offering him the deal. Judy was relieved. She could tell that Della was, too.

Mary asked, "What about little Luther? Jim's going to want to see his son. Will he agree to give up that right?"

Judy said, "When he attacked me, the mother of his son, he gave up all rights to him with that one act of hate."

Les came to the restaurant at nine o'clock the next morning for breakfast. He ordered two more breakfasts to go for the deputy and Jim. He asked, "What did Della decide? What are you going to do?"

"We agreed you should approach the court to offer him the deal just like we talked about."

"That's fine. Now, the first thing you should talk to Babcock about is filing for a divorce from Jim and full custody of your son."

"I've made an appointment with him. First thing is the divorce and custody, and the second is to settle the money matter."

Ten days later, Les reported to Judy that the court approved the deal with Jim. He would be released in two weeks. He advised her to have him served with the divorce papers right away. "He's still pretty sick and is going to stay with his family in Clay County. That's not too far away, but he's forbidden to step foot in Perry County for the next twenty years and to have no contact with you or his son no matter where you may go in the Continental United States."

"Mr. Babcock's already had me sign the divorce papers and he's drawn up a custody agreement. He's goin' to the jail tomorrow to get Jim's signature. He's going to tell him he has to sign the papers if he wants any of his money back on the hotel. When he gets his money, he's to give me a quit-claim deed for his partial ownership. That will then give me full ownership of the property."

"How much will you have to give him?"

"The lawyer is going to try to get him to settle for eight-hundred-dollars."

"Do you have that much money now?"

"I have that much, but let Jim think I borrowed it from the bank. I don't want to pay him this way, but it'll be worth it. He'll be out of our lives."

"I agree. The sooner you work that out the better. He'll be gone from the area in fourteen days and will probably be unavailable."

It took a week to handle all the legal paperwork. Jim gladly accepted the eight-hundred-dollars he was offered in return for a quit-claim deed. He had expected to get nothing because of the criminal charge against him.

Judy received a notarized and recorded deed giving her full ownership to the hotel and restaurant. Jim would be gone for good in another week. They began to breathe easier. If he came near her or the hotel, he could be arrested.

Les soon reported to Judy that Jim was gone. He had escorted him on horseback to the Perry county line. A young man who was his kin met Jim there and Les watched as they continued on their way toward Clay County.

It was now early November and they were preparing for Thanksgiving. Lance reveled in his new responsibilities. He was as reliable as the day was long. They made a good team. Betty Lou worked well with everyone. With Della working after school and weekends, the three of them managed to get everything done. Luther became accustomed to playing in the kitchen, dining room, or the hotel lobby. He was a well-mannered, happy little boy.

Judy found it was more involved now that she was doing the cooking and managing both the restaurant and the hotel.

The daily specials were such hits that at suppertime every day, the dining room was packed. The working men had the daily specials memorized and anticipated ordering them each day before they came to the dining room.

Monday was meat loaf day; Tuesday was chicken and 'slick' dumplings; Wednesday was Swiss steak; Thursday was open-faced roast beef sandwiches, and Friday was deep-fried catfish with macaroni and cheese.

Judy served the same daily specials for both dinner and supper. Anything she could do to make the work easier was worth trying. Judy's sayings, "*WORK SMART*" and "*DON'T MAKE WORK*," became their slogans. Della made attractive signs bearing the slogans for the wall in the kitchen. Then she made a companion sign that helped to explain the first two:

"CLEAN UP AFTER YOURSELF SO NO ONE ELSE HAS TO"

Della, Mary, and Betty Lou quoted the signs while laughing and talking. Judy was pleased that they made working together so much fun

Judy's big worry this year was whether or not they could go on their Christmas trip. On Sunday after Thanksgiving, Judy went to visit Isaac and Sylvia. She asked, "Could the two of you manage the restaurant for me this Christmas? If your folks can be left alone during the middle of the day, I figure that if Isaac can do the cooking, Betty Lou can handle the breakfast crowd so that Sylvia could feed the stock and handle the morning chores before riding in to help with dinner and supper. Then Sylvia can leave to take care of the evening chores while Betty Lou cleans up and helps Isaac get ready for the next day."

Sylvia assured Judy, "Ma and Pa Blevins are still able to take care of themselves and should be all right while we work at the restaurant. They stay alone on Saturdays when we go to the Farmers' Market."

Isaac asked, "How long will you be gone?"

"Christmas comes on Saturday this year. We'd leave on Thursday to get to my sister's on Christmas Eve. Then, we would forget about our normal trip to Harlan and start home on Sunday morning. We'd be here late Monday night. I can cook Tuesday morning's breakfast."

"Sylvia and I can use the extra cash right now. How much will we be paid for working the five days you're talking about?"

"I'll pay you double what you used to make."

Isaac laughed, "No, you won't. You go see your father and take the extra two days you normally take. That way you'll pay us for seven days instead of five. Will that be all right?"

"Isaac, I could kiss you!

Sylvia laughed, Miss Judy you go right ahead. I don't mind! You know we'll do anything we can. I'm lookin' forward to workin' a few days in town."

Then Sylvia looked concerned, "What about the hotel. Will Lance be on the front desk?"

"Yes, He won't be able to bus the tables and do dishes for you."

"That's all right. Between Betty Lou and me, we'll take care of it."

"Oh, I forgot to tell you Sheriff Les Cornett and his deputy Lloyd Campbell take their meals with us three times a day, and they also order meals for any prisoners in the jail."

Isaac asked, "What's Sheriff Cornett like?"

"He's been a good friend. You'll like him."

Sylvia hugged Judy and said, "I'm so sorry about your trouble with Jim. You know that I'm always here for you if you want to talk to someone later on."

"Honey, I know that. We've got to figure out a way to visit together more often. You're both real special people to me."

Judy told Mary and Della they were going to leave on Wednesday before Christmas and wouldn't be back until Tuesday evening, three days after the holiday. If you're taking presents to Grandpa Alex and your Aunt and Uncle, you need to get them ready."

Mary grumbled, "We've never taken anyone presents before."

"I know, but you're both working and can afford to buy some gifts. Della, you should think of Lance and Betty Lou. They're good friends to you."

Della was enthusiastic about the idea of gift-giving, but Mary wasn't. She grumbled, "Ma, if we give anyone presents this year, they're going to expect something for Christmas every year! If you start giving, how do you ever stop?"

"If you have a friend and care about them, why would you want to stop?"

Mary pouted, but Della asked, "How much should we spend altogether?"

Judy suggested, "Why don't you set a limit of three dollars to pay for all the presents you buy for other people? You'll need to make a list of the people and write down what you want to buy for each of them. As you buy the gifts you'll need to mark them off the list. Don't forget wrapping paper and ribbon!"

Later, Mary asked Della, "Why don't we go together and each put in half of the three dollars. Each gift we buy we can put both of our names on it as the giver. That way we each save a dollar and a half."

Della didn't know what to say, but she shook her head. Finally, she said, "No. I think that'd be cheap. When you buy someone a gift they need to know it's from you, alone. Miss Myrt once said it's the thought that counts."

"You're being stubborn and mean. I don't want to spend my money on people who won't give anything to me. If I knew they would buy me a present, too, I wouldn't mind it so much."

Della frowned at her sister. "I think you miss the whole idea of giving Christmas gifts. Where did you get the idea that you only give a gift to someone if you're sure they mean to give you one, too?"

"I didn't get the idea from anyone. It's just the way I feel!"

"Well get over it! You can't have a joyful Christmas with a selfish feeling like that in your heart."

Mary was in a mood the rest of the day. However, at work she put on her usual happy face and rang up a lot of sales. Her bonus would be a big one during this Christmas buying-season. After work that night Mary went to the kitchen to find Della. She could see her head over the top of the swinging doors and knew her sister was sitting on the counter. Still angry at her for making her feel guilty, Mary swung open the doors as hard as she could.

Della screamed in pain and surprise. She was studying her American History book and had one hand holding onto the side of the counter top for balance while she read. When Mary swung the door hard it caught her left thumb between the door and the counter top and smashed the nail. Mary cried, "Della, honey, I didn't mean to hurt you. I'm so sorry. Ma, can you fix her hand? I didn't mean for her to get hurt!"

Della wasn't in a forgiving mood as she nursed her injured hand. It was beginning to swell and blood was oozing from underneath the thumb nail. Judy went to the cooler and grabbed a package of breakfast steaks. She took out two. "Keep your hand and thumb between them for about an hour. That'll help with the pain and with the swellin'. After that, we'll soak your hand for thirty minutes in luke-warm Epsom salts water to keep down infection. Then I'll put some healin' salve on it and wrap it up good. You can't get it wet for a couple of days 'cause it can still get infected where it's bleedin'."

Then she looked at her other daughter, "Now, Mary, what were you so mad about that made you swing those doors that hard?"

Mary had tears brimming in her eyes and the most woe-be-gone look Judy had ever seen. "Ma, Della made me feel guilty this morning over my not wanting to spend my money on Christmas presents. I'd been thinking about it all day and feeling mad at her. I didn't know her hand was anywhere near the doors when I slammed them back like that. I'd never intentionally hurt her!"

"Well, you did. She'll have a bad hand for weeks. The nail may come off. We have to wait and see. She's not goin' to be able to wash dishes or help with the cookin' where she needs two good hands. You'll have to take her place on a lot of things until well after Christmas. If you don't feel like buying other people presents, then don't. Presents need to be freely given with love to the people we care about. When Della buys the gifts she chooses, you'll have to wrap them up for her since she can't use her left hand."

Mary was sniffling and standing with her mouth open while Judy told her all the ramifications of what she had done. Della was painfully hurt, but it was Mary who would bear the brunt of the consequences.

That day was a turning point in how Mary looked at her family and the people around her. It didn't completely make a Christian out of her, but it was a good start. She made a silent vow and a conscious determination that she wouldn't ever again let anger rule her head and her heart. Each passing day that she had to fill in and do some of Della's work for her strengthened that resolve.

Isaac and Sylvia came to help out a day early. They both said they needed to learn where everything was now that Jim was gone and Judy was cooking. She showed Isaac her week-day menu, particularly the specials. He said he didn't have to change anything.

In response to the questioning look Sylvia gave her when she saw Della, Judy explained what had happened to her injured hand. She was shocked to learn that Mary was responsible. Judy said, "Mary's been good as gold ever since. She's doin' everything she can for Della in tryin' to make amends.

Judy changed the subject, saying, "This is Luther's second Christmas and this time he's excited about it. We took him to see Santa Claus at Newberry's and he was afraid of him until the white-bearded man in the red suit gave him some stick candy Then, he wasn't afraid any more!"

"What about the girls? Mary's grown, and Della's almost grown."

"For the girls, I've bought them both young riding horses, with saddles and all the traveling gear they'll need. Tomorrow morning they'll see them for the first time. I hope the weather holds and it doesn't rain or snow. I always pray for a dry trail. They've made some graveled roadways here and there on the Harlan Trail, but if it's the large limestone kind, it's hard on the horses. Where we can, we walk them over to the side on dirt to avoid the gravel."

Isaac and Sylvia left just before dark. She said, "Isaac will be here at six o'clock in the morning. I'll be here by nine o'clock. I don't want you to worry about a thing. Your gun's in its usual place isn't it?"

"Yes. It's behind the stack of kitchen towels under the reach-through. Sheriff Les drops in even between meals to check on things. You'll like him."

The next morning there were squeals of delight when she rode Curly to the front porch, leading Ned and the two young horses. Mary said, "Ma, these horses are beautiful. How much did it cost to rent them for the week?"

Both girls' eyes grew huge and they broke into big grins as Judy said, "I didn't rent them this time. I bought them. Della's is the black with four white stockings. Mary, yours is the red roan. You have to give them names. They're your Christmas presents. You'll have to spend time with them every day and take good care of them."

Della asked, "What about the saddles and other gear?"

Judy laughed gaily for the first time in a long time. "Honey, everything you see on your horse is yours. Mary, the same goes for your horse, too. Now before we start packing to leave, what are you going to name them?"

Della studied a moment, "I'm calling him 'Socks!"

Mary decided and her royal-blue eyes lit up as she exclaimed, "Ma, he isn't very tall. He's just right for me. I'm calling him 'Little Red!"

With naming of the new horses settled, they slung their packing-sacks over the horses' backs and secured them. They quickly rode through Hazard. When they came to the Harlan Trail all three broke into song. They sang a favorite old Christmas Carol they all learned to love at Pine Mountain School. Della's mountain twang was heard above Judy's and Mary's voices as they sang,

The holly and the ivy are both now full well grown;
Of all the trees that are in the wood, the holly bears the crown.

Refrain: *Oh, the rising of the sun,*
                 The running of the deer;
                 The playing of the merry organ,
                 Sweet singing in the choir;
                 Sweet singing in the choir.

The holly bears a blossom as white as any flower.
And Mary bore sweet Jesus Christ to be our sweet Savior.

Refrain

> *The holly bears a berry as red as any blood.*
> *And Mary bore sweet Jesus Christ to do poor sinners good.*

Refrain

> *The Holly bears a prickle as sharp as any thorn.*
> *And Mary bore sweet Jesus Christ on Christmas day in the morn.*

Refrain

> *The Holly bears a bark as bitter as any gall.*
> *And Mary bore sweet Jesus Christ for to redeem us all.*

Refrain

> *The Holly and the Ivy are both now full well grown.*
> *Of all the trees that are in the wood, the holly bears the crown.*

Refrain.

The blending of their voices in Christmas carols and Old-English ballads passed the time pleasantly until it was time for dinner. They didn't build a fire, but pushed on to reach the half way place before dark. There, they built a fire, ate a warm supper, and bedded down the animals. Both sisters spent some time with Socks and Little Red. They were in love with them. Judy overheard them repeating over and over, again, "Oh, what a wonderful Christmas!"

The next day, just before dark, they arrived at Jonie's and with joyful hugs and kisses, greeted Alex and the rest of the family. Judy waited until after they ate supper and cleaned up the kitchen to talk about the happenings of the year in Hazard. She didn't start until the younger children were in bed and asleep.

Della and Mary excused themselves and went to bed with Alta, Mellie, and Clara. Only Otis and Gib remained in the room with the grownups.

Judy was sitting next to her father. As she related the troubles she had with Jim, she saw the hurt and sadness wash across his face and how it was reflected in his blue-green eyes. Jonie and Enoch remained silent, but Alex asked, "Did you kill Jim when you shot him?"

"No. He lived, but the doctor said he'll never be completely well because my bullet nicked his liver and caused permanent damage."

"What did the sheriff do about it?"

"Sheriff Les witnessed it happen and I wasn't charged with anything. Jim was charged with assault with intent to kill."

Alex sucked his breath in and let out a big sigh, and asked," What did the Judge do to Jim?"

"The County Prosecutor gave him a deal that I agreed to. In exchange for my one-time payment of eight-hundred-dollars to cover his part-ownership in the hotel, he would leave Perry County and not return for twenty years. No matter where I live, he's to have no contact with me or little Luther. He gave me a quit-claim deed on the hotel, and now the legal deed is only in my name."

Alex was thoughtful, and asked, "What if he violates the agreement he made? He could still hurt you."

"Then the court will revoke his rights and he'll go to prison. They said that he most likely would serve a sentence of twenty-five years."

Jonie spoke up, "Pa tell Judy about the dream you had back in the fall when the leaves were turning where you said she was in danger. In your dream she was really bad hurt and calling to you for advice."

Judy's eyes grew huge. She looked directly into her father's eyes, "Pa, I was praying and in talking with the Lord, I told Him I needed to talk to you because I needed advice. I'd cut my leg really bad and was in danger of bleeding to death. I had surgery and was in the hospital for ten days. Sheriff Burnett was sure that Jim had deliberately caused the accident. He filed a report saying he suspected criminal assault, but no charges were filed.

Alex asked, "What really happened?"

"Jim said he just bumped my arm. The paring knife rammed into the back of my leg all the way to the hilt, cutting through all of my clothes and apron. It severed an artery. The sheriff said there was no way that just a bump on the arm could cause that to happen."

"The dream I had was more like a vision, because I thought I was awake at the time and my eyes were open. I saw Jim with his face all screwed up in a rage. Then I saw you lying flat out with blood spewing out from under you and getting on walls and all over the floor. That vision haunted me for days. We never got any word from anyone that anything was wrong. I just prayed to God to keep you, the baby, and the girls safe. I had a real bad feeling about Jim, though."

"Pa, I think God answered both our prayers. God was with me when the sheriff was right there to witness what Jim did. He saw me shoot Jim, and said if I hadn't shot him, he would have. Della saw it all happen, too. The child has nightmares."

Enoch had remained silent while Judy talked about Jim and her troubles. Alex and Jonie both had tears on their cheeks. Each gave thanks to God that Judy was not killed. The two boys had looks of disbelief and shock on their faces.

Judy felt bad to be bringing this story to her family on the sacred Christmas Holiday. She stood up and asked, "Jonie, honey, do you have a stack cake made? I'd love some. Let's forget about what happened in Hazard."

Jonie almost giggled, "No, I'll make the cake tomorrow, but I've got some fried dried-apple pies still warming on the stove. I'll make us some tea. Everybody come to the kitchen and sit down!"

Judy asked, "What are we doing tomorrow?"

"Cook and bake most of the day. Israel and Id's family said they won't have Christmas dinner with us this year. Id's family has grown too big. He and Rhodie keep having a baby almost every year. Their two older girls are Pauline and Katherine, but there are a passel of younger ones. Over the last week two of Sadie's boys came to see us. Their son, Freeland (they call him Frill), told the other boys about going to their Cousin Della's graduation. They wanted to come by over Christmas to meet her and Mary. I asked who was coming. They said Hugh and Jim."

Judy said, "It's been too long since I've seen any of them. Anyway all the boys looked so much alike; I doubt I could tell them apart."

The next day around noon, two young men riding very tall horses turned into Jonie's front yard. Enoch was coming from the barn and signaled them to bring their horses over to the hitching rail and get down. When they dismounted, Enoch invited them in, "We're just sittin' down to dinner. You're just in time!"

The two were decidedly brothers. They were tall and slender. Each had thick, black-curly hair, dark brown eyes, and they were ruggedly handsome young men. As they came in the house, Judy was standing in the kitchen doorway. She smiled when she saw them, "I can tell you two are Bish's and Sadie's boys, but tell me your names."

It was Hugh that answered, "I'm Hugh, Aunt Judy, and this is my brother Jim. We knew you were plannin' to be here today and Ma and Pa wanted us to come to see if you had time this visit to come to see them?"

"I don't know for sure. We'll see how the weather is on Sunday, and will try. It's been so long since I've been up to Turkey Fork. I'd love to see Sadie."

Hugh and Jim stepped over the benches and arranged their long legs under the dining table. Mary and Della, along with all their girl cousins aligned themselves on both sides of the large table. Hugh and Jim paid a lot of attention to Mary and Della. Both boys were impressed that the girls had jobs that paid real money. Mary told them she worked for Newberry's in Hazard. Hugh was quick to point out that Harlan had Newberry's and Scott's. "Both are five and dimes!"

Judy assured them that she and the girls shopped those stores in Harlan all the time. Jim asked, "If you can't come to visit Ma and Pa on Sunday, when will you come back to Aunt Jonie's again?"

"Unless something happens not until next Christmas."

Christmas day came and went all to soon. On Sunday morning, the sun came over the mountain shining bright and it warmed up to near seventy. Judy asked

Otis, Gib, Della, and Mary if they wanted to ride with her up to Turkey Fork to see their aunt and uncle.

Mary asked, "Have I ever been to Turkey Fork?"

"No. Your Uncle Bish and Aunt Sadie came to see us here on Little Greasy Creek when you were small, but we never went to see where they live."

All four young people decided to ride along. With Luther safely in front of her on the saddle they followed the spring-fed creek up the mountain trail. They arrived at the Boggs' huge farm right at dinner time. Bish was grumpy and showed that he wasn't happy to see company come. Sadie was delighted. Judy followed her into the large kitchen. She laughed, "Don't mind Bish. He's just actin' normal. Hugh and Jim told me to expect you all today. I made some extra special cakes and pies. I know how young'ins like to eat!"

After the huge meal, while the cousins visited and played games, Judy helped clean up the kitchen. Otis and Gib said they would look after Luther. Sadie was proud of her pantry room and showed off her floor to ceiling shelves that included dozens of quart and half gallon jars of green beans, tomatoes, acorn squash, apples, peaches, blackberries, huckleberries, black raspberries, Cherries, winter greens, and pickles. There were shelves of pint jars of all kinds of jellies, jams, and preserves. She had two large barrels of sourer kraut. Under the pantry floor was a dark cellar that held Irish and sweet potatoes, turnips, sugar beets, and other root vegetables. Sadie gave Judy two pint jars of spicy chow chow.

Judy was properly impressed. "Sadie, honey, you make me jealous. I really miss being able to can and preserve my own food. You've done a ton of work. Do the girls help you with all this cannin'?"

"They sure do. Even the boys help with keeping fresh meat on the table. If they want to eat, they all have to do their part for the family. The one who doesn't do much and don't like to work at all is my Jim. Bish says he takes after him. When he was a young man, he let me do all the work. After we had a passel of young'ins, he had to work or not eat! I think he's been grouchy ever since."

The two sisters had a nice laugh together at Bish's expense. Sadie said, "What he don't know sure won't hurt him. I'll never tell!"

Judy enjoyed her visit with her older sister immensely. Emily was the oldest of the girls. Ranie was next in age order, but had died in child birth some years ago. That left Emily, Sadie, Judie, and Jonie. The youngest girls were closest to Alex. Emily and Sadie were kept so busy caring for their large families they seldom got a chance to visit him.

When Judy stepped out on the porch, ready to leave, she saw Mary and Della in a deep conversation with Hugh and Jim. Both brothers were promising to make a trip all the way to Hazard next summer to visit with them. Mary wasn't very impressed with the two young men. Della, however, seemed smitten by Jim. Judy remembered that Jim was the one his mother called the lazy one.

She called out, "Della, Mary, lets get the horses, it's time for us to go. Where's Otis, Gib, and Luther?"

Della answered, "Freeland, Art, Floyd, and Alex took them over behind the barn to a fenced clover-pasture to look at their horses. They said there were more than a dozen back there."

"Then you go tell them we have to go."

Jim spoke up, "I'll go with you. There's one that's all black. He's mine. I expect to have five horses of my own in another year."

Judy frowned in displeasure. Sadie's lazy Jim was spending entirely too much time with her younger daughter. Della's keen eyes hadn't missed her mother's disapproving look at Jim. She didn't want to give Judy any new grief. She cut their trip to get Otis and Gib very short. As soon as she got in earshot of them, she yelled, "Ma said we have to go!"

They followed the downward trail that ran along the side of the spring-fed swift-flowing water. Turkey Fork was one of the headwaters of Little Greasy Creek. They soon reached the main road leading to Jonie's.

The next morning came too soon. It was heart breaking for Judy to say goodbye to Alex. Each year they both feared they wouldn't see each other again in this life. When they left this time, Judy broke her habit and looked back several times to see her father leaning his weight against a porch post. She knew he had tears on his cheeks the same as she and Jonie did. To save himself the emotion of a goodbye, Enoch found something to do with the animals in the barn.

Judy and the girls missed not taking the annual shopping trip to Harlan. However, by having the extra day, they did go to visit with the Boggs'. Mary and Della kept up a lively conversation about all the tall, dark, and handsome Boggs brothers. Mary liked Freeland the best.

When they arrived back in Hazard, they found everything in tip-top shape. Isaac and Sylvia, with the help of Betty Lou and Lance, did a super job running the hotel and the restaurant in their absence. Although, they got back late on Tuesday night, Judy wanted to begin her regular routine again the next morning, but they wouldn't hear of it. She had to admit she was overly tired.

Mary chose to go back to Newberry's. She was anxious to tell her friends at work about Little Red, her special Christmas present, Della didn't have to go back to school until after New Year's Day, the following Monday. She and her mother slept in the next morning and had a late breakfast. They sat at their usual table in the corner, with their backs against the wall. Betty Lou took their orders. Della and Judy both thoroughly enjoyed being waited on.

They were just finishing when sheriff Les came through the front doors for breakfast. He told them that Hazard enjoyed a quiet and peaceful Christmas holiday. He said, "New Year's is never as quiet. People tend to drink too much and get careless with guns. Even before I was sheriff, I dreaded New Year's!"

Judy said, "I'm not going to let worrying about it spoil our holiday. People will always be people. Whatever happens we just have to deal with it. The Good Lord seems to protect drunks, fools, and children. It's all of us other folks that have to look out!"

Les laughed, "Is your life always so simple?"

Della chimed in, "No, Sheriff Les, Ma just likes to fool herself into thinkin' there's good in everybody. I happen to know that there are some people who are pure evil. It's them kind that good people have to watch out for!"

Judy was shocked by the emotion Della displayed in saying what she did to the sheriff. It was the first indication of the lingering ill effects that her daughter suffered from her ordeal with the Cantrells and in coping with the two life threatening incidents involving Jim and her.

January and February passed quickly. Mary worked six days a week and received a hefty sales bonus every payday. Judy talked to her about opening a savings account at the bank, but Mary was firm in her mistrust of anyone else touching her money. Her folding money stayed safe in her lady's money-sack,

Mary went out with the Ricketts boy, but she told Della and Judy that she only went with him so she would have an escort for social affairs.

Della looked forward to school being out in May so she could work full time at the restaurant. She would be seventeen on April 30. Her junior year at Hazard High School was going well for her. There was one boy that she liked, but she had yet to have a real first date.

Judy settled into a routine and for the first time since before Jim came into her life she was comfortable. It was in March that Judy began to worry about their risk of being held up and robbed. If she was on the desk when such an attempt was made, she was sure she could stop any robber in their tracks. Lance, however, was a different matter. If he tried to stop a robbery, he could get hurt.

She talked to the bank about their making a night deposit of each day's receipts. They gave her a locking, bank-bag with two keys. She kept one and the bank had the other key. She deposited the bag in the designated drop-slot at the bank building each night, and each business-day morning they opened the bag in the bank and deposited its contents in her second savings account.

Finally, Judy decided to close the older account and keep the new one. After she paid Jim eight-hundred-dollars, and bought horses for the girls, she had a little over five-hundred-dollars left. She thought of Mary not trusting banks and taking a cue from her, she wanted to keep her money safe under her clothes.

Chapter Twenty-One
THE HAZARD FLOOD

During the first week of April, 1927, it began to rain. The Kentucky River, North Fork, and Town Fork crested high, but were still within their banks. The water subsided by the third week. Before they were threatened with a flood again, Judy decided to take almost all of her money out of the bank. Bill told her in 1913 when the flood reached the top step of the hotel, the water was deep inside the bank on Main Street.

Della's birthday was coming on Monday, April thirtieth and thoughts and plans for that took the place of flood worries. Judy rode out to the Blevins' farm to ask Sylvia to help with a party for Della on Sunday afternoon, the twenty-ninth. She learned from Mary that the name of the boy Della liked was Joe Carter. He would be invited and Mary would bring the Ricketts boy as her date. Betty Lou, Judy, and Sylvia put up party decorations in the restaurant on Saturday night. It would be the first boy-girl party that Judy had ever been involved with. Sylvia and Betty Lou were laughing and giggling.

Judy wanted to know what was so funny. They told her she had to find a wine bottle for the kids to play spin-the-bottle.

"What's that game like?"

Sylvia and Betty Lou fell to their knees in fits of laughter. Judy began to get angry with them. "You all tell me right now what's so doggone funny. Is spin-the-bottle a dangerous game?"

Betty Lou winked at Sylvia, and asked, "Did you ever hear that kissin' could be fatal with teenage kids?"

Judy stamped her foot, "Kissing? What's kissing got to do with it?"

Sylvia got to her feet and hugged Judy. "A girl spins the bottle as hard as she can. If it stops while pointing at another girl, it's a pass. But if it stops pointing at a boy, then the boy gets to steal a kiss in front of everybody."

Judy's mouth flew open and she didn't say anything. Betty Lou said, Miss Judy all the young kids play spin-the-bottle. It's a harmless, fun game."

Judy looked at them both now with suspicion. "What else do they play?"

"Well," Sylvia said, "There's Post Office, too."

Betty Lou spoke up, with a giggle, "Sylvia, I don't believe Miss Judy is old enough to hear all this stuff that kids do. When they get to the party, let's just let them choose the games they want to play."

Judy finally figured they were teasing and grinned, "That's a good idea. You two imps will be putting all kinds of notions in their heads!"

With April behind them and it's proverbial April showers, Judy thought the flood threat was over. However, in the middle of the first week of May, it started to rain again. Two days later it stopped. On May the eighth, Luther's second birthday, Raff Pennington came into the restaurant wearing knee-high rubber boots. He didn't stop in the dining room but pushed through the swinging doors into the kitchen where Judy was putting the finishing touches on Luther's birthday cake.

Judy looked up in surprise. The significance of the knee-high rubber boots hit her as he said, "We're moving all of the horses across Town Branch to higher ground. Something strange is happening. The water's coming up too fast. Curly, Socks, and Mary's Little Red will be saddled. You should come and lead them to safety. I heard the businesses are closing and so is the High School, so your girls will be here soon."

Judy was removing her apron as he talked. She pulled on her knee-high boots and told Betty Lou to take over for her in her kitchen. Then she opened the door to the lobby and called to Lance to tell him where she was going and to watch Luther until she got back.

She crossed the porch and when she stepped off the bottom step, she was in ankle deep muddy water. She looked both directions and saw Mary coming on Main Street and Della coming down the cross street from the High School. As she followed Raff around the side of the hotel she was able to call to both girls. I'm going to the livery to move our horses to higher ground. Raff thinks this water is going to get deeper. Mary, put some clean clothes on Luther and then stay with him and Lance. Della, you help Betty Lou, although I doubt we'll have much of a dinner crowd!"

Judy hurried as fast as she could. Raff, Tom and his younger brother, Sid, were driving a dozen horses and mules toward the wooden bridge that led to a well-traveled road up the side of a sloping hill to their pasture. Judy led Curly, Socks, and Little Red about half way up the hill and tied them to the lower branches of a big maple tree. She talked to all three horses, patting each one in turn, "Now you guys should be fine. If that water gets all the way up here, there won't be a town left!"

When Judy got back to the hotel, the water was to the top of the first step. She grumbled, "Raff's right. Something's causing the water to rise too fast. It's not raining right now. It's either raining buckets up-river, or something's damming up the river down below. If that's it then this is backwater."

Les came to see about the dinner meal for the jail. Judy told him about Raff moving all of his animals to their high pasture and that she had moved her horses, too. "Judy, that's probably the wise thing to do. Lloyd has orders to move a prisoner to the second floor of the court house if the water gets over a foot deep. It's just eleven o'clock, but I thought if you had anything ready for dinner, I'd go ahead and take it now. If they have to move, they'll have already eaten."

"I'll fix something right away. Don't you think it would be a good idea to take a look downstream? We can't do anything about rain up stream, but we might be able to do something if the trouble's downstream. If this is backwater, it's going to get a whole lot deeper."

As he left, he assured her that he would take her advice as soon as he dropped the food off at the jail. "I'll come back to let you know what I find out."

Judy was watching as Les reached the street. The water was already a foot deep! She went inside and found Mary playing with Luther by rolling one of his rubber balls back and forth to him. Della was sitting up on the kitchen counter reading a school book. Betty Lou was nervously looking out the front window at the deepening water on deserted Main Street.

Judy asked, "Betty Lou do you have any rubber boots here?"

"Yes. They're in the back room."

"What do you want to do? This water looks like it's going to get a lot deeper. Will you get flooded where you live?"

"I don't know. The water's comin' up so fast, it's scarin' me. If you don't mind, I'd like to go home!"

"You go ahead. I think Lance should leave, too."

She watched as Betty Lou stepped into the street. The water was almost to the top of her boots. She had to walk slowly to keep it from sloshing over the tops of them. It was too soon for Les to come back. They all ate a quick dinner while they waited. She cut each of them a piece of Luther's birthday cake. Then, she asked Lance what he wanted to do, stay with them or go home. "Miss Judy, if it's all right I'll stay here with you. I don't have any boots and my room's on the third floor where I live, so it should be all right."

"Lock the front door and put a closed sign on it. No one in their right mind will cross Main Street today!"

Les came back and he was red faced with anger. "I found out what's wrong and why the water's rising so fast. Someone has thrown a full size mattress into the river. It's jammed tight against a big tree with a lot of branches. The tree is caught between two big boulders at the narrows on the river below the North Fork. Tons of debris has piled up behind the mattress and the tree limbs. It's dammed up. This is backwater just like you said. It's going to take a large charge of dynamite to dislodge all of that, and you can't set off dynamite under water, so we have to wait."

"Wait? How long? If the dam isn't opened right now this water's going to reach the second floor of the hotel!"

"I think you're right. Move all you can at least up to the next floor."

Judy asked, "What about the jail"

"I have to go now and move my records over to the court house. My dinner's waiting at the court house. You all stay safe!"

Judy told Mary to go upstairs and pack some clothes for her and Luther in travel-sacks. She went to the kitchen and told Della to do the same. Della said she would be there in a few minutes.

Before she went upstairs, Judy quickly gathered up a cookbook she had used at Pine Mountain School and other loose papers containing recipes. Some of them were hers and some were Jim's. Looking around, she knew it would be impossible to save anything else. There wasn't time.

She told Della that they would be on the second floor. "Don't wait too long, this is a serious flood!"

Della got down off the counter and walked over to the front windows. She saw high water in the street, but none up over the porches. She went back to the kitchen and sat on the counter again, reading. It was only a few minutes later that she looked up from the book and thought something was wrong with her eyes. She squealed, "Oh, my goodness!"

Della jumped down into knee-high water. Hugging her book to her chest, she waded slowly toward the stairs in the lobby. The door was open so she was able to get out of the dining room. "She scolded, "What a dummy I am! Ma told me to come on and I didn't believe the water could rise that fast."

When she got upstairs and found Judy, Mary, Luther and Lance, they were all in the corner bedroom where they could see both ways on Main Street. Judy took one look at Della and yelled. "Why did you wait so long? Get out of those wet clothes and go wash off. We don't know how long we can stay here on the second floor. Mary and I have packed our clothes. I'm taking all of Luther's. I grabbed everything I could to take with us. I put our things on a bed in the first room at the top of the stairs on the third floor.

Lance wants to stay in the hotel. You've got to hurry! As soon as you're ready, we're going out the window on the third floor to the roof of the building next door. We can move from one rooftop to another until we reach the wooden bridge that I used when I took the horses to the hillside pasture. We'll stay with the horses until we're told we can come back."

Della was in tears because she could tell that her mother was heart-sick. With the water already that deep in the kitchen she knew it was ruined. Mary was terrified. She only wanted to get to higher ground where she could feel safe.

Judy looked at the older man and reassured him, "Lance, I think you'll be all right. I hate to leave you here alone, but I don't think you can jump with us from the window to the roof and then from building to building. We'll tell people that you're here alone. You'll be rescued by someone with a boat."

Della had never dressed so fast in her life. Judy made the girls go first and then Lance. She had Luther in her arms. As she started up the stairs to the third floor she saw a wave of water came over the landing to the second floor. Judy was sobbing; she couldn't help it. That wave meant the water was all the way to the ceiling of the hotel lobby and the restaurant.

Lance walked with them down the hallway to the end room. He sat on the bed and watched as Judy opened the window. They were almost even with the building next door and the space to step over to it barely one foot. She looked down and saw the murky water a scant ten feet below them. First, Mary went out the window and stepped across to the next building. Then Della did the same. Each of the girls put down several travel sacks and turned back to take Luther from his mother's arms. Judy had four travel-sacks with her, two tied together over each shoulder. She quickly stepped over to the other roof.

Judy looked back and saw Lance in the window watching them. This building's roof was flat and easy to walk on. When they got to the other side and looked down, they saw it was a four-foot drop to the next building, but the water was only about five feet below the roof. Della said, "Ma, if we get down there and can't go any farther, we won't be able to get back up here to this roof. The water's rising and we'll be stuck there. It would be over Luther's head!"

Judy knew that Della was right. Mary was too terrified to speak. Judy asked Della, "Do you want to go back to the hotel and wait with Lance? You know we can wait here for someone to come with a boat to rescue us. I'm afraid if we don't get across that bridge before dark, we'll have to stay here all night!"

Della reacted quickly, "Ma, we shouldn't go back. We can be seen more easily by someone in a boat if we stay right here on top of this building."

Mary had been silent the whole time, but now she seemed to wake up, she shouted, "There's someone! They came around the hotel from Main Street."

The boat was a block away. She could see that it was Les rowing towards them. The flood had climbed higher and the other building was only a foot above water. From that roof they could easily get into the sheriff's boat. Judy waited until he was along side the building. He told Judy to bring one bundle each and leave the rest behind. "Now," he said, "You have to jump. Della, you go first. Judy hand Luther down to Della. Mary, you go next. Judy, it's your turn. You're all down now. Step in the boat one at a time. Judy you go first. Della hand Luther to your mother, get into the boat and sit down easy. Mary, sit down easy!"

Judy remembered Lance, "Les, Lance is alone on the third floor. Don't forget that he's there and will need rescuing."

Les started to row away from the building, "Where do you want to go? There's nowhere to go in town that's not mostly under water."

Judy said, "I told you that Raff took their horses to their pasture above the wooden bridge that's a block away. We'd planned to use the rooftops to get there, but they were all under water. I took Curly, Socks, and Little Red over that bridge two hours ago. It should still be okay to cross over if we can get there."

Les quickly rowed in the direction of the bridge. When he got there, they could see that the flood waters were lapping at the floor boards. Les pulled his boat over to the high ground and one at a time they got out. Luther hadn't made a whimper the whole time. He was fascinated watching all the activity around him.

The sheriff was casting a doubtful eye at the bridge. He said, "If you're going, go now! I'll stay here until you all get across."

Mary and Della were in front. Judy had Luther hugged tight against her heart. The girls leaped off the bridge onto the solid ground. They carried the travel sacks. Judy left the bridge last. As she struck solid ground, she sank down and rolled away from the water. Les screamed, "Look out! Get back! Run!"

He frantically rowed his boat backwards to get away from the bridge as it collapsed into the swollen waters. A wave of water washed toward Les and the boat danced backwards. He waved at Judy and the girls as they stood up and started the upward climb toward the big maple and their horses.

Mary broke the silence by saying, "Ma, the fact that we're alive and together is a miracle. I want us to thank God for His being with us today. How could the three rivers flood the town that quick? It wasn't even raining!"

"Sheriff Les told me a little while ago that it was caused by some thoughtless person throwing an old double-bed sized mattress in the river. It got stuck in the narrows against a big tree with a lot of limbs that was wedged hard into the rocks. Then a lot of trash stacked up behind it, making a dam. This is a flash-flood caused by backwater."

Della sobbed broken-heartedly, "Ma, what are we going to do? The hotel and restaurant are ruined. It would take more money than we could count to fix it back the way it was. This dirty water will make everything in the kitchen and dining room just destroyed. We don't have jobs! How will we live?"

"We may have to leave. Restaurants are always looking for good cooks and waitresses. We'll get jobs."

Mary said, "You're already thinking about our ruined business and how to live without it. This just happened. Shouldn't we wait until we see how bad it really is, and then decide what to do?"

Judy said, "The water isn't going to go down anytime soon. They have to wait for it to get low enough on the far side of the dam to set a dynamite charge. Once they do that all of this water will rush through the opening and flood whatever is downstream. It may be days before they get the water down low enough for us to go back into the hotel."

Judy saw Raff, Tom, and Sid coming around the hill toward them. Raff was shaking his head in disbelief, "I've never seen anything like this. We got our animals out, but my place is ruined. When the water goes down it'll leave a sea of mud and mold. We'll have to tear it down, burn it, and build a new livery."

Judy asked, "Will you be able to re-build?"

"Yes, I think so. I'll have to borrow heavily from the bank to build it back, but it's the only thing I know."

Judy shook her head, "Well I can't. The hotel is brick. It's water-logged and there will be the mud and mold you talked about. I just bought it and I've not owned it long enough to have money or credit. We're going to camp here now, and tomorrow, we'll visit my sister in Harlan County until I decide what to do."

Raff asked, "Will you write someone here so we'll know where you are and that you're all right."

"We'll write to Sylvia and Isaac, and I'll be in touch with Sheriff Les. Will you let Les know that we went to Harlan? Ask him to let Newberry's know what happened. Tell them Mary lost her home in the flood and had to leave."

"Yes, I will, but I hope you change your mind!"

They didn't leave the next day. The last food they had eaten was at noon yesterday. They were starving. Luther cried uncontrollably. Judy was desperate to find them food. She prayed, saying over and over, "God help me."

It must have been about ten o'clock that morning when Ethan came around the hill from the east. He carried in front of him on his horse a large wicker basket. Mary saw him first and jumped up, frantically waving her arms.

He dismounted and handed the basket to Judy. When she opened the lid she sank down to her knees. "Thank God for you, Ethan Brownlett. Everyone's almost starved. Luther especially is so hungry he can't stop crying. He wore himself out, but he's sobbing in his sleep."

"There's a cloth in the basket you can use to spread on the ground. There's hot coffee in the bottom of the lunch bucket. I brought a bottle of milk for Luther and water for the girls.

The church was saved. It's on higher ground than our house where the water is just on the first floor. This food was prepared in the church kitchen."

Luther was still asleep. Mary and Della were eating like a couple of cave people, grabbing at the food and stuffing it in their mouths. Judy scolded, "Slow down. You'll get sick! Use your good manners!"

Ethan laughed. "They're fine. Our whole family forgot their manners when the church ladies prepared this food and brought it to us this morning."

"How did you find us? How did you get here?"

The sheriff came by boat to check on us and found us in the church. I asked about you. He told me about your narrow escape when the wood bridge collapsed. "Thank God you're all safe!"

"But how did you get here? There's no dry road that you could have taken from the church that I know about,"

"From the church I rode to the southeast edge of town and then went up the mountain. There's an old little-used trail near the top that circles around and leads over to this mountain. That's how I found you."

Judy burst into tears, but they were tears of gratitude. "Ethan, you and Anne are such good friends. I know that Isaac and Sylvia are safe because their farm's in the highlands. When you can, let them know we're all right."

He asked, "What're you going to do? You can tell them yourself."

"No. I've decided that we're going to take what we salvaged last night and go to Harlan County to stay at my sister's, Jonie Lewis. Her mailing address is Big Laurel, Kentucky. I want to hear from all of you. Make sure Lance is all right. He stayed alone on the third floor of the hotel. He'll be starved, too!"

"Are you going to abandon the hotel?"

"I don't know anything else to do. I just bought it and bought Jim out. There's no money to restore it. The water's ruined everything. The mud and mold makes it unhealthy to use anything in the restaurant. I have no way to save the building. Maybe the city can find someone with money who'll restore it. I thought I would do a quit-claim deed to the City of Hazard if they'll take it."

"What will you do in Harlan?"

"There are several restaurants in Harlan. I'm sure I'll be able to get a job cooking at one of them. Mary has a good record at the Newberry's here and I think she can get a job at the one in Harlan. Della can go to school in Harlan and help take care of Luther. You've given us enough food to last a good two days, so we'll start for Harlan as soon as you leave. We can use the same trail you used to cut across the mountain. We'll save time and miss all this water."

Ethan's eyes were tearing up as he hugged Mary goodbye. "I want you to promise to write to us. If you see Miss Pettit, tell her that we're safe from the flood. I'll miss all of you. May God be with you!"

Then he was gone. Judy was all business. She woke Luther to feed him and urged him to drink as much of the milk as possible. Then she repacked the food basket and gave it to Della. She said, "Honey, you're responsible for our being able to eat, so be careful with the basket!"

"I will, Ma! Where'll we camp tonight? We can't get to our half way place, leavin' this late."

"There's another big rock that I know about. We can build a fire there. The days are longer now and we'll leave earlier in the mornin' and get to Jonie's before dark tomorrow night. Now that we have a plan, let's get movin'!"

From their vantage point high on the mountain, they had a good view of the devastation caused to Hazard by the back-water flooding. Main Street was built on low ground. The flood had reached almost to the second floor of the court house. Judy knew that Les, Lloyd, and their prisoner were all right. She could see the hotel. The water was half way up on the second floor and the canopy of the restaurant was completely covered by the dark and murky water. She guessed it would be another day or more before the water began to go down.

Judy resolutely put the hotel and the restaurant out of her mind. She felt in her heart and soul that God's plan for her now was relocating in Harlan. She would be near Alex and Jonie's family. She and Mary had good job possibilities. They needed a house to rent somewhere near Harlan so they could walk to work. She had a prayer in her heart and on her lips as they traveled that morning. "Dear God, I trust that You will make this work out for me, my girls, and Luther."

When they arrived at Jonie's they were welcomed with open arms. Jonie exclaimed, "What a surprise! We've had supper, but it'll only take a minute to get something on the table. Alta, go to the spring house and get some sweet milk for Luther and the girls. Judy, I have coffee made and still hot on the stove. While I get things ready, tell me what's happened. I know it can't be good!"

Judy didn't know where to start. She looked at her father who had pulled up a chair to sit near her at the table, "Hazard was almost destroyed by a flood. My hotel and restaurant are ruined. We had no where to go so I decided to come home to you. We'll find a place to live in Harlan and Mary and I will find jobs there. Della can go to Harlan High School and take care of Luther for me."

Judy saw Alex's slow grin and was surprised. "Pa, I thought you'd be unhappy with me and my decision. It was hard to abandon all that I've worked for. I can tell that you're not too surprised that we're here!"

Alex smiled, "Yes. I'm happy you're all here. I'm not surprised to see you. I'm sorry about the flood and the loss of your property and business. Thank God you're safe! I'm not surprised because of another vision I had after your visit last winter. I knew some kind of natural disaster was going to happen that would involve you. I didn't know it would be water. After you eat, you must tell me what happened to cause a flood. It's not rained that much here, or in Harlan."

Jonie cleared the table and put food away, saying, "We can do the dishes later. Pa wants to hear about the flood. He'll soon go to bed. So let's sit here at the table and you tell us about it."

Mary took Luther into a bedroom to get him ready for bed. Della stayed at the table with her mother. It didn't take long for Judy to tell them about the tree, mattress, and trash that created a dam and caused the flood of backwater.

Alex stroked his long beard, deep in thought. He said, "God works in mighty and mysterious ways. Someone had a mattress that should have been burned if they wanted to get rid of it, but instead they just tossed it in the river so that it became someone else's problem. I'm sure they never meant to cause so much heartache and misery. Who knows, maybe they were flooded out, too. That would serve them right! Judy, honey, I think you have made the right decision to come home. I think its God's plan. I'm going to bed, children. Goodnight."

Hazard Hotel and Restaurant, Main Street, May 1927

Chapter Twenty-Two
STARTING OVER IN HARLAN

Judy and Mary planned to go to Harlan on Sunday, and job-hunting early
Monday morning. Judy would visit restaurants seeking a cook position, and Mary
would apply for a sales position at Newberry's and Scott's.

On Tuesday they would go house-hunting. They wanted a four-room house
if they could find one. To be comfortable they needed one with a living room,
kitchen, and two bedrooms. Judy and Luther would share a bedroom and so
would Mary and Della.

When they arrived in Harlan they checked in at the boardinghouse and
arranged with the owner to stay on a day-to-day basis. The lady told them to take
their horses to the Feed, Grain and Livery Stable behind the boardinghouse. They
made a day-to-day deal for boarding Curly and Little Red, too.

Early the next morning they started job-hunting. Judy told Mary to meet her
at the boardinghouse at noon so they could get the free dinner.

The first restaurant that Judy stopped at on Monday morning was located
near the building site for a new movie house. The sign said it was to be the Margie
Grand Theatre. The restaurant was owned by the Sizemore family. Mr. Sizemore
said they didn't need a cook right now, but might later on. Ackley's Restaurant
was closer to midtown. She was told to come back that afternoon to talk to the
owner. Another one was the Green Parrot. They had no openings.

Mary wasn't having any luck. Neither Newberry's nor Scott's had any
openings. They took her application and told her to come back to see them in a
week. Of the two, Newberry's manager was the most professional. When he asked
her why she left the store in Hazard and she told him about the flood, he was very
sympathetic. As soon as she left him, he wrote a letter to Mr. Stewart asking for a
reference on Mary Smith, Hazard Hotel, Hazard, Ky.

At noon Judy and Mary met and tried to decide what to do next. Although
Mary was discouraged, she didn't want to add to her mother's troubles. She was as
positive-sounding as she could muster, saying, "I saw some other stores that
looked interesting. What do you think about Powers and Horton? There's a
Bower's Department Store across the street from the A&P. Then there's a bargain
store on Main called Watson's. Until I know something from the Manager of
Newberry's, I could be applying for jobs at those other places."

Judy grinned. She knew that Mary was putting on a happy face in order to
cheer her up. She said, "Well, I'm going back to Ackley's about three o'clock this
afternoon. If I can talk with the owner, I might get something there. It was the
cleanest and had the most up-to-date kitchen. I know I'll not earn what Bill paid
me, but we need to have some money coming in."

Mary left to go put in more applications at the other stores around town. Judy stayed behind to talk with the owner of the boardinghouse about possible houses she could rent.

The lady was a goldmine of information. She said, "The Sunshine Coal Company closed this year. Most of the houses they provided their miners are empty and for rent. I hear they're in pretty good shape. You have to carry water from a pump, but it's not too far away from any of the houses. Each house has an outside privy that's maintained by the housing manager."

"Who's the housing manager and where can I see him?"

"His name's Harvey Fuson, a lawyer. He has an office in town, but to handle the rental business for the Sunshine Mine people, he has a little office set up across the street from the big Armory building there in Sunshine."

"I don't know Sunshine. What's the closest way to get there?"

"Take the railroad track west out of town. Go across the Railroad Bridge and veer to the left, you'll go past the L & N Railroad water tank. If you stay on the tracks and go a little farther, you'll see Frank Cole's Grocery on the left by the railroad-track crossing.. Then when you look the other way, you'll see the Armory. You can't miss it."

Judy thanked her. She left the boardinghouse and returned to see the owner of Ackley's. The man was tall. He had black bushy eyebrows and a thick shock of white hair that looked like it was too wiry to comb. However, he had kind eyes. His first questions had to do with previous employment. When she told him she managed the Hazard Hotel and Restaurant until last week. His eyes grew huge, he asked, "Why'd you leave that job?"

She answered, "The hotel and restaurant were destroyed by a flash flood last week that almost took the whole city. I lived at the hotel with my two daughters and son. We've lost our home there, so we'll live here in Harlan now. My family lives across Pine Mountain in Big Laurel. I'm staying with them until I find a job and a house to rent here in town."

"Who did you work for there?"

"Bill Jenkins, He's retired and moved to Florida."

"Would you consider a job helping in the kitchen until something else opens up? What I mean is the woman who's cooking now is talking of moving back to Tennessee somewhere. When she does, you'll be our cook."

"I'll be glad to take the job under those conditions if it'll pay enough for us to live on."

"I pay kitchen helpers a dollar twenty five a day for six days a week. Because I'm asking you to take the job temporary, I'll raise the pay for you to a dollar fifty a day. That's nine dollars a week."

"When I'm your cook what is the pay?"

"It'll pay fifteen dollars a week to start, with a pay raise after six weeks. Your meals are free."

Judy smiled in appreciation, and asked, "What are the hours?"

"We open at seven, so you would need to be here at least by six. We close each night at eight. I don't have to tell you that you have to prepare for the next day's breakfast the night before. We have daily specials that you help prepare. You help bus the tables and do dishes. In general, anything else you're asked to do to help the kitchen and dining room to run smoothly."

"My younger daughter's seventeen. School's out now and she'll care for my son who's a two year old. She's a senior and will attend Harlan High School in the fall. When she goes back to school, I may have to bring Luther to work with me part of the time."

"I think we can work that out when the time comes. When your young son is here with you his meals will be free, too. You said you need to find a house to rent. After you do that and get settled, let me know when you can start!"

Judy said, "I talked to four other restaurants today. None of them are as clean or well equipped as yours. I thank you for talking with me. I'll be back to see you as soon as we're settled."

Mary had no luck finding a job at the other stores. No one was hiring. The only one that would take her application was Watson's. Judy told Mary that if she gave it time she would probably get the next position that opened up at Newberry's. Then she told her about the job she was offered at Ackley's.

"I want you to go with me in the morning to see this Harvey Fuson about getting a house to rent in Sunshine. If he has more than one empty house, you can help me choose. We'll want to be able to walk to work, so keep that in mind."

After breakfast the next day, Judy paid the owner for another day at the boardinghouse. Then they went to the Livery Stable and saddled their horses. It was an opportunity to give Curly and Little Red some exercise.

They took the lady's directions and followed the railroad track around a bend until they saw Frank Cole's Grocery Store. It was ten o'clock when they found Mr. Fuson's office located in a small green clap-board building. He was standing on the steps with his keys out ready to lock up.

Judy called to him, "Mr. Harvey Fuson?"

The man turned and looked at them. He was taking in the strange sight of two handsome women riding horses on the main street through Sunshine. People walked everywhere in the village. Horseback riders were rare.

Judy was sizing him up. He was dark haired, slightly balding, short, rather portly, and a handsome man. She liked his kind eyes and smile. He asked, "Yes, ma'am. I'm Harvey Fuson, and what can I do for you?"

"I was told to see you to find out if you have any empty houses for rent?"

289

"Yes, Ma'am, I do. There're two on this street, not too far down. Then there's an empty one over near the water pump. It's not a paved street over there; it's just hard dirt around the house."

"I see you were about to leave. Do you have time to show them to us now? If not, we can come back later."

"No, I can show them now."

He opened the door to his small office to get his ledger book for the mining company's rentals. He locked the door behind him and started walking up the street. Judy and Mary dismounted and followed him, leading the horses.

He was talking as they walked, "The houses on our left are the odd numbers; the ones on the right are even numbers. The two empty ones are numbers 26 and 28. They're side beside. One is fenced and one is not. You can see that these houses aren't too far from Frank Langford's Grocery Store."

"You have two grocery stores in Sunshine? I didn't know mining companies allowed that!"

"This one did. Actually, there were four grocery stores. There's Paul Reasors' Store over by the Sunshine Grade School, and on up the road here near the little hill, is an all rock building that was a store, but I think it's closed now.

The first house, Number 26, was the one with the fenced front yard. All of the houses along this street had hard-dirt yards. None of them had any bushes or flowers growing anywhere. The yards were all swept clean. Each house had a front and back porch with steps to climb.

He unlocked the door with a skeleton key and they went in. Each room had exposed wiring and there was a drop light in the center of the rooms that was hanging about three feet below the ceiling. There was an on and off pull chain attached to each light.

The ceilings of each room were made of sheets of wood and painted. Judy guessed the walls were wooden, too, but the people had wall-papered over them. Each room was a different color and pattern. There were fire grates in all of the rooms except the kitchen, where there was a brick chimney with two sections of stove pipe hanging loosely from the flue opening. There would need to be another elbow section added to the stove pipes to accommodate a wood or coal-burning stove. The house was clean. Just the windows needed a good washing. Judy looked out the back door and saw that the privy was located at the far left side of the back yard. She asked, "How much is the rent?"

"It's five dollars a month. I need one month in advance as a deposit, and the rent paid every first of the month after that. If you move without notifying me you lose your five dollar deposit. If you notify me that you're moving and the house is left in good condition and clean, your five dollars will be refunded to you. If you like the house and want it, I'll save it for you for three days."

Mary asked, "Ma, can we see the other two?"

Mr. Fuson answered, "Sure you can. I'll lock up and we'll go next door."

House number 28 was identical to the first one. The only difference was that it didn't have a fenced front yard, and Frank Langford's Grocery was closer.

The third house was numbered 107 and was located on an unpaved area near the village pump. Inside, it was clean, but the ceilings and walls were the same. There wasn't any wallpaper in any of the rooms. Judy asked, "Is that pump the only place to get water?"

He said, "Yes, ma'am, everybody has to carry water from that pump. You'll notice several worn paths from the houses you looked at first; those are short-cuts through people's yards to get to the pump easier. No one complains about anyone taking a short-cut to the water."

Mary said, "Ma, if we took this one we would be closer to the water pump. That'll make a big difference in the winter time."

Judy asked, "How much is the rent for this one?"

"It's not on a paved street. The rent is three dollars and fifty cents a month. But I still need five dollars in advance as a deposit."

Judy and Mary looked at each other and nodded in agreement. Judy said, "We'll take this one. I do need to ask, if we decide to wallpaper the house, will you pay for the materials if we do the work?"

"Just give me the receipts itemizing what you bought for improvements and I'll deduct the costs from the rent."

"When do you expect to move in?"

"It's going to take a few days. We're staying with my sister's family across Pine Mountain at Big Laurel. We were in the big flood in Hazard and lost everything. I have to find new or used furniture and all new kitchen equipment."

Mr. Fuson had a look of sympathy in his eyes, "Let me ask around, I may be able to locate some for you. Are you particular about color, material or style?"

Judy nodded her head in appreciation, "No, we won't be that particular. Anything you can do to help us to begin all over again will be appreciated."

"Whatever I find that I think you can use I'll go ahead and set up inside the house for you. Give me the weekend to work on it. Before you buy anything, come back and look inside the house."

Judy thanked him and handed her new landlord the five dollar deposit. He took the money and sat down on the porch steps to record it in his ledger. She gave him her name as Judy Elizabeth Smith-Collins along with the information that she was employed at Ackley's Restaurant in Harlan.

As he handed her the skeleton key to the house, Judy asked, "Is there any place in Sunshine where we can board our horses? We have three."

He thought for a minute, "None of the mining camp houses have out-buildings, but I have a barn behind my house. I live just up the little hill beyond the pump and over the mine-spur of railroad tracks. My house is the large white two-story. I have a handy-man who also drives for me name of Redmon. I'll ask him if he would agree to take care of your horses for a little extra money. He's been with me for a while and is reliable. If he agrees, we'll clean up the stalls that are already there and get straw and hay for them. I'll let you know what he says."

Judy thanked him again. She asked, "Do you want me to give you the first month's rent today?"

"You can if you want. This is almost the middle of May. Now I know you won't be moved in and settled for some time yet. So the rent you give me today will also cover the month of June. There won't be any more due until the first of July. I'll leave the electric in my name until you move in. They'll want a small deposit when you put it in your name to start the first of June."

She gave him another three fifty and he recorded it in his ledger. They said goodbye to him, and watched as he walked back toward his office.

Mary squealed, "Ma, I can't believe it. You have a job already and we have a house!"

"Yeah, honey. We have an empty house! It cost me almost a whole week's pay, but it was sure nice of Mr. Fuson to offer to help us find some furniture for the living room and bedroom, and stuff for a kitchen. We're going to need beds and bedding, dressers and chests, curtains for the windows, and some kind of divan and chairs for the living room. I'll need a stove, table and chairs, kitchen cabinet, and an ice box. Money's going to be scarce if we buy all that!"

Mary said, "I know that Della doesn't have much saved, but you can use my money to help get our bedroom stuff. If I get the job at Newberry's in time I can use my sales discount to help get the bedding for both bedrooms. Oh, and they have curtains and window blinds, too."

Judy said, "It's still early. Let's ride around Sunshine and see where everything is. Luther's no way near ready for the Primer yet, but I want to see how far he'll have to walk to school."

They locked up the house and mounted Curly and Little Red. The pump was only a few feet from their front door. There was a path that led gradually up to the railroad spur-line and the horses easily climbed it to walk along the tracks. Mr. Fuson's house was easily spotted. It was the largest one around. Judy was interested in the barn. It was in good repair and only needed some weeds and trash removed from around the building.

They rode on a little way and saw the gray boxy school house. There was a big play ground all around it with two slides, and a large swing set.

Turning left they saw Reasor's Grocery Store. Mary laughed and said, "Well we'll have three choices for trading for groceries. Our house is right in the middle between Frank Cole's, Frank Langford's and now Reasor's!"

Judy grinned, "You know, I've lived so long in just one room, first at Pine Mountain School and then in the hotel that I've forgotten what it's like to even say *our house*! It rolls off the tongue real nice, doesn't it?"

It was still early when they got back to the boardinghouse. After they left the horses at the Livery Stable, Judy said, "Let's celebrate tonight! We'll head back to your Aunt Jonie's in the mornin'."

"Celebrate? How and where?"

"Let's skip supper here and eat at Ackley's Restaurant where I'm going to be workin'. I want to get an idea of how they handle the supper crowd."

When they walked into the restaurant it was five o'clock. The room was about half full. The supper special was chicken and dumplings. Only a few people had ordered it. "Let's order the supper special. I want to see what its like."

"Oh Ma, I want my usual, ham and eggs over easy!"

"Okay, then you can tell me if it's made as good as how we did them in Hazard! It's important that I know how well they cook basic dishes."

A sweet faced young girl smiled at them as she approached their table to get their order. "Hello, my name's Anna Mae. It's good to see you this evenin'."

After they ate, Judy was satisfied that her cooking would be 'head and shoulders' better than what was offered now. The chicken stock was thin and watery and the dumplings were doughy and not completely cooked. She exclaimed, "No wonder only a few customers ordered the supper special!"

Mary said her ham was too stiff. The eggs were hard, not soft like 'over easy' should be. The home fries that came with the standard breakfast dish were cold and not cooked enough to be soft so they could be mixed with the eggs.

"Well, now I know that whoever they have cookin' here sure can't beat my cookin'. I needed to know that ahead of time. I've learned that the good Lord expects us to be prepared. We can't always see what's comin', like that flood, but He always makes a way. He has really blessed us today!"

They left Harlan the next morning and arrived at Jonie's late in the afternoon. Judy and Mary were beaming as they dismounted and, Jonie said, "I can tell from your faces that you have good news. The boys will put up your horses. Luther's still nappin'. Della's down in the orchard helpin' to pick ripe June apples. Our two trees are loaded this year. You and Mary come on in and have a snack. You can tell me your news while I finish cookin' supper!"

Judy and Mary enjoyed a barbecued pork sandwich and coffee. Judy let Mary do most of the telling. She ended up talking about the house they rented. "Aunt Jonie, we have a nice house, but right now it's just an empty house. Ma says we have to start all over again by buying new or used everything!"

Jonie raised her eyebrows. "You remember that you stored some of your things in the far end of the hayloft in the barn. It's been there for about ten years.

After we eat, let's go and see if you can use any of it now. If you can't, maybe Enoch and the boys can use the wood to make you something for the house."

While they were eating and then cleaning up the kitchen, Judy was remembering a lot more about what she'd stored away so long ago. There was lots of daylight left when they climbed up in the hayloft, but the storage area was dark. Otis brought two oil lanterns for them to use. Jonie pulled matches out of her apron pocket and lit them.

The bedding Judy had stored was tied up with brown rope. When she untied the bundle, she found six hand-made quilts she'd forgotten about. They spread them out over the sweet smelling hay and examined them. Only one had streaks of mildew along one edge. Judy felt like she had found gold! Jonie said, "I know how to get that mildew out. Tomorrow, we'll wash and boil them. They're so pretty. Tomorrow they'll look like new!"

They pulled out more wooden boxes. She found a set of dishes, platters, glasses, pots and pans, tools she needed to cook with, and pewter table flatware. Della came up into the storage area to see what was going on. She took one delighted look, "Ma, every time we go to Harlan we can load as much as we can carry of this stuff into travel sacks and take it with us on our horses' backs."

"I don't believe I've got anything else I can move over the mountain. Let's see what Mr. Fuson can come up with. We'll clean everything good and transport all that we can. We'll go to Harlan this Sunday, but until I get some beds, we'll stay at the boardinghouse. I need cleanin' stuff, too. Della, I need you to stay here to take care of Luther. All of us will go on the next trip."

Judy and Mary arrived back in Harlan in mid-afternoon on Sunday. After they checked in at the boardinghouse, they followed the railroad track again to Sunshine and then to their house.

When Judy unlocked the front door and walked inside, she was speechless. There were some furnishings in every room. Mr. Fuson had really been busy. Everything she saw was used, but in good condition. In one bedroom there was a full-size metal bed set up with springs and a mattress in place. In the other bedroom there were two three-quarter size beds in place and each one had springs and mattresses.

Across the foot of each bed were sheets, pillows, and pillow cases. In the living room there was an overstuffed divan with a matching chair. Another chair that had been slip-covered stood alone in a corner.

There was a dish cabinet in the kitchen that was in need of a coat of paint. A table with four chairs was in the middle of the room under the drop light. An empty ice box stood against the far wall. On the table was a set of red and white dishes and several dish rags and tea towels. Against another wall was a homemade wash stand. There was a coal bucket, water bucket, water dipper, and a pan for washing faces and hands.

Judy said, "Tomorrow I want to clean and wash everything afore we use it and put it in place. Let's unpack Curly and Little Red. Then we'll decide what else we really need. Tomorrow, we'll go shopping!"

Mary said, "We don't have any curtains, but there are brackets for window blinds on each window. Let's use the bed sheets to cover the windows. We don't want someone to break in and steal anything."

They got an early start the next morning. The Frank Taylor family that lived next door offered to heat water for them. The cleaning and putting away of their meager possessions didn't take long. Katherine (Kathy) Taylor brought over a kettle of steaming beef/vegetable soup and hot cornbread for their dinner.

After they ate, Mary made a list of all they needed to buy, beginning with window blinds and curtains. While she was writing the list, Harvey Fuson's driver, Dan Redmon, drove up in the front yard in an open-window, four-door Chrysler sedan. On the back seat was a big copper kettle for boiling clothes. He'd filled it with other things, including a wide washboard, a clothesline and a large bag of wooden clothes pins. There were blinds to fit each window except for the kitchen and six pairs of long lacey ecru color window curtains with curtain rods.

Also, on the seat was a large galvanized wash tub. It, too, was filled with more home furnishings and some basic food items like flour, meal, sugar, pure lard, and dried pinto and great-white-northern soup beans. Judy was embarrassed by the generosity of Mr. Fuson. She asked, "Where did all this come from?"

"The furnishings in the rooms there I picked up with Mr. Harvey's wagon and mules. His business friends said they were donations from them and their neighbors for a flooded out family that was moving here from Hazard."

"We can't accept charity!"

"No, Ma'am, Mr. Harvey said you might feel that way. I was told to tell you that this ain't charity. It's just what you would do for someone else who'd lost everything. You'll never know where it came from. That's what he said. You can depend on everything that Mr. Harvey says. He's a good man!"

Judy was silenced for the time being. Then she asked, "Are you bringing us anything else? I need to know before I go to town to buy some things."

"Yes, Ma'am, I'm to take the car home and get the wagon and mules again to pick up a cook stove with stovepipes and a thick, metal platform for it to set on. Somebody's gonna to be there to help me load it and then come with me to unload and set it up for you. It's a wood and coal-burning stove. I need you to stay here 'til I can fetch it."

Judy didn't know what to say. She just dumbly nodded her head, and silently watched as he unloaded the car. Then she found her voice, "Did Mr. Fuson say anything about us boarding' our horses with you?"

"Yes, Ma'am. I'll be happy to take care of them for you. They're fine lookin' animals. The big one looks like he's gettin' old. What're their names?"

"Curly is mine. He's the older one. The younger one is Mary's. His name is Little Red. What will you charge for feeding, exercising, grooming, and talkin' to them?"

Dan grinned, showing he'd lost a front tooth, "He told me you had three horses. I asked at the Livery what they charged. They said for three horses it would be twenty five cents a day each. I'll take care of all three of them for you for two dollars a week. Will that be all right?"

"Yes, that'll be fine, and I thank you. I saw Mr. Fuson's barn and I liked what I saw. Do you live there with him in that big house?"

"Yes, Ma'am, he gives me my own room. He's a good man!"

He drove away and she and Mary began to put away the food items. "Ma, we shouldn't buy too much 'til we see what all the man's bringing."

Kathy Taylor came over to see if she could help. Judy told her a cook stove was coming yet. "Do you know where I can order a ton of coal?"

"We get our coal for the kitchen stove and the fireplace grates from Hobart Harber. He lives straight across from you, but up the hill, on the side of the mountain. His house is above the road that runs behind the Sunshine Baptist Church. You can see the two houses up there. His is the last one on the end."

"We have to stay here 'til they come with the kitchen stove and set it up for us. After that I'll go to see him to order the coal."

They didn't wait long. Then after the used kitchen stove was in place and Dan had left, Mary stayed at the house while Judy went to see Mr. Harber.

She climbed the small hill to the railroad spur and crossed the tracks. There was a worn path between two camp-houses that led to another small hill. She climbed that and crossed the graveled road to the steep stone steps leading up to the Harber house. When she stepped onto the large wrap-around front porch she turned to look down at Sunshine. The view of the neat well-maintained little village, the snaking river that flowed past, and the opposite mountain peaks were breathtaking.

As she stood there taking in the landmarks she recognized, a tall, pleasant man came out of the house and greeted her. She explained who she was, where she lived, and that her next door neighbor, Mrs. Frank Taylor, had recommended him for the delivery of a ton of coal. He said he would bring it tomorrow and unload it in the corner of the front yard where coal had been piled before. She asked, "How much do I owe you?"

"It'll be clean, block coal, no slack. I'm charging three dollars. You can pay me when I bring the coal tomorrow."

Judy thanked him and made her way back down the three distinct little hillside paths until she reached the level where the pump and her house was. If all went well, this would be the last night they would spend in the boardinghouse.

While Judy and Mary were putting the finishing touches on their new home in Sunshine, Della was helping Jonie can the luscious fruit from the June apple trees. She and Alta were peeling and quartering the apples. Otis and Gib were picking more from the trees for them to put up. In addition to canning the quartered fruit, Jonie was making applesauce and apple jelly.

Luther entertained himself with building blocks. Dolly watched him build a good sized tower out of the blocks and then she pretended to sneak up on him and knock them down. Then they both fell over in giggling fits.

Finally, Jonie told the girls to stop peeling apples so she could begin dinner. The two girls went out on the front porch, taking Luther, Dolly and Delphia with them. They made pallets for the three little ones out of heavy, patchwork-quilts and watched while they fell asleep.

Jonie's house sat a little below the Little Greasy Creek road. You couldn't see anyone coming from either direction. Alta and Della were surprised when Hugh and Jim Boggs rode into the front yard. Della mumbled, "Well they have timed it right again. It's dinner time!"

The young men dismounted and tied their horses to the hitching rail. Hugh doffed his hat with a mock flourish, "My, but you ladies are looking fine today. Della, is your mother here?"

"No, she and Mary are in Harlan. We've rented a house. Ma got a cooking job. We're moving. They'll be back tonight. What do you all want?"

"We just wanted to visit with Aunt Jonie and Uncle Enoch, and to see you two pretty girls again."

Alta and Della both blushed. Jonie heard men's voices and came to the front door. "I thought I heard someone here. You two boys go down in the orchard for me and tell Otis and Gib to come on to dinner. I'll set two plates for you. Girls, wake up Luther, Dolly, and Delphia. You can feed them first."

When she got them all in the kitchen, she looked sternly at Alta. "I heard what those two young men were sayin'. I think it was Hugh doing the talkin'. They're your first cousins. They can't be actin' like they come a courtin'. I don't like their coming around and talkin' like that. Now I want you to pay them no attention. After they eat, I want you both to be too busy helpin' me and they'll get tired of workin' with Otis and Gib and leave."

The two Boggs brothers were back the next day. Hugh sat in the kitchen talking with Jonie. Enoch started to come in the house from the barn and saw Jim holding hands with Della. She kept looking around anxiously. Enoch could tell she wanted to get away from him, but was too polite to hurt his feelings.

He came up behind Della and scolding, asked, "Girl, why ain't you in the kitchen helpin' your Aunt Jonie? Where's Luther? You're supposed to be watchin' him. Jim, you come on in the house now. I 'spect dinner is 'most on the table. Gib and Otis will be here soon. They're always hungry!"

Under Enoch's disapproving glare, Jim continued to make 'sheep' eyes at Della, and smiled knowingly at her, "I guess we better do as Uncle Enoch says. I'll have to leave after we eat, but I'll be back to see you agin on another day."

"If you're coming to see me, there's no need. I won't be here. I told you before that we're moving to Harlan. I'm going to school there."

Jim reached for her hand, but she jerked back away from him. He smiled pleasantly, slightly blaring his dark eyes, "Don't you worry, I'll find you. We'll see you again, and soon. When you see Aunt Jude, tell her we said hello."

After the Boggs boys left, Della with tears in her eyes, asked, "Aunt Jonie, what am I going to do? I don't want that Jim Boggs coming here. I know it upset you, Uncle Enoch., but it's not my fault!"

Enoch grinned, "Honey, I know that. I was pretendin' to be mad so he'd leave you alone, but it didn't work. He's got more nerve than a brass monkey!"

"What am I going to do? He said he'd find me even when we move."

"Don't you worry any more; I think your Ma will fix his wagon! When she does, he won't bother you any more."

The next day, Israel and Id stopped by to ask about Judy. They had heard about the Hazard flood and seen Della in the yard. Jonie assured them she was fine. "They lost everything in the flood, but she's found a job in Harlan and has rented a house. Now she's rounding up some furniture and kitchen stuff."

Id said, "When we saw Della in the yard, she was holdin' hands with Jim Boggs. He's her first cousin. He's been comin' down here for about six months now to call on Dora Mae Helton. It looks like he's making a move on Della. I'm sorry to say it, but that Jim's always tryin' to win over every pretty, young girl he meets. He's no good! Be sure you tell Aunt Judy what's going on. That Helton girl's crazy about Jim and she's not one to mess with. She'll hurt Della."

Judy told the boardinghouse lady they wouldn't need their room anymore. Then they went to the house to wait until Mr. Harber came to unload the ton of coal. He was true to his word. It was clean, block-coal with no slack.

Kathy Taylor said she would keep watch so no one stole their coal. She advised Judy to get a tarpaulin to put over it to keep it dry when it rained so it would make a better fire. "I've got extra kindling wood that I'll put in a box on your porch. Be careful when bringing in kindling and coal. Watch for snakes."

Early the next morning they got ready to return to Big Laurel. Curly and Little Red were saddled. They locked the doors and mounted. Judy grinned, "Mary, honey, we have what we need to cook, do the wash, and sleep in our own house. This is God's plan for us now. He'll provide all we need!"

Della was so happy to see her mother and sister, but Judy knew something was bothering her when she saw tears welling in her eyes. Joni greeted her with a happy hug, wanting to hear all about the new house. Enoch gave her a half-hearted smile, but kept a serious look on his face.

They ate a late supper, but it was still a long time until dark. Judy loved the long days of May, June, and July. She was having a piece of Jonie's June apple tree's applesauce stack-cake. "Della did most of the work makin' that cake. She's a hard worker. Luther's a little angel when she's watchin' him."

Everyone had left the kitchen except the grown-ups. Alex sat with his chair leaned back against the wall and listened to the talk. Enoch started, "Judy, Hugh and Jim Boggs came back to visit twice while you were in Harlan. Jim's making himself a nuisance talking like he's courtin' Della. She tries hard to make him leave her alone, but he won't take no for an answer."

"How do things stand right now?"

"She told him to not come back to see her 'cause she's movin'. He told her it didn't matter where she went, that he'd find her. He said to tell you hello. I told her that Jim has more nerve than a brass monkey!"

Jonie spoke up, "That's not all, and Id told us that Jim's been courtin' the Helton girl, Dora Mae. That's why he's been down here so much. They said that she's crazy about him and might try to hurt Della."

"Don't worry so much. You know I'll take care of Della. She's a good girl and wants to finish school like Mary did. As far as Jim Boggs and Dora Mae Helton are concerned, I'll take care of them in my own way!"

Alex was grinning again and stroking his long, white beard. He asked, "When are you all leavin' to go back to Harlan?"

"Tomorrow morning. You wouldn't believe all the stuff people have given us. They told me to not think of it as charity, but just people doing for me what I would do for them if the need arose."

The next morning just as Judy, Mary, Della, and Luther were ready to leave, Loretta and Dora Mae Helton came stomping upon Jonie's front porch. Judy met them at the door and blocked their way to keep them outside of the house. Loretta shouted, "We want to talk to you about your little slut of a girl, Della! Where is she? Bring her out here!"

Judy reached out and took Loretta by the hand. Judy's lips moved silently. Then her words were soothing, but belied the outraged look and narrowing of her eyes, "Why Mrs. Helton, Loretta, isn't it? And this is Dora Mae, all grown up! Have you finished High School already? Della has another year yet. What is it you want to see me about?"

"Not you, we want to see Della!"

"Della is a child. You'll talk to me or not at all!"

"We hear she's makin' a play for Dora Mae's boyfriend, Jim Boggs. Della's trying to take him away from her!"

"Why would she do that? She wants to graduate from High School and get a good job. She has no interest whatsoever in Jim Boggs. We're moving to Harlan and she'll attend High School there. That's far away from Dora Mae's boy friend.

Anyway, if you want to get mad at someone, get mad at him, not Della! He's the one who makes the long trip from Turkey Fork to come here. Now, unless you want to apologize to my sister and her family for your unfriendly visit to her home, I think its time you left her property."

Judy reached again. This time she touched Dora Mae's beautiful thick black curly hair. Her lips moved silently. Then she said, "What beautiful hair you have, child. Some people begin to lose their hair when they have mean thoughts about others for no good reason. It would be a shame if that happened to you."

Loretta grabbed Dora Mae's arm and spun her around. "Girl, I don't want you talkin' to her! Let's go."

She got in a parting shot at Judy, "It's a good thing you're movin'. You do anything to my Dora Mae and you'll regret it the rest of your life!"

"You've already done a lot of evil to me and my girls. You have a lot to answer for, maybe for the rest of your life!"

For the first time a shadow line of fear crossed Loretta Helton's face. Her eyes grew huge as Alex looking like a figure out of the Old Testament stormed out of the house onto the front porch. He shook his fist at the astonished woman. She and Dora Mae quickly ran down the steps and to their horses.

Judy couldn't keep from laughing as she took Alex's arm and helped him back into the house. "Pa, you scared that evil woman to death. You couldn't have timed your coming out here on the porch any better! We'll give them at least ten minutes to get home and then we'll leave. Jonie, if you come to Harlan to trade afore we come back to see you, I'm working at Ackley's Restaurant near the Court House. It's a block from the building site for a new Theatre. Come to see me there and maybe I can get off to show you where we live in Sunshine."

Judy felt a surge of excitement race through her. As she rode along on the Little Greasy Creek Road, she prayed, "Dear Lord, I'm going home! I'm feeling like this is your plan for me and the fulfillment of Pa's visions. With Your help, I'll be able to provide for Luther. My girls have good educations and are willing to work hard. They'll be all right. Bless Jonie and her family. Bless Pa and keep him safe. It's 1927. He's a hundred and five this year. Forgive me for rushing to vengeance against the evil doers in the world. I'll give you all the praise. In Jesus' name I pray, Amen.

Noble (Nobe) LangfordBrother to Frank Langford, owner of Frank Langford's Grocery in Sunshine

Chapter Twenty-Three
AN UNLIKELY ROMANCE

When they arrived in Harlan, the first thing they did was stop at the A&P Super Market to buy basic food items. Tomorrow she would order an ice delivery for the ice box. Tonight, she bought a small loaf of sliced white bread, canned goods, non-perishable fresh fruit and vegetables and very little meat. Judy did buy a quart each of sweet milk and buttermilk. She bought bacon and eggs for breakfast. She already had all she needed to make biscuits.

Della was excited about seeing their new home. She couldn't remember much about ever living in a house. She was six years old when they left their farm and she went into the Primer at Pine Mountain Settlement School.

The coolest place in the house was the back bedroom. That was where Judy placed a small wooden box that held the bacon and eggs, a small beef roast, sliced bologna, potatoes, onions, a cabbage head, and the two quarts of milk. She placed it near a window that she would open later to let the cool night air in.

While Luther ran gleefully from one room to another, they put up the window blinds and curtains. It was a huge improvement. With the sheets off the windows, they made up each of the beds. Judy used three of her quilts as bedspreads. She had some of her own clean pillowcases to use on the pillows. Luther would sleep with her in the double bed in the first bedroom. Della and Mary would each have their own bed and sleep in the back bedroom.

Tomorrow, she intended to go to one of the second hand stores and try to buy dressers and chests. Della asked, "Ma, what if this Mr. Fuson brings us some for the bedrooms?"

"We can't have too many. We have our clothes and towels, wash cloths, sheets, quilts, and a lot of other things that we need drawer space for."

The next morning, Mr. Redmon was there before nine o'clock with the wagon and mules. He had a young man with him who helped unload one dresser base with a detached mirror, and two chests. He set up the dresser in Judy's bedroom. As soon as he was done, he left.

Judy asked Kathy Taylor, "When will the ice man come again?"

"He comes twice a week. He's due today. I'll tell him to add you to his list of customers. He'll give you two cards. One says 50 and one says 100. If you want fifty pounds, put that sign in your window. If you want a hundred pounds, use that sign. He brings it in the house and puts it in the ice box for you."

How much does it cost for delivery twice a week? How do we pay him?"

"It's fifteen cents for fifty pounds and thirty cents for a hundred. I pay him every two weeks on Friday. He'll ask to be paid in advance. He said too many people move away without payin'."

"We can pay him today and up until school starts in September. After that, Della will be in school and. Mary and I will be workin', and then could we leave a key and our money with you so he can take the ice in the house and you can pay him for us?"

"I'll be glad to. Who'll be watchin' Luther for you if everyone is workin' or going to school?"

"I may have to take him to work with me unless I can find someone willin' to watch him for nothin'. I won't make enough to pay for it and live, too. Della will be home from school at about three thirty. She'll watch him then."

"Would you trust me and Frank to watch him for you? He's a darling little boy. We wouldn't charge you anything."

"Kathy that would be an answer to a prayer, but you ask Frank first and then let me know. God bless you!"

That night when Judy climbed in between the cool, clean sheets in her own bed in her own home, she was close to tears again in gratitude. Luther was sound asleep beside her. She grinned at the memory of the little parade they made on their way to the privy out back before bed. Luther was sure something ugly was going to get him if he sat on that 'black' hole.

There was no sound coming from the girls' room. She slid out of bed on her knees. Her prayers were silent and long tonight. There were so many nice people to remember and to ask for God's blessings in their lives. Dear Lord, I was so afraid that I couldn't do this for my girls and my son. I spent almost all of my money buying the hotel and paying off Jim, but You've been with me all the way. Tomorrow I'll know just how much money I have left. We'll have to live on what we earn. When Della finishes school and gets a job that'll help us to begin to save again. Please be with me Lord. Bless my family, bless Pa and keep him safe. In Jesus' name I pray. Amen.

Ike, the ice man came early the next morning. Judy paid him sixty cents for two weeks. What a relief to put their precious milk, meat, and eggs away in the ice chest. Ike chipped off a few small pieces to give to the girls and Luther to chew. They thanked him for the treat, and he left them grinning with delight.

Except for a few odds and ends she needed to buy they were in very good shape, thanks to Mr. Harvey Fuson. The people who had helped her so freely didn't want to be known. She told no one about Mr. Fuson's role in it except her family in Big Laurel. In Sunshine, only the Taylor's knew it was his handyman and wagon that delivered the heavy items.

Judy got up first and started a fire in the cook stove. While it was getting hot, she sat down at the kitchen table to count her cash money that she had with her and to speculate what she actually had in the bank in Hazard. She was surprised. She counted almost four-hundred dollars in folding money. Her little yellow bankbook said she had a balance of one-hundred seventy-nine dollars. The last night deposit she made hadn't been recorded in her book yet.

Everything she bought for the hotel and restaurant was on a cash only basis. She owed Lance, Betty Lou, the maintenance man and housekeeper some money. She'd like to give each a month's pay to tide them over until they found something else, but she didn't dare. She would write to Sheriff Les and send him enough money to give each of them a week's pay. She would write to Isaac and Sylvia to see if Lance could live with them. She quickly figured up how much it would take to pay her people.

Today was Saturday. The Harlan County Savings and Loan was only open until noon. She would open an account there and ask them to arrange a bank transfer of her savings account in Hazard to her account in Harlan. Then she would pay for a bank draft to send to the sheriff.

Judy believed in being prudent about her money. She wanted no one to know how much she had. She put two hundred dollars in her lady's money-sack under her clothes. She used the rest to open the new savings account.

Tomorrow she would get Curly, Socks, and Little Red taken care of with Mr. Redmon. When Mary found a job, she would help pay their board bill. In the meantime, Judy knew she had to pay for all three horses.

On Monday she would let Ackley's know she was ready to start work. Mary was going back to Newberry's again to ask about a job. Della would take care of the house and watch Luther. Thinking about Della, she remembered she had to write to Ethan to ask him to get her school records and send them in the mail so she could register Della at Harlan High School.

With Della on her mind, she decided she had to do something to nip this unwelcome romance in the bud. So far it seemed to all be in Jim Boggs' mind. It wouldn't do any good to talk to Sadie. Jim was a grown man. He was in his mid-twenties and Della was seventeen. Della had too much intelligence and ambition to succeed to be taken in by his smooth talk. His own mother said he was lazy. If he showed up here in Harlan, she would quickly send him on his way.

Judy started her new job on Wednesday. Mary's new boss was Mr. Stahlsworthy, the manager of Harlan Newberry's. He told her that Mr. Stewart in Hazard gave her a fine recommendation. Her permanent assignment would be the Notions Department, but he wanted her to be a swing employee. She would fill in wherever he needed her when people called off sick or were on an extended leave for vacation, illness, death in the family, or any other reason.

Mary realized what such as position required. She asked, "Will I be expected to know enough about each department's merchandise to be helpful to the customers like I can be in the Notions Department?"

"Yes. Mr. Stewart assured me that you're capable enough to learn all you need to know in a very short time."

"What will I be paid?"

"You will receive a dollar twenty five a day to start."

"What are the hours?"

"A normal work week is five days. We stay open until nine on Fridays because that's payday for the miners."

"That's not enough hours. I worked six days a week in Hazard."

"I know that, but if you're filling in for someone else, you'll be expected to work Saturdays, if that's their schedule."

"But you're saying six days a week is not sure. Five days a week's not enough. In Hazard I received a bonus based on my sales. Here, if I'm a floating salesclerk, you won't be able to figure my total sales."

"You're right. I can see he was correct in saying you're intelligent and motivated. I plan to raise your pay to one sixty a day after thirty days. That would more than equal any bonus Mr. Stewart gave you."

"Oh, yes sir, Mr. Stahlsworthy; that will be fine. I can begin tomorrow if that's what you want."

"Be here at nine o'clock in the morning, and we'll get you started."

With both Mary and Judy working and promises of raises in pay, they knew the money they earned would cover their living expenses.

Both Mary and Della had savings, but since most of their clothes had been left on the rooftop in Hazard, they had to buy all new. Mary used her own money to buy under clothes and stockings, three work outfits, a Sunday best dress, and new shoes. Judy let Della choose her own clothes, but reminded her that what she bought would have to be for school, too.

Luther had outgrown all of his clothes. Judy felt they weren't wasting any money in buying him play clothes for summer and all new outfits for fall.

Judy was given the full-time position of cook for Ackley's. Mary was given her promised pay raise after thirty days. Reverend Brownlett sent Della's school records which stated she had enough credits to be a senior in the fall. Sheriff Les sent receipts signed by Lance, Betty Lou, and the maintenance man and housekeeper along with thank you notes from them. He said the Perry County Board of Health condemned the hotel building as unsafe and the city took possession of the abandoned property. They would contact her at her sister's address if they found someone with funds to renovate the hotel, and required a quit-claim deed from her. He had been unable to rescue their travel bags from the rooftop. Someone beat him to them and they were gone.

She got a note from Isaac and Sylvia saying that Lance was now living on their farm and would be with them as long as he wanted to stay.

Judy and Mary settled into a comfortable routine. School started for Della right after Labor Day. Kathy Taylor was wonderful with looking after Luther. They gave her a dollar a week to use for his snacks and dinner.

As soon as Della arrived home from school, she went next door to the Taylor's to get him. If the weather was good, she took him for a long walk all the way to Reasor's grocery to buy his favorite penny candy: the 'Guess What' that contained two pieces of chewy peanut nougat and a neat little prize. While eating the candy, they circled around past Sunshine school and stopped at Mr. Fuson's barn to pet all three horses.

Mr. Redmon was taking excellent care of them. Every day he exercised one of them, making sure that each one was ridden once every three days using a large pasture owned by Mrs. Louise Gilbert and a well worn trail that stretched gradually upwards from the Fuson barn to the top of Sunshine Mountain and then riding back down again.

With so much to do between school and caring for the house and Luther, Della had forgotten all about Jim Boggs. Across the street from the High School there was a small diner. It was a favorite hangout for the richer students who always had money to spend. Della was not included in this clique of rich kids. Four days a week she ate a lunch that was packed in a paper poke. But, on Wednesdays she used fifteen cents of her money to buy a delicious foot-long chili-hotdog and a large RC Cola.

It was a warm fall day in late October that she found Jim Boggs waiting for her near the diner. Always in a hurry to get home to pick up Luther, she didn't see him. She was half-a-block away from the diner when she heard her name called and turned around. Her first reaction was to ignore him, but she couldn't do that once she saw him and knew who he was.

She stopped to allow him to catch up with her. He smiled and asked, "Where are you going in such a hurry?"

"I have to go straight home after school to take care of my little brother."

"I'll walk with you. Then I'll stay for supper with you and Aunt Jude, if that's all right?"

"Mary and Ma won't be home until almost dark. I have to get supper for them. What will you do until then?"

"You and I will visit with each other. I haven't had a chance to really talk to you because we can never be alone together."

"Ma wouldn't like you being in the house alone with me. She would say it's not fittin' and I agree. I'll put a chair on the front porch and you can sit out there while I make supper."

"Do you think that's being polite to your kinfolk?"

"My being polite has got nothing to do with it!"

"What do you do 'til it's time to cook supper?"

Della answered, "Today, I'm taking Luther for a walk to the grocery store and to see our horses where they're boarded."

"Then I'll go with you on your walk, too."

Della didn't know how to tell him, "No," but she wished the earth would open up and swallow him.

"How did you get here in Harlan, anyway"?

"I came to see you!"

"Why? You have a girlfriend. Dora Mae Helton said you've been her beau for almost a year. You'll cause a lot of trouble if you cross those Heltons in any way. You can visit because of Ma, but I want you to forget about me!"

"Dora Mae and her mother told me all about you. We didn't know you were at Pine Mountain School until my brothers Frill and Art went to your graduation about four years ago."

Della turned on him in a fury, "The Heltons have been pure evil to my Ma, Mary, and me. I can just imagine what they told you. And, none of it's true!"

Jim opened his mouth in surprise and then shut it. He was silent after that. They used the railroad bridge to cross the river and followed the tracks to Sunshine. From Frank Cole's store it was just a short distance to their house. She went next door and picked up Luther. Jim was waiting by their front porch. Della talked low to Kathy, telling her the man with her was a cousin, but he was a bother. She asked, "Will you come over later so I'll have someone with me for a little while until Mary or Ma gets home. I don't want to be alone with him!"

She promised she would. Then Della said in a loud voice, "We're taking Luther for a walk to see the horses and will be back in a little while."

Kathy nodded, "I'll see you when you get back!"

Della could tell that Jim was a little put-out because there was a next door neighbor that would be watching them. She knew she was right not to trust him, and she was not going to be in the house alone with him.

They were gone about an hour on their walk. Luther was between them all the way with Della holding his hand. When they bought their penny candy, she wrapped the second piece in paper and put it in Luther's bib overall's pocket. All three horses nickered when they approached the barn. Jim didn't remember having seen them before. He petted and talked sweet to all three of them. "They're mighty pretty. Which ones yours?"

"The black, his name's Socks. Little Red is Mary's and Curly is Ma's. The man who owns this property and lets us board the horses here is the one we rent from. He manages all the rentals for the Sunshine Mining Company."

Della dawdled all the time away that she could and then she started back home. She put a chair out on the porch for Jim and told him to watch Luther while he played in the front yard. Kathy Taylor was already sitting in her porch swing. She had a sweater with her and Jim knew she meant to sit there a while.

Della went in and lit a fire in the cook stove to begin supper. She had plenty of water on hand. For supper, she prepared fried and steamed pork chops with cream gravy, made buttery and creamy mashed potatoes, and warmed up the soup beans they had the night before. She had a pone of cornbread. She sprinkled a few drops of water over it and put it in the warm oven. When it was taken out later, it would taste like it was fresh baked.

It was six o'clock when Mary came home. She was shocked and surprised to find Jim on the front porch and Kathy Taylor sitting at the kitchen table with a cup of hot coffee.

She went to the bedroom and removed her sweater and hat. Della followed her to explain about Jim, "He waylaid me at school and insisted on walking home with me. I couldn't get rid of him. I told him he had to stay on the front porch until you or Ma came home. I asked Kathy Taylor to come over to make sure he stayed put. I didn't know what else to do!"

"Wait until Ma gets home, she'll handle it. No, she won't get home until almost nine o'clock. Let's put supper on the table. Maybe he'll eat and leave. Supper smells delicious!"

Mrs. Taylor went home. Della set four plates and invited Jim to come in to eat. She had prepared one pork chop for each of them, but Jim took two. Della was satisfied to finish what Luther didn't eat of his chop.

After supper Jim went into the living room and stayed while Mary and Della washed dishes and cleaned up the kitchen. Della set a full plate of food in the warming closet at the top of the stove. If Judy wasn't hungry when she got home Della intended to eat it; she was still hungry!

Mary hung up the dish towel, and looked toward the living room. Her brilliant-blue eyes were sparking with anger. She went in to confront him, but her good manners got the best of her. Instead, she asked, "Jim, where did you expect to sleep tonight? We only have beds for four people. You can't stay here."

"What time does Aunt Jude get home?"

"Ma works from six o'clock in the morning until eight at night. She'll be home about nine o'clock You need to make sleeping arrangements elsewhere and be gone when she gets here."

He showed his shock and surprise at the directness of the small young woman who dared to talk to him like that. He stood up, towering over her. He was trying to intimidate Mary by looking down at her.

She didn't give an inch. Then he said, "Well, I do have another cousin who just moved recently over near the Sunshine school, his name's Nathan Turner, his Pa's Uncle Rob. I'll go over there to stay the night. I've done that afore. I didn't know you all lived in Sunshine until today."

Then he was gone.

Della was near tears. She was angry and frustrated. "Mary, how do you get rid of boorish men? I can't bring myself to run him off. Ma didn't raise us that way. You did that so slick. You have to give me lessons!"

Judy was enraged by Jim's brashness. Also, it was news to her that Rob's Nathan lived in Sunshine. "I don't know his wife or if they have children. Since Rob fell out with Pa and Jonie, I don't get any news about them."

Della was to the point of wailing, "Ma, what are you going to do about that Jim? I don't want to be afraid to leave the school building because of him."

"I'll see if I can get two days off together and I'll take Luther with me and go to see Sadie, but spend the night with Jonie. She's got to help me to put a stop to his being a pest. Mary, I'm proud of the way you got him to leave!"

"I've learned how to deal with difficult people at Newberry's. You wouldn't believe the stuff they try to pull. Some are openly thieves or dishonest. My boss says I handle them better than he does. If I catch them stealing, I have someone get the police for the store. Mr. Stahlsworthy is the one that presses charges against them. He listened to me when I told him he had to do that or they would think they could get away with it all the time."

It was another two weeks later before Judy could take two days off and, with Luther riding in front of her, made the trip to Turkey Fork to see Sadie. This time she rode Socks instead of Curly. She found Sadie sitting on the front porch peeling potatoes from a bushel basket. She put Luther down to play in the yard, telling him to not go anywhere. Judie didn't have a lot of time and she got right to the point, "Sadie, did you know that Jim came all the way to Harlan to see Della? He's still acting like he's courtin' her."

"Yeah, he told us she let him stay with her until Mary came home and that she cooked a big supper for him. He said your little Mary told him he couldn't stay the night and he went to Rob's Nathan's and stayed."

"Well, in the first place, Della didn't cook supper for him. She cooks supper every night for me and Mary. He just happened to be there and she fixed him a plate because it was good manners. She made him sit outside on the front porch the whole time until Mary came home. Della got the next door neighbor to come over and stay with her so Jim wouldn't come in the house while she and Luther were there alone. Jim's not telling it true. Della doesn't want to see him. She's finishing High School this year and doesn't have time for any boy friend, much less a first cousin! Can you or Bish put a stop to him bothering her?"

"Judy, Jim's a grown man. He's twenty-seven and doesn't listen to us. I told you he's lazy and he likes to try to win favors from young teenage girls. That Dora Mae Helton told him your Della had loose morals and for him to stay away from her. That was like waving a red flag. He's a man. Bish told him if Della was just seventeen and could cook like that, he should marry her!"

"What do you think we should do about this?"

"Tell Della to ignore him if he comes around again. If she does that each time, he'll get tired of it and stop coming on his own."

Judy was doubtful that would work, but she nodded her head, "Well, we'll see if you're right. I have to go now. How 'bout you coming to see us the next time you're in Harlan. We can make room for you so you can stay all night."

Where do you live in Sunshine?"

Judy gave her good directions, but told her if she couldn't visit the house to come and see her at Ackley's Restaurant.

She put Luther in front of her on the saddle and left. It was a steep road down to Little Greasy Creek. She turned right and went to Jonie's. When they arrived, Luther ran ahead to find his Aunt. Id and Rhodie Miniard were sitting in the kitchen. They each had a piece of apple pie and a cup of coffee. Jonie jumped up to hug and kiss Judy and Luther, asking, "Oh, how long can you stay?"

"Just tonight, Where's Pa?

"He's lying down. I'll get him up in a little while or he won't sleep tonight. He'll be so happy to see you."

Id and Rhodie stood up. Id said, "We had better get on home. Aunt Jonie, you all come and see us when you can. Tell Grandpa Alex bye for us."

After they left, Judy told Jonie why she made the trip to see her. "It's that Boggs boy, Jim; he's bothering Della again! Sadie says there's nothing she can do about it and that Bish advised Jim to marry her because she's seventeen and can cook! Oh, I'm so mad at Bish and Jim that I could spit!"

Jonie said, "Sadie's the one that told you Jim won't work. She might as well have called him a mountain bum. We know he's in his middle twenties and likes to try to take advantage of teenage girls. What did she say you should do?"

"She thinks that I should do nothing. Della should ignore him long enough for him to get tired and then he'll leave her alone. Did you ever hear of a man getting tired of bothering a girl? I guess I'll have to be the mean one and forbid him to come to the house again!"

"When Pa gets up, we'll ask him what he thinks you should do. Now, I have to start supper. You sit there and talk to me while I work."

She got out a dishpan and filled it with potatoes to peel. Judy took them away from her. While Judy peeled potatoes, Jonie went to the smoke house and brought back a big ham. She used a big razor-sharp knife to cut off six generous slices. Then she cut them into smaller portions ready to fry. "I'm going to make a big skillet of home fries so I need you to slice the potatoes, too. I'll be frying the meat and making up two biscuit pones. I'll open two quarts of green beans and they'll cook quick. That should be enough for supper."

They made quick work of getting supper on the table. Alex smelled the ham frying and came into the kitchen looking very sleepy eyed. When he saw Judy, he whooped. She got up and gave him a big hug and kissed his cheek. He asked, "Honey, what brought you here; is something wrong?"

Judy waited while Luther climbed on Alex's lap, then she said, "I'm having trouble with the Boggs boy, Jim. He's bothering Della. Acting like he's courting' her. Bish advised him to marry her because she's seventeen and can cook! Sadie and Bish say he's a grown man, and they can't tell him what to do. I wanted your advice on this."

"Didn't I hear you say the boy don't like to work? Maybe that's how to get rid of him. Let Della tell him he can't come back until he's worked at a job for at least six months! She'll be almost through school, ready to graduate before he could even see her again, if he does get a job. That may do the trick." Then Judy saw him grinning as he stroked his beard and added, "Don't count on it!"

"Oh, Pa, what if that don't work."

"Then use your gun and run him off!"

Judy got a strange look on her face. She frowned, "Pa, I just remembered that I left my handgun in a drawer under the front desk in the lobby of the hotel and my rifle on a shelf in the kitchen at the restaurant. They were underwater for a long time. I'll have to buy a good hunting rifle. I can't be without a gun!"

Alex asked, "Jonie, do you think Enoch would mind if I gave Judy my huntin' rifle? It may need a good cleanin', but it's a good gun."

"Pa, I'm sure Enoch wouldn't mind. It's your gun and you can do with it what you please. I think it's right and fittin' that you give it to Judy."

Alex slowly got to his feet and went into the bedroom where he slept with the boys. He came back with the old rifle that Judy knew so well and loved because it belonged to Alex. She took it and looked it over. It was a beautiful gun with a handmade stock. A long time ago he carved the initials, "DAT" for David Alexander Turner, sideways on the end of the handsome, wooden stock.

"Pa, I'll treasure this forever!"

Alex winked, "Use it to scare off this lovesick nephew of yours! Tell Della I'm real proud of her for havin' more good sense than he does, and him ten years older than her!"

When Judy returned home the next day, she told Della what her Grandpa Alex advised her to do. She grinned, "Are you saying that Jim Boggs wants me to marry him? I never dreamed that to be true. Ma, should I take his attentions seriously? He's good looking in a rugged mountain-man kind of way. I just thought he was a royal pain. Maybe I should be nicer to him, but I don't want to be alone with him! I'll do what Grandpa Alex said, but he may never come back. Mary was really rough on him!"

Except for worrying about Jim Boggs showing up unannounced, Judy's life in Sunshine and Harlan was peaceful. She liked cooking for Ackley's Restaurant and was getting quite a following for her daily specials. The most popular one was the chicken and slick-dumplings made in a delicious and slightly thickened cream sauce. She prepared this special a day ahead so that the pronounced chicken flavor and special seasonings were tastier. People made the trip to Harlan from miles around on "Chicken and Dumpling Day."

Ackley's and Newberry's were closed one and a half days for Thanksgiving. With Christmas coming on Sunday, Judy and Mary were only free from Saturday noon until Monday morning. Mary had to be at work by seven on Monday to get ready for the After-Christmas-Sale. They were all happy because this year they could celebrate Thanksgiving with family for the first time, and didn't have four days of travel in order to spend Christmas in Big Laurel.

On both holidays, Jim and Hugh Boggs showed up at Jonie's to have dinner with them. Their real reason for being there was so Jim could see Della. To Judy's dismay, Della was nice to them. The truth was that Della felt more grown-up since she now realized she was being courted by an 'older' man.

After they arrived back in Sunshine late on Christmas night, Judy sat and had a long talk with Della. She wasn't scolding. Judy was wise enough to know that to forbid her younger daughter to see or talk with Jim would cause a rebellion and if she didn't continue to see him openly, she would slip and see him anyway. The best argument she could come up with was the fact that they were first cousins. Della had a serious questioning look on her face as she asked, "Ma, do you really believe it's wrong to fall in love with a cousin?"

"That's not for me to say. I know cousins marry, but usually it's distant cousins. I know Turners who married Turners, Lewis' who married Lewis', and so on. In your case it would be Smith marrying a Boggs, but all of your children would be double first cousins to Jim's brothers' and sisters' children. Do you see what I mean? It would complicate all of our family's relationships."

"Ma, you know that it's not very likely that I'll get married anytime soon. I've got to figure out a way to get the money together for my graduation and Senior Prom. I've got some of my own money yet, but not much. I want to put my application in at Newberry's and Scott's so I'll be first in line for a job with them when I graduate. You know, maybe Jim will be my date for the Prom."

Judy was satisfied that Della wasn't seriously thinking about Jim Boggs yet as someone she would marry. Her thoughts were skipping along from one thing to another. Her plans included graduation, the Senior Prom, working to earn her own money, and most imminent was the money she needed for an evening dress for the dance, senior pictures, yearbook, class ring, and invitations. Also, on her mind were her grades and receiving her High School Diploma.

In order for Della to feel she was earning money, Judy began to pay her a dollar a week for taking care of Luther and preparing supper every night. Because Judy had to work weekends and Mary worked most Saturdays, the bulk of the housework fell on Della's shoulders. All of them except little Luther knew what it meant to not make work. They cleaned up after themselves and helped each other in every way they could. When she did extra chores like the washing and ironing on Saturday, Judy added fifty cents to her savings. When it was time to pay for graduation expenses, she had the money she needed.

The Senior Prom was on April 28, two days before Della's eighteenth birthday. She had a date for the dance with Jerry Cotterall, a senior classmate. She hadn't talked with Jim since Christmas and wasn't thinking of him anymore.

After school on the thirtieth, Della stopped at Newberry's and Scott's to check on her job applications. She saw Mary working in the Notions Department, her favorite assignment. Mr. Stahlsworthy told her there weren't any openings, but for her to keep checking with them.

Mr. Denning, the Manager of Scott's told her there was an opening and he would hold it for her until school was out. "I have a son who's graduating this year, too. Your graduation ceremony's on Saturday, the nineteenth of May. Come and see me on Monday, the twenty-first."

Della was so excited she didn't ask about pay, hours, or duties, When Mary came home and they ate supper and cleaned up, she asked Della, "What are we going to do about Luther and the housework if you're working, too?

"I don't know yet. We have to talk to Ma about that. If she thinks we can't manage with me working full-time, maybe I can work somewhere part-time. I want to earn money that's not coming out of Ma's pocket."

When Judy came home on that Monday night they sat down and had a long discussion about how they could manage to keep up with the housework and make it possible for Della to work full time. They came up with a plan that followed the long-time mountain women's tradition, 'helping out the morrow.' Each night before going to bed, they prepared the next day's supper and put it in the ice box to stay fresh. The first one who arrived home at night picked up Luther and began to put supper on the table. Washing, ironing, and cleaning house would be done by both Mary and Della on Sunday. Judy's day off was now on Wednesday each week. She spent that time with Luther and took care of any unfinished ironing, and did some cooking and baking.

The three of them made a great team. Then Mary found a serious beau. He was a dark-haired, brown-eyed, handsome twenty-three year old teacher named Maynard (Manny) Howard. Mary was five foot-two and he was five foot-six inches tall. They made a good looking couple.

On weekends, sometimes Mary and Manny went to the movies at the newly-opened and beautifully-ornate Margie Grand Theatre, took long walks down along the clear, swift-running river, or they exercised Socks and Little Red by riding up to the head of Sunshine Holler beyond the mine's huge slate dump. On Sundays when there was a warm summer rain they sat on the front porch with a good book and reading aloud to each other.

It was on Wednesday, the Fourth of July, when Jim Boggs called on Della again. Both girls were home because the stores were closed for the holiday. He looked at Mary, expecting trouble with her, "I don't want you to worry; I'm visiting with Nathan and Birdie and I'll sleep there tonight. I thought Della and I might take Luther for a walk to see the horses."

He looked surprised when Della accepted his invitation. With Luther walking between them and each holding his hands, they didn't touch each other. They walked in a big circle. When they passed the school house, he pointed out Nathan's and Birdie's house. It was a new home. The lush green lawn was neatly mowed and lovely multi-colored rose bushes grew in the front and side yards.

Della asked, "What does Cousin Nathan do that they can afford to live in a house like that?

"He sells insurance for some company from Tennessee."

"Do they have any children?"

He laughed like it was some kind of joke, "Yes. He's got no boys, just three girls. Their names are Callie, Denise, and Janice, the baby."

"Do Uncle Rob and Aunt Becky ever come to see them?"

"I don't know. I've never seen them there."

They continued on until they came to the Fuson barn. All three horses nickered to be petted.

When they arrived back at the house, Manny was there to see Mary. He had bought her a lovely gift at Freed's Jewelry Store in Harlan. She was showing her delight, holding up a gold and jet-black chain-link evening bag. She handed it to Della to examine. Although it was gold, it was soft as any cloth. Della opened it and the inside was gold, but smooth to the touch. Jim was irritated and being facetious when he growled, "Buddy, that must have cost you a pretty penny!"

Della knew Jim was never going to buy her anything that beautiful or expensive. She didn't care about that, but she didn't want him hurting Mary's or Manny's feelings. She dragged him away, saying "Come, let's take a bucket and you go with me to the pump. You can carry it home for me!"

A random thought popped into Della's head the moment she saw the frown on Jim' face when she suggested that he carry a bucket of water. She was walking ahead of him toward the pump and she grumbled silently, "It's almost like he's made a vow to not work at anything. He considers carrying water women's work and that it's beneath him to help with anything!"

Jim was startled when she blind-sided him. In her sweetest voice, Della delivered her Grandpa Alex's message. "Jim, to spend time with me or to be my beau, you must get a job and work at least six months at it. When the six months are up, you'll have some money saved. Then, you come back to see me. I like you, but you have to show me you can hold down a job."

His eyes grew huge and slightly blared, "I don't intend to work for no man! I'm going to be like my Pa. He didn't go anywhere to work when he and Ma got married. I'm going to hunt, fish, and trap. You'll keep house and raise our food. We're going to live off the land!"

She retorted, "What land? You've got no land that I know about!"

"If we got married, Pa would give us some land."

"Are you asking me to marry you first, and then hope your Pa gives us enough farmland to make a living on? You're out of your mind! Get a job and work for six months, or show me a deed to at least forty acres of land with your name on it. When either of those things happen, come back to see me. Then maybe I'll think about marrying you!"

Jim was furious, "Okay, you don't want to see me 'til I prove myself to you, huh? I'll see you in six months!"

He left and she was still standing at the pump. She was chuckling as she carried the bucket of water to the house. "Grandpa Alex was right. I probably won't see him again."

When she went into the kitchen with the water, Mary was sitting at the table looking at the gold mesh purse. She kept rubbing it and putting it against her cheek. "I've never seen anything like this. Della, I wish he'd got me a ring instead. He never talks about getting married. I don't want to wait 'til I'm as old as Ma was when she married. I'll be twenty-one in November! I see you have the water, but where's Jim?"

I did what Grandpa Alex told me to. I told him if he didn't work at a job for six months he couldn't see me again. Mary was stunned, "What? You silly goose, I thought you liked him."

"I do like him, but I won't marry a lazy man. Remember what our Pa did to Ma. He wouldn't work and help Ma do anything, and Jim is just like him."

It was late October and the mountains were vivid with autumn colors. Della loved the fall season best of all. It never lasted long enough. When the leaves lost their hold on the trees and fell, winter was waiting in the wings, ready to take over the world.

About a week later as they walked to work, Indian summer was still lingering and they were enjoying the warmth of the rising sun. It came up over the mountain like a big orange ball. They were talking about Thanksgiving and going to Aunt Jonie's for the holiday. Jim Boggs was the farthest thing from Della's thoughts.

Both girls were startled when they saw Jim leaning against one of the front windows of Scott's. He was waiting for her. Della flushed red in anger. "What are you doing here? I have to go to work! If you want to talk to me, come back at noon. We can talk while I eat my dinner."

Jim smiled. With his eyes slightly blared, all he said was "Okay."

Then he was gone.

Della was flustered all morning. It was hard to concentrate on her work. She grumbled, "Doggone Jim anyway. It would be just like him to not show up at all. I hope he stays away. Six months from the fourth of July is January. Next year! I wonder what he wants. I'll take him around the block to the benches at the court house. We can talk there while I eat."

Knowing that Della was going to meet Jim, Mary ate her dinner at eleven-thirty. Della found Jim waiting for her as she stepped outside on the sidewalk at twelve. They walked a block away to the court house benches and sat down. She looked at him, thinking, "My, he's handsome." Then, she demanded, "Well, what do you want?"

He smiled at her in that sweet, commanding way, that both pleased and irritated her. "I want to marry you. I want to marry you right now!"

Her eyes grew huge. Then she recovered from her surprise and shock. "Do you have a job?"

"No."

"Did you get a job or even look for one?"

"No."

"Did your Pa give you any land?"

"No."

"What have you been doing for the last four months?"

"I've been thinkin' 'bout you night and day!"

"You think that we can live on your just thinking about me?"

"No."

"Well, what then?"

"You marry me and I'll get a job. They're hiring miners up at Lynch. We'll move up there. They furnish a house to their miners."

"What would we furnish it with? Nobody's going to give us anything."

"Let's get married first and worry about that later."

"You're out of your mind! Go get the job. Get the house. Have a bedroom furnished, a kitchen ready to use, and a living room with something to sit on, then come back to see me!"

"Is that a yes? You'll marry me?"

"That's a maybe! I'm not settling for a pig in a poke!"

"I'll see you again, soon. I figure we'll be married before Christmas!"

Then he was gone!

Della sat on the bench starring into space. She was stunned. "What have I done? Ma's going to kill me! I have to admit that I like Jim Boggs. I like him a lot! I don't believe for a minute that he'll really get a job, a house and furnishings for it just like that!"

But he said he did.

Jim purposely came to Jonie's on Thanksgiving Day to tell Judy and Della he had a job at Lynch. He said, "The mining company has assigned us a house. Ma and Pa are helping to round up enough furniture and kitchen stuff. I thought that maybe you, Aunt Jude, could help us, too."

Judy was speechless. Della was stunned.

Finally, Della found her voice, "Jim Boggs do you expect me to marry you just like that? You want to get married with no planning at all! I want to see a pay stub, see this house that you say is assigned to us, and talk to your Ma and Pa to hear what they're saying about us."

Della turned to her mother and asked, "Ma, what should I do? I don't want to get married and have nothing to live on. Will you go with me to Lynch to see the house he's talking about?"

Judy had to fight back tears, "You mean you want to marry Jim?"

"Yes. I do, if he's telling us the truth. He's supposed to keep a job for six months. I only said that we might get married. He's jumping the gun on me. I told him I wouldn't buy a pig in a poke. That's why I need you to go with me to check out this house. We can take the train from Harlan to Lynch."

Judy said, "Della, honey, you take your day off next week on Wednesday and we'll go check it all out. Jim, what's the house number?"

"Aunt Jude, they've not told me yet. I'll find out by next Wednesday and if you stop by the mine's business office, they'll tell you the house number and how to find it. Lynch is a really big coal-mining camp."

Mary had been listening to the conversation with Jim with a scowl on her face. When he left, she cornered Della in the back bedroom and demanded to know why she now wanted to marry a man she had been barely able to tolerate just a short time ago. Della was put on the defensive. "Why are you mad at me? I thought you'd be happy to see me move out and give you a room all your own. What're you really mad about?"

"I'm the oldest! I should get married first."

"What about you and Manny? He gives you great presents and I thought you would marry him."

"He hasn't asked me yet. If I say anything about a wedding or tell him about another friend getting married, he changes the subject. He doesn't really want to get married. As soon as I find someone else, I'm going to break up with Manny. But that's not the point. You're not supposed to get married before I do!"

"If Jim's lying to me, with Ma going with me to Lynch I'll find out next Wednesday and there won't be any wedding."

"Do you really want to live in Lynch? We'll never get to see you."

"No. I've got a feeling that Jim isn't telling the full story, but we'll have to wait and see."

Judy and Della took the whistle-stop train out of Harlan. They made stops at Rosspoint, Putney, Totz, Cumberland, and Benham/Lynch. When they left the train at the Lynch depot, they went straight to the long-narrow, gray-building that had a sign on the front that read 'Mine Office.'

The room they entered was set up like a bank lobby. There were benches against the wall where people could sit. However, a short, portly man bounced out of one of the small, side offices and asked, "May I help you ladies?"

Judy did the talking. "We're here to find out the employment status of my daughter's fiancé. They're planning to be married in December."

"Congratulations young lady! What's the man's name?"

"Jim Boggs."

"What are your names?

I'm Judy Smith-Collins. My daughter is Della Smith."

The man was searching through a long list of men. Their names weren't listed in alphabetical order, but by date hired.

"Do you know when he was hired to work here?"

"It would be very recent. He said that a house had been ear-marked for him in the mining camp,"

"He was mistaken then. The houses are only furnished to married men. He's not married yet, apparently. I'll keep looking at the list. I've not found his name. Oh, here it is. He's listed to be called next to fill any available opening. He hasn't started to work yet, but he's been approved for employment."

Judy asked, "You're saying my daughter and Jim should go ahead and get married and then you'll assign a house to them. Is that right?'

"First, we have to find a place for him. When we do we'll be in touch with him to begin work. That may take a while. If they're getting married in December, they'll most likely have the wedding before he has a job!"

Judy thanked the man for taking so much time with them. He was very gracious and wished them a good day. As they walked back toward the train depot, Judy looked at her daughter. Della was red faced with anger. She exclaimed, "That Jim! He never tells anything the way it is. He doesn't outright lie, just shades the truth. I bet he was counting on us taking his story at face value, and hoped that we wouldn't take the time to come up here."

"You're probably right. But I've been thinking. You say you do want to marry this rascal, right? I don't like the idea of you moving to Lynch. It's so far away from me and Mary. Jim should get work closer to Harlan. There are jobs at Tway, Bardo, and Liggett. I hear men talking at the restaurant. There's a three room shotgun house for rent in Sunshine Holler. It's past the graveyard, but before you get to the large, slate-dump. I can help you rent it and also help you get some second-hand furniture."

"What's a shotgun house?"

"It's a house that's built long and narrow. If the front and back doors are open, you can see through them like looking through the barrel of a shotgun."

Della laughed, "That sounds a little strange. Ma, if you help us to get married in December and for some reason Jim doesn't get a job, what then?"

"I advise you to not quit your job until he's working. Don't worry, I'll build a fire under him and get him moving!"

Judy went to see Mr. Fuson about renting the shotgun house in Sunshine Holler. He told her she needed to guarantee the two dollars a month rent until Jim showed him a pay stub. On December fifth, Judy paid the five dollar deposit plus two dollars for a months rent. He said, "Mrs. Collins, this means that the rent's paid until February first. If he isn't working, I'll have to see you for the money.

They set the date of December 12, 1928 for their wedding day. Della bought a princess-style ankle-length white eyelet dress, a lot like the one she wore when graduating from Pine Mountain School. She bought a pair of white patent-leather shoes to match. Judy went with them to get the marriage license. Jim still didn't have a job and Della was paying for everything.

Mary and Della spent the next week getting the house ready. Judy had a second-hand store deliver their furniture, including a bed room suite, two overstuffed chairs, a kitchen table and chairs, cook stove, ice box, and a cabinet.

Mary used her discount at Newberry's to buy her sister wedding presents of bedding, including pillows, and different kinds of towels. Judy gave her another hand-made quilt. Sadie gave Jim some mis-matched dishes, a washtub, and washboard, a brand-new water bucket and dipper, and a few old beat-up pots and pans. Della used her discount to buy window shades and curtains for the bedroom. To let more light in the house, she left the rest of the windows bare.

Judy and Mary went with Della and Jim to the Harlan Court House where they were married by the Justice of the Peace on December 12, 1928. Della was eighteen and Jim was twenty-seven.

Della used her own money for the basic groceries they needed at the A&P store in Harlan. She bought a ton of coal from Hobart Harber.

They used the heat from the kitchen cook-stove and built a fire in an open grate to heat the living room. To save their coal, the bedroom was unheated.

Della wasn't all that thrilled with the institution of marriage. It seemed to her that everything was heaped on the woman. In her case the man expected to be taken care of like he was a child, with no responsibilities.

It was Judy's and Della's day off. Della was glad her mother came to visit that morning. She was worried because Christmas was coming and she had used up most of her money. Judy told her to forget about presents this year and to spend her money to buy what she needed for the house and for more groceries.

She said to Jim, "Mr. Fuson's taking care of the electricity until the first of January. You go down to the Kentucky Utilities office and open your own account. You need to have a job before you do that. Anyway, you'll have to give them a five dollar deposit because you're renting."

"I'm not renting, Della is. Let her pay the deposit and put the account in her name. She has a job."

Judy looked at Jim with unmistakable disgust on her face, "When are you going to start looking for work? You're married now; it's been a week and you've done nothing. You said you would get a job. I told you to go up to Tway, then to Bardo, Yancey, or Liggett. They're all hiring."

"I'm not going to look for a job right now. I'm going to hunt, trap, and fish. Come the spring, Della can share-crop a big garden and we'll grow what we need to eat. Maybe we'll use her money to get us a Jersey milk-cow."

"What about your promise that you'd get a job after you got married? Somebody else got you a home, furnished it, and helped with coal, food, and electricity. You have free water from a mountain spring. Have you carried in a bucket of water or a bucket of coal? I think you're a lazy, good-for-nothin' liar!"

"Now, Aunt Judy, there's no sense in getting all riled up! What me and Della do's our business. We have everything we need now, so leave us alone."

"I'm not talking to you as your Aunt Judy. I'm talking to you as your mother-in-law! I'll kill somebody that tries to hurt one of my girls. Ask your Cousin Id about his mangled ear. He got that from my gun when he shot up your Uncle Rob's house with my girls inside it. You don't want to mess with me where Della's concerned. Now you get your self cleaned up and go get a job!"

Jim visibly paled. "Okay, Aunt Judy, I'll go first thing in the mornin'"

"No, you won't! You clean up and leave right now. When you come back you better have a job! The closest mine is at Tway. Go there first. I'm staying with Della. If you want to eat today, you better come back with a job!"

Jim had been about twelve years old when he first heard about Judy shooting Id after the raid on Uncle Rob's home. He knew that when his Aunt Judy said something she meant it. He also was sure she would shoot him!

Jim was dressed and out of the house in a half an hour. They both watched as he went down the hard dirt trail past a big rock and out of sight.

When she first came in the house that morning, Judy had put a big box on the kitchen table. Inside the box was the last thing that she intended to buy Della and Jim for their "setting up house-keeping." It was a cheap set of red and white paisley patterned dishes. She got them at Newberry's using Mary's discount privilege. Judy had carried the heavy box all the way from her house to theirs in the head of Sunshine Holler.

Della was thrilled with the set of dishes. Judy said, "Use these for special times and those beat up mis-matched ones that Sadie gave you for ever-day."

"Ma, I was thinking the same thing. These are so pretty. Thank you for them. And, thank you for what you did with Jim this morning. He's lied to me so many

321

times about finding work, and what he's going to do that I can't believe a word he says any more. I've got to keep my job even if he does get one because I can't depend on him keeping a job. If I don't work, we'll starve!"

"You've got to get some back-bone yourself. You know how I gave in too easy to your Pa and look what he did. Don't let Jim get away with shirking his duty to provide for you. Let me know if he gives you any real trouble. You know that I'll deal with him in my own way, but just short of shootin' him!"

They spent the day putting things in order. Judy had given Della a second hand-sewn quilt on her wedding day to use like another spread. She and Jim were able to sleep under a sheet, blanket, and two quilts in a room with no heat.

Luther was busy playing with lined paper and a box of colors that Della gave him. His art work wasn't that bad for a three and a half year old. She laughed, "Ma, look, his horsey even has four legs!"

Luther was indignant, "Not horsey! It's my cow!"

The three of them sang songs with Luther's off-key, baby-voice joining in. When they put him down for his nap, he was asleep in a minute. Della said, "Ma, we've built a memory today. I'll never forget this time we've spent together. Now if Jim just gets a job! Oh, I pray to the good Lord that he does!"

It was late in the day and Judy was still there helping Della put a delicious baked ham supper on the table when Jim came home. He came in the door with a big grin on his face. "Lord, but that smells good. I'm starved! I smelled ham as soon as I passed the big rock and ran the rest of the way home!"

Della was impatient, "Well, what happened, did you find a job?"

He pulled a piece of folded paper out of the top pocket of his bib overalls and handed it to Della. She unfolded it and began to read. A big grin was spreading over her face. "Honey, you did it! You're going to work for The Tway Mining Company. It's a Mr. Tway that owns it. I wondered why it had that funny name! You start next Wednesday, the day after Christmas!"

Judy said, "Well, Jim, that's a nice Christmas present for Della. Do you need anything for the job? --- Lunch bucket, helmet, carbide light, and carbide? Do any of your brothers have any of it they can give or loan to you?"

"I don't think so. I'm gonna need heavy work gloves and steel toed safety shoes, too. It's winter time and it's warm in the mine, but I know in the summer I'll need heavy clothes 'cause then its cold down in there."

"I'll give Della the money you'll need to buy those things. Go to town Friday night when the stores are open late."

"Thanks, Aunt Judy!"

"I told you that today I'm not talking to you as your Aunt Judy. Today, I am your mother-in-law! If I invest this much money in your job, you sure had better keep it! We're having supper with you and then we're going home. It was too cold for Luther to play outside. He's worn himself out running from one end of the house to the other."

Jim was happy he had a job. He was not so happy that his Aunt Judy, Mother-in-law, or whatever, had threatened to shoot him. He grumbled, "She would shoot me. I know it! I'll work for now, but I don't have to like it. That's what a woman's supposed to do for a man. That's what my Ma always said."

They spent the first part of Christmas day with Alex and Jonie's family. After they ate and before the women folk began to clean up the kitchen, Jonie took Judy into the big pantry room so they could talk privately.

She had a big grin on her sweet face and her eyes twinkled as she said, "Honey, I'm with child. I'm about three months along. I think it'll be 'round the fourth of July when I'll get down. Alta is old enough to take over the house for me, but I'd like you to take some time away from work and stay with me the first three or four days. Do you think you could do that?"

Judy stood still, staring, with her mouth open. Finally she found her voice, "I've been at Ackley's for well over a year. We'll be able to plan the time closer in June and I'll arrange to take a six-day vacation. Oh, honey, I'm so happy for you. What did Enoch say?"

"For about a week he was walkin' around in sort of a daze.

"Does Pa know?"

"Yes, you can't hide anything from him! I had to make him promise to not say anything 'til I had a chance to tell Enoch."

Judy, Mary, Della, and Jim all had to work the next day. It was hard to say goodbye to Alex and Jonie's family, but they knew they had to leave right after the kitchen was cleaned up in order to be home before dark.

Alex held Judy's hand a long time when she was ready to go. His blue-green eyes showed his deep love for her as he spoke in a quavering voice, "Daughter, you're very dear to me. I'll be a hundred and eight years old soon. I won't be with you much longer. Our heavenly father is calling me home.

The Lord Jesus has prepared a place for me and for you. Don't fret when it's my time 'cause you'll know in your heart that we'll be together again. The Bible says we should weep at the coming into this life and rejoice at the going out. We all have a hard race to run in life. But if we run a good race, then we know our job is well done and the Lord has helped us to run it.

That's the way I feel today. Now, that's enough of these thoughts. Merry Christmas, my darling! Come back to see me soon!"

Louise Gilbert - owner of 2 acre garden plot and cow pasture in Sunshine

Chapter Twenty-Four
DELLA'S FINAL ULTIMATUM

Jim surprised everyone and kept his job. The winter was over and there had been an early spring. Jim wanted Della to talk to the owner of a two-acre piece of level land right next to Harvey Fuson's house to see about planting a garden on it with an offer to share half of it with them.

The same person also owned the hillside above the garden patch of land. Their property line began where the road dead-ended that was in front of Hobart Harber's house and included all the land that lay from there to the other side of the mountain. On that side of the mountain the owner's property line ended next to the road that led up to Della's and Jim's house. Jim wanted her to see if they could use it to pasture a cow. If so, he wanted her to buy a Jersey milk cow.

Della asked, "Why is it that you want me to do the talking to make a deal with the owner? Mr. Fuson told Ma the owner is Louise Gilbert. She's a widow. Her daughter married Doctor Jones, a dentist in Harlan. I'll talk to Mrs. Gilbert. If she says yes, you're the one who has to plant and care for the garden."

"Why is that?"

"Because I get one day off a week and you get two. We'll put our money together to buy the cow. You'll have to build a shed of some kind to keep her out of the weather. I'll milk her in the morning before I go to work, but you have to take care of her at night. If we're going to use Mrs. Gilbert's pasture, we'll have to give her some of the milk."

"Where would I get wood to build a shed?"

"Talk to Mr. Fuson. He may know where you can get some. It would be improving the property here and he might help you to get it built."

"You talk to him; you're the one that rented the house."

Mrs. Gilbert agreed to let them plant a garden, but only wanted enough of a share for her own use. Also, they could pasture a cow, if they got one, on her land. She said, "Della, I have a whole orchard of apple, cherry, and peach trees that bear well every year and the fruit goes to waste. You plan on getting all you want this year. It does my heart good to see ambitious young people."

Mary and Della had their dinner time together every day. Now that the weather was warmer, they usually went to sit on a bench under a tree at the Court House. They both liked to watch passersby. Most of the women they saw worked in offices and they liked to see what they were wearing. Mary said it was like watching a fashion parade. In 1929 the latest thing in women's dresses was ones with low waist lines and leather belts buckled equally low.

Mary thought the style was lovely. Della said it looked ridiculous. They talked about Manny Howard, Mary's beau. "You never say anything about a wedding. When are you going to get married?"

Mary flushed red, "He says he isn't ready to get married. I don't know what to do. I'm not getting any younger. I'll be 24 next November!"

"Do you love him?"

"I thought I did, but each time I talk about getting married, he puts me off like it's the last thing in the world he wants. I'm not sure if I love him now."

"Have you seen any one else you might be interested in? Do you like anyone else? There are some single men who work here and live elsewhere!"

"I know that. There's one man who comes in the store to talk to me. I think he works at the Bardo Mine. He stays in the boardinghouse. I see him on Friday nights, payday for the miners. He buys some little something and hangs around until I'm not busy and then we talk. He has a truck and goes home the next morning and comes back on Sunday to go to work on Monday."

"What's his name?"

"I call him Ray. His full name is Raymond Pascal Fannon."

Della laughed, "Pascal is a funny name. It must be for some relative.

Mary agreed, "He told me it was for a grandfather on his mother's side."

"You seem to know a whole lot about him. Why don't you see if he'll be your date to see a movie on Saturday night? He doesn't have to go home. If he does take you to a movie, then you should break up with Manny."

"I can't ask a man to take me to a movie. It's not fitting!"

"You don't have to ask him outright. Find out what's showing at the Margie Grand and tell him you'd like to see that particular movie. Then it's up to him to make the next move. If he asks you to go with him, then you'll know!"

Two weeks later, on Monday, when Mary met Della on the street corner by Newberry's at noon for their walk to the Court House, she was excited and anxious to talk. Della sensed it was about this Ray Fannon. They sat down and opened their dinners. Della asked, "Well, are you going to tell me or not?"

Mary took a big bite of a sandwich and with twinkling royal-blue eyes, finally said, "I took your advice last Friday. Ray asked if he could take me to the Margie Grand on Saturday night. I said yes. We had a very good time. He's a perfect gentleman, but soft spoken and shy."

"I can tell you like him even more than you liked Manny from the start!"

"You're right, I do! I'm going to break up with him this week. I'm going to give him back all of his gifts that he gave me. I think that's the right thing to do. If he won't take them back, I'll keep them."

"Now you're having a real romance. Let me know what happens."

Jim worked for five months. It was May and he was itching to go hunting and fishing. Without any warning, he quit his job at Tway. On Friday, May 17, he came home and handed Della his pay envelope. Instead of half cash and half script, it was all cash. He said, "This is my last payday. I'm going to work in our garden, hunt, trap, and fish like I told you last Christmas. I don't intend to work any more for somebody else."

Della was speechless. After a few moments, she found her voice. "That's all well and good for now, I suppose. I'm earning enough for us to live on in the summer time. But when we have to buy coal, what then?"

Jim acted incredulous, he asked, "Coal? Is that what you're worrying about, coal? All I have to do is go over to the slate dump and pick up all the coal you need. I'm not the least bit worried about anything."

"Well, I am. I'm worried because we're going to have a baby in about seven and a half months!"

Jim whooped joyfully, jumped up, grabbed Della in his arms and swung her around, "Darling, that's the most wonderful news. Seven and a half months, you say? That's around New Year's."

"I figure the baby will be born around the first week of January."

Jim asked, "How long do you think you'll be 'lowed to work after they know you're expectin'?"

"I don't know. I'll try to hide it as long as I can by wearing big clothes. If I'm lucky, I can probably work 'til Thanksgiving. When I have to quit my job, you'll have to go back to work in my place."

"We'll cross that bridge when we come to it. Your Ma won't let you and her first grandchild go without. She'll give us money."

"We're not going to go begging to my mother! She has Luther to care for! She needs her money. She's warned you what she'll do if you stop honoring your responsibilities. For once why don't you be fair? Just agree that when I stop working to have this baby, you'll take care of both of us!"

"Now, honey, I told you that we'll cross that bridge when the time comes. I like to eat, too. We won't go hungry. I'm gonna have one of the largest and prettiest gardens you ever saw. And, we have our cow, don't forget."

Della bought two smock tops for work. She let out the seams and waist bands as far as they would go on her skirts. Then she bought two new skirts four sizes too big and lapped the waist bands over and pinned them with two safety pins so she could wear them. She grumbled, "This having a baby wastes a lot of money on clothes. Afterwards, I'll seam up the ones I let out and cut down the oversized ones. The material that's left over will make pretty quilt pieces."

Mary and Ray dated every Saturday night and Sunday for a month. He didn't go home at all during that time. Seeing movies was the only entertainment that was available. Mary convinced Ray that going to church together on Sunday morning was part of dating. When she accomplished that it meant they were together all day on Sunday. She told Della, "If we're together every Sunday all day, and after six months we still like each other, then maybe we'll get married."

Della laughed, "That's a lovely romantic way of thinking, Sister. And, that's a lot of movies! Doesn't Ray own a truck? Why don't you save your money and go fishing? If you catch sun grannies or catfish, give me some!"

It had been a while since all of them had been across the mountain to visit Alex. His hundred and seventh birthday was the fifth of June. They left after work on Saturday to stay until Sunday evening. Judy, with Luther in front of her in the saddle, Della, Jim, Mary and Ray all rode their horses over the mountain.

Alex's eyes lit up with excitement when he saw the two girls and their young men. He was meeting Ray for the first time. He looked up at him and said, "Mary, honey, he's a tall, good looking fellow. He suits you to a 'T' and I can tell by looking, that you two will be married afore too long! Am I right?"

Mary hugged Alex tight and kissed his cheek, "You have to ask Ray that question. He's not asked me, yet."

Ray grabbed her up in his arms and kissed her firmly right on the mouth. She was so surprised she almost fell backwards when he put her down. "How's that? We just sealed the deal, and Mr. Turner, I do want to marry Mary when she gets around to saying yes."

Alex clapped his hands gleefully. "I never thought I would live to see the day when Mary got swept off her feet!"

Mary was red from her lacy collar to her eyebrows. She looked up into Ray's soft blue eyes and said, "Yes. I'll marry you!"

Ray grinned delightedly and asked, "When?"

"When do you think you'd be ready? Where would we live?"

Mary's head barely came up to Ray's chest, but he still had his arm around her shoulder, he answered, "The sooner the better! We can get a house in Sunshine, too. That way you'll be near your mother and Della."

Not to be outdone, Jim began bragging about his big garden and all the vegetables he had grown.

Alex was impressed, and asked, "You did all that and worked every day, too? Della, honey, are you still working. When is that baby due?"

Jim didn't answer Alex. Della said, "The baby's due in January. How did you know; I've not told anyone but Jim? Well, everybody knows now!"

"Honey, you have that look women get when they're bringing new life into the world. I've lived a long time, so I surely do know that look!"

Grandpa, Jim isn't working anymore. He says he's planting a big garden, hunting, trapping, and fishing,"

Alex's eyes grew huge, "And, honey, what're you doing?"

"I'm going to work at the store as long as they'll let me. I figure that'll be around Thanksgiving. Then, Jim will have to do something about money in order for us to live."

"What's your Ma saying about this?"

Della laughed, "She's not pleased with Jim. In fact she's told him that if he doesn't honor his responsibilities, she'll shoot him!"

Alex fixed his intensive eagle-sharp eyes on Jim who was visibly squirming with embarrassment, and thundered, "Who could blame her! You're my grandson; Della is my granddaughter. I don't know you very well 'cause you ain't bothered to visit me while you were growing up. I'd say you're nigh to thirty years old. Della's a beloved grandchild. I've watched her grow since she was a baby. If you ain't good to her, if I'm able, I'll shoot you myself!"

Della was anxious to change the subject. Alex was showing his growing weakness from old age and Jim's situation made it worse. She looked at her Aunt Jonie who was huge with the fast approaching time to deliver her baby. She asked, "Aunt Jonie, when do you expect the baby?"

"Honey, I do believe its two babies. The doctor said I was having twins!"

All three, Judy, Mary, and Della chorused "What!??"

"Yes. He said they can come any time after the first of July. I think they'll wait 'til after the Fourth of July. Judy, honey, I want you to come back for the Fourth and plan to stay with me for a week."

"I've been at Ackley's almost two years and I believe I can be off at least five days to be with you. I'll come back on the seventh of July to stay with you until the twelfth. You tell those babies to cooperate! They can't come before the seventh and can't be later than the ninth!"

Jonie laughed, "I'll try to make 'em listen to you but they may not!"

Over the next two weeks, Jim did nothing but grouse about all the work he was doing. "I don't see why a garden has to be hoed out three times. Once should be 'nough. Then just let the stuff grow up with the weeds. I think women just invent work to keep a man busy."

Della laughed, "That's a nice try. If you just hoed a garden once, the weeds would take it over and nothing would grow or produce anything. If you just hoe it twice, then weeds would make harvesting impossible. They would grow waist high! You have to grit your teeth and hoe the garden at least three times. Some people go back over it again to make the harvest easier. I've seen gardens to be ashamed of and if the weeds take it, people will talk about you!"

"How about you helping me after supper and on Sunday?"

"No. I've got the house to keep clean, washing and ironing, and all the cooking. You get a job and we'll both find a way to do the garden. Until you're working like I am, churning to make butter, and taking care of the garden is all yours."

"What about when we start the harvest. Beginning in August, we'll have beans, corn, tomatoes, and a whole bunch of other stuff. You're going to help me with all that ain't you?"

"I'll buy the canning jars and other supplies you'll need for putting up your harvest. You can string some of the beans to make shucky beans for winter. You have to dig a hole and line it with coffee sacks to store potatoes, turnips and any other root vegetables you grow. I'll ask Ma to get us a small barrel or a crock to make sauer kraut. If you manage to do all of that, we'll eat good all winter."

"I suppose you want me to take old lady Gilbert up on her offer to give us apples, peaches, and cherries. You want me to put them up, too?"

"Jim, honey, I suspect that you've waited too long on the cherries. They've ripened and are gone. Now, the peaches and apples ripen in August, so you could still can a lot of them and dry some of the apples."

"If I go pick the fruit, will you help me with the peeling and canning on your day off or at night?"

"Yes. I'll help you, but you're in charge. I'm not doing it all for you!" Remember, I'll probably have to quit work before November. We need to have the harvest put up and out of the way so you can find a job for the winter."

"I told you that I'm not gonna work at a job. I'm gonna hunt, trap, and fish this winter. When do you think you'll have this baby?"

"I think the first week or so of January. What will we do for money?"

"You'll have some saved. You always do. We'll manage and if we need anything really bad, your Ma will come through for us!"

While Della was dealing with Jim and his stubborn determination to not get a job, Jonie was getting closer to her due date. The Fourth of July came and went. On Saturday, the sixth, after she got off work, Judy mounted Curly and remembering to take a lantern with her, started for Jonie's. There was still some daylight left when she reached Putney and started up the mountain on the Laden Trail. When she saw the huge Rebel Rock looming in the gathering dusk, she knew it would be pitch black on the mountain in a matter of minutes.

She lit the lantern and held it high so her eyes could see the trail ahead. When she arrived at the crest of the mountain, she hit the level surface of the road the school built. She exclaimed, "Bless Miss Pettit for building this road! I should be at Jonie's now in about three hours."

Judy knew it wasn't safe for a woman alone to be on Pine Mountain in the dark. Besides the danger of snakes, panthers, and bears, people had been murdered on the Little Shepard and Laden Trails. She shook off the thought of danger, but quickly placed her hand on the rifle hanging from her saddle. She always kept the gun loaded and she wouldn't hesitate to use it.

She was about five hundred yards from the end of the Laden Trail and near the Divide general store when she suddenly came face to face with two bearded and scruffy looking men riding mules. She didn't know either of them and was instantly suspicious. She lowered her lantern with one hand while easing the rifle off her saddle with the other until the gun was in front of her lying in the crook of her arm and her finger was pressing against the trigger. A gentle squeeze with her knees signaled Curly to keep on walking.

The men pulled their mounts over to the side of the road as though to let her pass. When she came even with them, one reached toward Curly to grab his reins. Judy swung the Lantern hard and knocked his hand away. The lantern fell to the ground, but still gave some light. The first man could plainly see that she held a gun level with his chest. The second man began to circle around Judy.

She spoke in a strong commanding voice that put the fear of God in the first man. She asked, "Which one of you fellows wants the first bullet?"

The man she had hit with the lantern yelped, "Ike, Ike, don't do anything! Go on up the trail or she'll kill me!"

The man named Ike did as he was told. When he disappeared around the first bend in the road, Judy told the other man to follow him. He did. When she couldn't see him anymore, she carefully dismounted, retrieved her lantern, mounted Curly again, and kept a close watch behind her as she put him to a swift trot. When she reached the entrance to Pine Mountain School, she stopped, blew out the lantern, and sat motionless on the opposite side of the road behind a large growth of mountain laurel and waited. No one was following her.

It was almost midnight when she arrived at Jonie's.

The next morning Judy told them about being stopped by the two men near the Divide store. Enoch didn't know who they were, but guessed they were the Dillon brothers who lived in a log shack on the other side of the mountain where the Little Shepard Trail branched off from the Laden Trail.

Judy said, "Well, I learned my lesson. Never again will I be on that mountain alone in the dark. The good Lord was with me last night because as soon as I thought of danger, I put my hand on my gun and was ready for them."

Jonie was standing by the kitchen table, finishing the last of her breakfast coffee. She hugged Judy, "Thank God for protectin' you!"

Judy kissed her cheek, "Sister, you are huge! You are a little woman and I sense trouble with this birthin'."

Jonie's eyes widened, "Don't even think that. It's been almost four years since I birthed a child. I pray to God that this time will be easier. The doctor in Harlan won't come all the way over here. I'm dependin' on Sarah Harris, a midwife, and you to deliver me!"

Judy grinned, "I knew that! As soon as Sarah gets here I'll have lots of help. Just relax and let the Good Lord work with you to bring two new little lives into His world."

On Monday, July the eighth at around noon, Jonie's water broke and the terrible pain of birthing began almost immediately. Judy tried to distract Jonie's concentration on the pain, "You have to tell me where everything is so I can take care of you and be ready for the babies when they come. Where are the extra sheets, wash rags, and towels? I know you made a lot of diapers and little clothes for these two babies."

Jonie insisted, "I need to get up! In between my pains I can finish gettin' dinner ready for Enoch and the young'ins!"

"Oh, no you don't! I sent Enoch up to Israel's to ask Id to go get Sarah Harris. Enoch and the boys will finish gettin' dinner ready. Alta will help them. He said they'd get supper, too. You stay in that bed!"

When Id came back he had Sarah Harris with him. She was all business and told Judy to have everyone else stay out of the way. It was almost one o'clock on the morning on July 9, 1929 that the first of the twins were born. Sarah took care of Jonie after she handed the little girl to Judy. She barely had time to get the first baby cleaned up before Jonie closed her eyes uttered a low moan and the second one was born.

Sarah Harris acted as though it was the most natural thing in the world to give birth to twins. Jonie came through the birthing just fine and the twin baby girls were strong and healthy. Sarah changed the bedding and bathed Jonie. Together they arranged her hair and helped her to get dressed in a pretty new gown. Then Jonie wanted her babies. Judy placed them in bed with her, one baby on each side of their mother and called Enoch in to meet his daughters.

Judy asked, "Enoch, have you decided on names for them yet? They look so much alike, it's hard to tell them apart!"

Jonie nodded, "We agreed that if they were girls, we would name them Ineda and Alfreda. When I made their little clothes, I put yellow threads in the hems of one set. We'll use those clothes for Ineda. The others will be for Alfreda. Enoch, I want you to decide which one of them is to be called Ineda!"

They finally decided the best way to tell them apart was to use scissors to trim one little girls' fine baby hair to make a bang on her forehead. She would be Ineda and wear the clothes with yellow threads. The other little girl's hair would be left alone and she would wear the unmarked clothes. She would be Alfreda.

After making sure the twins and their mother were all right, Sarah Harris went home. It was about three o'clock and another three hours until daylight. Enoch woke up Otis and Gib to ride home with Sarah.

Judy stayed at Jonie's until Saturday. She left at first light and thought she would be in Harlan well before Noon. Other than the time she was in the hospital with the cut on her leg, this was the only time she had willingly spent a whole week away from Luther, and she was anxious to get home.

The summer had been perfect for growing a garden. It rained just enough and at the right times, mostly at night. Della laughed, "Jim, honey I do believe you have a way of making it rain. Every time you hoe in the garden all day, it rains sometime around midnight. Then it stops before daylight and the ground dries out just enough so you can spend another day hoeing!"

No one ever saw a neater and more weed-free garden. Everything that Jim planted and cared for grew and flourished.

Jim proved one thing. He could work when he had to. With advice and some help from Judy and Della, he put up over a hundred quarts of Kentucky wonder green beans, beefsteak and big-boy tomatoes, sour and sweet apples, and peaches. When the sweet corn came in, he brought several ears in every night to prepare for the next day. They had corn-on-the-cob, fried corn, creamed corn, corn pudding, and even added grated corn to their cornbread.

Della laughed when she told Judy, "Ma, I hope I never see another ear of corn! Well, at least, not 'til next year!"

Judy was very serious, "I can't tell you how surprised I am that Jim has pitched in and worked like he has this summer. He's workin' harder to get out of workin' than he would have at a regular job!"

"Ma, I know that. He still says he's not going to work ever again for somebody else. He thinks we can live off the land like Uncle Rob did with Aunt Becky doing all the farm work. If it wasn't for Mrs. Gilbert, we wouldn't have any land for a garden or a pasture for the cow."

"What are you goin' to do?"

"There's nothing I can do 'til the baby comes. If we can keep meat on the table, we have canned fruit and vegetables. Still, we'll need to buy pinto and great-northern beans, lard, flour, corn meal, and the other makings for bread. Without me working, it won't be long 'til all my money's gone."

"I've been workin' on some baby things for you. How many things have you gotten together so far?"

"Well, almost nothing. I've been afraid to spend the money."

"I've been busy hemmin' diapers in my spare time. You'll have three dozen pair for the baby."

"Isn't that too many? Surely, I won't need three dozen!"

"You'll be surprised how many it takes to keep a baby dry. You don't want to let him stay wet or you'll cause a terrible diaper rash. Next Wednesday, you and I will go shoppin'. You have to get ready for this child. If you manage to work until late October, you'll only have two more months to go.

It was Monday, the twenty-first of October that Nathan Denning, the manager of Scott's Five and Dime, noticed that Della came to work that morning wearing a smock and then changed into the store's uniform smock. Even with the loose fitting clothing, the fact that she was pregnant couldn't be missed. He called her into his office and asked her if she was with child. She blushed red and stammered, "Yes, but Mr. Denning, I need to work as long as you'll let me."

"Doesn't your husband have a job?"

"No, sir, he doesn't. That's why I need to work at least another month."

"Another month will be almost Thanksgiving. If you feel you won't endanger yourself or your baby, you may work until the Holiday. I don't want you to do any heavy lifting. When my wife is pregnant, standing a long time puts a terrible strain on her back. I'll put a chair in the Notions Department so you can sit down when you aren't busy with customers."

Della's eyes were brimming with tears. "Mr. Denning, I thank you, sir, with all my heart."

"Just be honest with me. If working becomes too much for you, come and tell me. We don't want you to put yourself or your child in any danger."

Jim was happy that Della would be working until Thanksgiving. "Let's stay home this year and have our own big dinner. That way, we'll have leftovers to last almost a week. When we go to Aunt Jonie's, we never bring home any leavin's. Anyway, I don't think you should be bouncing around on a horse!"

When Della told Judy that Jim wanted them to stay home for the holiday, and that he didn't think she should be riding a horse in her condition, she was surprised when her mother agreed with him. "At that time, you'll be due in a little over a month. We don't want anything to happen that can hurt you or the baby. In fact, you shouldn't lift anything heavy or hang clothes outside by lifting your arms over your head. Even that can cause the cord to wrap around the baby's neck. Make Jim hang the clothes on the line and take them down for you."

"I've only seen the twins once; on Labor Day. I loved watching Grandpa Alex sit with both little girls on his lap. He had the sweetest smile on his face when they cooed at him and pulled on his long white beard. When you go, give Aunt Jonie and Uncle Enoch a hug for me. Tell them I'll not be there for Christmas, but I'll come see them next spring when the baby's big enough."

Judy's face showed she was deeply concerned about something, Della asked, "Ma, what's troubling you?"

"I'm going to ask Jonie and Enoch if they'll put Curly out to pasture at their place. Will you give me Socks 'til you're able to ride again and need him? You know I'll take good care of him."

"Of course, you can have him, Ma. Consider him yours. I'll miss Curly. He's been with us all my life. Anyway, we have Jim's horse. He never likes to visit Aunt Jonie. He says she makes him feel guilty just for livin'. When I go with you to visit them, I'll ride his horse."

On October 29, 1929, the New York Stock Market crashed and President Herbert Hoover declared a bank holiday to try to ward off a national disaster as bank failures happened all over the country.

Judy had no way of knowing such a national tragedy was going to happen. Anyway, she didn't have to worry about losing her money. She had very little money left after relocating from Hazard to Harlan and helping Jim and Della to set up housekeeping. After the Hazard Bank transferred the small amount of money she had left in her account to the Harlan County Savings and Loan, she closed her account and kept her money on her person.

A week later, on November 5, 1929 Alex died in his sleep. When she went to wake him for breakfast, Jonie found him with a smile on his face. All she could think of was what her father had said to Judy last year at Christmas time. "Weep at the coming into this world and rejoice at the going out. Don't fret for me because we'll all be together again in heaven."

With tears streaming down her cheeks, Jonie went to the side door that opened onto the large wrap-around porch and called for Otis and Gib. Both boys were with their father in the barn. All three came in answer to her call. After telling the boys that their grandfather had died, she asked them to saddle their horses and ride to Harlan. She told Enoch he needed to go with them. She said, "Go to Ackley's Restaurant and tell Judy her father died this morning. Tell her to come as soon as she can and to bring Mary and Della, too."

Enoch had the presence of mind to ask Jonie about notifying the Harlan Newspaper. "Alex Turner has a lot of friends throughout Harlan County. There's going to be relatives that we may not be able to notify. If it's in the paper, that'll help. Do you want Alex taken care of proper by a funeral home? He talked about liking the folks that run the Mount Pleasant Funeral Home. They've been in business way before the city was called Harlan."

Jonie said, "Yes. We'll set his coffin up in our front room. There's no way to get him to Harlan and then back here. Enoch, you should talk with the Newspaper people and then see the people at Mount Pleasant Funeral Home. Make what arrangements you can. Ask them to provide a preacher to conduct Pa's funeral. I'll feel better when Judy gets here to help with the arrangements. I want him buried here in Alex's Branch graveyard so we can be close to him."

While the boys were getting ready, Enoch helped Jonie to examine Alex and make sure his arms and legs were straight in the bed. They were. "Jonie what clothes do you want him to wear to be buried in?"

"He would want his dark blue trousers, white shirt, black string tie, blue and white checkered vest, and dark blue frock coat. They're the clothes he always wore to Harlan. I'll brush them and put them on the bed for the funeral home people for when they come. I hope they get here by tomorrow."

Enoch did everything just as he and Jonie planned. He arrived in Harlan at about three o'clock and went to Ackley's to tell Judy. She asked him to go to Scott's and Newberry's to tell the girls. They each arranged to be off work on Monday and Tuesday. Judy helped Ackley's make arrangements for someone to take her place. Della and Mary were told to take three days of bereavement leave. Through her tears, Mary explained to Della what that meant. She said, "It means you can take up to three work-days off, but without pay."

Della told Enoch, "We'll stay on the job for another two hours. The store closes at five. Mary lives with Ma, but will you tell Ma that I'll get ready as fast as I can and come to her house? We can leave from there tonight."

Enoch said he would do that, but he and the boys had to stop at the Harlan newspaper office to notify them, and then go to the funeral home to see about making funeral arrangements. "That's going to take some time. If you come to Mount Pleasant Funeral Home when you're ready to leave, we'll all leave together. Is that agreeable?"

Della had farther to go to get home. This gave Mary time to go to Nathan's house by the school to tell them his grandfather Alex died this morning. Birdie said they would probably come to Big Laurel tomorrow.

They were all ready to leave at six o'clock. The days were so short it was already getting dark, and it would be much colder and pitch-black dark going across Pine Mountain. Della and Jim brought his miner's hat with its carbide lamp that she could light when it got dark. Judy and Mary didn't have any kind of light, but Enoch had thought to bring three coal oil lanterns.

Judy said, "Your arms are going to get awful tired holding those heavy things up high enough for us to see. We will take turns with you. We're lucky to have a clear sky and when the moon comes up it should be bright."

They made good time traveling to Putney, but it was slow going on this side of the mountain. As soon as they got to the top of the mountain, they were on the new section of the road that the school had built. .

Everyone had been concentrating on the journey, worrying about having enough light to see to travel, and saving the horses from getting too tired, especially the aging Curly. As they got closer to Jonie's, the realization that they had lost Alex began to weigh on them. To each of the travelers, Alex's life and love for them had different meanings. Otis, Gib, Della, Mary, and little four year old Luther thought of him as their beloved grandfather. He was the head of the family, and the wisest of men.

Jim was the only one in the group that didn't care for or appreciate Alex. To him Alex was a meddling old man who should have minded his own business. He would never forget nor forgive either Alex or Judy for threatening to shoot him over how he treated his wife! The only reason he came tonight was because it would be too hard to explain to his mother a reason for not coming.

To Enoch, Alex was not just his father-in-law. He loved Alex for the kind, gentle soul that he was. When Alex first came to live with him and Jonie, he never complained and was constantly working around the farm. He taught Enoch so much that was simple, good, and practical knowledge about running a hard-working farm and to respect the woman who works by your side. Jonie learned from her mother, Stacy, about a mountain woman's role on a hard-working farm, but Alex taught Enoch from a man's viewpoint.

Judy felt that she must be outwardly strong for the sake of her children and Jonie, but inside her heart and mind she was inconsolable by the loss of her father. Alex had been the head of her world for as long as she could remember.

When she was married, her father was in her thoughts more than either Bob Smith or Jim Collins. His wisdom and faith in God sustained her through the trials the two men heaped upon her, the death of Stella, and the heart rendering loss of faith in the goodness of people. She would continue to live her life according to how she perceived God's plan for her. She couldn't suppress a sob as she uttered the thought, "But, dear Lord, it will be so hard to go on without Pa's wisdom and counsel."

It was very late when they arrived at Jonie's. They all had a snack and went to bed, knowing tomorrow was going to be a long, hard day.

Enoch engaged local men to dig the grave for Alex next to Stacy's. Alex' youngest son, Preston, was on the other side of his mother. Judy's daughter, Stella, was on the other side of Preston. Alex's daughter, Rana Miniard, was buried in a different section of the graveyard. Rob's daughter, Martha, mother of Denver Turner, was also buried in a different section.

Early that morning, Otis and Gib rode to Alex's sons' and daughters' homes to tell them about his death. They made a big circle so as not to back-track to notify his sons, Dave, Liege, and Rob; his daughters, Emily Lewis, Sadie Boggs, and Rana's husband, Israel Miniard. Otis and Gib asked all the men in the family to serve as pall bearers.

Two Mount Pleasant Funeral Directors arrived at Jonie's in Big Laurel at eleven o'clock the next morning. One was an older man who was a long-time friend of Alex's. The other was much younger, but both Della and Mary had seen him in Harlan. The men drove a hearse over the mountains by using the barely passable road through Bledsoe past Pine Mountain School and on down to Big Laurel. They walked over to the Alex's Branch Graveyard and decided they would park on the main road and have pall bearers carry Alex's casket around the side of the hill to reach the level path leading to his open grave.

The Funeral Directors pulled a blue-green metallic coffin from the back of the hearse and with the help of Enoch and Id, carried it into the house. Then they carried in the metal collapsible coffin stand and two tall pillars that served to hold a dark red velvet valance designed to frame the coffin.

Enoch pushed several chairs and a settee to one side of the living room in preparation for Alex's wake. When the funeral directors finished, Alex was in his coffin and dressed in the clothing that Jonie had provided. The metal support stand was skirted in the same deep red velvet material as the valance.

Jonie provided them with a large oval framed picture of Alex to be displayed on an easel. The picture was taken when he was ninety-three years old and showed his piercing blue-green eyes, dark hair and eyebrows, and long flowing white beard.

People began coming to Jonie's for Alex' wake around two o'clock on Sunday afternoon. The women folk brought bowls and pans of prepared food. The kitchen table was so full there was no room to sit and eat there. The people filled their plates and went outside to sit on the porch and in the yard to eat. The sun was bright and there was little or no wind. Still, all the mourners kept their coats and sweaters on against the late autumn chill.

Jonie asked the girls, Della, Mary, Alta, and Mellie to keep up with the dishwashing so that when other friends and relatives arrived, they'd have clean plates and silverware. Two of Sadie's daughters, Ethel and Mary, immediately upon their arrival, started to help with the dishes without being asked.

The wake lasted all night. Some of the men in the family brought jugs of home-brew, and quart and half-gallon canning-jars of moonshine to pass around. Enoch told them to take it out of the house. They could use the barn and the back yard, but he wanted none of them drinking around the women and children.

The funeral was held at eleven o'clock the next morning. In response to Enoch's request, the funeral directors provided a minister to conduct the service.

There was standing-room only for mourners inside Jonie's house, on the large wrap-around porch and even in the front yard. Jim sat by Della and then stood alone outside and watched as the men carried the coffin out to the hearse. He made no effort to be one of the pall bearers.

After the graveside service, family members and friends left one-by-one, or in groups. Only Israel, Id, Rhodie and their daughters, Pauline and Katherine, came back to Jonie's. The funeral directors gathered all of their equipment and packed it inside the hearse. They told Enoch he would receive an itemized bill.

The next day was Wednesday and there was no work for Judy, Mary, and Della. Each of them was taking advantage of their regular day off. They spent the night with Jonie and Enoch. There was a sadness that settled over them. It couldn't be helped. The younger children were playing quietly with dominoes, checkers, and a deck of cards. The older children were sitting outside on the porch talking in hushed voices. The grownups, including Della, Jim, and Mary were in the kitchen. Jonie said, "I'm not one bit sleepy. We have a lot of cakes and pies that people left and I made a big pot of coffee."

With that she passed out saucers of pie and cake along with steaming cups of coffee. Otis and Gib drank milk instead of coffee. After they finished eating they both went to bed. The children on the porch were shooed inside and put to bed. It was almost midnight when the rest of the family finally gave up and soon all were asleep.

Morning came way too soon. Judy regretted staying up so late. She joined Jonie in the kitchen. Only Otis and Gib were up, but they were in the barn taking care of the milking. Judy asked, "Will you and Enoch have enough money to pay for Pa's funeral? If not I'll help with the cost."

"Pa held back money from the sale of the old place to cover what he called 'puttin' him away nice'. I'm pretty sure there'll be 'nough money, but if there ain't, I'll let you know."

Della and Jim prepared to have their own Thanksgiving feast since she wasn't supposed to ride a horse until after the baby came. So, on Thanksgiving eve, only Judy, Mary, and Luther made the trip to Jonie's. Judy rode Socks and led Curly. Mary rode Little Red. Ray Fannon was invited to go with them, but he said he needed to spend the holiday with his folks, Mammy and Pappy Fannon.

Enoch and Jonie were pleased that Judy trusted them to care for Curly during the last, few years of his life. Alta and Mellie volunteered to exercise him, feed, and groom him. Judy told the girls that in return they could consider that the gentle old horse belonged to them.

Ineda and Alfreda were over five months old and sitting up. Judy was smitten with the darling little girls, but noticed that Jonie's other daughters were getting very little attention because of the twins. After the babies were in bed asleep, she asked Jonie if all the girls could gather in the kitchen to have a 'sing' while they worked on dinner.

Jonie's eyes showed her surprise as she said, "Yes. That'll be fun, but what made you think of that?"

"I believe that your other girls are feeling left out because of people making a fuss over the twins. All of us singing together will make them feel they're important. Don't you agree with me?"

"I sure do. You're right. I'll call all of them in with us right now and we'll make the rafters ring!"

A month later Judy, Mary, and Luther made the same trip. Christmas came on Wednesday this year. They left Harlan at noon on Christmas Eve and arrived at Jonie's just as night closed in. It was their first Christmas without Alex. That thought was uppermost in their minds when they gathered around the table for stack-cake and coffee for the grownups and cake and milk for the children.

Judy smiled and nodded toward the end of the long table. No one sat there. She said, "Jonie, honey, we forgot to pour one more cup of coffee."

"What? Who needs a cup of coffee? Who did we miss?"

"Pa is here with us tonight. I can feel his presence. Let's welcome him with his favorite cup filled with coffee just for him!"

Jonie's eyes were brimming, "We sure will. We'll do it for Pa! Every year that we're all together, we'll pour Pa a cup of coffee on Christmas Eve!"

On Sunday after Christmas, Mary had a date with Ray Fannon for church in the morning and a movie at the Margie Grand in the afternoon. Judy and Luther spent the better part of the day with Della and Jim. It was about two weeks until

Della's baby was due. Jim was grumbling because Della hadn't bought him any Wild West dime novels.

Judy ignored Jim and asked, "Della, honey, when was the last time you saw Doctor McCall?"

"I saw him sometime back in October. I don't like going to him because he always has whiskey on his breath. If he's going to drink before he sees his patients, he should at least chew some peppermint leaves. Jim interrupted, "Why should she waste money on a doctor, when she can't give me twenty cents to get us two new books to read?"

With a warning look at Jim, she asked, "Do you think it's wise to wait 'til you're ready to birth the baby to call him? I'll be with you, but you should have the doctor here, too."

Jim declared, angrily, "I'm sayin' that she don't need no doctor. She has you! I know that I'm gonna go huntin' when she starts the baby foolishness!"

Judy was disgusted, "Jim, the best thing in the world for you to do is to go huntin' and get out from underfoot!"

Della interrupted them, "Ma, McCall's office is in Harlan, near the Howard Drug Store. Can you stop tomorrow to remind him that I'm due the first or second week of January?"

Judy laughed and asked, "Do you want me to tell him to stay sober?"

"Ma, that's not funny. I hate the smell of whiskey. If he's drinking, I don't even want him to breathe on me!"

The sign on the building read R.A. McCall, M.D. Judy opened the door and walked into a small, dimly lit, and depressing waiting room. She grumbled, "No wonder Della didn't want to come back here."

She left her message with the nurse and went on to work.

Judy's day off was on Wednesday and she planned to take Luther and spend the entire day with Della. When she arrived at about ten o'clock that morning, she found Jim still in bed reading the last half of one of his 'Stories of the Wild West' dime novels. She asked, "Why is the book torn in half?"

Jim said, "We have a system. I read the book first 'til I'm half done, then I tear it in half. I give her the first half to read while I finish the last half."

Jim was still talking when Judy looked at Della's face and saw the first sign of pain that signaled the beginning of labor. Judy barked an order to Jim, "Get up out of that bed. Clean yourself up. Stop at Fuson's barn and get your horse. Go to Harlan and find Doctor McCall. His office is usually closed on Wednesday's. You don't have time to walk everywhere to find him. The best bet is that he's probably in one of the taverns getting liquored up."

Jim asked, "Now? You want me to go now? She ain't even whimpered yet. The baby is hours away!"

"At the rate you're moving, it'll be hours afore you get the doctor here. Take your gun and dress warm enough so you can go ahead and leave for your hunt. Go by Ackley's and tell them I'm with your wife who's birthin' your baby. I won't be to work tomorrow. Now, I don't expect you to get back home until late tomorrow evening. Be sure you bring me something you've killed so I can put meat on the table for you and Della!"

Jim retorted, "I don't know why you're making all this fuss over something that women have done on their own since the beginnin' of time!"

Judy fired back, "Well, now it's past time that men got in on the act, too. She didn't create that baby all by herself. You had a great deal to do with it! Now, come on and get going!"

With Della watching and trying hard not to laugh, Judy all but pushed Jim out the door. She stood outside on the little porch and watched him walk past the big rock and disappear from sight. Judy knew he would cut across Louise Gilbert's pasture. That was the shortest route to Fuson's barn.

It was after six and dark outside when Doctor McCall showed up. Judy turned her head away because the smell of whiskey was so strong. He weaved himself to the kitchen table, pulled out a chair and sat down. She poured a cup of strong coffee and sat it down in front of him. "Don't you have anything a man can drink? I've come a long way and it's all uphill. I need a good strong belt of whiskey! Where's the little mother-to-be?"

"You're not touching her 'til you sober up!"

"I'm the doctor here. You have to do as I say. Who're you, anyway?"

"I'm her mother and you'll do as I say or I'll help you out the door and half way down the hill with my foot! Now drink your coffee!"

R. A. McCall's eyes grew huge. He didn't argue with Judy. He sat at the table sipping on the steaming brew while Judy went to the bedroom to check on Della. Even when the pain was overwhelming, Della hadn't once cried out. Judy smoothed her hair back and mopped sweat off her forehead. "Honey, it's all right to yell, scream, and holler if you want to. Nobody's goin' to fault you for it."

"Ma, if I give in and do that, I'm afraid I won't be able to stand it at all. As long as God helps me to not yell and holler, I'll bear it better that way. Where's the doctor? Did Jim come back?"

The doctor's here, but he's drunk. I made him take a cup of hot coffee to help sober him up. No. Jim didn't come back. I told him to go huntin' and to stay away all night. In his grouchy mood he would just aggravate the both of us!"

Judy started back toward the kitchen and was just in time to see Doctor McCall replace a flask in his coat pocket. She stormed into the room, ranting at him, "You're going to be useless tonight. I saw you pour whiskey in your coffee! What a poor excuse of a doctor you've turned out to be!"

Doctor McCall ignored her, stood up and weaved his way through the living room to Della's bed. He went through the motions of examining her, turned around, sat down on the foot of the bed, and said. "She's hours away from delivering. I'm going to stretch out here and take a nap. Call me when she's ready to give birth."

With that little speech, the doctor fell over on his side and was out cold. Judy pushed him all the way down to the foot of the bed. She sat by Della for hours, holding her hand and giving her comfort through the worst of the pains.

It was almost two o'clock in the morning when Della gave birth to a healthy baby girl. Judy bathed the baby and dressed her. She pinned on a diaper, triple-folded to fit a new born. From the clothes they had bought and hand-made, she took a belly-button support cloth and double-pinned it tightly in place. Then she dressed the baby in a wrap-round infant shirt, and a kimono gown. After that she wrapped her in a receiving blanket.

Della asked, "Is she all right? I want to hold her!"

Judy assured Della that as soon as she was bathed and dressed in one of her new home-made gowns, she could hold her little girl. "You need to see if you're able to nurse her. If you don't have enough breast milk, I'll have to make up some cow's milk for her to take using the bottle and nipple that we bought. Della asked, "You said make up some milk, what's mixed in with it?"

"I made up milk for Luther by mixing four parts milk and one part white Karo syrup to start with. As he got older, I changed how I mixed it. If she can't tolerate it, we'll have to try something else."

Judy asked, "Did you and Jim pick out a name for the baby?

"Yes, her name is Rosezelle. If she'd been a boy, he was going to name him George Washington Boggs."

Is there a reason why he wanted to name a baby George Washington?"

"Uncle Bish named him James Jefferson Boggs after Thomas Jefferson, only he didn't get the man's name right!"

Judy nodded toward Doctor McCall who was still passed out on the foot of the bed. "Well when your good-for-nothing doctor wakes up, we have to be nice to him so he'll write down the birth certificate information correctly."

It was almost four o'clock that morning when Judy decided it was past time to wake up Doctor McCall. He opened his bleary, red eyes, sat up and looked around the room. He didn't know where he was. Then his gaze rested on Della propped up on pillows with a little bundle in her arms. "Well, little mother, I see the baby has been born. You did a good job. Let me take a peek at you."

Della snapped at him, "You needn't bother. We're both fine. My mother took care of me when you couldn't!"

The doctor took affront at Della's show of anger. He turned to Judy to ask for the information that he needed to apply for the baby's birth certificate. Judy told him that the father was James Jefferson Boggs, Sunshine; the mother's maiden name was Della Smith, Sunshine; the baby's name was Rosezelle Boggs.

When the drunken doctor filled in the information for registering the birth, he had the father's name as James Jefferson Boggs, Big Laurel; the mother as Sarah Ann Smith, Hazard; and the baby as Baby Girl Boggs, Sunshine.

Judy offered the doctor a piece of apple pie and another steaming cup of coffee. As he sat at the kitchen table eating and drinking his coffee, he asked, "Do you mind if I stay here 'til daylight? I'm afraid of snakes in the dark."

Judy said, "You can stay as long as you like. My daughter needs to rest now and the only place for you to sleep is here in the kitchen. I'll wake you when I'm ready to make breakfast. You should eat something before you leave."

The doctor left after breakfast. Judy let Della sleep until she woke up on her own. Della tried to nurse her baby, but had almost no breast milk. For the third time in eight hours, baby Rosezelle took about three ounces of the cow's milk and white Karo syrup mixture. Then, she was sleeping again.

Judy insisted that Della remain in bed. "You can get up and stir around on Saturday, but you're to do nothing but take care of the baby. I'll tell Jim what he needs to do. You let him do it, too. The lazy lout will try to get you to do everything for him while he does nothing but don't let him get away with it."

Jim finally came home about four that afternoon. Judy was surprised when he pulled two squirrels out of his burlap sack. She quickly skinned and dressed them. Soon they were simmering in brown gravy. "These will be good with the green beans and mashed potatoes I made. I was wishing for some meat to fix, and here you came with two squirrels. The Lord loves you, Jim!"

Jim blushed red because this was the first time his Aunt Judy had thanked him for anything. Actually, it was the first time she had said anything really nice to him. He walked out on the front porch so he could grumble in private, "Well, I can't believe she's being nice to me. I'm glad she's not threatening to shoot me again!"

Jim followed as closely as he could all of Judy's instructions on how to take care of Della and the baby. He was pleased that Della used the name he chose for the little girl.

There was no place to weigh Rosezelle, but they guessed she weighed about seven pounds or so. When her weight seemed lighter, Della told Jim that all babies lost a little at first, but she would gain weight again in about five days.

Della was surprised and pleased because Jim seemed to really care for baby Rosezelle. He helped with bathing and dressing her, but refused to change a diaper. He refused to do any washing or ironing. Judy had to work, so Mary brought Luther and came to stay Saturday night and all day Sunday. She did the washing and most of the ironing. Judy brought Luther and came on Wednesday to do the same thing all over again.

Judy counted off the days on a wall calendar, "Della, honey, ten days will be up on Sunday. After that, you can do whatever you feel like doing. You need coal for the living room grate and the cook stove. Have Jim take a coffee sack and go down to the Sunshine railroad spur near the river after dark and pick up the coal that's dropped off the railroad coal gons that are setting there. You make sure he goes to gets the coal. You mustn't try to carry it!"

When Judy went home, Jim heaved a big sigh of relief. "Now, finally we're alone. I know you love your family, but I get tired of the bossiness of your mother. My Ma was never that way with us boys. She bossed my sisters all the time, but never made us do anything. The girls did 'most all the work at home."

Della laughed, "Well no wonder you get your back up when we suggest you get a job or do something here at home. You've not been raised to take on any real responsibility. I'm glad to say that you seem to be turning away from living that way. While you were in town, did you hear anymore about the national banks failing and the lack of jobs for men and women?"

"Hey, it's really serious for the people who want jobs. It's not going to hurt us none 'cause I don't want a job. You have the baby to take care of and I don't want you to ever work for somebody else again."

"Jim, honey, we have the baby to worry about. What will we do for money when she needs more clothes, shoes, and special baby food?"

"Ma never worried about that stuff. We'll plant the garden again this year and grow our food. I'll hunt while you tend the garden. If we need money, we'll sell the animal hides that I get with my traps."

"The mountains are about trapped out. That won't get us enough money to live on."

"Then we'll sell Socks. I've got my horse to use for hunting."

"Ma is using Socks when she goes to visit Aunt Jonie and Uncle Enoch. You know she's put old Curly out to pasture!"

"Then, let her buy Socks from us. That's only fair!"

"No, you go get a job just for a little while, 'til I get back on my feet. Then you can stay home and watch Rosezelle while I work. You can still hunt, trap, and fish after I get home at night."

"My wife's goin' to take care of our young'ins, and grow our food just like my Ma did. You're not working any more."

Does that mean you'll get a job?"

"I told you that I'm not working for somebody else ever again. I mean that. We can get some cash money by selling Socks to your Ma."

"I already gave Socks to Ma. We can't sell him to her!"

"Then we'll sell the cow!"

"We can't do that. We need the milk for Rosezelle. I use buttermilk and the churned butter for cooking!"

"There ain't no pleasin' you anymore. I'm not workin' for somebody else. Get that through your thick skull! If you say we need money, then you figure it out yourself. You can't have everything your way!"

"Jim, it's a good three months before we can break ground to plant a garden. You can take care of the baby and the house while I work. I'll see if I can get my job back at Scott's. Ma says that jobs are getting as scarce as hen's teeth. If I wait any longer, there may not be any jobs left!"

"You're not going to work. I won't take care of Rosezelle and the house. Get 'nough money from your Ma to tide us over 'til summertime. I'll get 'nough skins with my trapping, and catch 'nough fish to sell to the restaurants to keep us in cash money. Then, there's the garden. It's free to us from old lady Gilbert. We have plenty of seed saved from last year. See, I've got it all figured out. Just get the money from your Ma and she can keep Socks."

"I'm going to see if I can get my job back. If you won't take care of your daughter, I'll see if Kathy Taylor will keep her with Luther."

"The day you go back to work, I'll leave you and I won't come back!"

"You don't mean that!"

"Try me!"

Della didn't say any more. She was quiet the rest of the day, but her head was in a whirl. She had some money, but hadn't counted it lately. Jim didn't know that she had any of her savings left. She meant to keep it that way. The next day after he rode off to go hunting and to check his traps, she sat on the bed, removed her lady's money-sack from under her clothes, and counted her money.

What she counted equaled about three months pay from Scott's. It wasn't much, but if she borrowed the same amount from Judy, with the garden and Jim hunting, she could make the money last until late next fall.

Judy and Luther came to spend the day with her on Wednesday. That morning, Jim groused, "I wanted to stay home but I'm goin' huntin' 'cause I don't want to be fussed at by your Ma all day. She don't understand that a man has to be the man of the house. I wear the pants in this family!"

Della laughed, "Well, you better figure how you're going to have pants to wear. I've patched your other pair of bib overalls so much, the patches have patches. Don't you say a word about selling Socks or the cow. You think Ma's bad, you don't want to ever see me mad!"

Jim's eyes widened in surprise and he made a hasty retreat from what he saw as having to reckon with two angry women. Della fed Rosezelle, bathed her, and put her back in the middle of the big bed. To break the flow of a cold draft of air, she fluffed up two pillows and placed them on each side of the little girl.

She was cleaning up the breakfast dishes, when Judy and Luther arrived. After she poured two steaming cups of coffee and sat down, she told her mother of her dilemma over Jim's stubborn refusal to get a job.

"I've got a proposition for you, Ma. I've got about a hundred dollars yet of the money I've saved. Jim doesn't know I have it. I want you to keep it for me and give me some of it along as I need it for Rosezelle and to buy the foodstuff we can't grow. Jim will think you're loaning me money. When my money's almost used up, I'm asking you to lend me the money I'll need 'til I bring the garden in and put up the food. After that, I'll get a job somewhere and if Jim wants to leave me and the baby, then let him!"

"Honey, are you sure you want it to come to that? You know that as long as I have money and you have a need, I'm going to help you."

"Ma, I'll not support a lazy bum. Either he takes proper care of me and Rosezelle, or come the fall, he can leave and not come back! Not ever!"

Judy was surprised at the fierce anger shown by Della. It wasn't like her younger daughter to express her feelings so openly. She changed the subject by asking her if she had talked with Mary lately. "No, I haven't seen Mary since Sunday, is something wrong?"

"No. Ray has asked her to set a date for their wedding. She decided on June the eleventh. That's on a Wednesday, her regular day off. Just like with you, she didn't want to miss any work."

Della asked, "Where will they live?"

"They asked to stay with me 'til they find a house and get it furnished. Ray said his folks are going to help them set up housekeeping."

"Ray works at the Bardo Mining Company. Is he going to try to find work somewhere else? I know he could get a coal-camp house just for the asking where he works."

"I thought of that, too. It looks like he's thinking of changing jobs. We'll just have to wait and see. At least he's not like Jim. He wants to work!"

"Oh, Ma, I'm so disappointed with Jim. I loved him, but he's killing my love. He acts like he loves the baby. If he loved us, he'd provide for us."

Judy asked, "If it comes to your getting a job next fall, and he does as he says and abandons you, would you come to live with me after Mary and Ray move to their own home?"

Della said, "I think that times are going to get real hard with this bank-failing business. Living up here in Sunshine Holler is too far from town to have to walk to work. Your rent is five dollars a month. Maybe we should look for a cheaper house to rent. One of the girls I worked with told me that there are houses over by the river on the other side of the railroad tracks that rent for just two dollars a month."

"You're right. If the Taylor's move in with her folks on a farm in Knox County, I won't have anyone to watch Luther. He'll be five in May but won't be in school until September."

Della asked, "Didn't you tell me once that Ackley's said you could bring him to work with you if you needed to?"

"Yes, but you know that would get old real quick, and it would be an imposition on them. If Frank and Kathy Taylor do move away, I'll let you take care of him 'til school starts. He's a good little helper and will mind what you say. Do you think Jim will raise a fuss?"

"Let him try! Just let me know ahead of time. It's too far to bring him all the way up here and take him back home every day. So we'll plan on him staying with me all the time except on your day off, or until we decide something else."

Judy asked, "Are you plannin' for the worst? You think you'll have to get a job and that Jim will leave you?"

"Yes, I am. One of us may have to stay home to take care of Luther and Rosezelle. That's why I'm wondering about the cheaper houses by the river."

"Well, lets cross those bridges as we come to them."

Della's idea about giving her money to her mother and having her dole it out to them a little at a time worked like a charm. Jim wasn't so demanding because he thought all of the money she had was from small loans from Judy. He exclaimed, "Della, honey, you see now that I was right. This proves it! I don't have to work because your Ma gives us free loans!"

In late February, when Judy advised Della that the signs were below the knee and if they were going to plant potatoes, now was the time to do so. Jim used a three prong garden fork and a mattock to prepare the ground. Judy bought them a hundred pounds of seed potatoes. Even if it turned very cold in March, potatoes were hardy and would be fine. Della let Jim do all the work involved with that planting.

In late April, Della hired a man to plow and break up the clods on half of the garden. It was the second week in May when she and Jim sectioned off the prepared ground that would be for corn and beans, and began to plant the seed. On the third weekend, Della hired the man again to plow and prepare the ground in the other half. They planted cucumbers, Cushaws, squash, cantaloupes, pumpkins, and sowed mustard and kale greens in one part of it. In the other they bought plants to set out: beef steak and big boy tomatoes, Cabbage, red and yellow hot-peppers, and sweet, green-peppers.

Everything came up looking good. There hadn't been any late frosts and the tomatoes and peppers were thriving. Jim's hunting and trapping were paying off. He did a good job of bringing home rabbits, squirrels, possums, and even some field quail. Judy said, "Jim, some of the men were talking about good places to find deer. You have to go deep in the mountains away from any mining companies. I think if you went up to the top of the holler here and over the mountain toward Loyall, you would find deer."

Jim laughed, "Yes, and all kinds of snakes, a panther or two, and bears. I think you're trying to get me killed!"

"You've got your gun and know how to use it. You want to be a real mountain man. If you got a deer, you'd have meat on the table for a month!"

It was apparent to Judy that she and Jim were always going to be at odds with each other. She praised him when he worked hard in the garden, had good results from his traps and hunting, and gave him good advice about everything. But Jim remained suspicious of her motives, and never fully trusted her.

June the eleventh came and Mary and Ray were married by the Justice of the Peace in Harlan. Ray brought all of his belongings from the boardinghouse as he moved in with Judy and Mary. A little at a time over the next month, he brought odds and ends from Mammy and Pappy Fannon's farm to Judy's.

A week after Mary was married the Taylor's said a tearful goodbye and moved to Knox County, near the little town of Barbourville.

Over Jim's bitter protests, Luther moved in with him and Della. Judy decided it was easier to spend her day off with Della than to uproot Luther by bringing him home for just one day a week.

Jim was surprising them again and working hard at gardening. He loved to show off the results of his efforts to anyone who cared to listen. His one suit of work clothes were in tatters from being worn all the time. Because he thought Della had no money of her own, rather than ask Judy for money for new pants, he went to bed while Della washed and dried his one pair of bib overalls..

Ray took a mining job at Coxton up toward Evarts. They were assigned a nice camp-house with room for a good-sized garden. Mary took advantage of the previous renter's hard work and only had to hoe her garden one time. She was able to can a lot of green beans and tomatoes.

Ray and Mary combined their savings and furnished their new home. Both of them were working. Because of the failing economy, Newberry's was cut ting back on their store hours. That meant Mary would work only thirty hours a week. She began to look elsewhere for a job.

Ray had his truck and drove to and from work. Mary had to walk a long way to State Route #38 to take the Harlan-based VTC bus to and from Harlan.

By the end of September Della and Jim finished putting up the year's harvest of fruit and vegetables. Her only pair of shoes was so worn they wouldn't stay on her feet. The mornings were too cool to go barefoot. She tried to make a pair of boots out of burlap bags, but they were too scratchy against her skin.

The people who lived in the next house down the holler were named Maggard. Once during the growing season, Della gave them a bushel of beans and a half bushel of tomatoes along with some cucumbers, peppers, and squash. Mrs. Maggard mentioned that she had some barely-worn, low-heeled shoes that were too large for her. She asked, "Would you like to see if they fit you? They'll do to work in and will feel better than the burlap bags I saw you trying to wear."

Della tried them on and they did fit. She exclaimed, "Oh. My goodness! This is an answer to a prayer. The Lord love you for your kindness!"

When Jim noticed she had 'new' shoes, he groused about it. "I don't want my wife takin' charity from no neighbor. We're doin' all right now. We're all set for food all winter with my huntin',"

"I can't ask Ma for any more money. She's given us over a hundred dollars. I don't have anyone to keep Rosezelle now even if I was to get a job. Mary said that Scott's and Newberry's have both cut back on store hours because of the bank failings. They're calling it 'the Great Depression' because of so many people unable to find work."

"If we don't have any money, we'll just do without. At least we'll have full bellies!"

"Rosezelle has outgrown everything. She has to have warm winter clothes. She's having too many earaches. I'm going to see Mary today to ask her to use her discount privileges to get Rosezelle a cheap coat and some new shoes. You and I can do without, but our baby can't. I don't want her getting sicker!"

"You're tryin' to make me feel guilty so I'll get a job. I'm not feelin' one bit guilty. So, stop beatin' 'round the bush with me!"

Mary didn't hesitate about buying a coat for Rosezelle. She got it slightly too big so she would grow into it. There was a matching hat with ties under the chin and mittens to match. She also bought her sox and shoes.

Della had brimming eyes as she tried the bright red coat on the dark-haired, brown-eyed little girl and saw how sweet and cute she was in new clothes. She confided in Mary that she was going to have to get a job herself since Jim refused to work.

Mary came to see Della on the fifth of November to tell her she had a new job at O. B. Bailey's Eagle Laundry on the southeast side of Harlan. She exclaimed, "I'm so thrilled! The pay's seven dollars a week for working ten hours a day, five days a week, and six hours on Saturday. I'll be steam-pressing shirts mostly, but I'll also be pressing sheets for the hotel. I start next Monday."

"Do they have any other openings? It's getting colder and I need to buy a ton of coal for the kitchen stove and the fireplace grates. Jim won't go pick up coal when the train's sitting there on the railroad spur. He waits until it's gone on and then says the coal on the ground has been picked over and won't go at all. It's too cold in the house and Rosezelle's got another ear infection. I've got to find a job for myself."

"I'll ask Mr. Bailey on Monday and see what he says. I'll let you know next Wednesday."

Della did a lot of soul searching over the next few days. She went over her choices in her mind. She grumbled as she struggled to pray, "Dear Lord, I have really messed up my life here lately. I've neglected to follow my own plan to include You in every decision I make. I think I fell in love with the thought of love and made a huge mistake in my choice of marrying Jim."

Della paused, looked around the room and her eyes fell on Rosezelle who was sleeping in the middle of the big bed. "Lord, I can't even buy my baby a proper bed. She shouldn't be sleeping between me and Jim. She has the warm coat Mary bought her, but no warm dresses or sweaters to wear in the house."

She thought about the chance to work again and for seven dollars a week instead of five fifty. In her mind, she argued the pros and cons of the choices she had and prayed, "Dear Lord, just because I messed up my life by marrying the wrong man doesn't mean it has to be a permanent mistake. Lord, lead me to do the right thing to make this mess go away. I believe that Your plan for me is to get that job at the Eagle Laundry if it's possible! Dear Lord, I'll talk to Ma. Luther's in the Primer now and going to school half-days. Tomorrow, I'll take Rosezelle and go to see Ma at Ackley's. Lord, with Your help, I'll begin right now to try and get my life in order again. In Jesus' name I pray, Amen."

Judy was surprised to see Della and the baby come into the restaurant to see her. Della didn't mince any words, "Ma, I need to give Mary an answer on Wednesday about my working with her at the Eagle Laundry. I need to make my plans with you if I'm to do this. How's your job working out here? Mary was cut back in hours again at Newberry's and was only earning four fifty a week. That's why she took the job at the Eagle Laundry. Have your hours been cut, too?"

"Yes. Honey, I dip into my savings every week to keep up with the rent, Sock's and Little Red's board, the electric bill, and very basic livin' expenses."

"How much are you making a week?"

"With so many people out of work, the restaurant is really hurtin'. I'm being paid for thirty hours, but I work more. My pay's dropped to five-dollars and seventy-five cents a week, and may be cut again."

"Did you check into the houses by the river?"

"Yes. The rent is like you said, two dollars a week, but as is. Mr. Fuson said they won't pay for any improvements. It's on high ground above the river and he says they've never flooded out."

"Ma, if I earned twenty eight dollars every four weeks, could we make it on my pay alone? That's you, me, Luther, and the baby."

"If we rented the cheap house, I believe we could. It's worth a try!"

"Let's do it! I'll tell Mary that I'll take the job if it's open. The day I go to work, Jim threatened to leave me for good. Let's see if he does. We can plan to move into one of the houses by the river on the first of December ."

On Wednesday, Mary came to tell Della the job at the Eagle Laundry was hers if she wanted it. She needed to come in to see Mr. Bailey, sign some papers, and begin on Monday. The next morning, she dressed her baby as warmly as she could and went to Harlan to meet Mr. Bailey. He was businesslike, but took time to play patty-cake with Rosezelle. He asked about who would provide care for her little girl. She assured him that her mother was available for that.

Mr. Bailey said, "I'm offering you the same arrangement that I made for your sister. Your hours will be the same as hers. We give you all national holidays off with pay, including a day and a half for Thanksgiving and Christmas. The pay is seven dollars a week to start. After six months you'll be raised fifty cents a week. Then every three months thereafter, with satisfactory service, you'll receive a twenty-five-cent a week raise up to ten dollars a week. Is that agreeable with you?"

"Yes sir, Mr. Bailey. I want you to know that I thank you from the bottom of my heart."

All the way home, Della was rejoicing with a prayer on her lips. "Thank you, Lord! Oh, dear Lord Jesus, thank you!"

Sunday, November the sixteenth, was Judy's last day as cook for Ackley's Restaurant. She was now prepared to take care of Luther and Rosezelle while Della worked.

On that same Sunday, Della told Jim she was going to work the next day.

Jim told her if she left the next morning to take a job, he wouldn't be there when she came home that night. He gave her an ultimatum: "If you do this, you will not see me again!"

Della began her new job at the Eagle Laundry in Harlan on Monday, November 17, 1930.

Jim packed his belongings and left home the same day.

He never came back.

Jim Boggs - After deserting Della and Rosezelle, Jim served in the military in the
Panama Canal Zone

Legend

Hank Wilder	
Kathryn Pettit	
Ethel DeLong Zande	
Luigi Zande	
Reverend Ethan Brownlett	(Mary's foster home)
Mrs. Anne Brownlett	
Blevins Brothers	Josh, Gabe, Isaac (cook)
William (Bill) Jenkins	Owner, Hotel and restaurant
Lance Middleton	Older man, dishwasher, handyman
Sylvia Rae Johnson	(Waitress)
Betty Lou Partin	Waitress hired to replace Sylvia when she married Isaac and moved to the farm
Raff Pennington	(Owner of Livery Stables)
Tom Pennington	Owner's oldest son
Sidney Pennington	Owner's youngest son
Walter Middleton (Walt)	Sheriff 1921-1925
Lester Cornett	Sheriff 1926-1930
Tim Jones	Deputy 1921-1925
Lloyd Campbell	Deputy 1926-1930
James T. Farmer (J.T.)	Judge
Jim Collins	Judy's second husband and father of Luther
Doctor Lewis	Hazard Doctor
Liege, Rob, Dave, Alex, Preston	Judy's brothers
Sadie, Rainie, Emily, Jonie	Judy's Sisters

Luther is born May 8, 1925
Rainie married Israel Miniard (Rainie died in childbirth)
Israel is the father of Israel David Miniard, known as Id Miniard

Id married Rhoda (Rhodie)	Their two oldest children were Pauline and Katherine
Jonie and Enoch Lewis	Sisters married brothers
Emily and Robert Lewis	Sisters married brothers

Gilbert & Otis Lewis Alta, Mellie, Dolly, Delphia Ineda, Alfreda, Rhoda, Clara

Loretta Helton	Dora Mae's mother
Al Helton	Loretta's brother-in-law and Dora Mae's Uncle

Thelma Brackett   Overseer of hotel housekeeping staff

Roy Jackson   Hotel Maintenance man

Myrtle Baker   Judy's new older friend

(Dave married a Baker girl in Big Laurel)

Myrt lives permanently at the hotel

Gertrude and Roger Burnett   Myrt's daughter and son-in-law

Harvey and Sarah Cantrell   Farm family for Della's placement
                                    East of Hazard)

Lacey, 14; Winnie, 15

Harvey, Jr. 19; Jimmy 17   Cantrell children

Chad Owens   oldest of two brothers, killed Art
                                    Bailie over a horse deal.

Arthur Babcock   Myrt's attorney

Mr. Stewart   Manager of Newberry's, Hazard
                                    opened in 1919

Anna Mae   Waitress at Ackley's

Frank and Kathy Taylor   next door neighbors

Dan Redmon   Harvey Fuson's driver and handyman

Arthur Stahlsworthy   Manager of Harlan Newberry's

Nathan Denning   Manager of Scott's

Maynard (Manny) Howard   Mary's first beau

Wedding for Mary and Ray   Wednesday, June 11, 1930 - Mary is
                                    24

Della is 20 on April 30, 1930

Rosezelle is born January 9, 1930

For more information on the Pine Mountain Settlement School and its history, please visit the internet.

LaVergne, TN USA
04 November 2010
203579LV00003B/5/P